Craft-Tastic Adventures:
Unleash Your Imagination with Amazing Crafts for Kids Ages 7 and Up

Embark on a Journey of Creativity and Fun with Hands-on Crafting Projects

Contents

Getting Started

Make Your Own Printing Crafts

Apple Print Canvas Bag

Block Printed Cards

Stencil Art Plant Pot

Clay Printing

Cling Film Wrapping Paper

Button Print Trainers

Easy Screen Prints

Spotty Painted Mugs

Sandpaper Printing

Make Your Own Nature Crafts

Woodland Photo Frame

Sand Art

Shell Creature Fridge Magnets

Pressed Flower Coasters

Seed Mosaic

Japanese Blossom Tree

Pebble Zoo

Pine Cone Field Mouse

Lavender Hand Warmers

Make Your Own Jewellery

Pendant Necklace

Lucky Rabbit Earrings

Knotted Bracelet

Fabric Flower Ring

Funky Toy Hair Clips

Jewelled Cuff

Puzzle Piece Hair Comb

Button Bag Charm

Jewellery Tree

Make Your Own Paper Crafts

Cube Puzzle

Paper Pulp Monsters

Make Your Own Notebook

3-D Photo Art

Quilling Cards

Giant Crayons

Paper Globe Lampshade

Envelopes and Notepaper

Paper Bouquet

Make Your Own Recycling Crafts

Bottle Tops in Bloom

Stackable Rocket Boxes

Beach Hut Pen Pots

Bedroom Pinboard

Water Bottle Bracelets

Scrap Paper Daisy Chain

Peacock Bookends

Sunny Days Clocks

Plastic Bag Weaving

Make Your Own Textile Crafts

Cute Sock Owls

Rock Star Rag Doll

Toadstool Doorstop

Totally Brilliant Tote

Jean Genius Desk Mascot

Secret Diary Cover

Mini Bag Organiser

Cupcake Pincushion

Knitted Phone Case

Glossary

GETTING STARTED

Are you feeling crafty? Then you've come to the right place! This book is packed full of awesome projects that are quick, easy and fun to make. Soon you will be able to impress your friends and family with all kinds of unique creations!

Keep It Simple!

There's no need for expensive equipment. The projects have been carefully designed to make use of everyday items that can be found around the home – or garden. Clear, step-by-step photos and instructions will guide you through every stage of the process.

Tool Time!

On the opposite page is a list of the the tools you're most likely to use when making these crafts. However, each chapter also has its own toolkit, listing some special extra tools you'll need to complete the projects.

New Skills!

While creating your funky gifts and fun items to share, you'll also be learning lots of great new skills, such as paper quilling, screen printing, stencilling and sewing. So what are you waiting for? Grab some pencils, scissors and glue, pick a project and get crafting!

BASIC TOOLKIT

Pencils, Pens, Paints and Brushes

It's a good idea to have a pot or a pencil case full of pens, pencils and brushes. Start with a nice sharp drawing pencil (HB is good), a set of colouring pencils, some felt-tipped pens and any paints and brushes you can find.

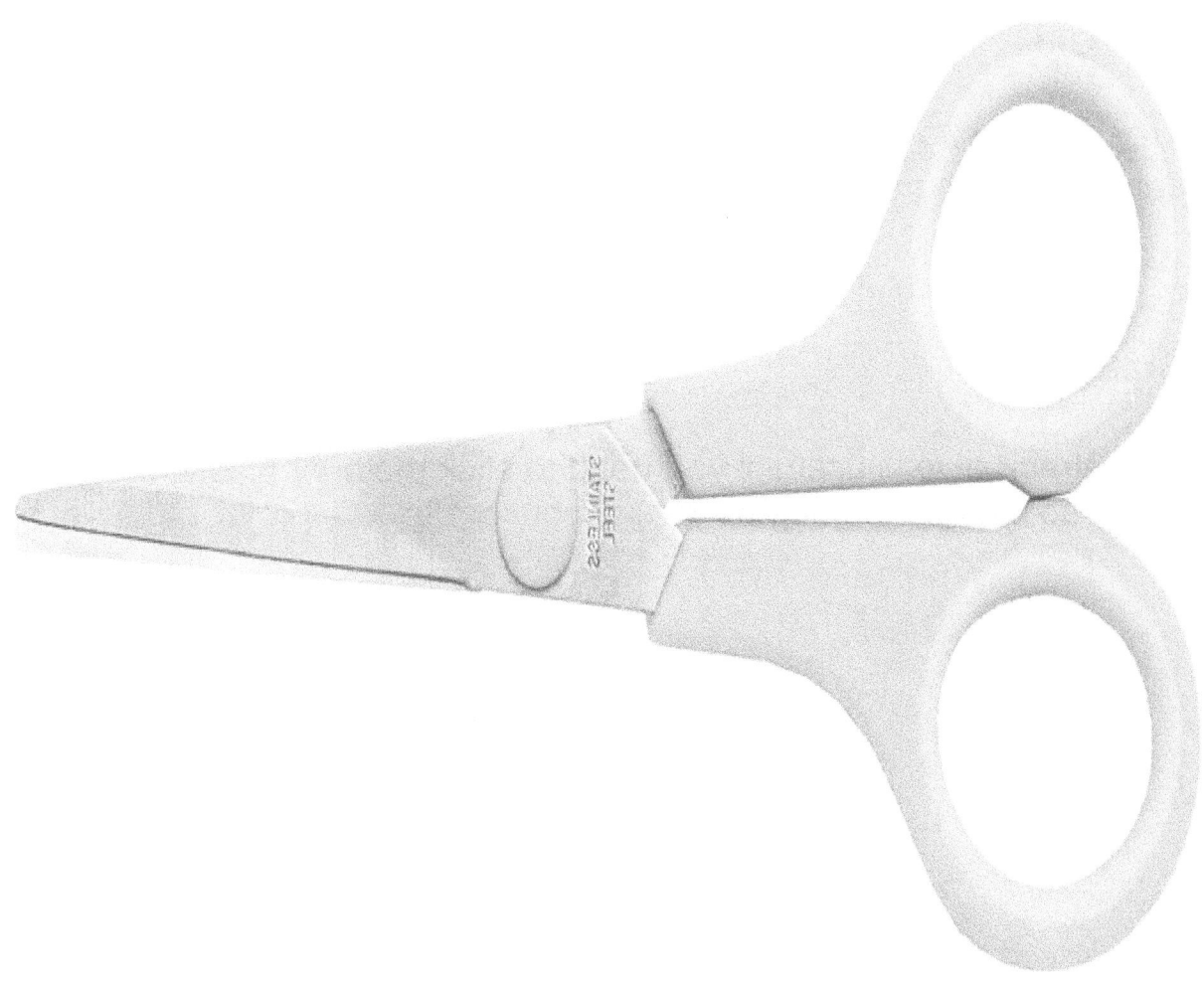

Scissors

Even though you can tear and rip paper, most of the time you will want to cut crisp lines. Always be careful when using scissors! If you need to cut tougher materials such as plastic, ask an adult to help.

Ruler

Sometimes you need to be precise. Use a ruler to measure and to draw straight lines.

PVA Glue

This is a crafts essential! PVA glue sticks most things together and can be used to make papier mâché.

Craft Glue

This strong glue is useful if you need to stick metal or plastic things (such as buttons or googly eyes) to your crafts.

MAKE YOUR OWN PRINTING CRAFTS

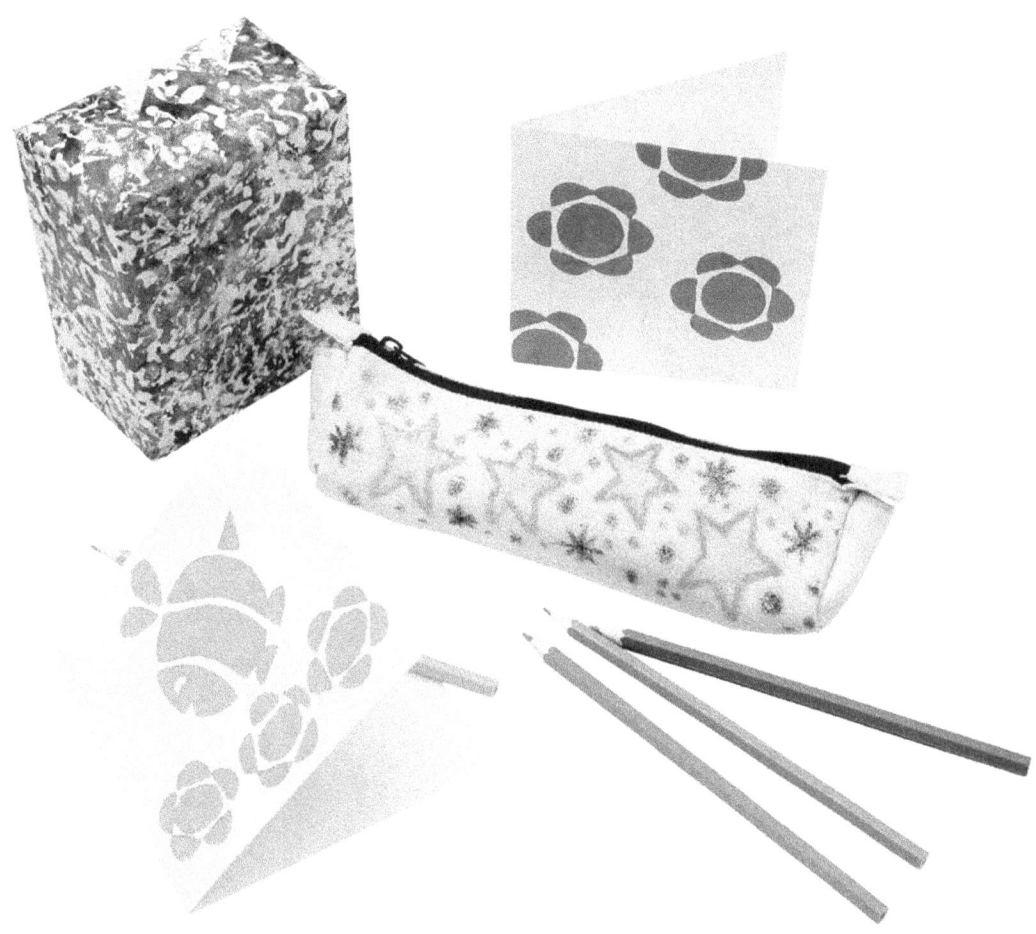

When you hear the word 'printing', what do you think of? Do you imagine your desktop printer at home or a printing press churning out thousands of newspapers? Well, think again! Printing can be a lot more fun than that.

Stop the Press! Let's Get Printing

You don't need computers or machines to print. All that you really need are your own two hands and some simple craft materials. This chapter is full of easy, step-by-step printing projects. So grab some paints, follow the intructions and you will be making perfect prints every time!

Get the Look!

One of the best things about print-making is that you can print onto just about anything. Once you understand the basics, you'll be able to transform your clothes, books, stationery and even your room.

Keep It Clean

Getting messy is all in a day's work for a print-maker. Always lay newspaper or plastic over the surface you're working on and have a damp cloth close to hand for any small spills or splatters.

PRINTING TOOLKIT

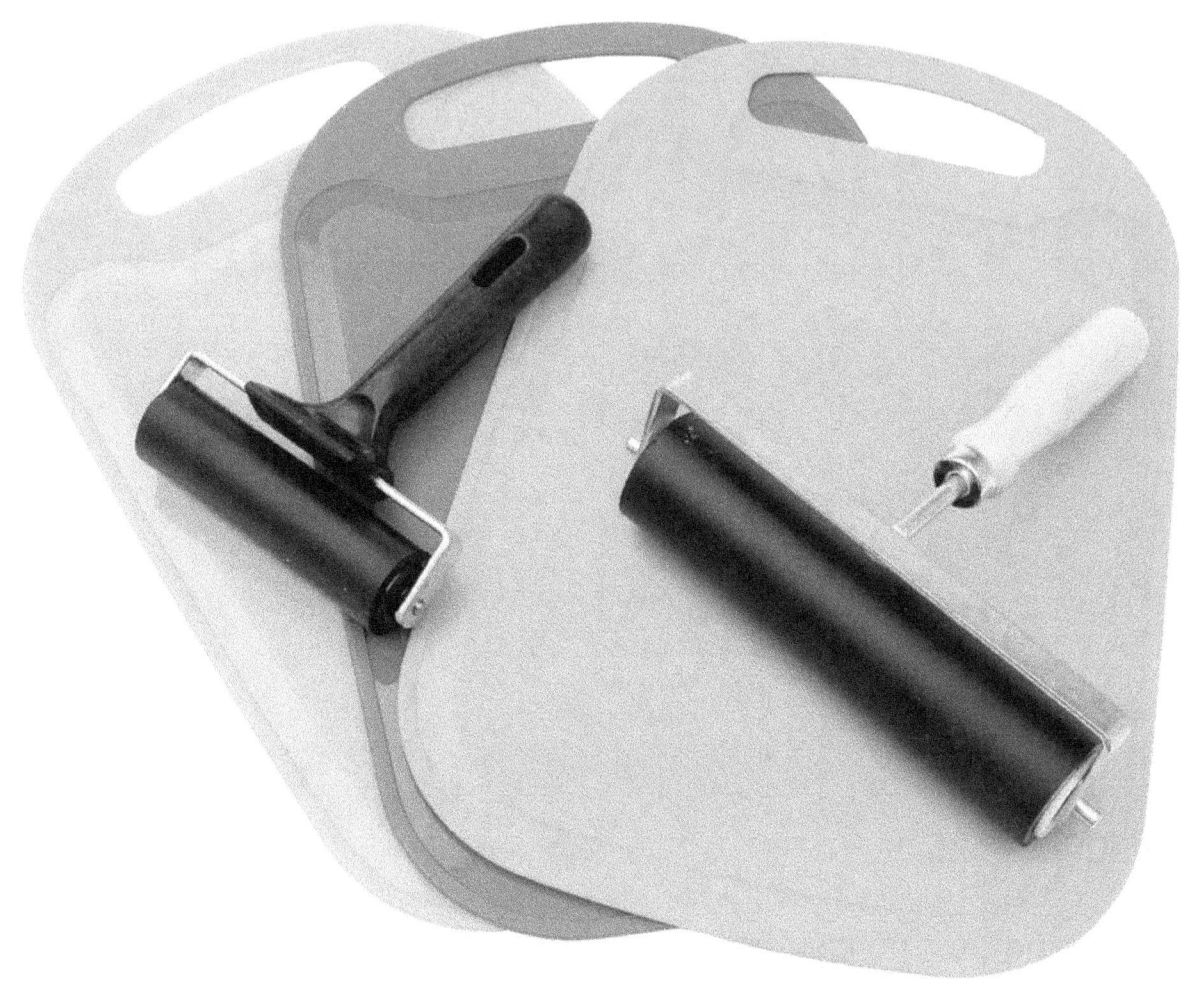

Rollers and Brushes

You will need two different types of rollers to create exciting prints – a fluffy roller to spread paint and a hard, rubber inking roller to spread inks and apply even pressure to create your prints.

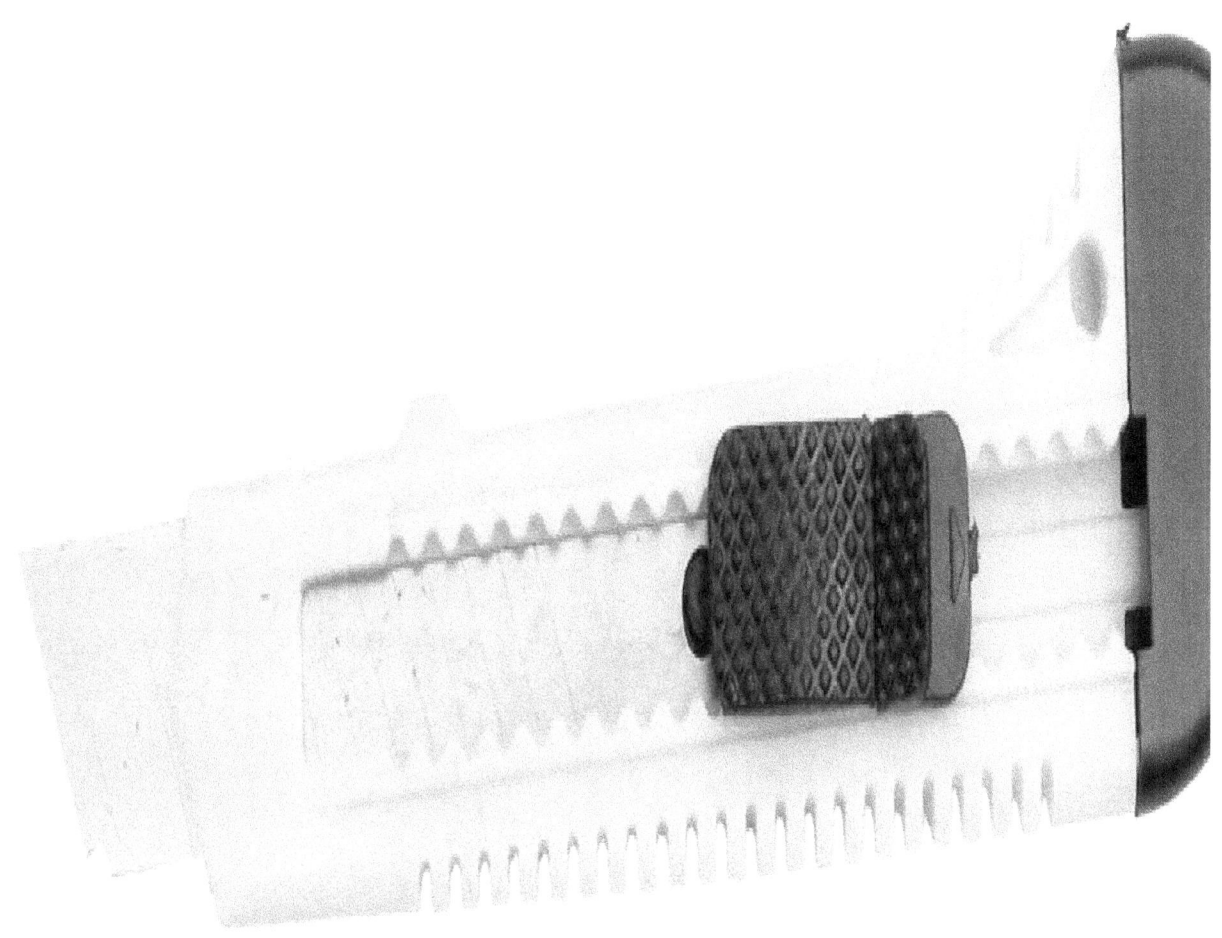

Craft Knives

Be careful! One of the projects in this chapter uses a craft knife. Please ask an adult to help you. NEVER use a craft knife without adult supervision.

Paints

For most printing, you can use acrylic or poster paints. When printing on clothes, bags or shoes, you will need to use fabric paint. Carefully follow the paint's instructions to make sure that it will be colour-fast. If the instructions say to use an iron, ask an adult to help.

APPLE PRINT CANVAS BAG

Printing with fruit and vegetables is easy and it looks great. This fruity canvas bag is perfect for making shopping trips. It saves on using plastic bags, so it's good for the environment!

You will need:

Blank canvas bag

Apples

Fabric paint

Table knife

Plastic chopping board

Paintbrushes

1. Cut some apples in half. You may want to ask an adult to help.

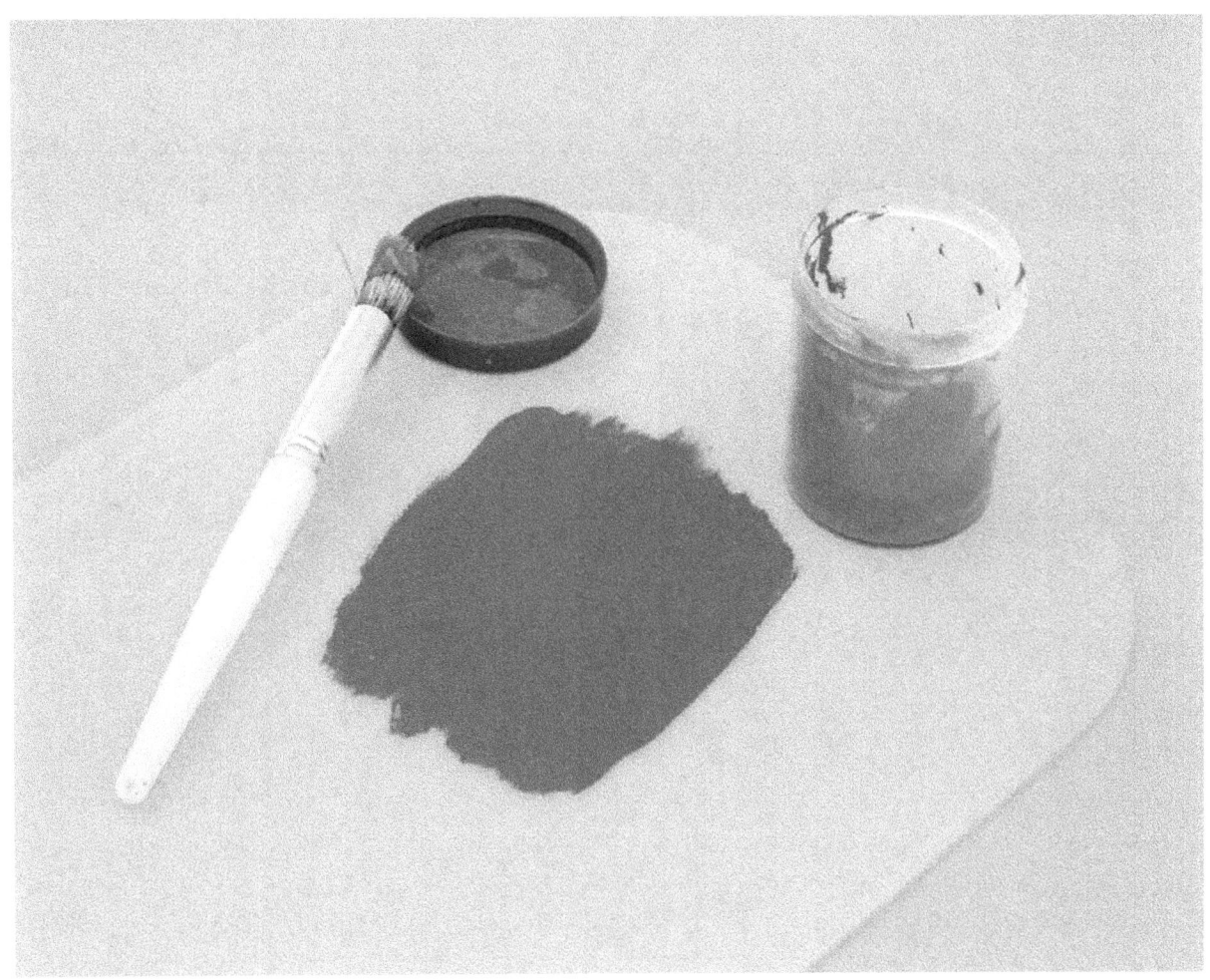

2. Brush a thin layer of fabric paint onto a plastic chopping board.

3. Press the flat part of the apple onto the paint, making sure that the whole flat surface of the apple is covered.

4. Firmly press the apple onto the canvas bag. When you lift it off, you will reveal an apple-shaped print!

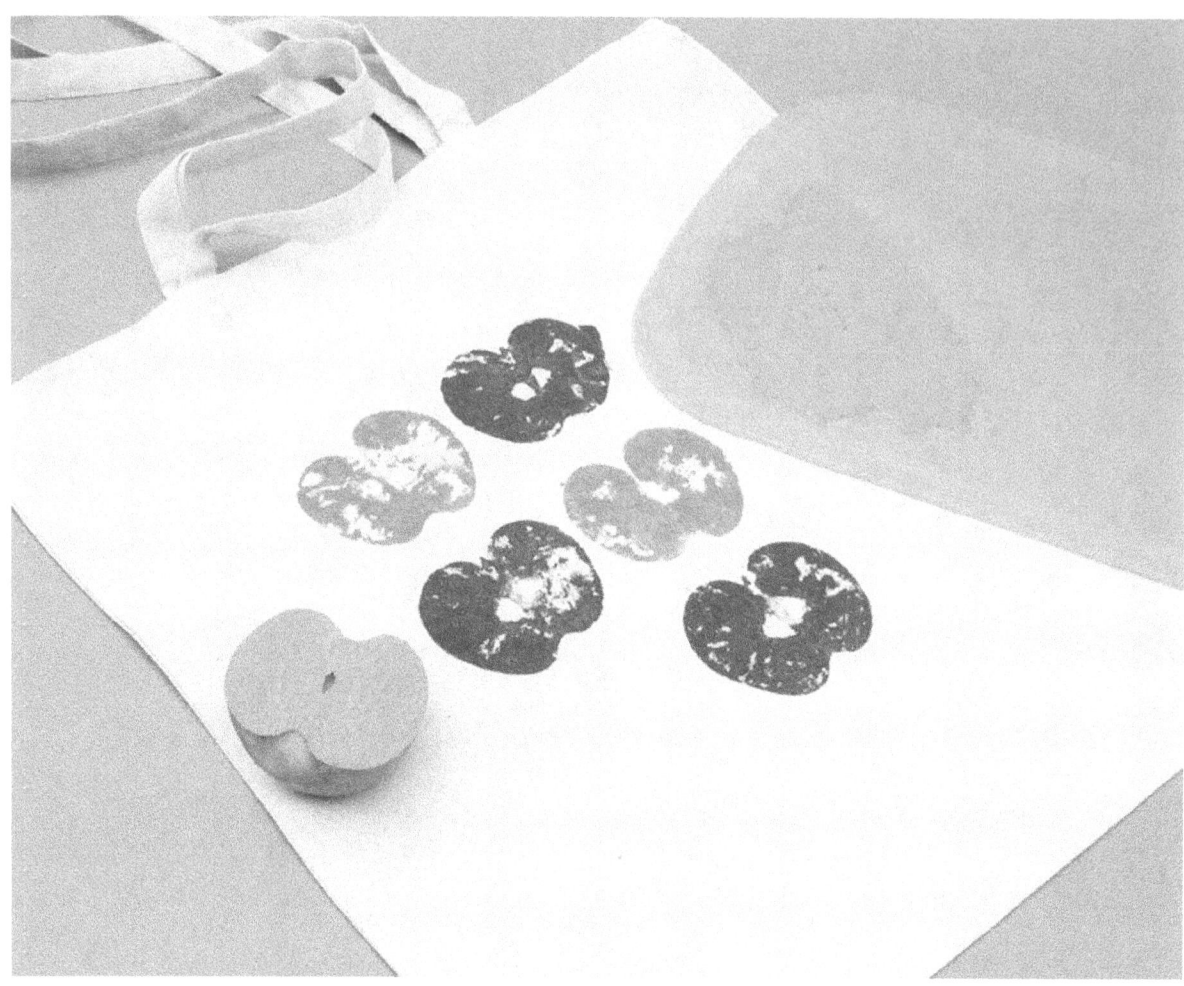

5. Repeat steps 3–4 until you have covered the whole bag, changing colours if you like. Leave to dry. Then check the instructions on your fabric paint. If the instructions say that you should use an iron to fix the paint, ask an adult to help you.

BLOCK PRINTED CARDS

Relief prints are usually made by cutting into wood. Here's how you can create the same effect with craft foam!

You will need:

A wooden block

Craft foam

Craft glue

Scissors

Poster paint

Paintbrush or roller

Blank cards

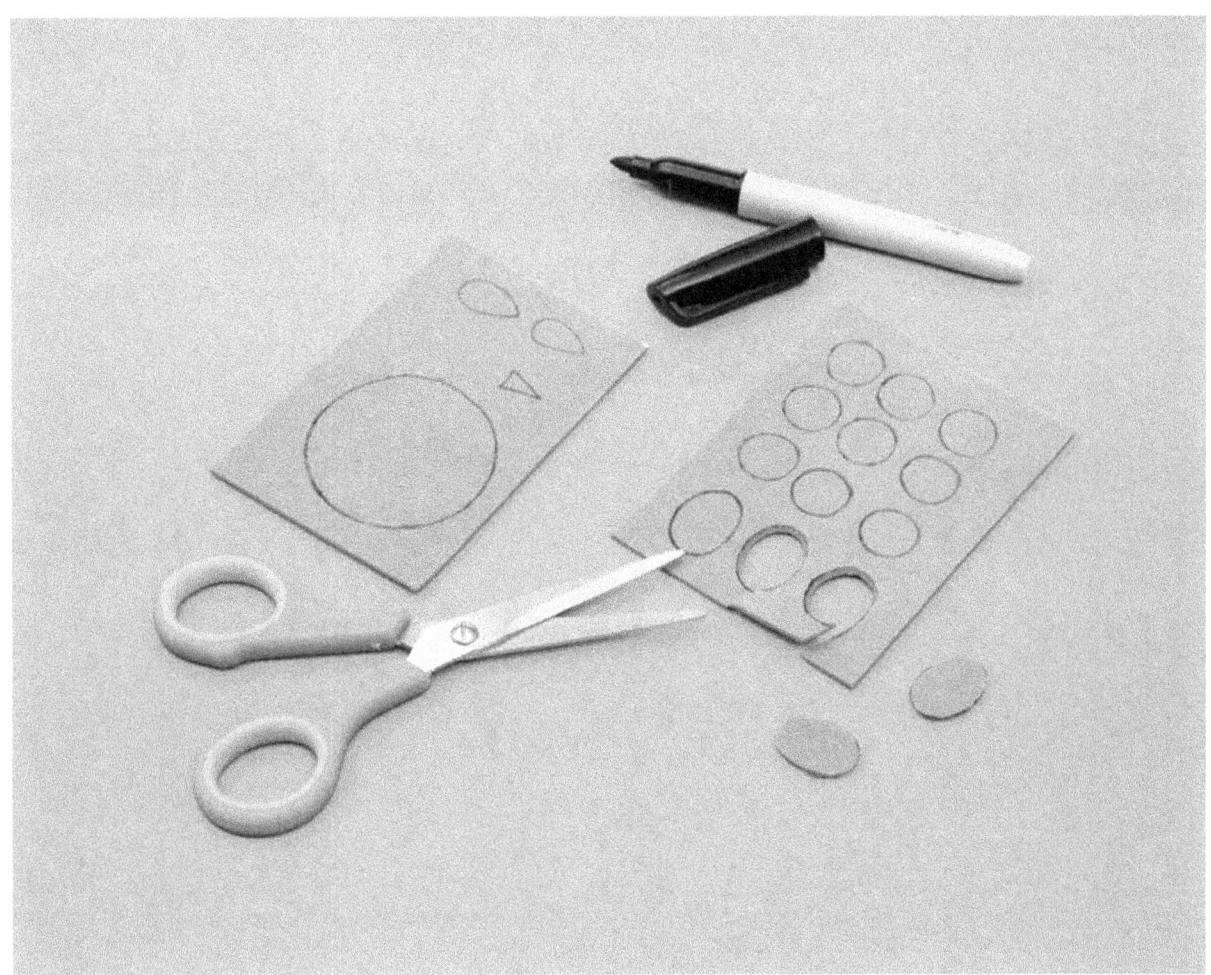

1. Draw shapes onto craft foam and cut them out with scissors. For a bee, you will need a large oval, two teardrop shapes, a triangle and a small circle. For flowers, you will need three large circles and eight small ones.

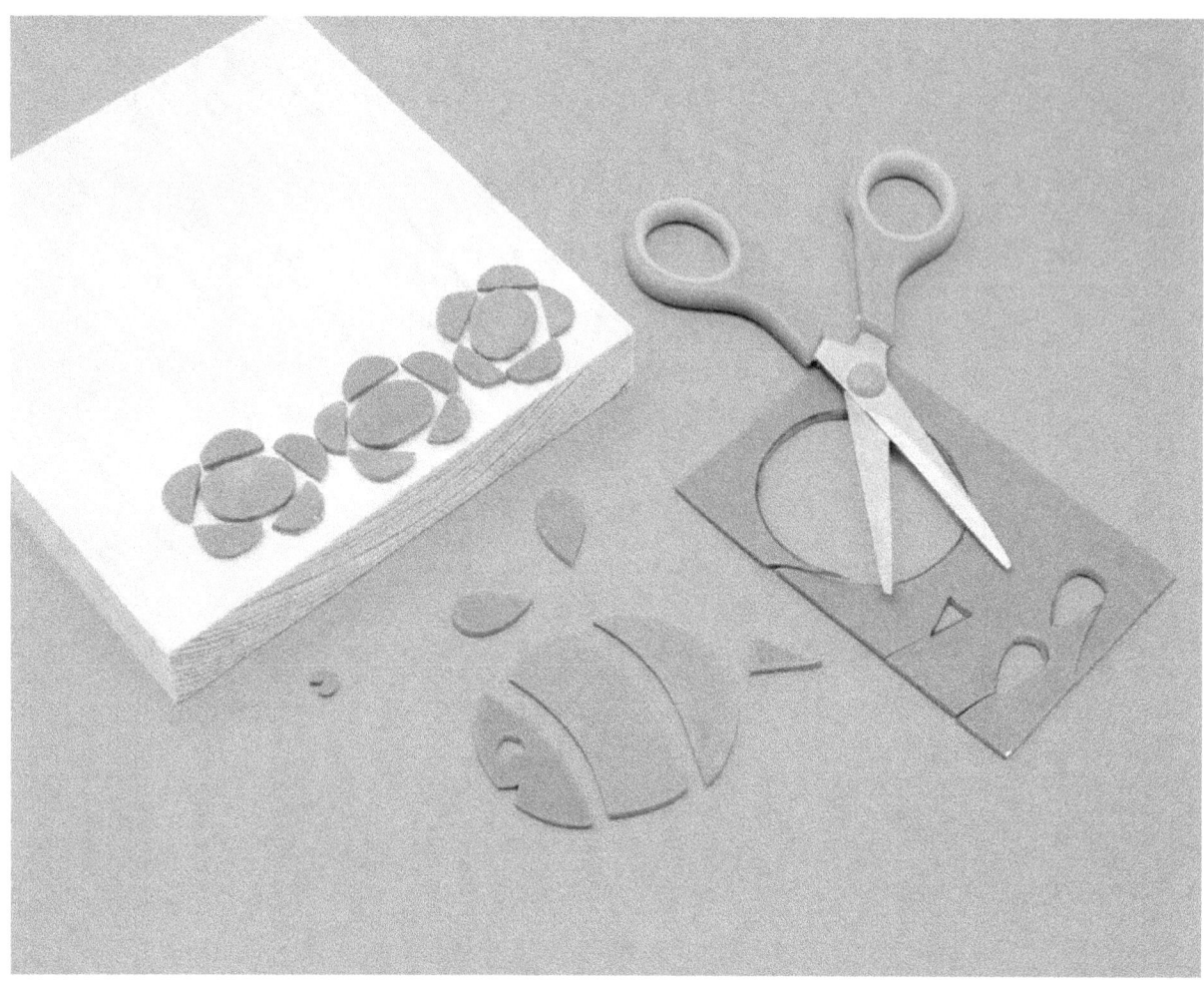

2. Cut each of the small circles in half. Cut the large oval into three parts, and snip into one part to give your bee an eye and a mouth.

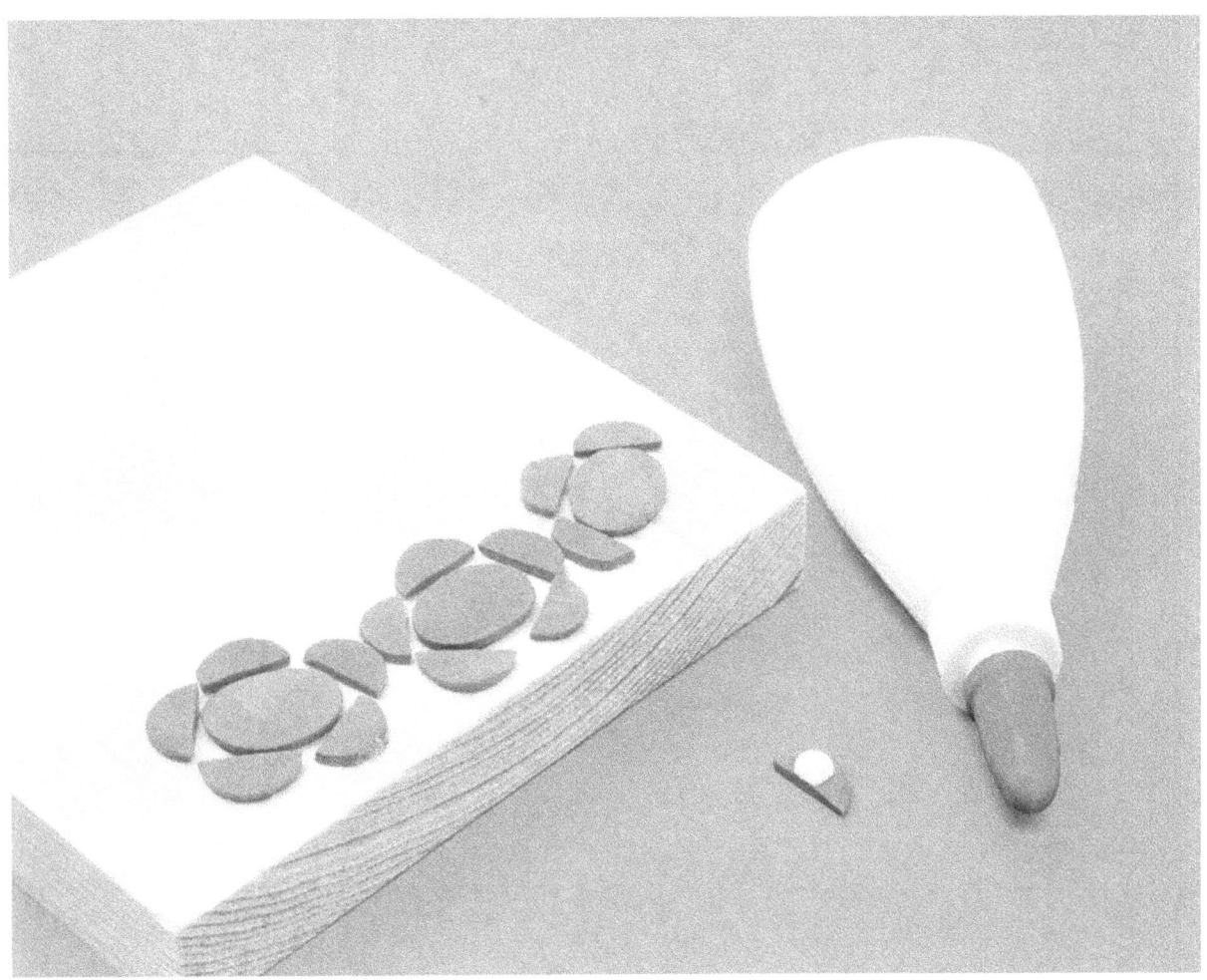

3. Stick the shapes onto the wooden block using craft glue. Leave them to dry.

4. Paint or roller a thin layer of paint onto the block. Then press it onto the card.

5. Carefully peel off the block to reveal your design. Repeat steps 4 and 5 if you would like to print more cards!

STENCIL ART PLANT POT

Because the stencils in this project are flexible, you can use them to print on curved surfaces! You will need an adult to help you with cutting out the stencils. Never use a craft knife without adult supervision.

You will need:

Paper

Black marker pen

2 sheets of acetate paper

2 sheets of tracing paper

Craft knife or scalpel

Paint

Clay plant pot

Brush

Masking tape

1. Draw your design onto a piece of paper.

2. Trace the lines of your drawing onto tracing paper, but leave little spaces in the lines. Then trace the outline onto a separate piece of tracing paper, and colour it in.

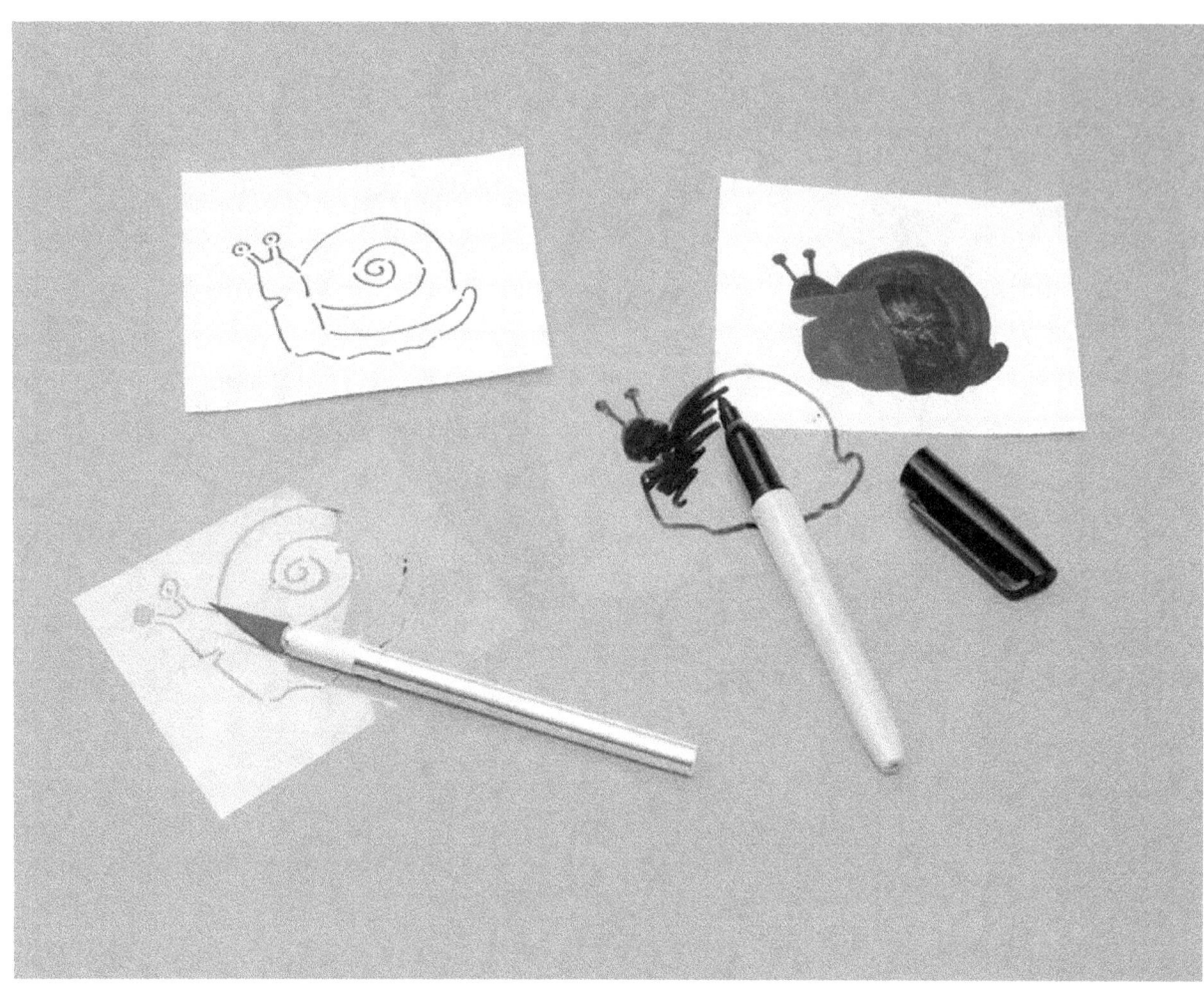

3. Trace the spaced-line drawing and the outline drawing onto acetate paper. Ask an adult to cut out everything coloured black on the acetate sheets with a scalpel or craft knife.

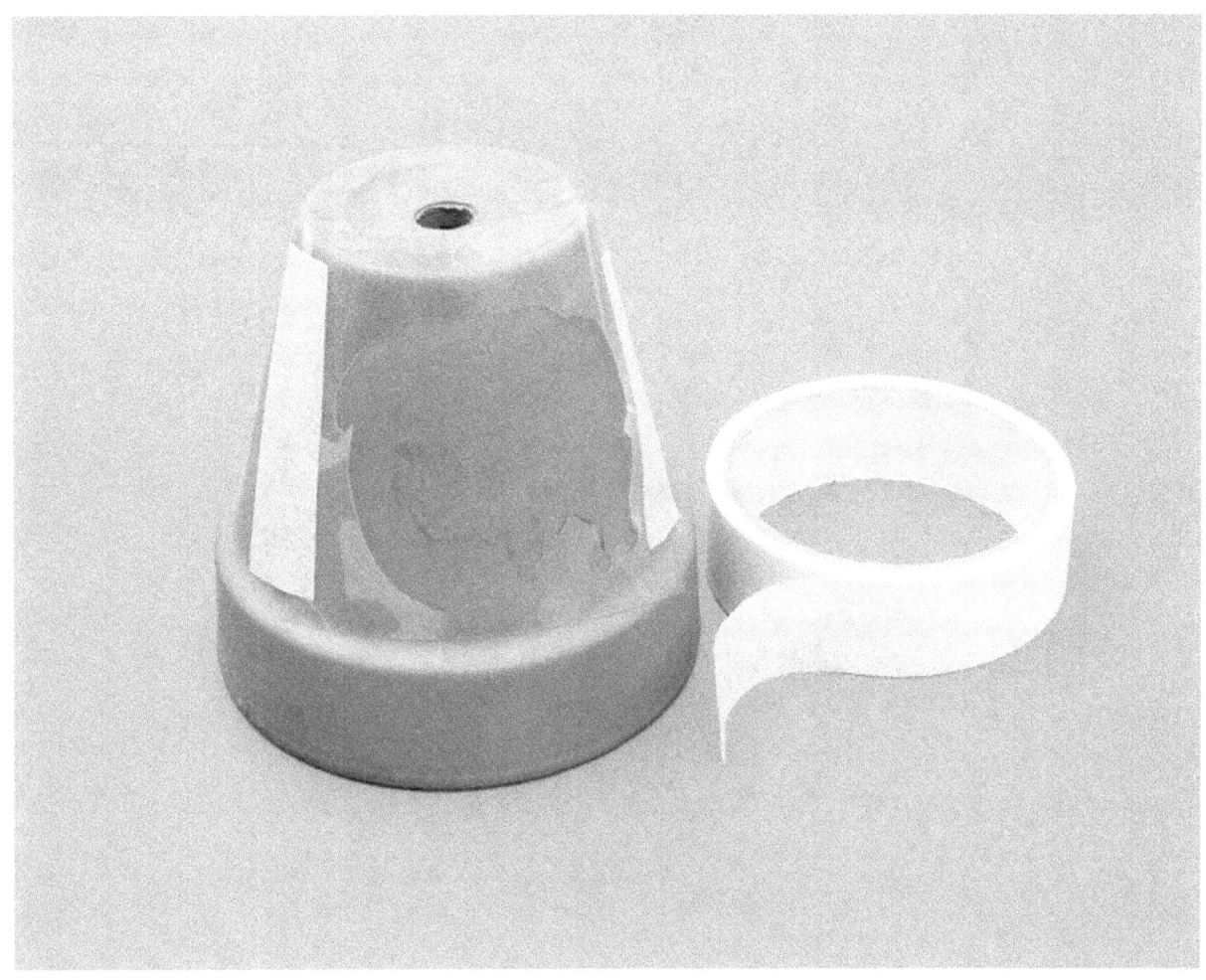

4. Fix the stencil with the larger cut-out areas to the clay pot, using your masking tape.

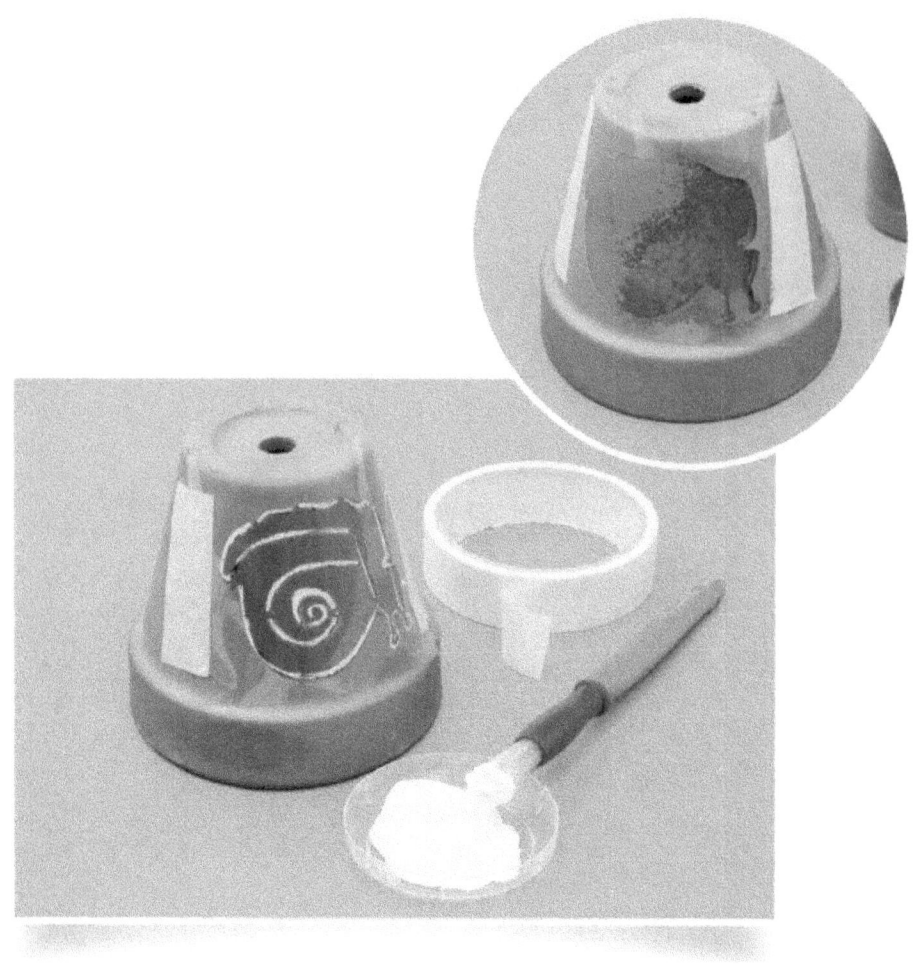

5. Paint everything inside the template area blue and leave to dry.

6. Now tape the other stencil over the top and use white paint to add the final layer to your design. Wait for it to dry.

CLAY PRINTING

You can make prints in wet clay and make prints from wet clay! This double printing method makes beautiful pictures. The prints look best when the clay is still wet, so you have to work fast!

You will need:

Air-drying clay

Clay tools (or ordinary cutlery)

Rolling pin

String

Printing roller

Foam roller

Paint

Sturdy paper

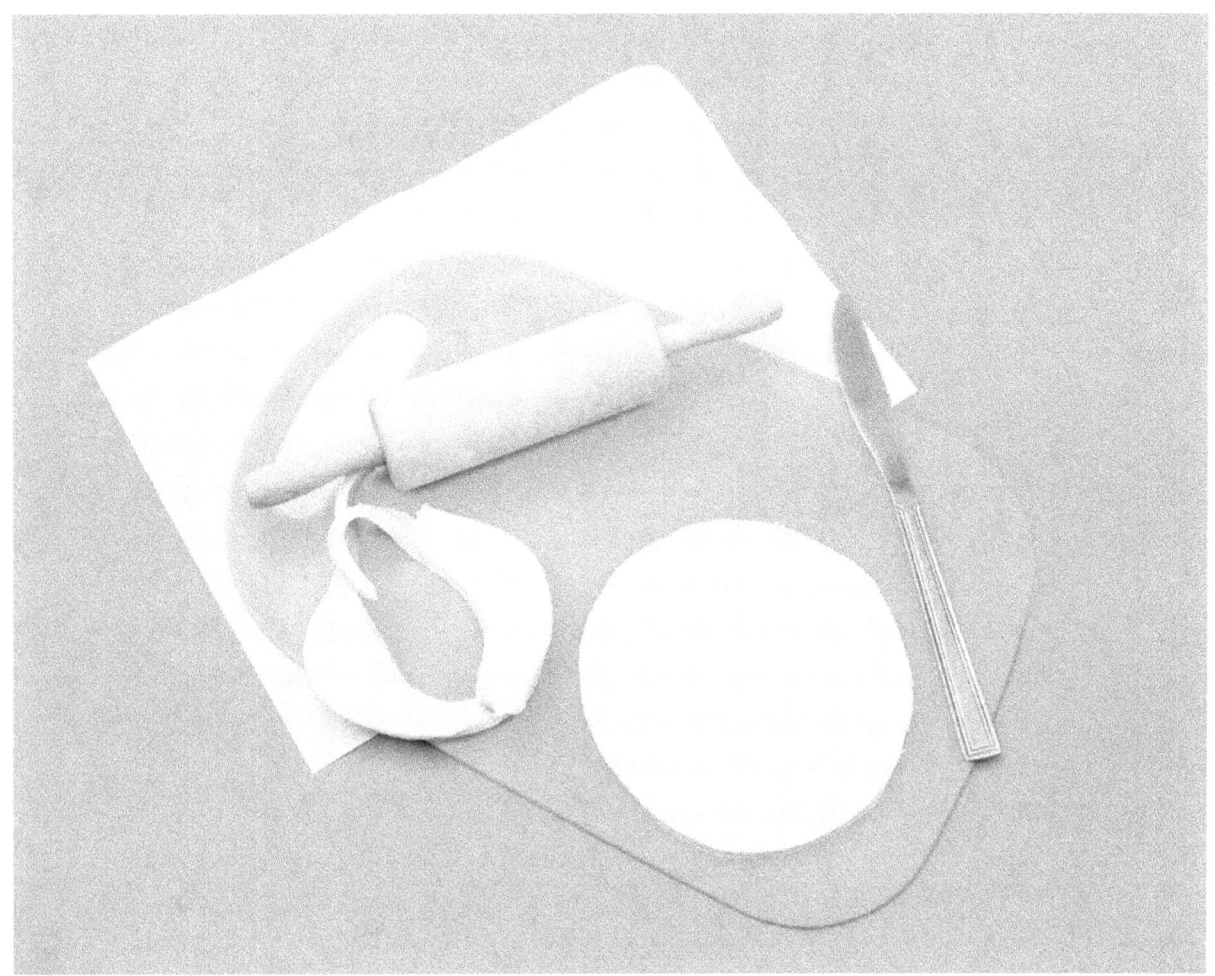

1. Roll out your clay so that you have a piece that is 1 cm (0.3 in) thick and smaller than your piece of paper.

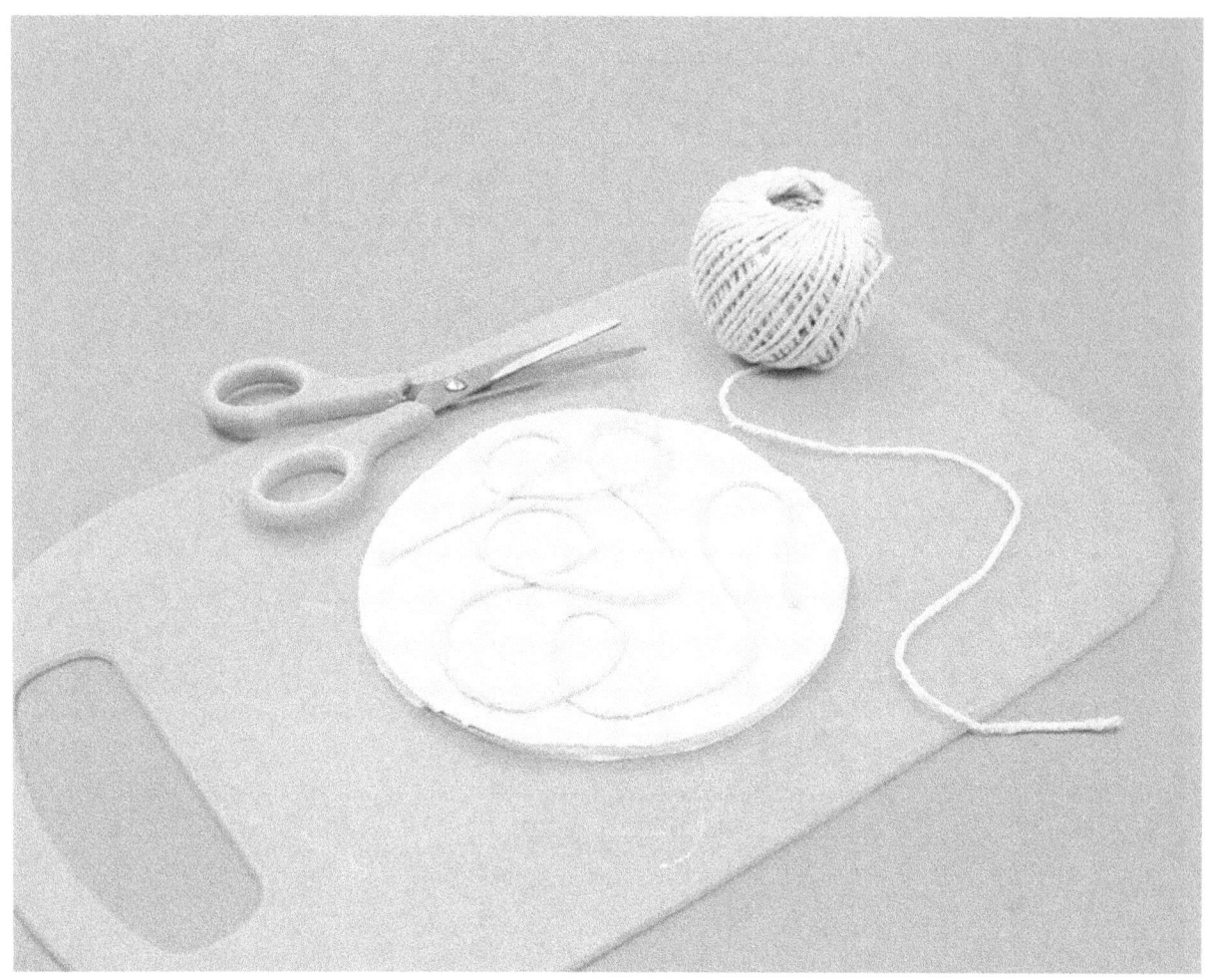

2. Place your string on top of the clay in an interesting pattern. Press down to make an imprint before you remove it.

3. Use clay tools (or a knife and fork) to add more details in the clay.

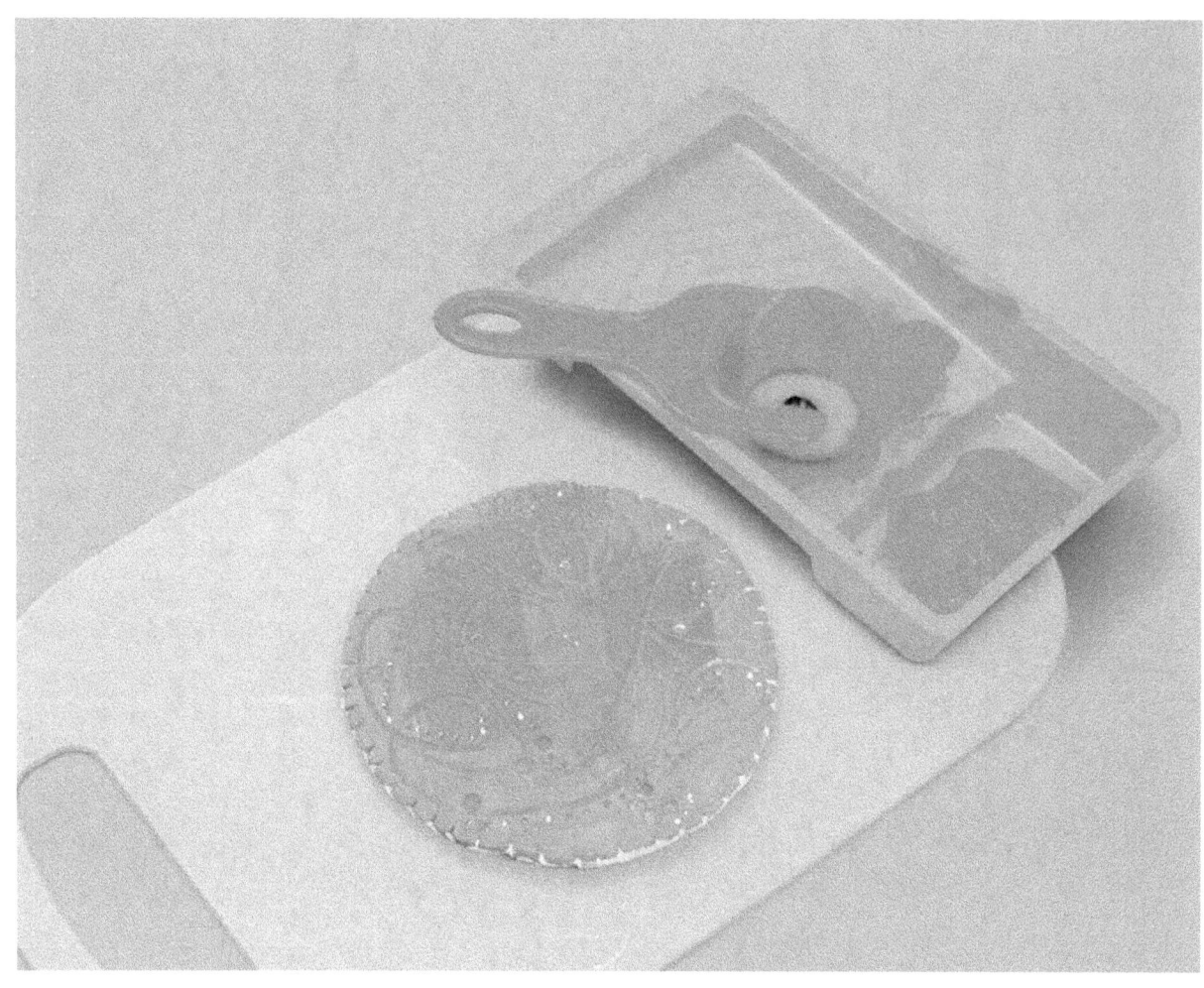

4. Roll a thin layer of paint onto the clay.

5. Place a piece of paper on top and use either another roller or your hands to press it down.

6. Remove the paper to reveal your print.

When you have finished your prints, make a hole at the top of the clay slab before leaving it to dry. When the clay has hardened you can hang it up as a plaque!

CLING FILM WRAPPING PAPER

Cling film may be good for wrapping up food, but it's also great for craft projects. This cool wrapping paper will really make your gifts stand out from the rest!

You will need

Plastic chopping board

Cling film

Aluminium foil

Paper and scissors

Poster paint and silver paint

Paintbrushes

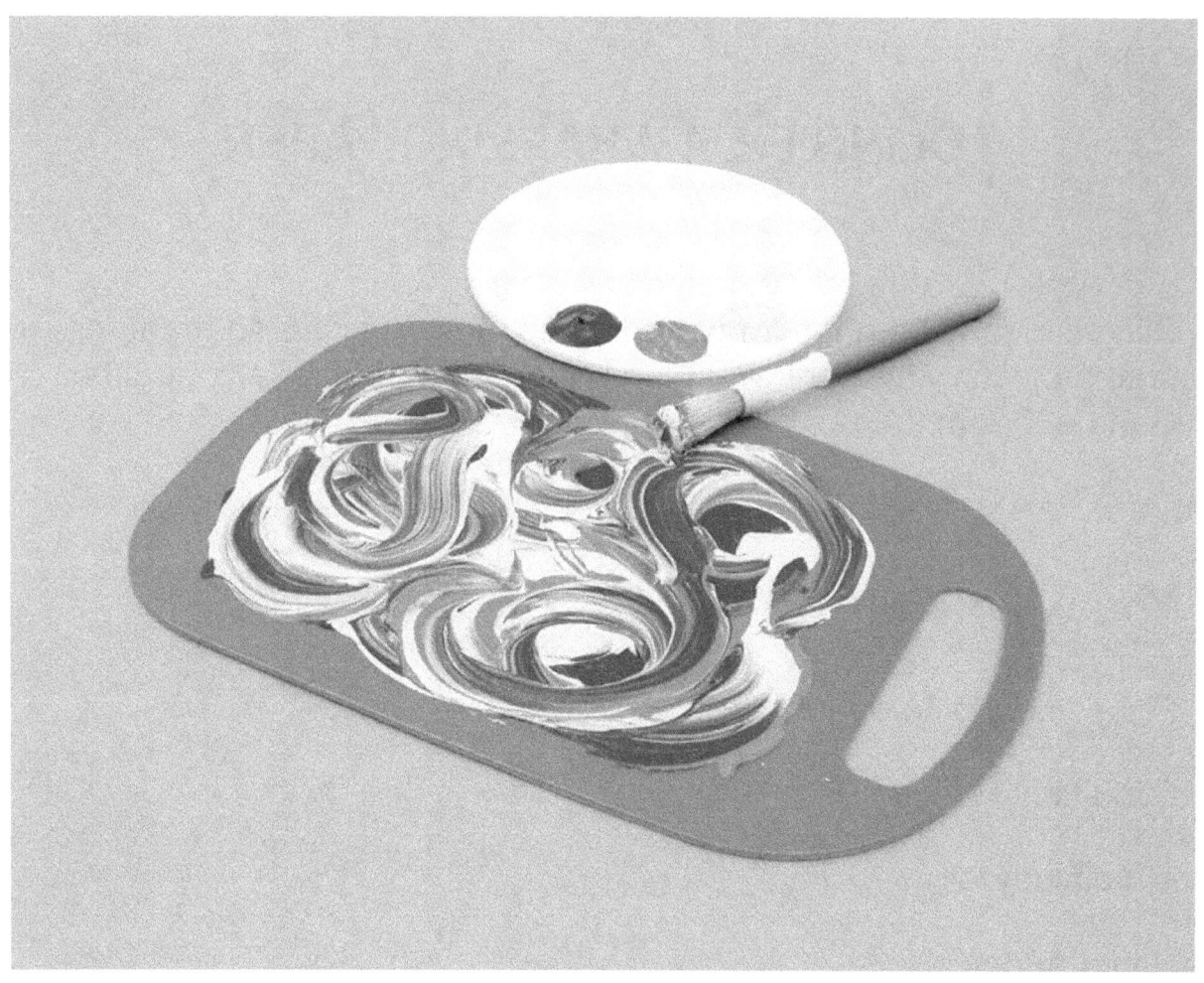

1. Spread three colours of paint onto your chopping board, swirling them together with your paintbrush to make a pattern.

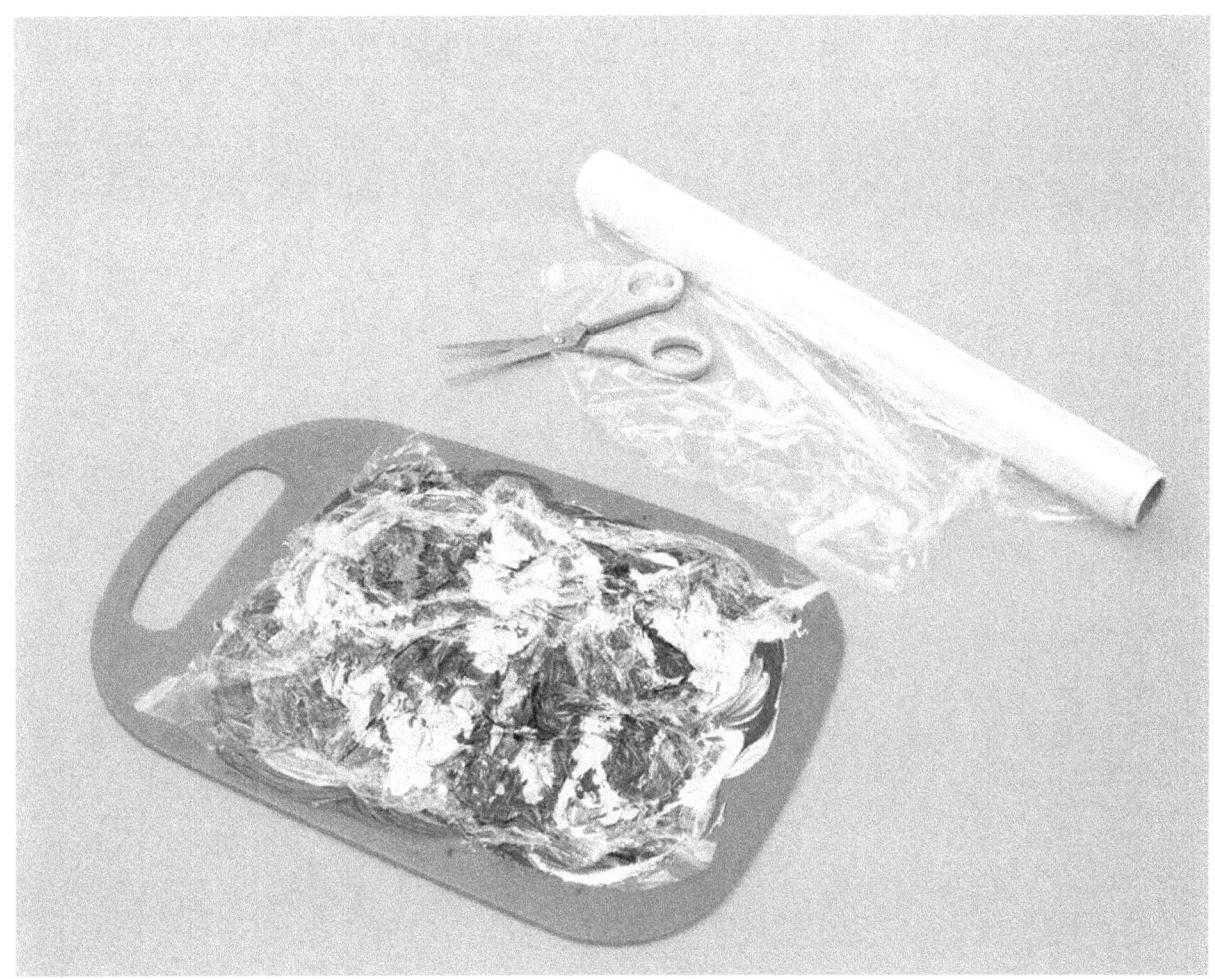

2. Put a square of cling film onto the paint mixture and press it down.

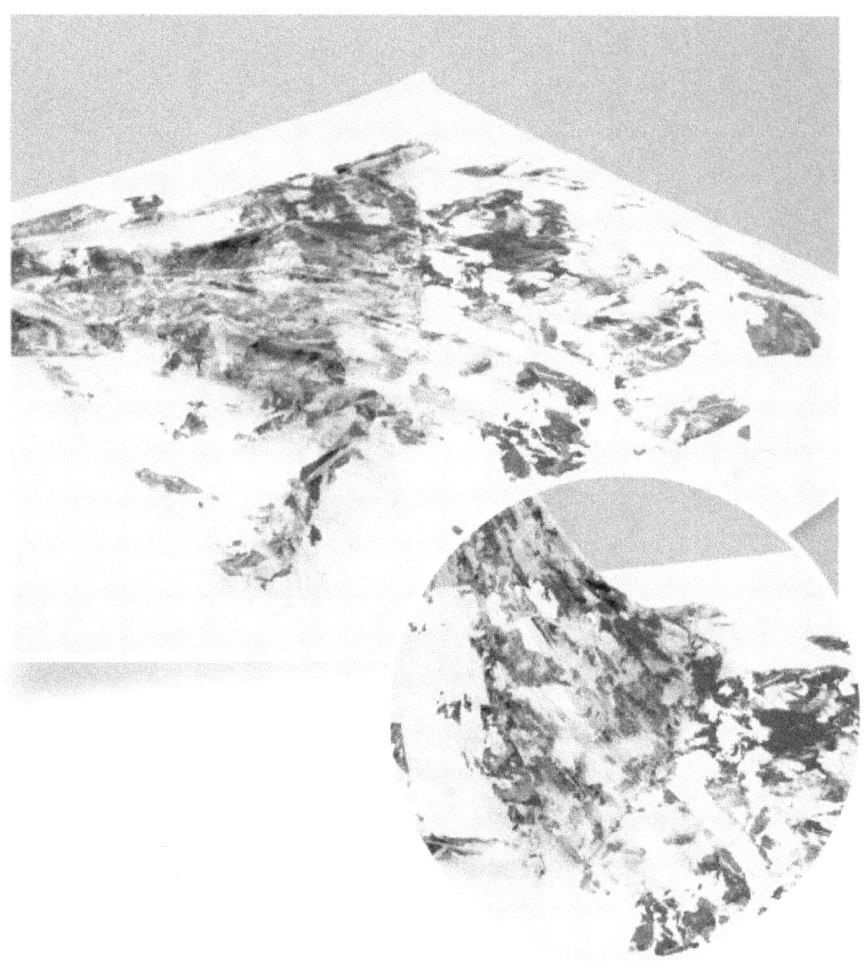

3. Carefully lift the cling film and lower it onto your paper. You do not want it to be a flat print so it doesn't matter if it scrunches up. Lift off the cling film to reveal your pattern.

4. Repeat steps 2–3 until you have covered the whole piece of paper. Leave to dry.

5. For some added sparkle, paint the chopping board with silver paint. Scrunch up some aluminium foil and press it onto the silver paint. Then press it onto the paper.

BUTTON PRINT TRAINERS

Here is how you can make your old trainers look fresh and exciting! This type of printing uses found objects. If you don't want to use buttons or don't have any to hand, you can try using bottle tops instead.

You will need

Bottle corks

Buttons

Craft glue

Old plain-coloured canvas trainers

Fabric paint, paintbrush and palette

Black felt-tip pen

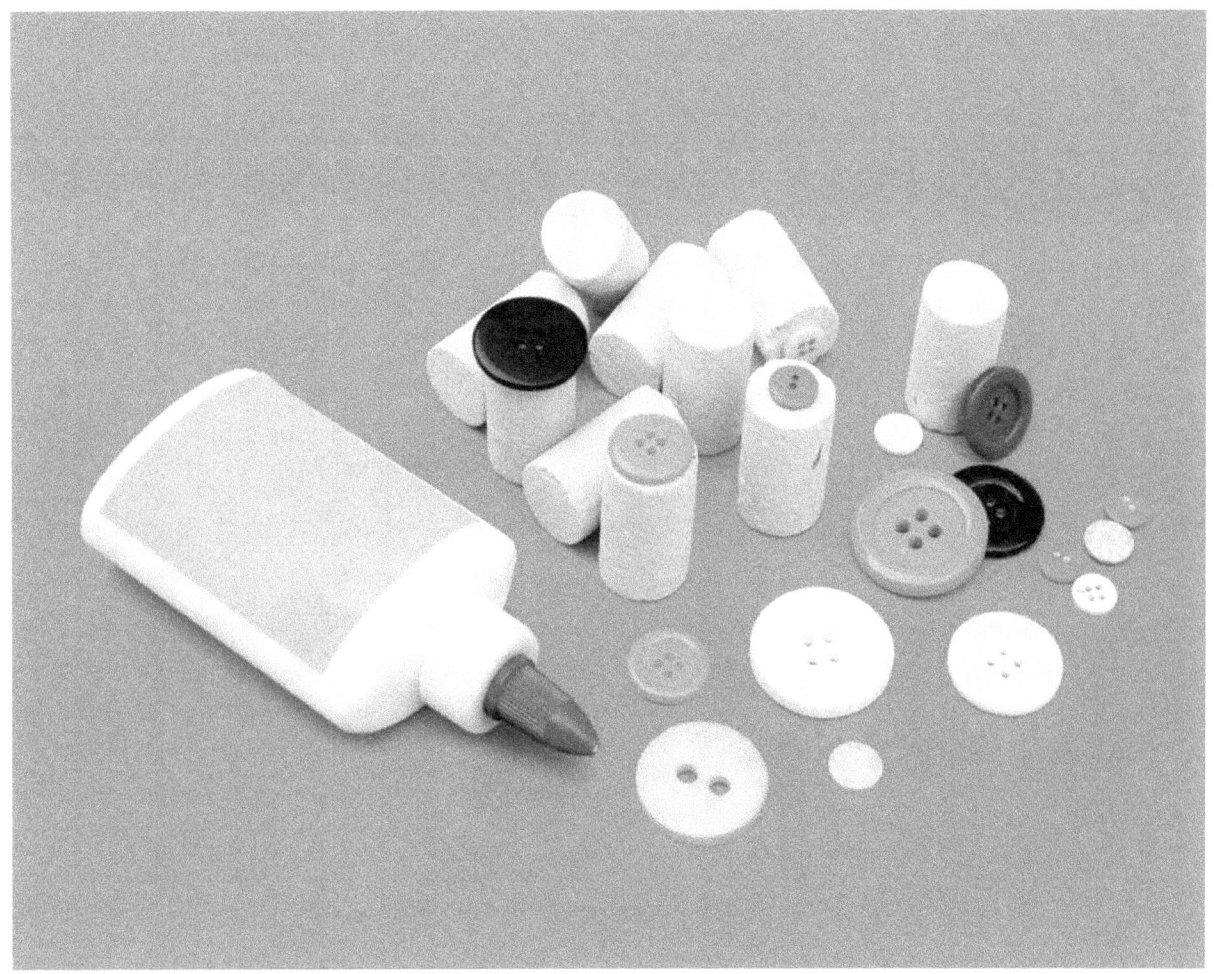

1. Glue some buttons onto the top of bottle corks, using craft glue. Leave them to dry.

2. Use a paintbrush to paint a layer of fabric paint onto one of the button stamps.

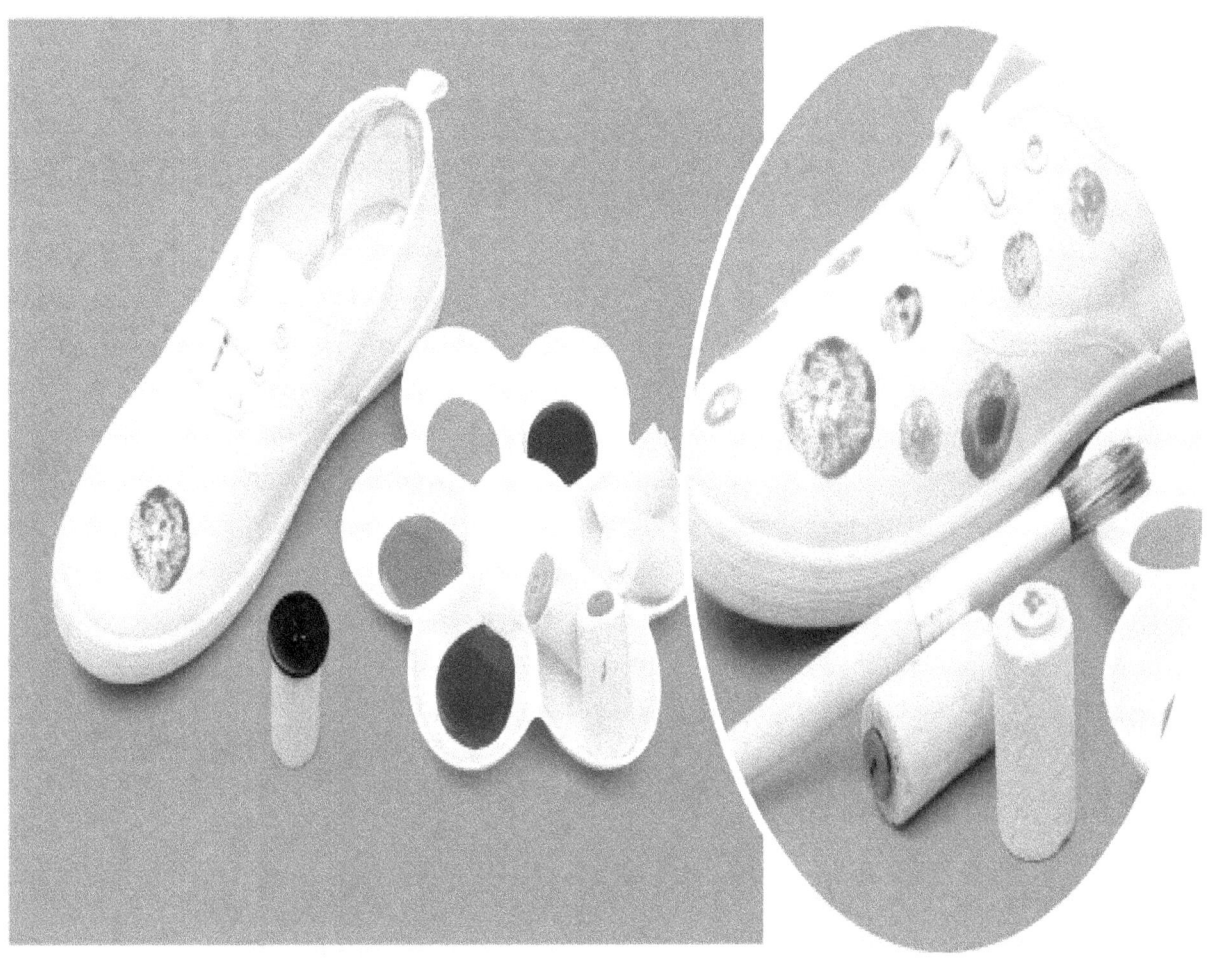

3. Press the stamp onto the trainer and lift it off to reveal your print. Repeat with all the other button stamps and cover your trainers with lots of prints.

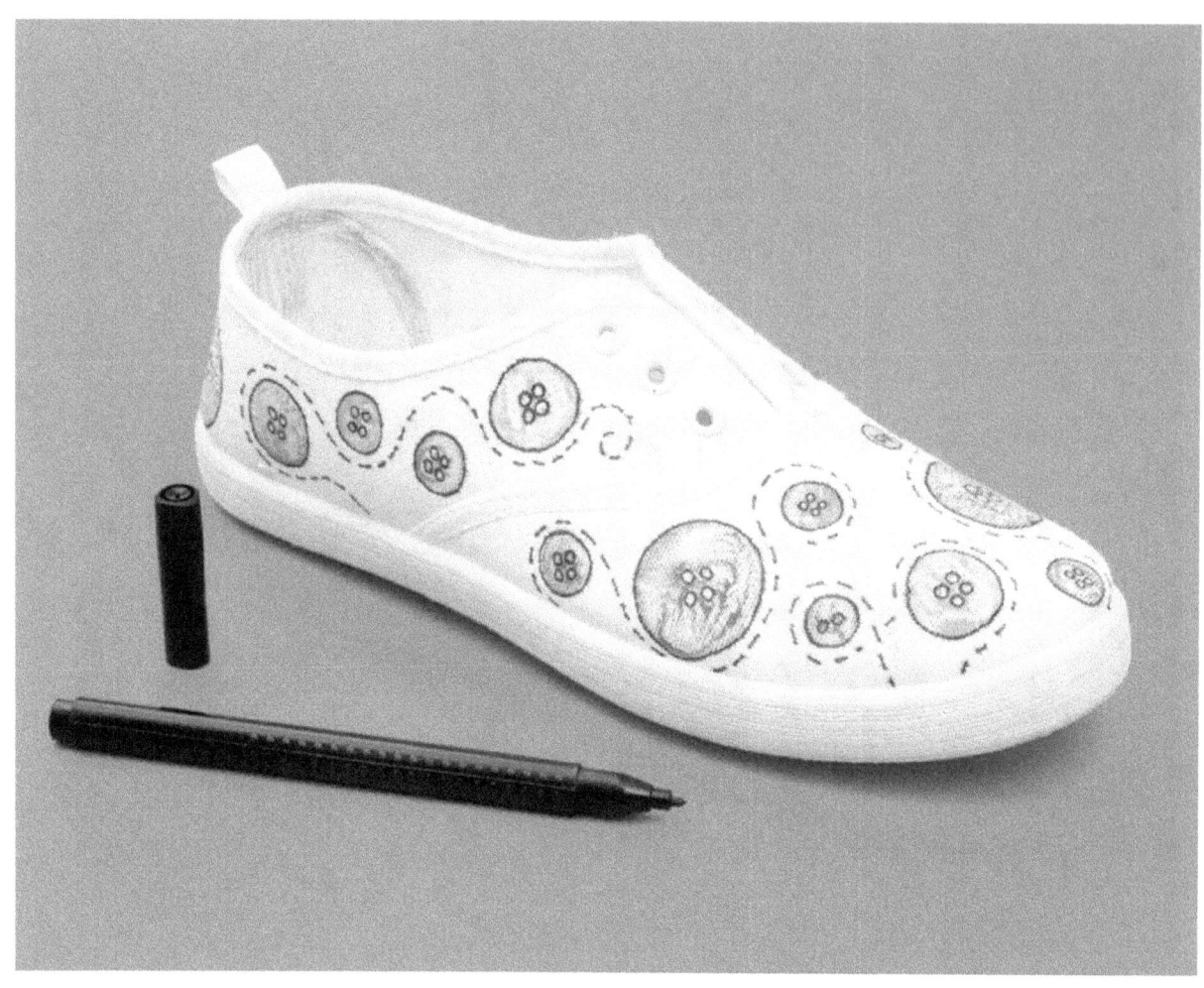

4. Add to your design using a black felt-tip pen.

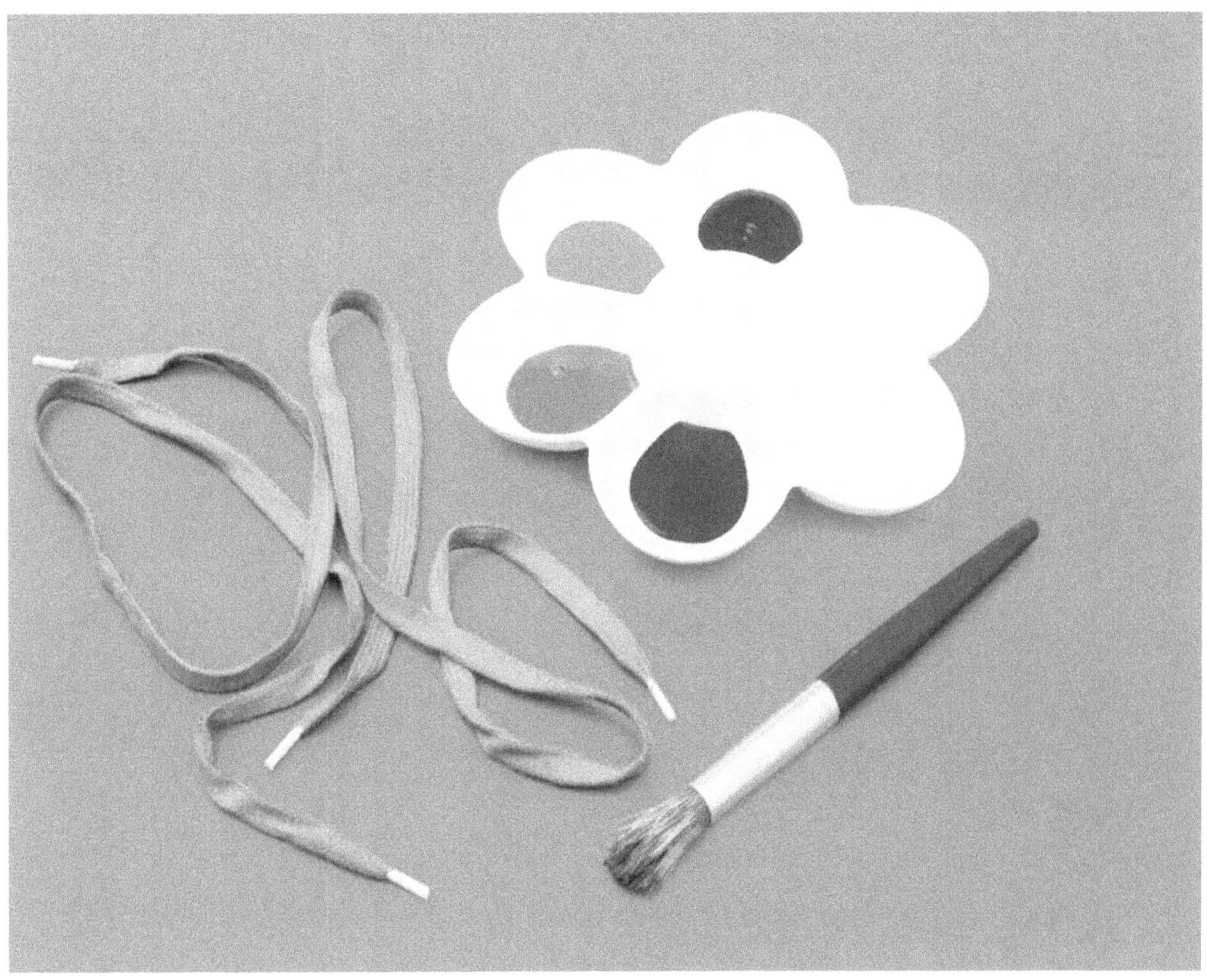

5. Paint the laces in a bright colour and leave them to dry. Finally, check the instructions for your fabric paint. If you need to use an iron to fix the paint, ask an adult to help.

EASY SCREEN PRINTS

Screen printing is similar to stencil printing, except that the ink is pushed through a mesh using a tool called a squeegee. If you do not have a squeegee, try using a plastic card instead.

You will need

Wooden frame (an old photo frame will work)

Drawing pins

Voile (fine netting)

PVA glue

Paint and paintbrush

Plastic card

Paper and pencil

Black marker

1. Draw a pattern or illustration onto a piece of paper, using bold, heavy lines.

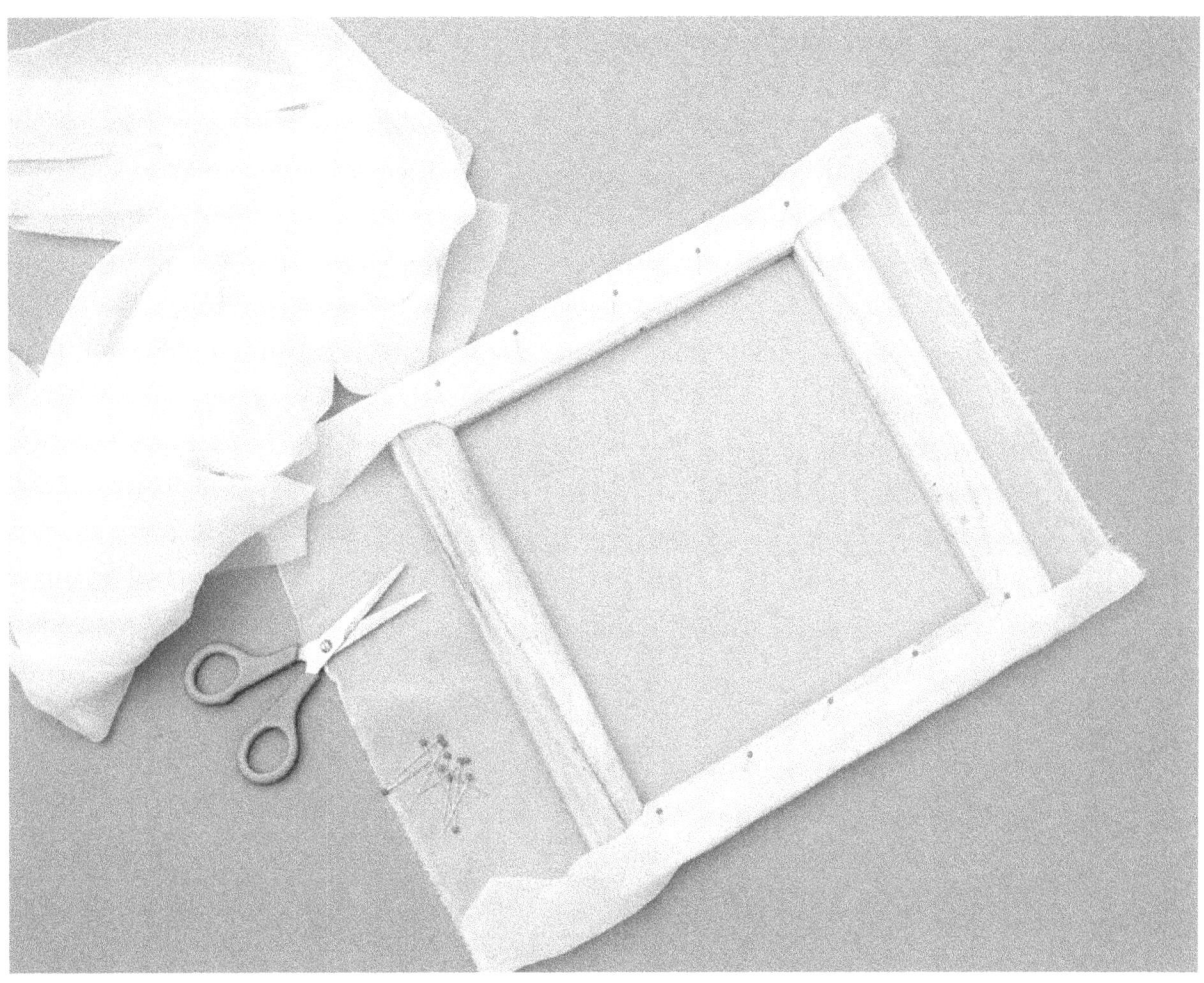

2. Stretch some voile netting across a frame, and ask an adult to pin it in place.

3. Trace around the outside of the black lines in your design onto the netting, using a fine pencil line.

4. First, protect your surface! Then paint over the whole screen with PVA glue, except for the areas inside your pencil lines. Do the same to the other side. Leave it to dry.

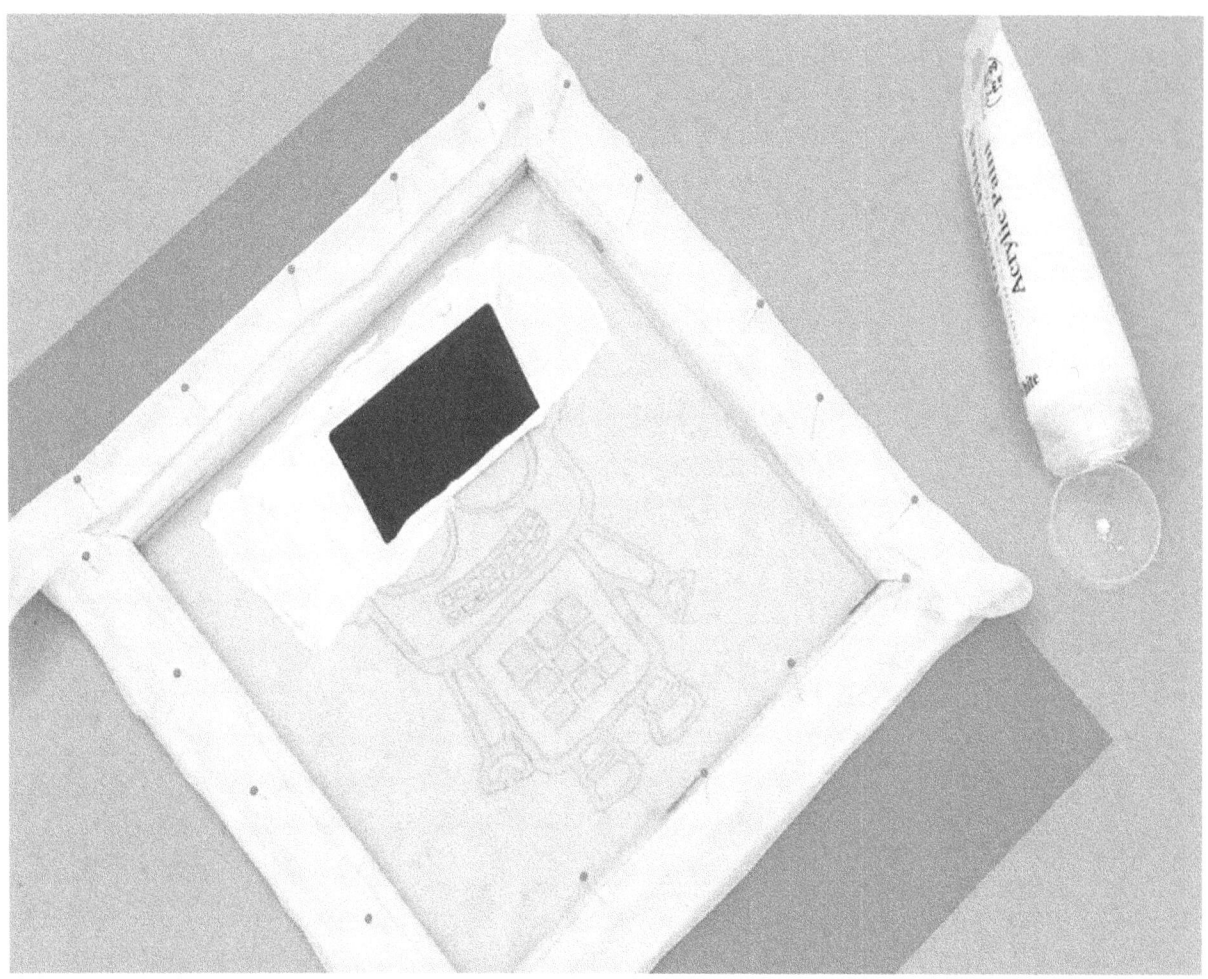

5. Place the screen on top of a piece of coloured paper. Ask someone to hold it in place for you. Brush some paint across the top of the netting, then use a plastic card to drag the paint across the screen. When you have finished, take another piece of paper, and repeat as many times as you like. Finally, cut around your prints with scissors.

SPOTTY PAINTED MUGS

Teatime will never be dull again with this personalised mug. But beware, once you have a mug that looks this good, everyone will want to use it!

You will need

Ceramic paints

Pencil and marker pen

Plain mug

Carbon paper

Paper

Scissors

Masking tape

Cotton bud

1. Measure around your mug, then measure the height and cut a piece of paper to the same size. Use this to draw your design onto.

2. Tape some carbon paper onto the mug, and then tape your design on top of that.

3. Trace over your design with a pencil, pressing hard. Then remove the papers from the mug to reveal a faint print.

4. Start to paint on the mug by dabbing on ceramic paint with a cotton bud.

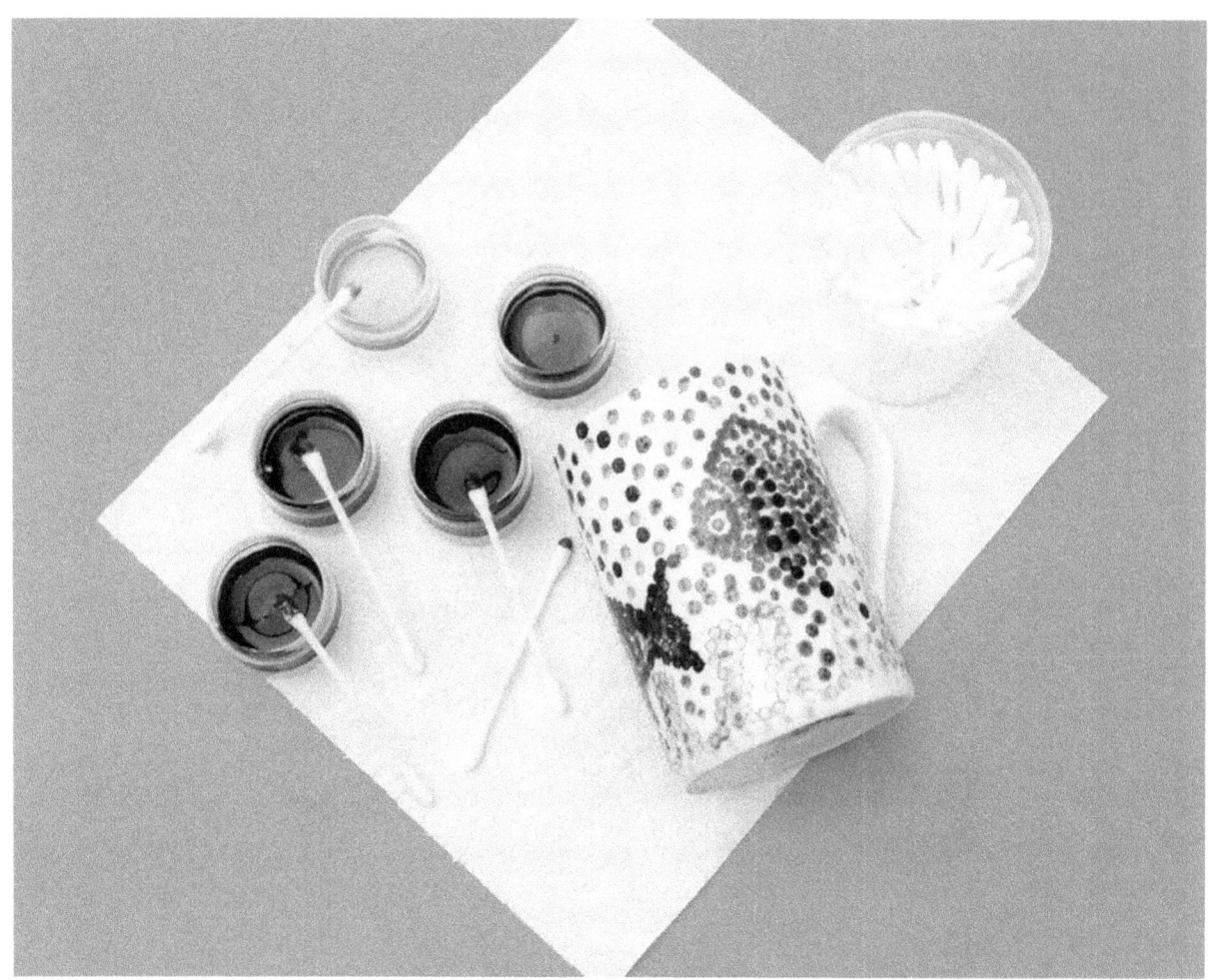

5. Keep stippling (dotting) on the ceramic paint until you have finished your picture! Then you will need to follow the instructions on the label of your ceramic paint to make it set. Most ceramic paints will need to be baked in the oven.

WARNING!

If the instructions for the ceramic paint tell you to use the oven, ask an adult to help. Don't do this on your own!

SANDPAPER PRINTING

You may think that sandpaper is only good for making things smooth... but think again! It's great for making one-off prints onto fabric too. We've used this technique to decorate a pencil case.

You will need

Medium coarse sandpaper

Crayons

Iron

A plain fabric pencil case

Card

Tea towel or piece of fabric

Scissors

1. Cut a piece of sandpaper to the same shape as the pencil case. Draw a design on it, using coloured crayons.

2. Keep adding to your picture to fill the whole space. Make sure that you press down firmly, to create a thick layer of wax.

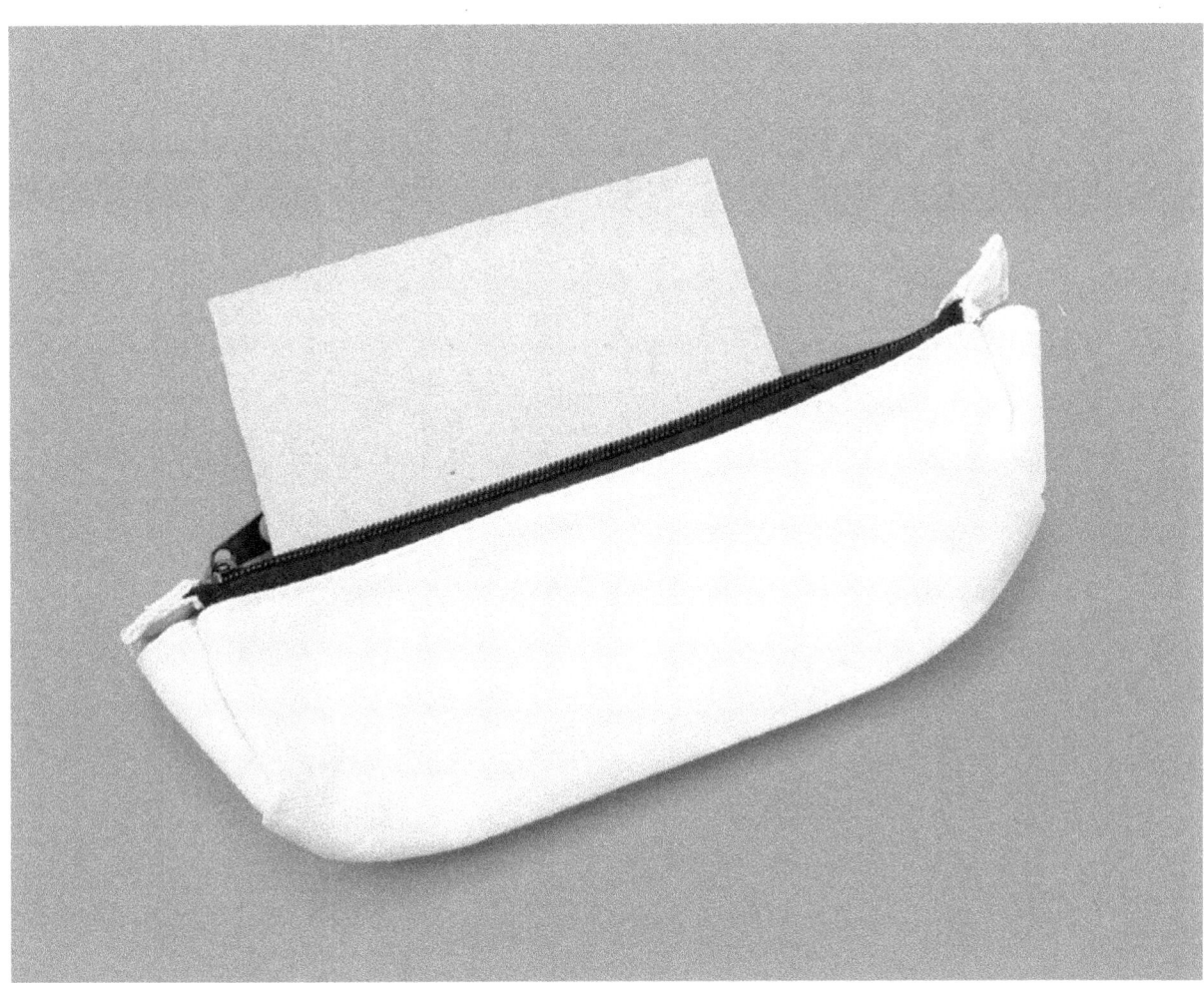

3. Place a piece of card underneath the fabric that you are going to transfer the pattern onto. If you're using a pencil case, place the cardboard inside.

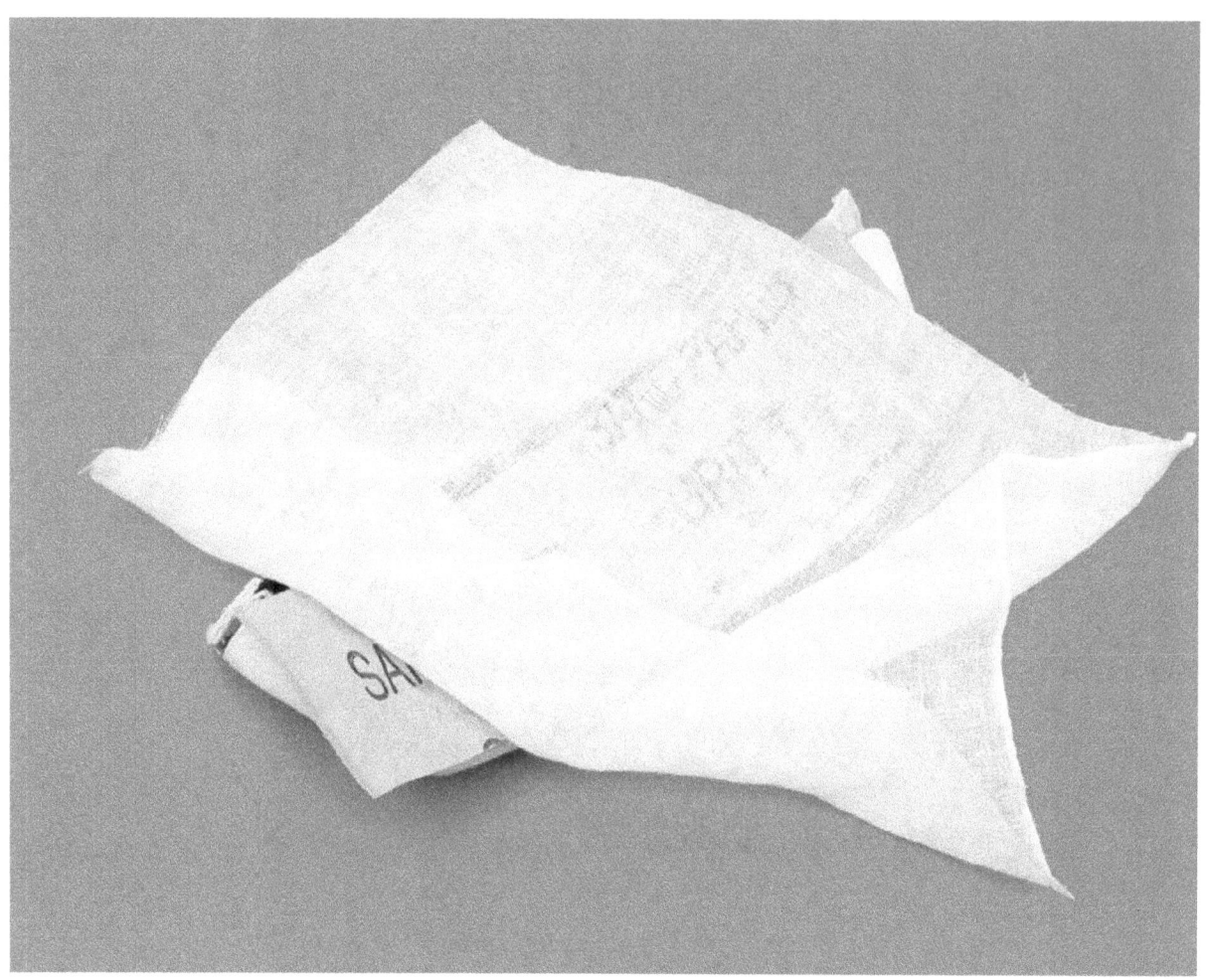

4. Place your sandpaper onto your fabric with the pattern facing down. Cover it with a tea towel or piece of fabric.

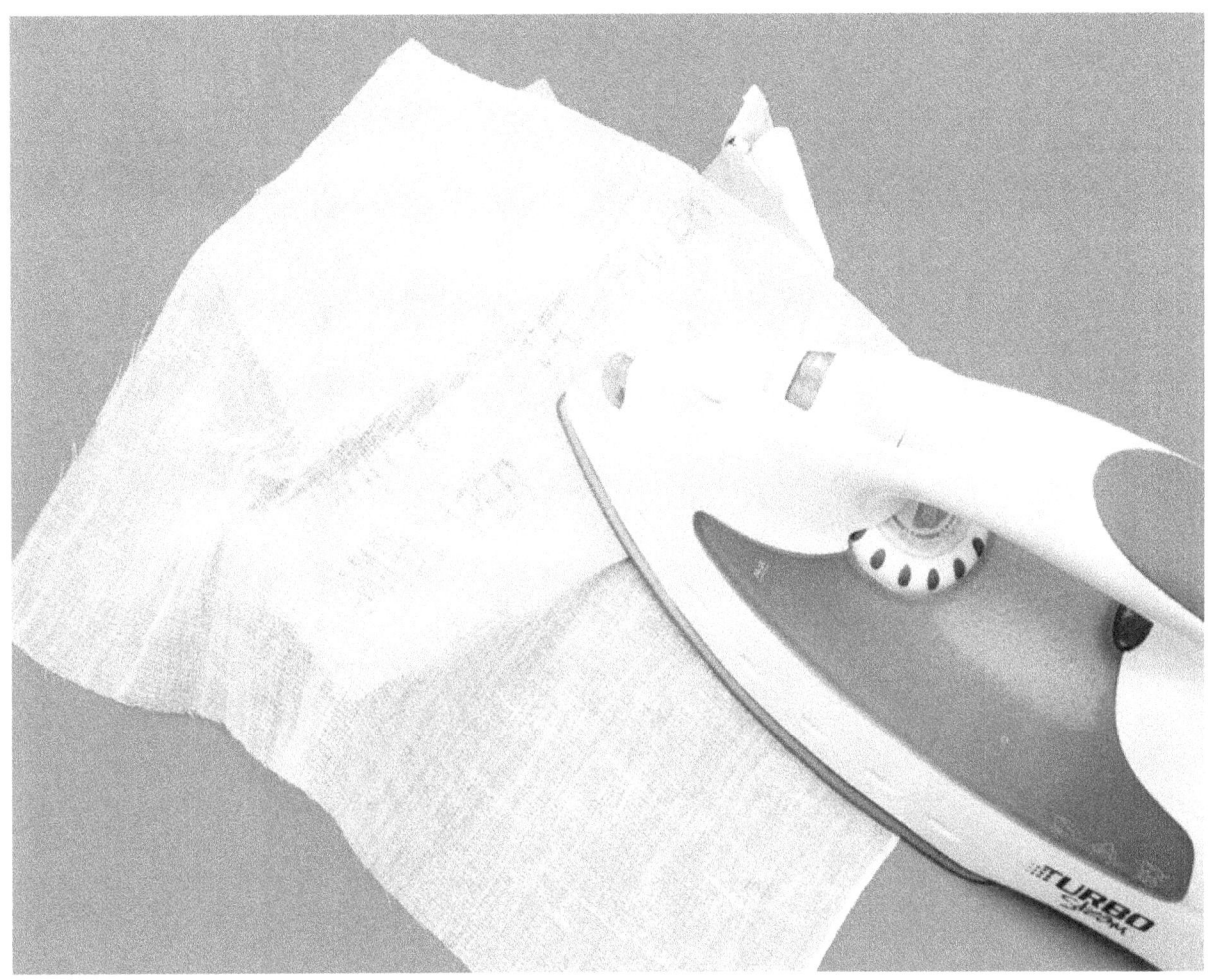

5. Ask an adult to iron on top of the sandpaper for two to three minutes. Then lift it off to reveal the pattern on your pencil case!

MAKE YOUR OWN NATURE CRAFTS

When you next take a walk through a wood or a trip to the seaside, stop and look around you. There are so many interesting shapes and colours – even smells! You can use the objects that you find to create amazing craft projects.

Foraging Fun

It's possible to use natural objects in art and crafts all year round: from fresh flowers in spring, to shells on the beach in summer. In autumn, acorns and conkers are ready for discovering, and in winter you can collect small stones or make rubbings from the bark of trees.

Outdoor Inspiration

You don't have to travel very far to discover a whole world of interesting creatures and habitats. Even in the smallest of gardens you can find interesting objects for craft projects and inspiration from plants and animals.

Look Before You Touch

Remember that not everything you discover from your outdoor adventures can be collected, so ask an adult first if you're unsure. It's important to wash everything you find before you use it, to get rid of any small bugs or dirt.

NATURE TOOLKIT

A Bag or Basket

A top tip is always to carry a small bag or basket with you wherever you go. Plastic or canvas bags fold up really small and can be carried in pockets or rucksacks, so you will always be ready to collect craft materials, wherever you may be.

Food Colouring

This is a great, simple way to dye natural objects, such as sand or leaves. It takes just a few drops to create an assortment of colours.

Stones and Shells

These simple natural objects, available from any woodland or beach, can – with a little crafting magic – be transformed into wonderful characters.

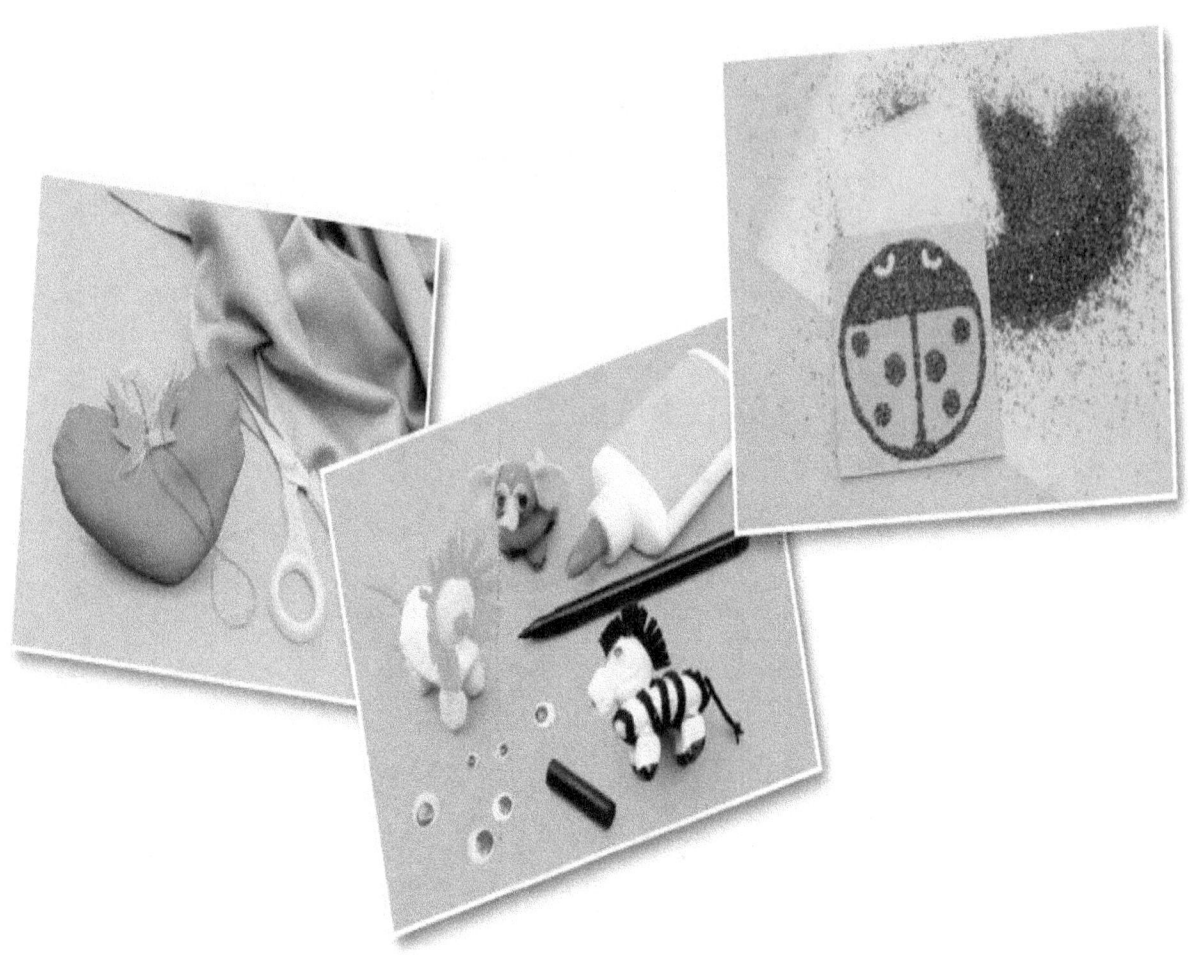

WOODLAND PHOTO FRAME

Bring memories of outdoor fun back into your home with this woodland–inspired photo frame. You could use it to show off holiday snaps of your friends or family, or photographs of nature.

You will need

Cardboard

Twigs

Craft glue

Scissors

Ruler

1. Cut out two cardboard squares that measure roughly 15 x 15 cm (6 x 6 in). Cut out a smaller, 9 x 9-cm (3.5 x 3.5-in) square in the middle of one of the larger squares.

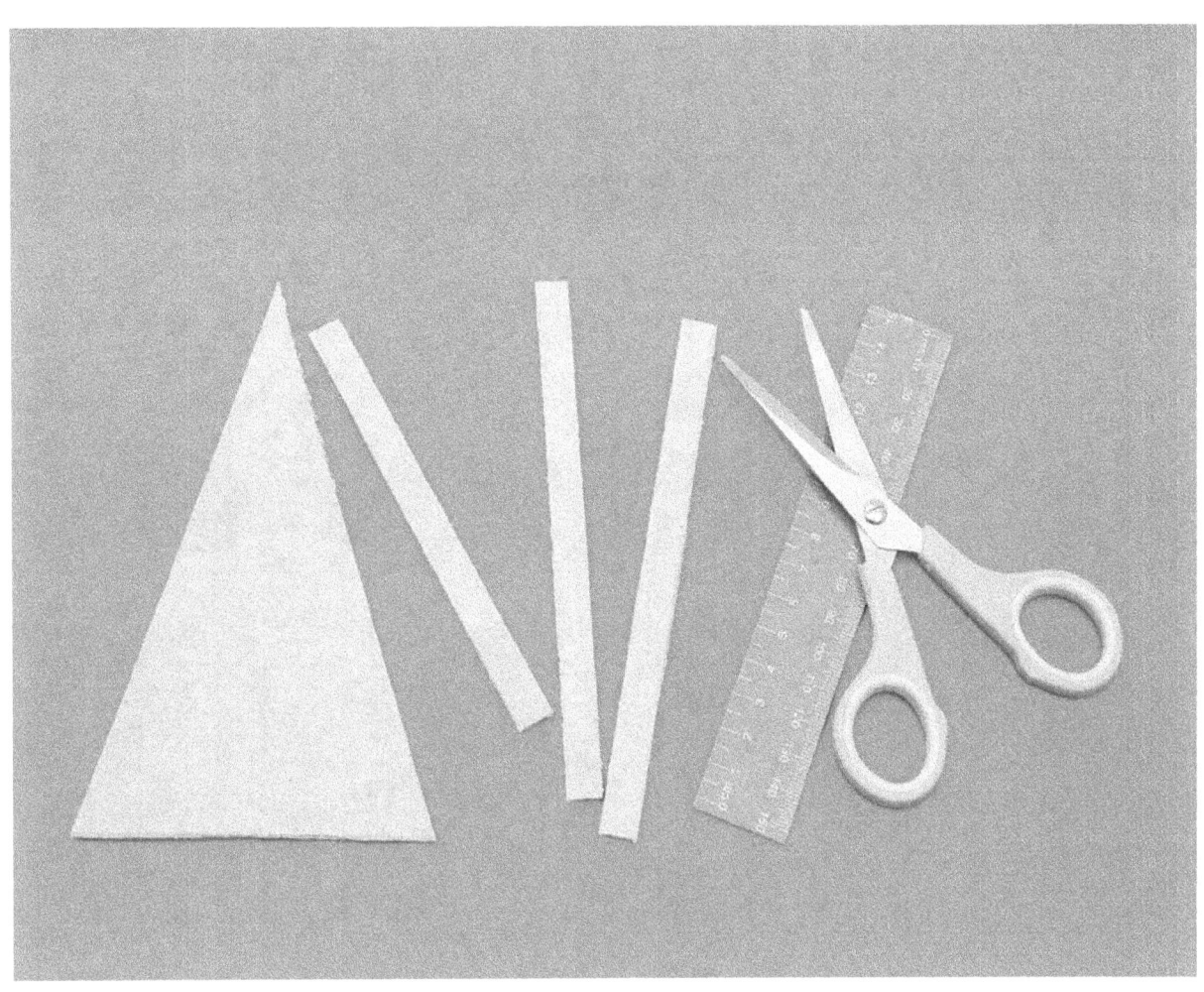

2. Cut out two cardboard rectangles that measure 1 x 15 cm (0.5 x 6 in) and another one that measures 1 x 13 cm (0.5 x 5 in). Then cut out a triangle about 15 cm (6 in) tall.

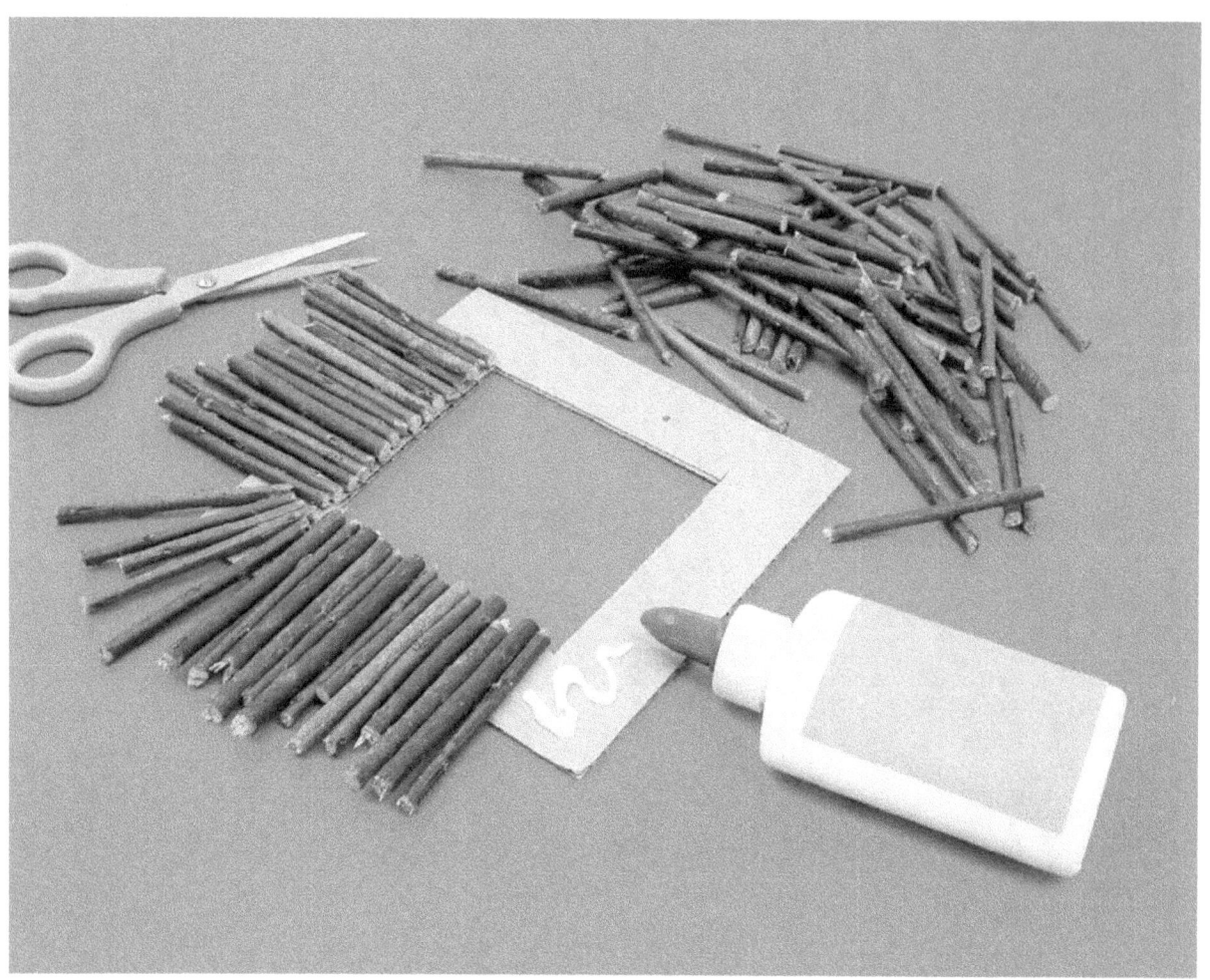

3. Snap the twigs into 6-cm (2.5-in) pieces and start gluing them onto your cardboard frame, using craft glue. Leave them to dry.

4. Turn the frame over so that the cardboard is facing you. Glue the two longest card pieces to either side of the frame using craft glue. Stick the shorter rectangle to another side (this will be the bottom). Then spread some more craft glue onto the card pieces you have just stuck down and stick the square card piece on top.

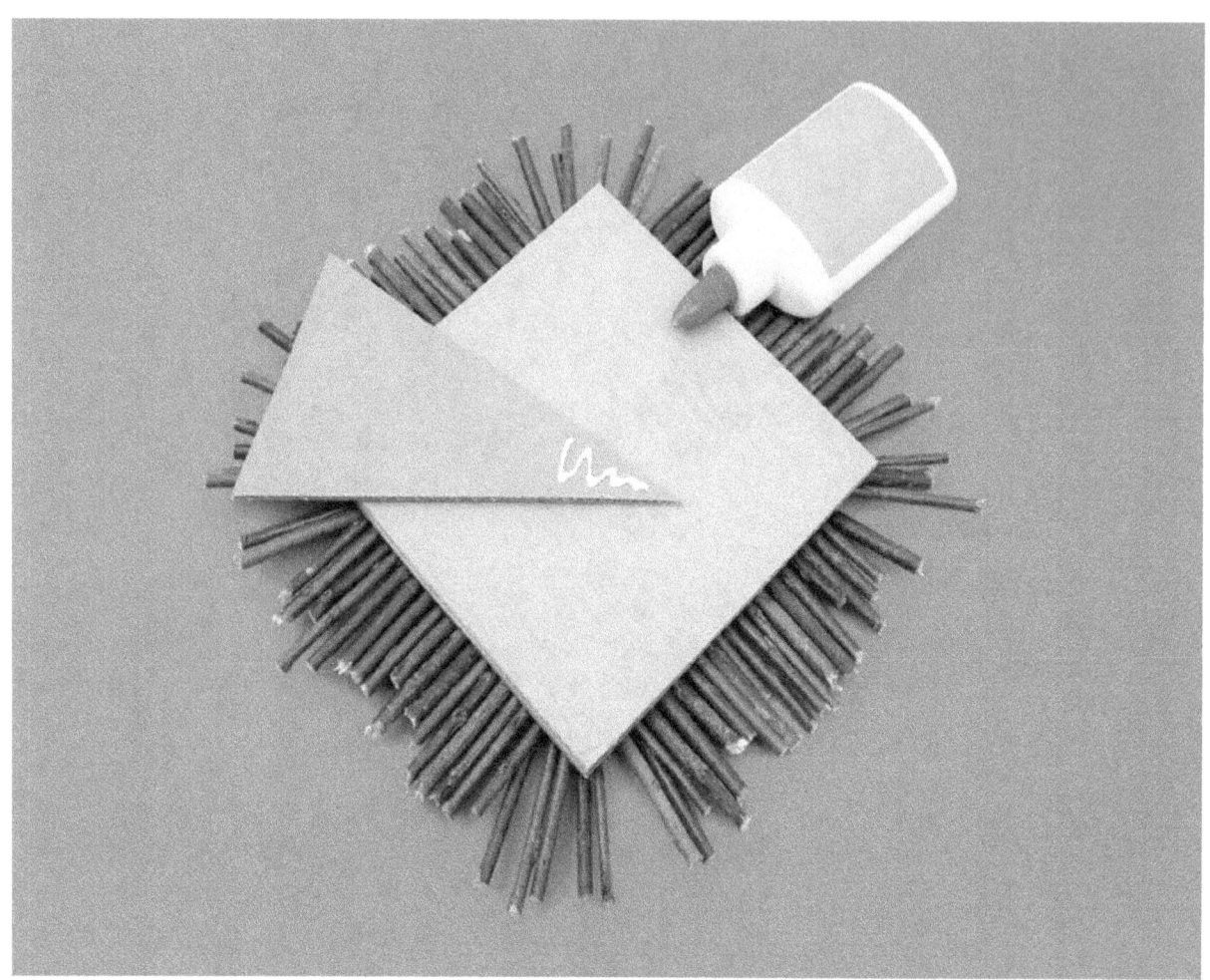

5. Make a fold near the top of the triangle. Put some glue on the point above the fold and stick it onto the back of your frame. Leave this to dry completely. Then stand up your frame, and slide a photograph inside.

SAND ART

Sand is fun to play with when you're at the beach. But did you know you can also use it to create awesome art? Here's how you can make coloured sand and use it for fab decorations that will remind you of those dreamy days in the sun.

You will need

Sand

Food colouring

5 plastic pots

Plastic sheet

Glass bottle

Funnel

Sticky tape

Coloured paper

Shells

PVA glue

Paintbrush

1. Pour some sand into five plastic pots. Add a few drops of food colouring to each pot so that you make five different colours of sand. Mix it well with the end of a paintbrush so that all the sand is coated with the colouring.

2. Spread the coloured sand onto a plastic sheet. This will help it to dry faster.

3. Using the funnel, pour the coloured sand into the glass bottle. You want to make a stripey pattern, so use one colour at a time.

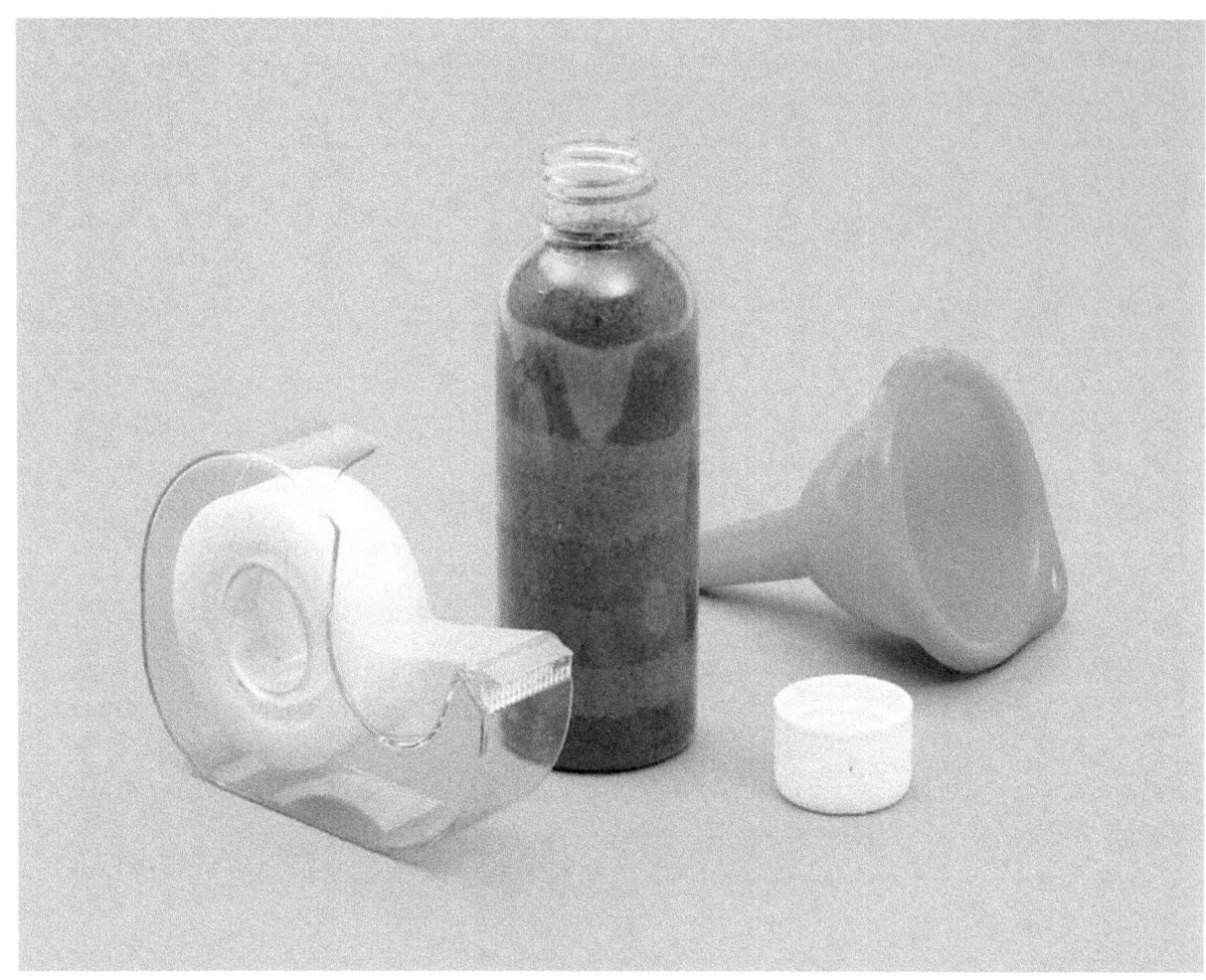

4. Once you have filled the whole bottle, screw the lid back on. If your bottle does not have a lid, you can seal it with sticky tape instead.

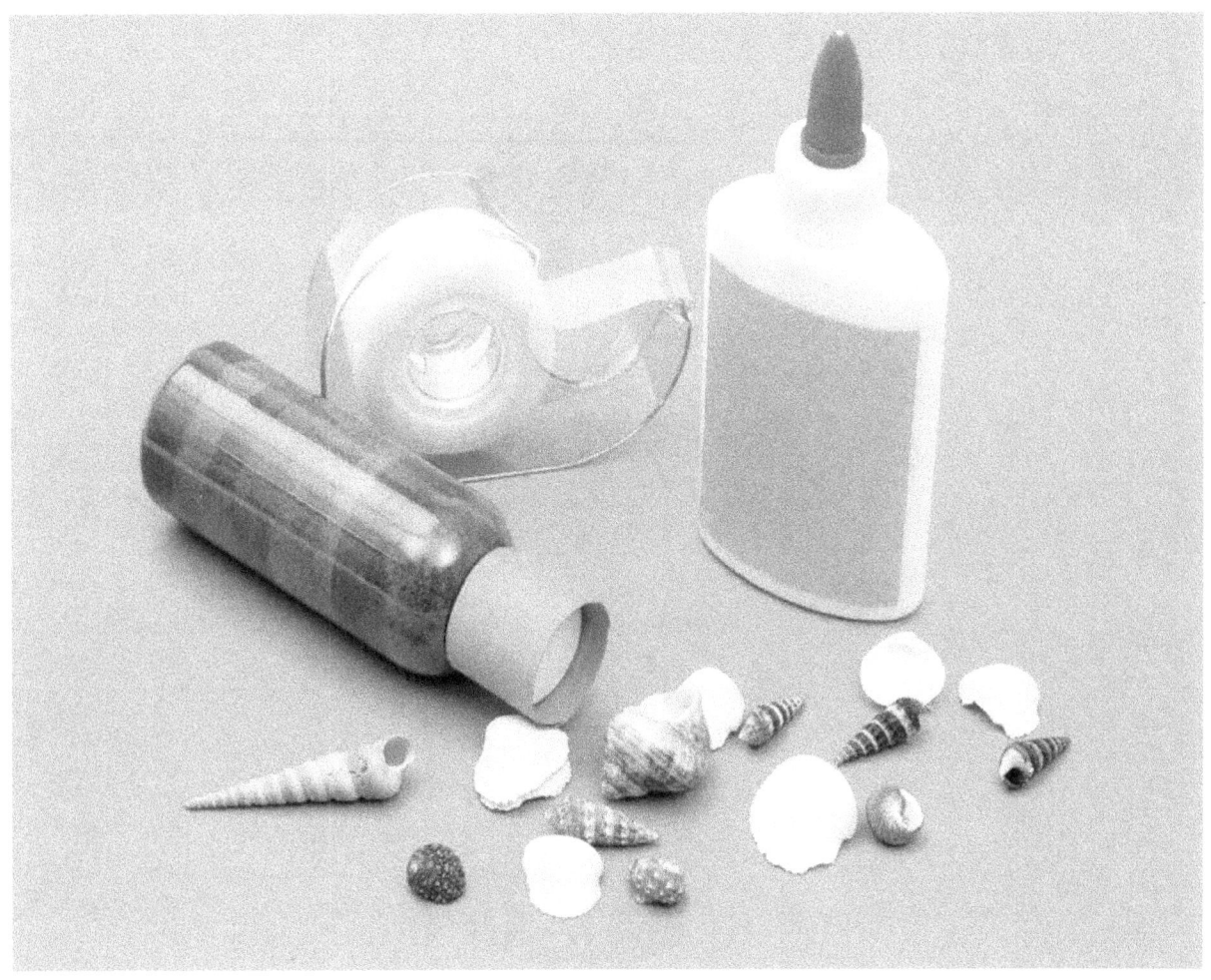

5. Wrap some coloured paper around the neck of the bottle and tape it in place. Stick on some seashells using PVA glue.

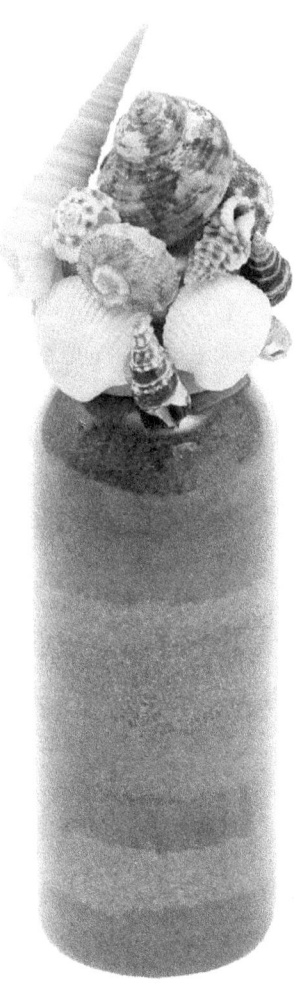

Will you make each coloured stripe level and even? Or will you shape the sand into curves and diagonal patterns?

SHELL CREATURE FRIDGE MAGNETS

Have you ever collected shells from the seaside? You can find them in many shapes and sizes. Here is the perfect craft for you to transform your shell collection into cute and crazy creatures!

You will need

Shells

Bowl, soap and sponge

Acrylic paint

Paintbrush

Craft glue

Googly eyes

Coloured card

Scissors

Magnets

Metallic pens

1. Use warm, soapy water and a soft sponge to clean all your shells well, making sure that they don't have any sand left on them.

2. Paint your shells in different colours using acrylic paint and leave to dry. You can also try painting some in different patterns such as stripes, dots or swirls.

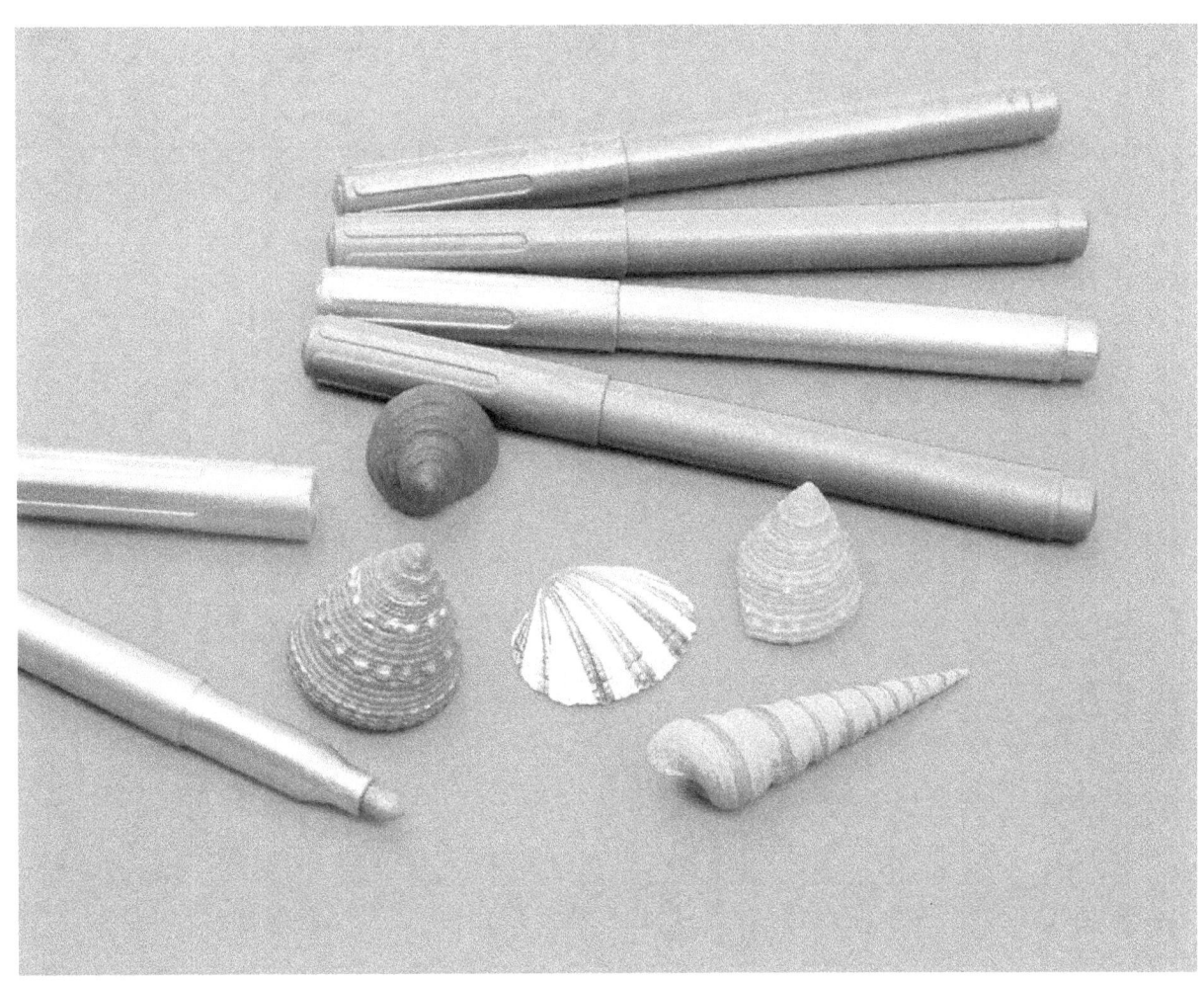

3. Add to your design using felt-tip pens. Metallic colours look especially good.

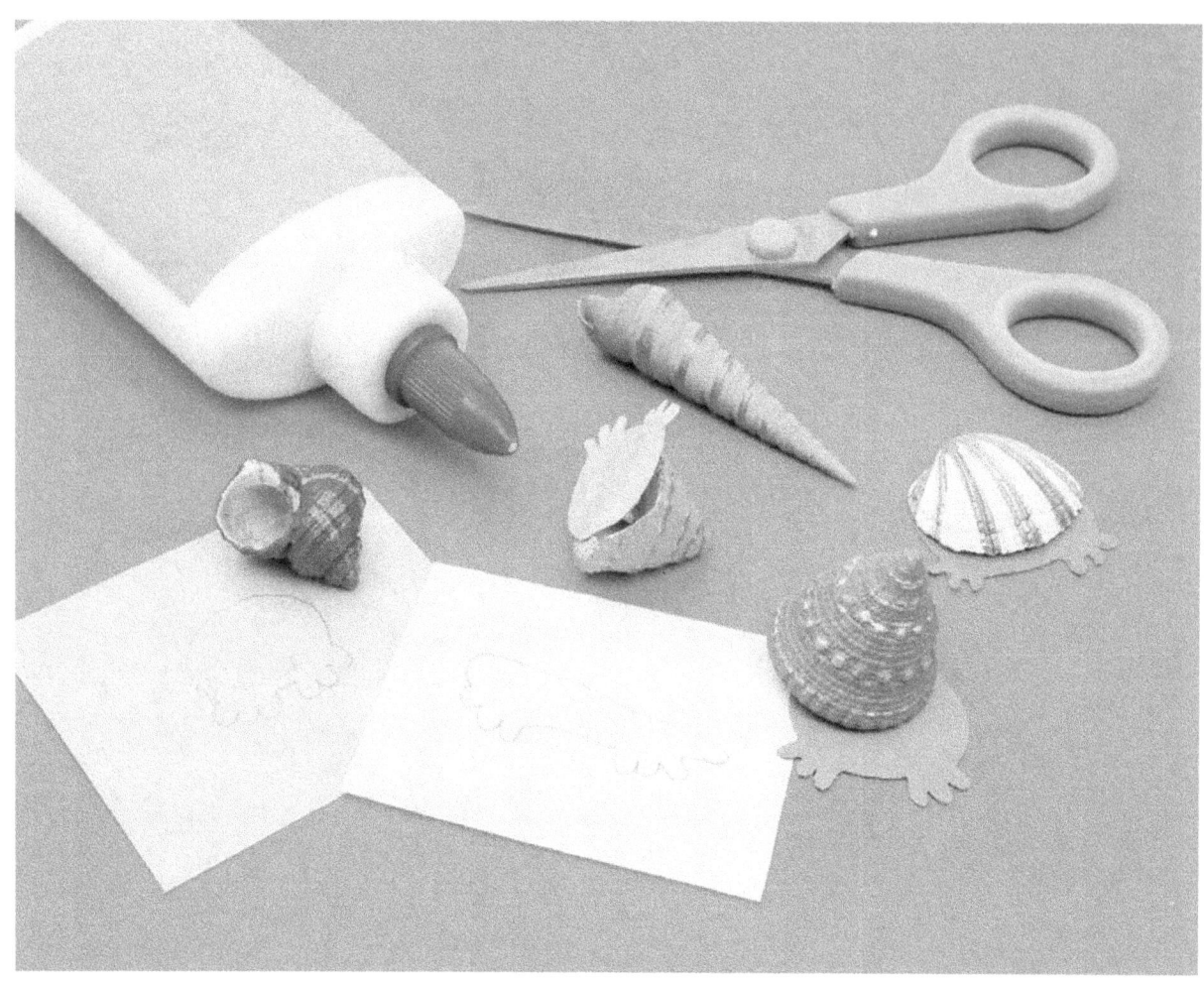

4. Cut out some feet from the coloured card using a pair of scissors. Then stick each of them onto the backs of the shells with craft glue.

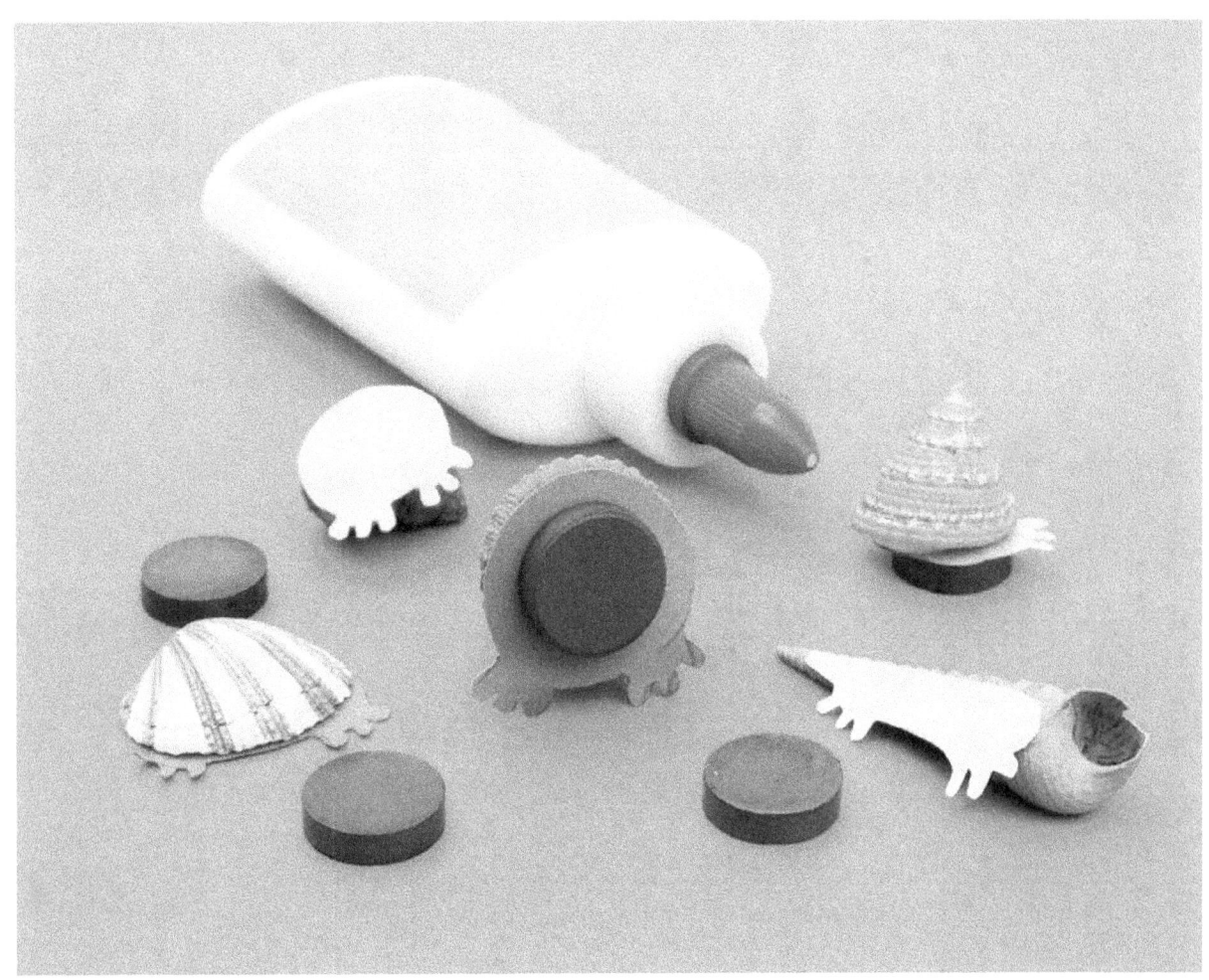

5. Stick a magnet onto the card on the back of each shell, using craft glue. Leave them to dry.

6. Stick one big googly eye and one small googly eye onto each shell using craft glue. Leave to dry.

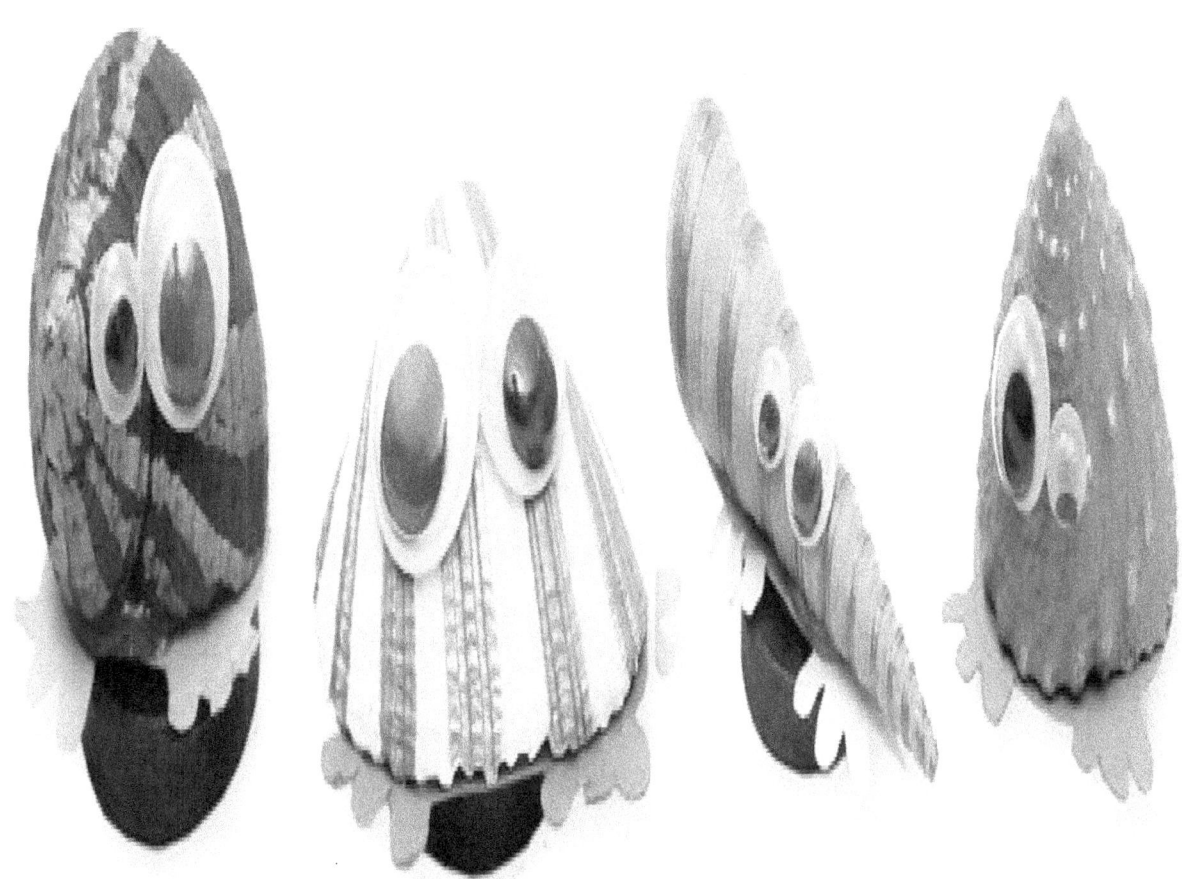

PRESSED FLOWER COASTERS

Keep flowers looking bright and colourful by pressing them before they start to wilt. You can preserve them forever by turning them into classy coasters. These make a fantastic gift!

You will need

Bathroom tiles

Flowers

Heavy books

Coloured paper

Felt

Kitchen towel

PVA glue

Fabric glue

Acrylic sealer

Scissors

Paintbrushes

1. Sandwich your flowers between two sheets of kitchen towel and two heavy books. Leave them to dry out in a warm, dry place for a few weeks.

2. Cut out squares of coloured paper that are slightly smaller than your tiles. Stick them onto your tiles using some PVA glue.

3. Coat each tile in PVA glue and stick on your pressed flowers. You could also stick on leaf shapes cut from paper. Leave to dry.

4. Ask an adult to help you with this step. Give each tile a coat of acrylic sealer. Leave it to dry and then apply another coat.

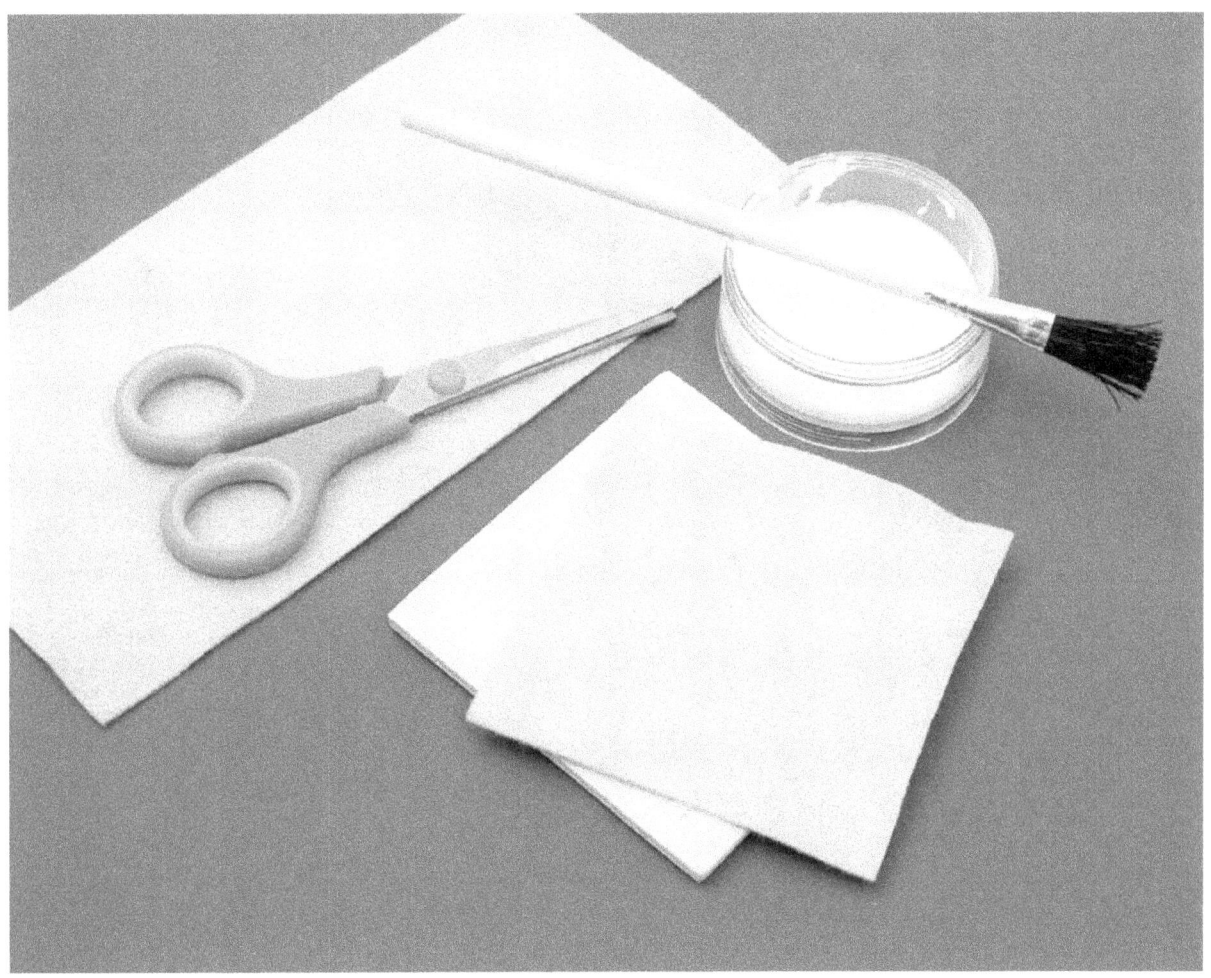

5. Cut some squares of felt to the same size as your tiles. Stick the felt to the back of the tiles with fabric glue.

If your family are redecorating the house, you could make several tiles to decorate the bathroom or kitchen.

SEED MOSAIC

All plants come from seeds, so there is plenty of choice when it comes to making this craft! We have used black poppy seeds, but you could try using sunflower seeds, pumpkin seeds or even mixed bird seeds!

You will need

Seeds

PVA glue

Card

Scissors

Ruler

Black marker pen

Poster paints

Paintbrush

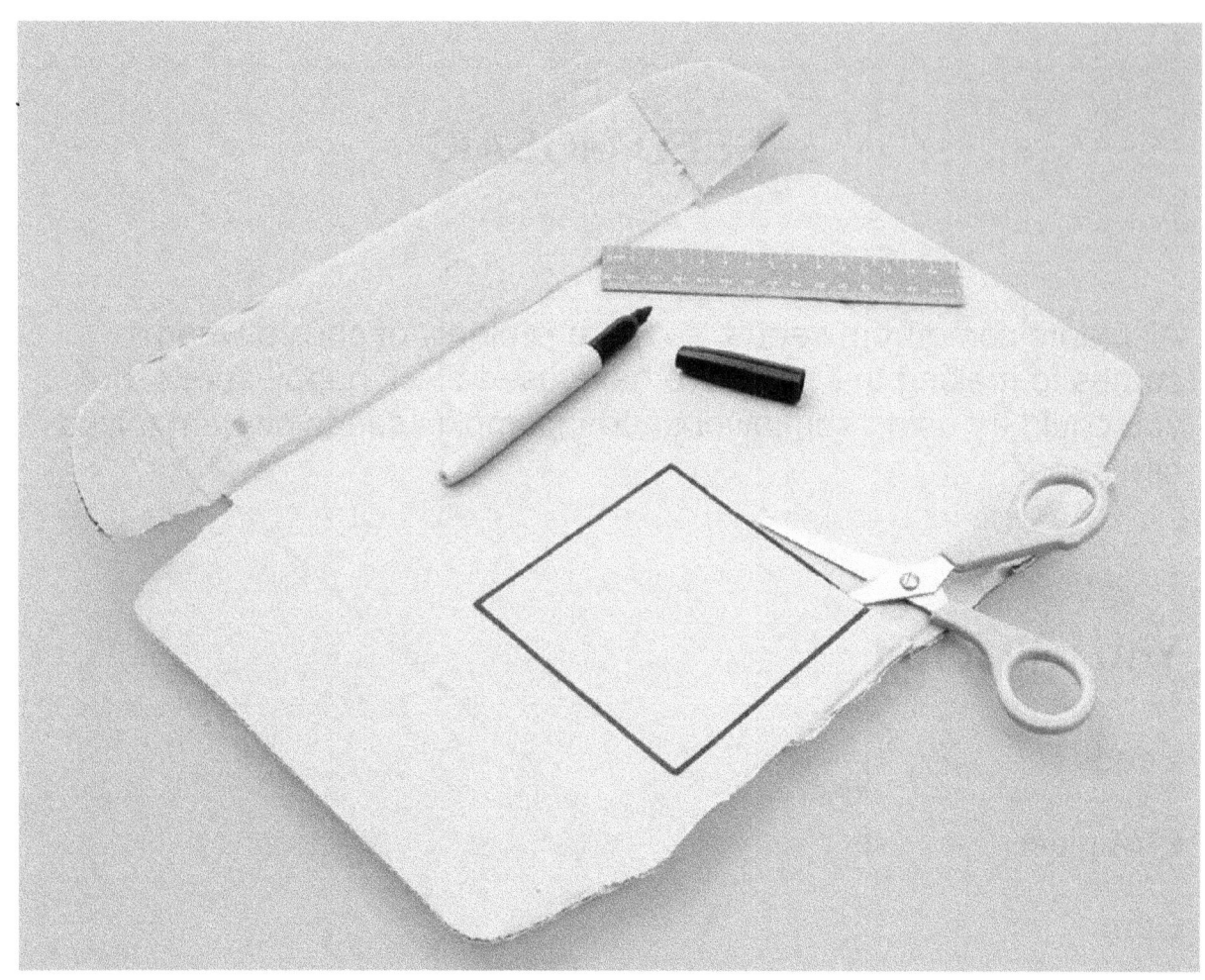

1. Measure and cut out a 15 x 15-cm (6 x 6-in) square of card.

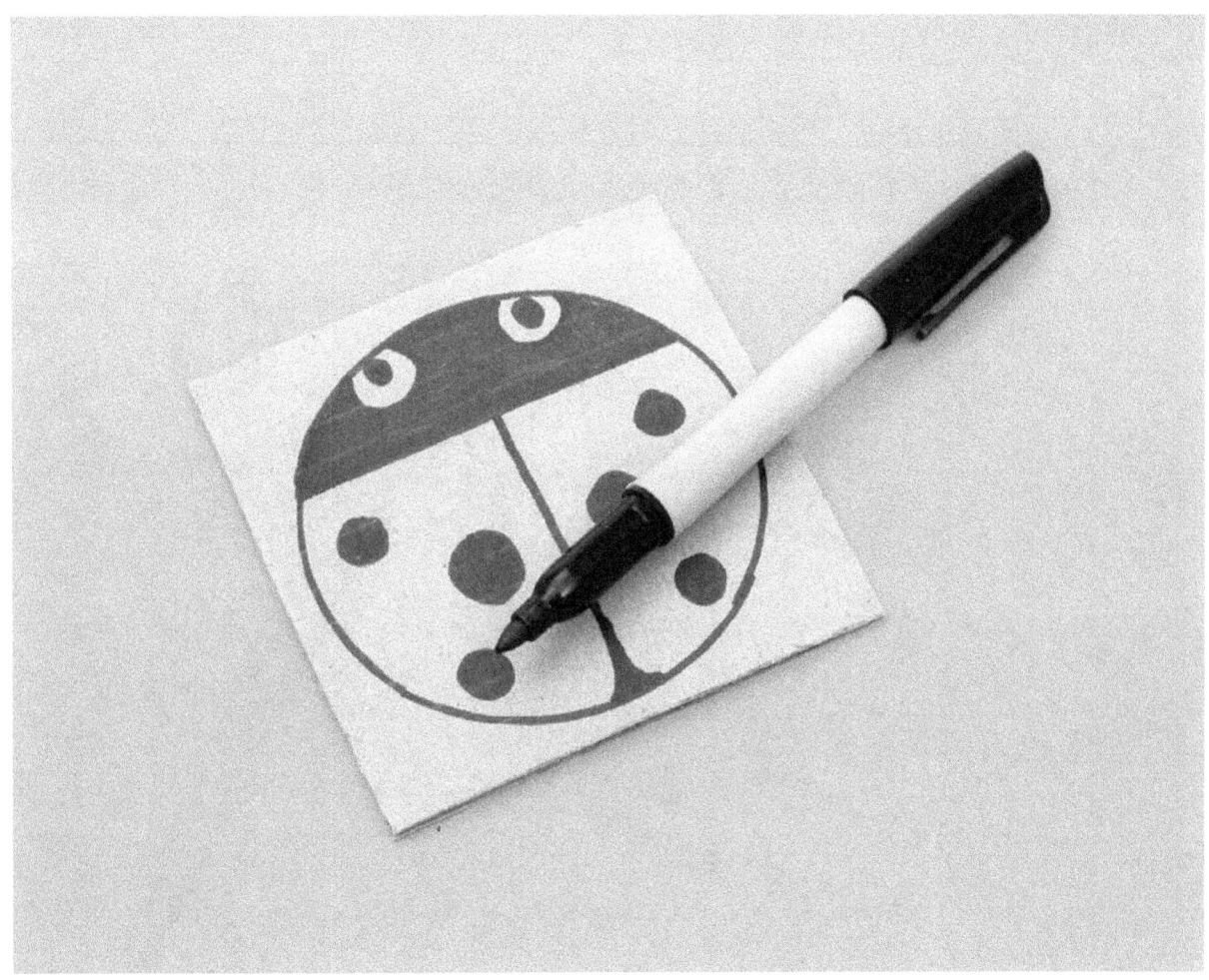

2. Draw a pattern on the card using a black marker pen.

3. Paint your design a bright colour. Then leave it to dry.

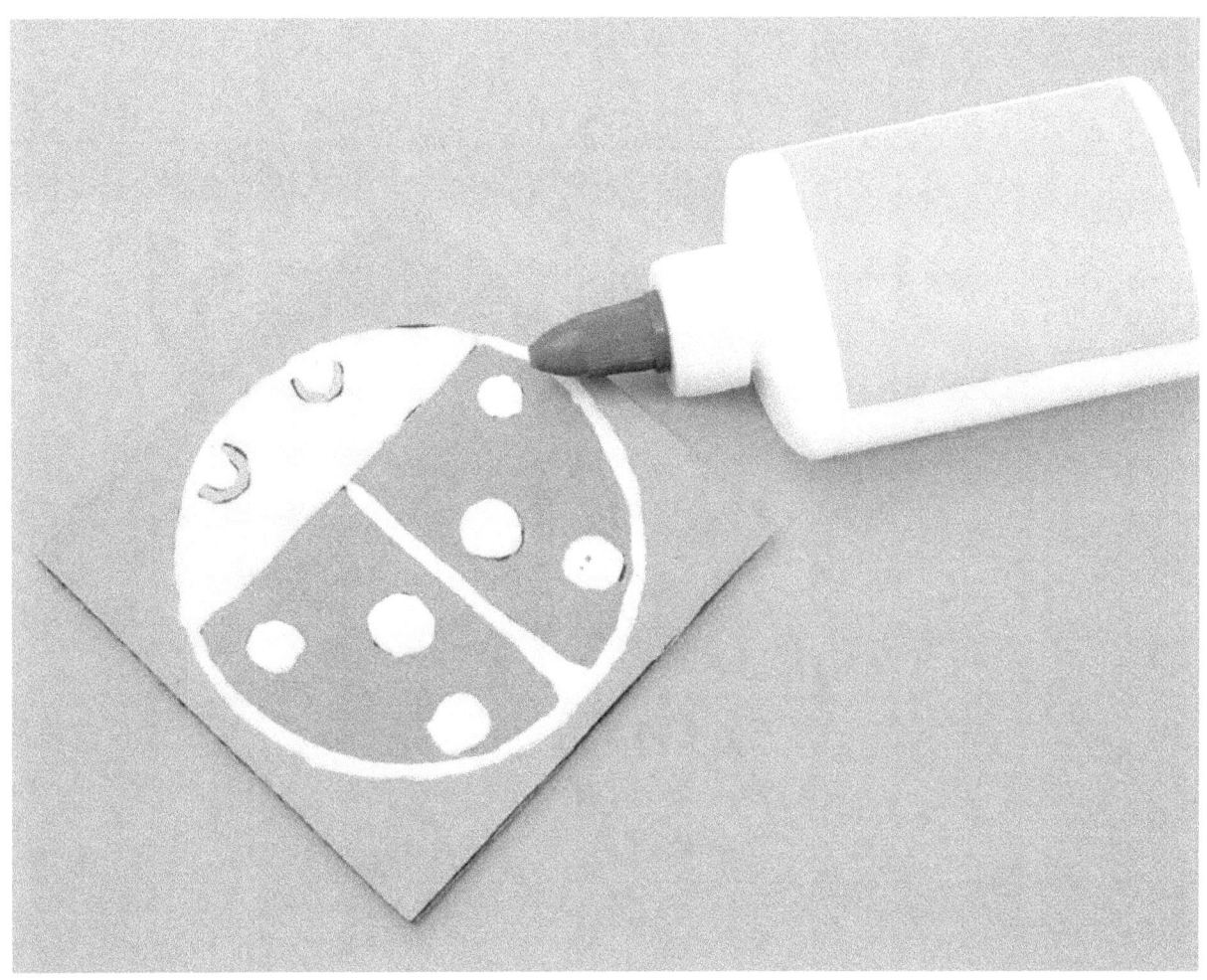

4. Squeeze glue over the sections you have drawn in black marker pen.

5. Scatter seeds all over your picture.

6. Shake off the excess seeds to reveal your pattern.

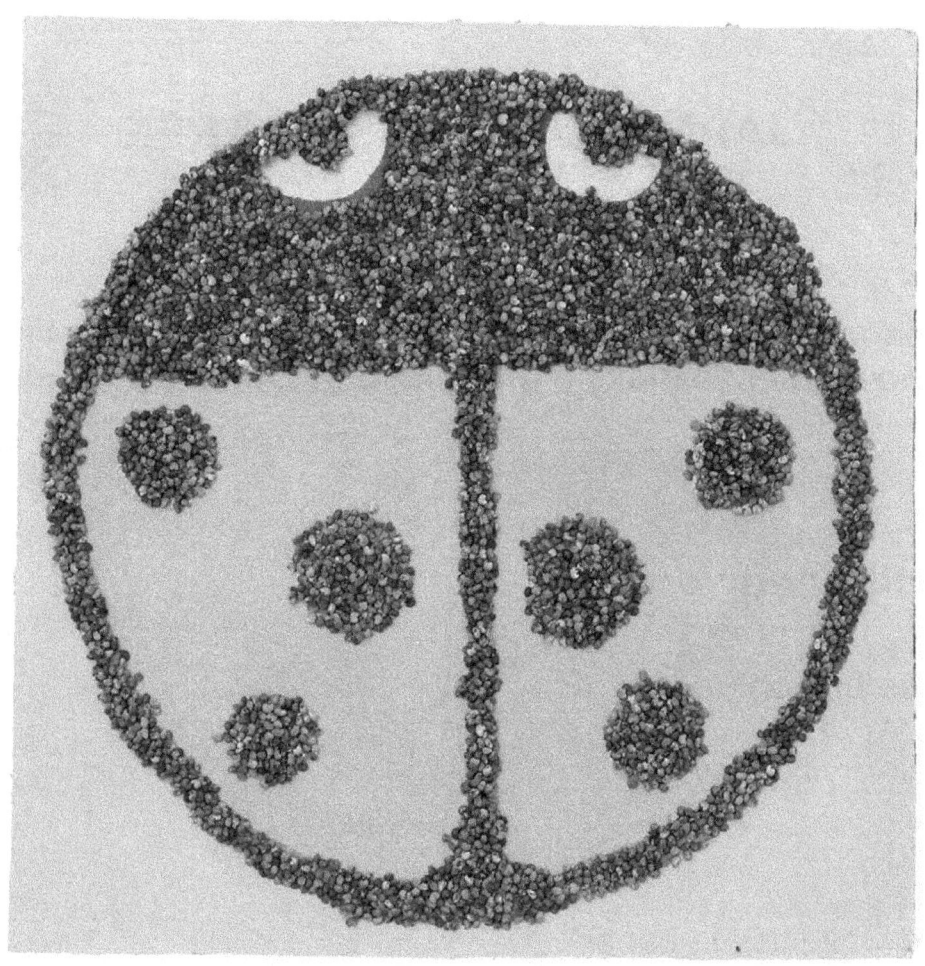

Why not try using other natural materials for collages? For example, you could swap the seeds for pine needles or flower petals.

JAPANESE BLOSSOM TREE

The Japanese art of bonsai involves carefully pruning tiny trees. Here's how you can make a tiny tree that needs no pruning at all!

You will need

Small tree branch

Brown air-drying clay

Plastic lid

Pink and white tissue paper

PVA glue

Drinking glass

Scissors

Pebbles and sequins

1. Put a lump of air-drying clay onto a plastic lid to make the base of your tree. Press the tree branch into the clay and mould the clay around the branch, so that it looks like a tiny hill. Leave it to dry in a warm place.

2. Trace around a drinking glass 20 times onto pink and white tissue paper. Cut out each circle and fold it over three times.

3. Cut a petal shape into the top of each piece of folded tissue paper. Open it up to reveal a flower! Place each white flower on top of a pink flower and twist them at the centre to hold them together.

4. Stick the flowers onto your tree branch with PVA glue and repeat until you have covered the whole branch.

5. Fill the base with the pebbles. As a finishing touch, you could decorate your blossom tree with sparkly sequins.

PEBBLE ZOO

Collect stones of different sizes and shapes to make these cute creatures. You could use them as paperweights, bookends or decorations for your room.

You will need

- Stones
- Craft glue
- Fabric glue
- Acrylic paint
- Paintbrush
- Felt
- Scissors
- Googly eyes
- Black marker pen

1. Stick a medium-sized stone to a large stone using craft glue, to make a head and body for your creature. Then glue four smaller stones to the large stone to make some legs.

2. Repeat step 1 twice. To make the zebra, stick another small stone onto the front of the medium stone. This will be the muzzle.

3. Paint the animals using acrylic paint. Use yellow for the lion, white for the zebra and grey for the elephant.

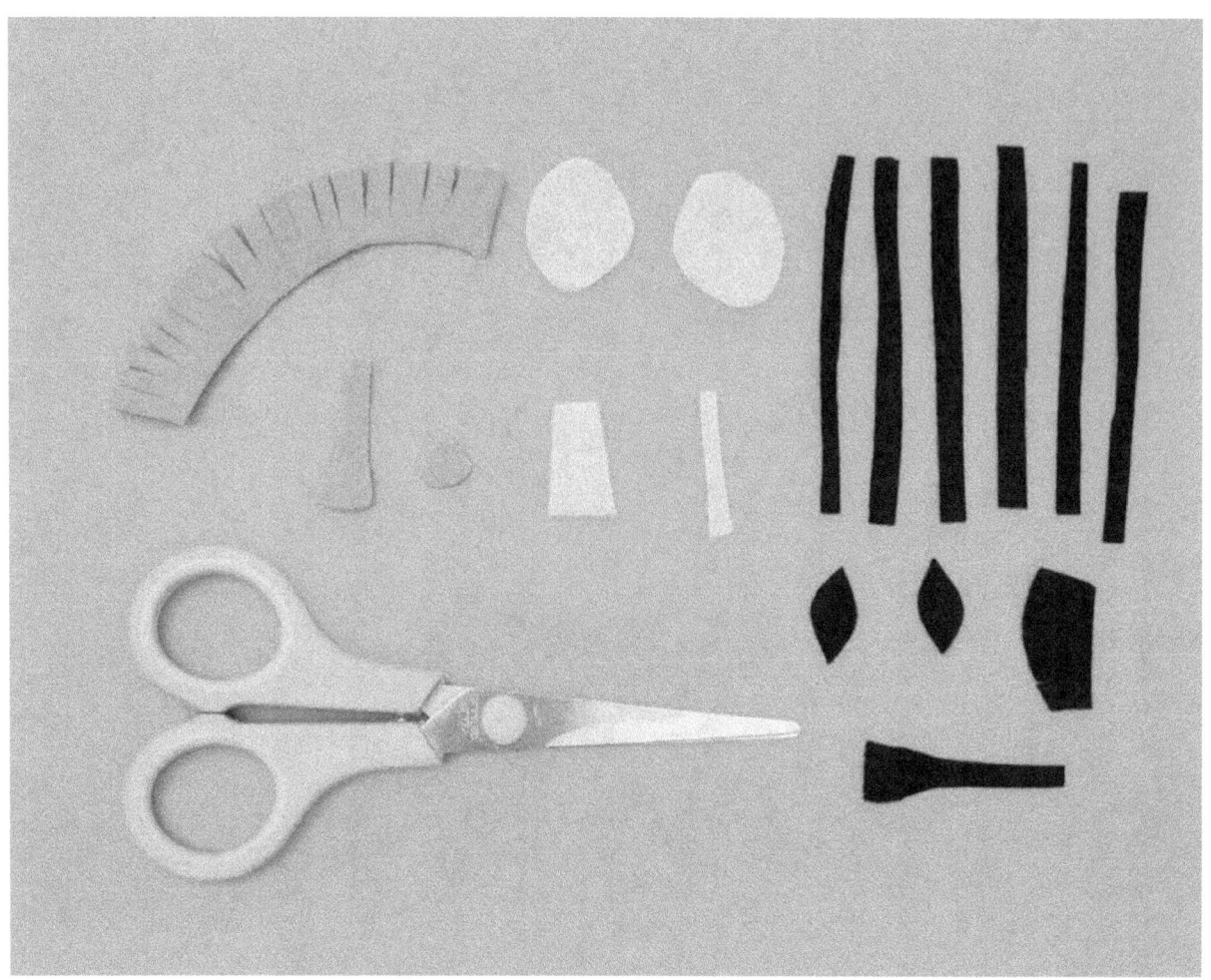

4. Cut out an elephant's ears, trunk and tail from blue felt. Cut out a lion's mane, tail and nose from orange felt. Cut out a zebra's stripes, mane and tail from black felt.

5. Stick the felt shapes onto the animals with fabric glue. Draw more details onto the animals using a black marker pen and finish them off by sticking on googly eyes with craft glue.

PINE CONE FIELD MOUSE

Pine cones are plentiful in autumn. Why not turn one into a cute little field mouse of your own?

You will need

Pine cone

Felt

Scissors

Googly eyes

Craft glue

Wool

Pipe cleaner

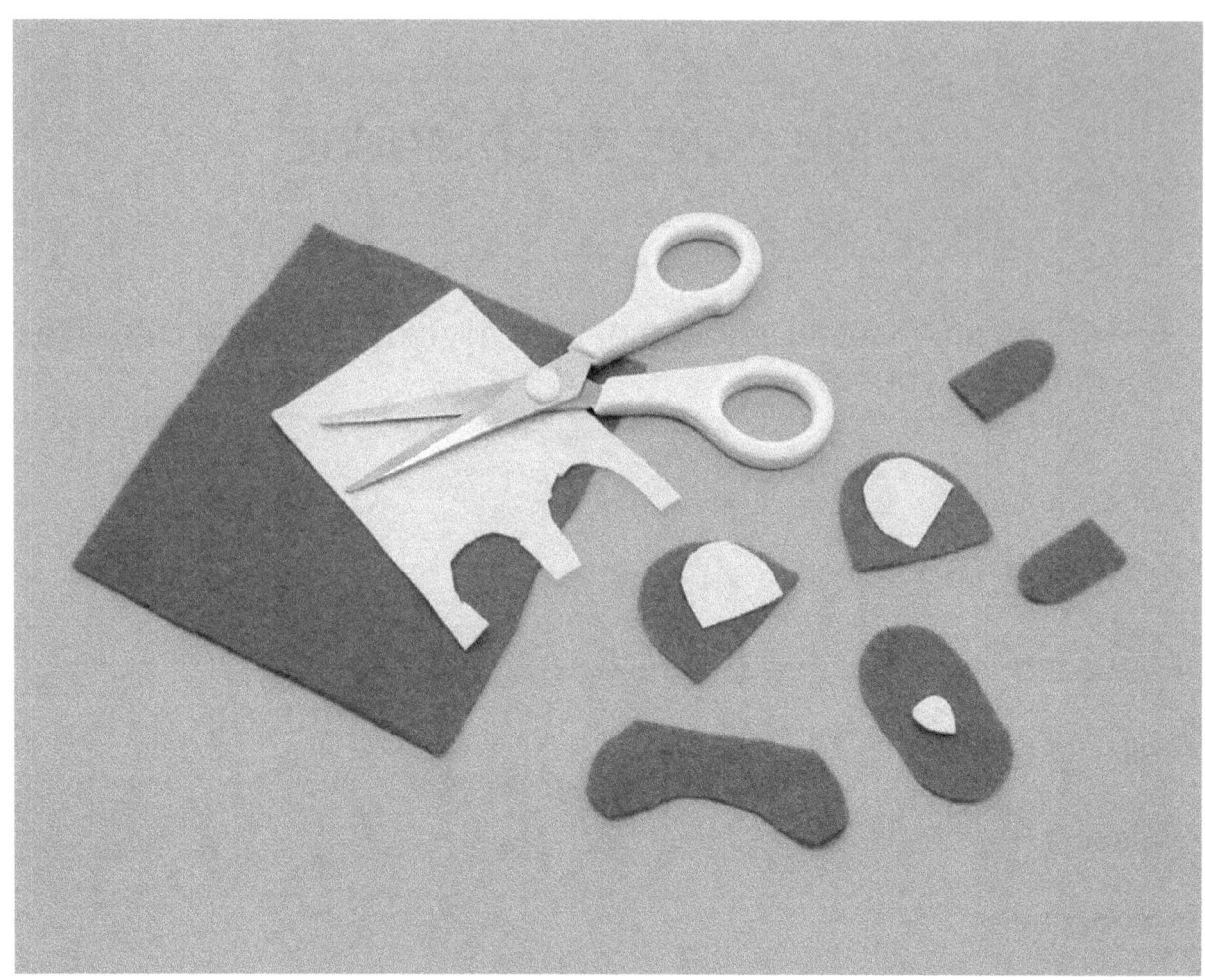

1. Cut out some round ears, an oval face, two arms and some feet from brown felt. Cut out smaller ear shapes and a nose from pink felt.

2. Stick together the pink and brown parts of the ears with craft glue. Then glue all the felt shapes except the nose to the pine cone.

3. Using the craft glue, stick some googly eyes to the face.

4. Cut some brown wool into short lengths to make the whiskers. Stick them just under the mouse's eyes with craft glue. Glue the nose on top of the whiskers.

5. Stick the pipe cleaner tail to the back of the pine cone and curl it slightly.

LAVENDER HAND WARMERS

Dried lavender smells great, and you can use it to stuff all sorts of things – such as this heart-shaped strawberry! You will need to ask an adult for help with the sewing.

You will need

Red and green cotton fabric

Rice

Dried lavender

Large cup or bowl

Scissors

Needle and white thread

Black marker

1. Fill a large cup or bowl two thirds of the way up with rice, then fill it to the top with dried lavender. Mix them together.

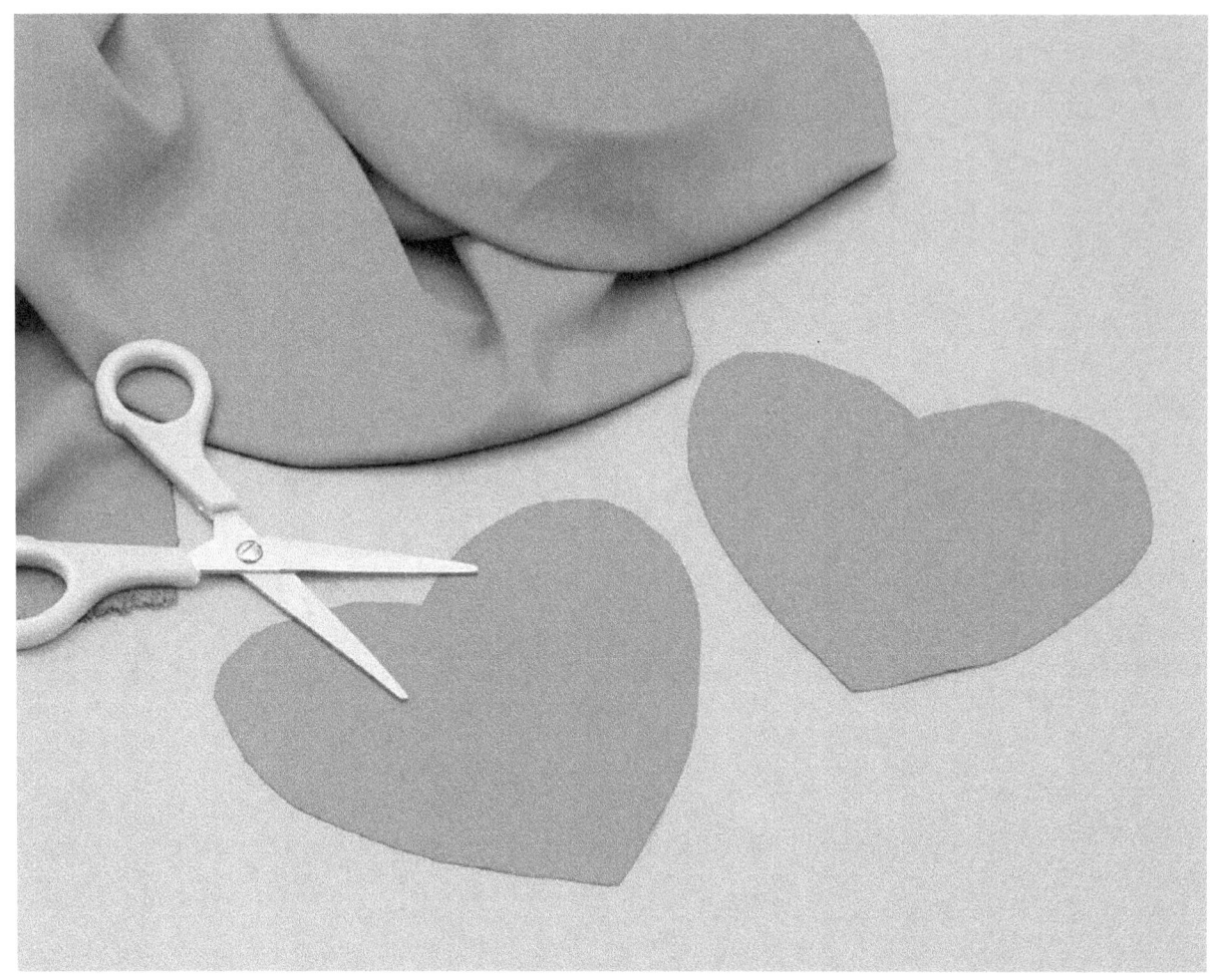

2. Cut out a heart shape from red fabric measuring about 12 cm (4.7 in) across. Trace around it with a marker, then cut out another identical shape.

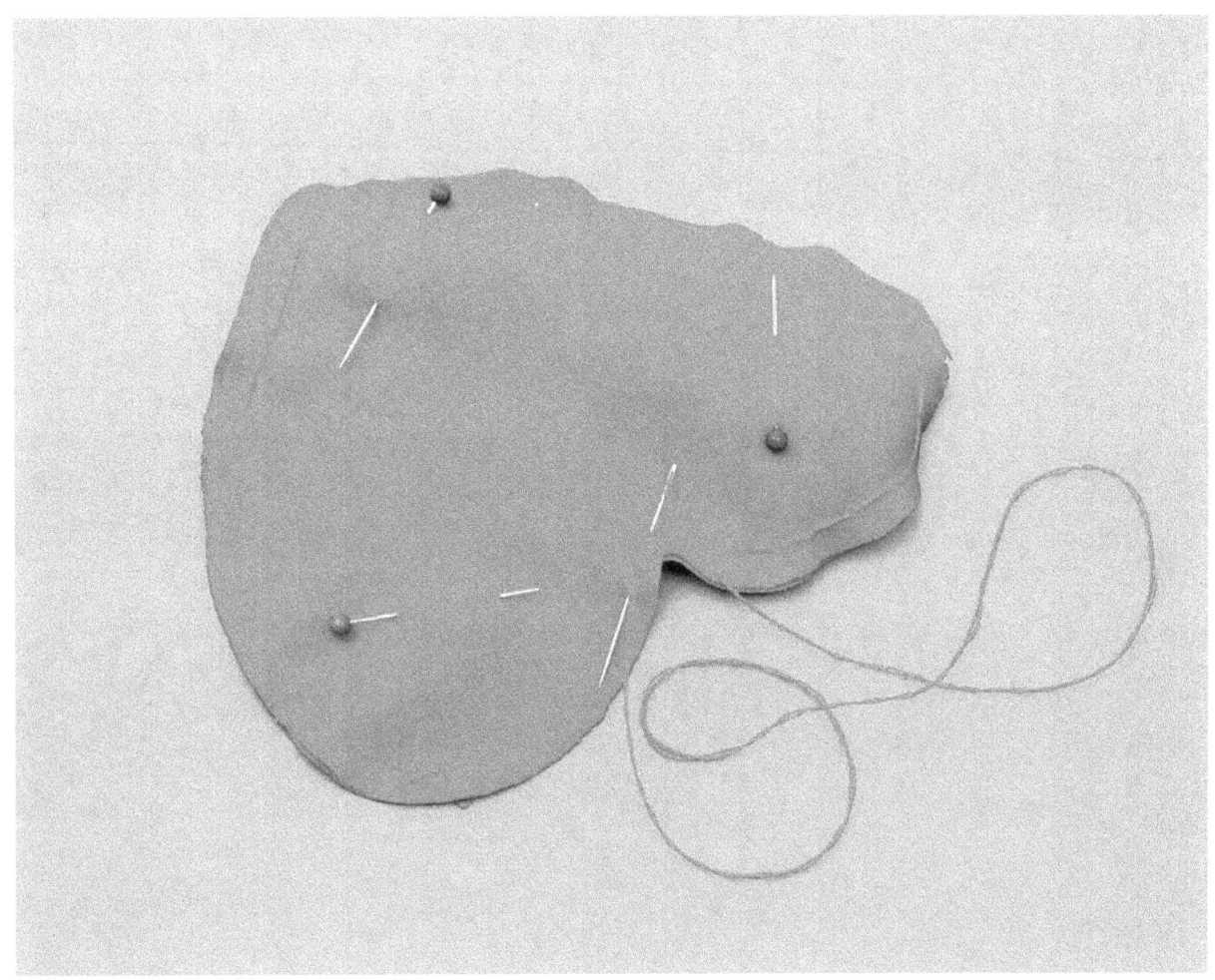

3. Carefully sew the two hearts together around the edge, making sure you leave a small 5 cm (2 in) gap somewhere.

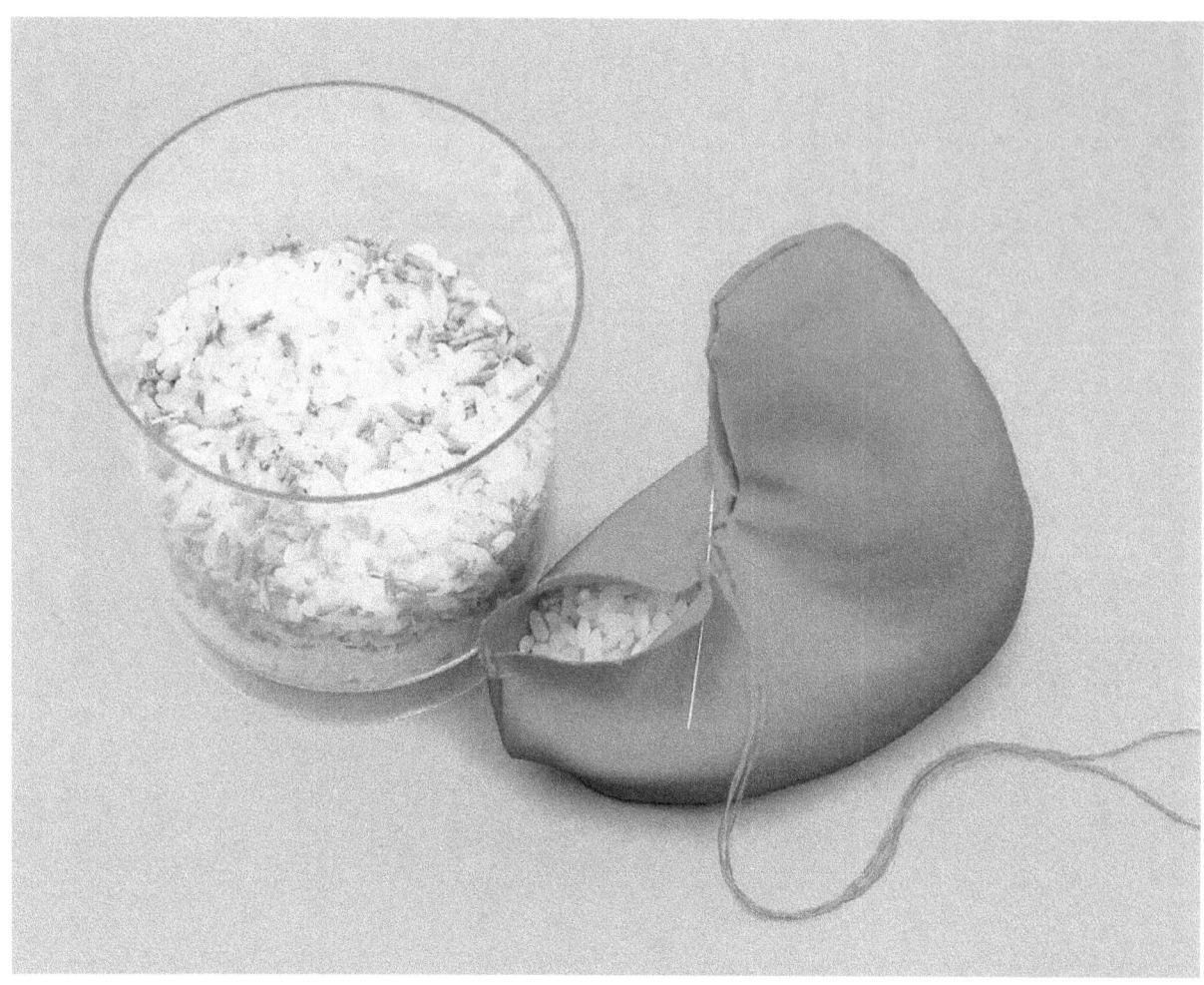

5. Cut out two stalk shapes from green fabric and sew them onto each side of the strawberry. Sew on white seed shapes using your white cotton thread. Do this on both sides.

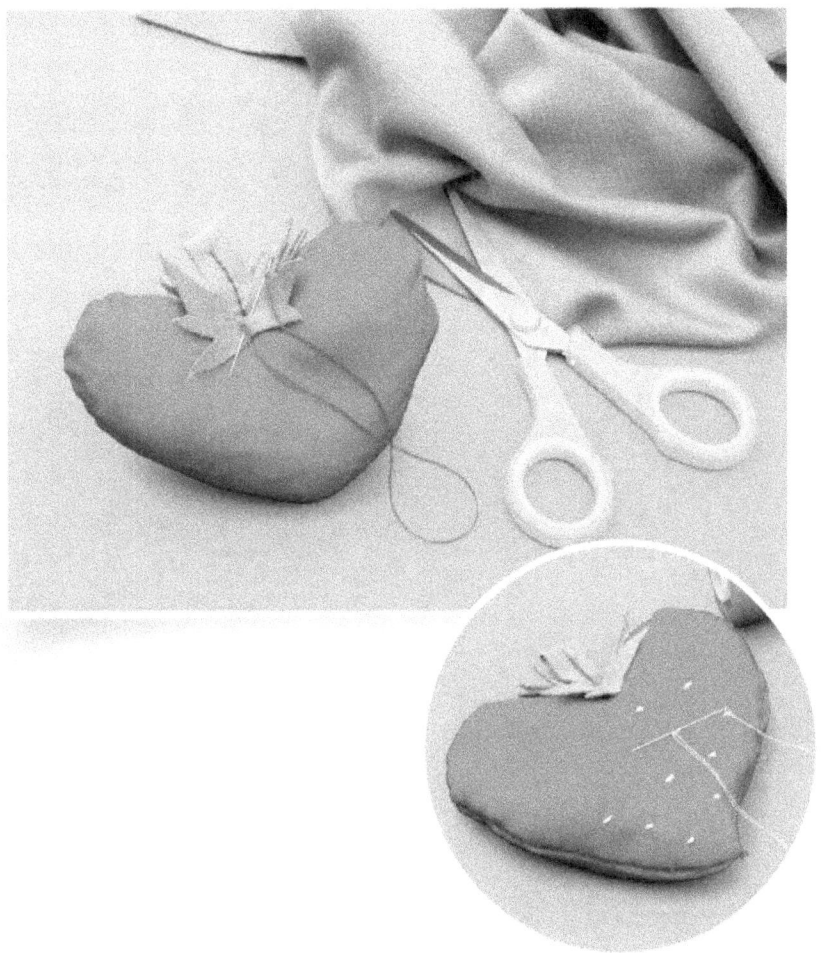

4. Turn the heart inside out to hide the stitching. Fill it with rice mixture. Then sew up the gap to make sure nothing spills out.

Now pop the bag into the microwave for 10 seconds to warm it up. The smell of lavender is very relaxing, and warmth can help to relieve aches and pains.

MAKE YOUR OWN JEWELLERY!

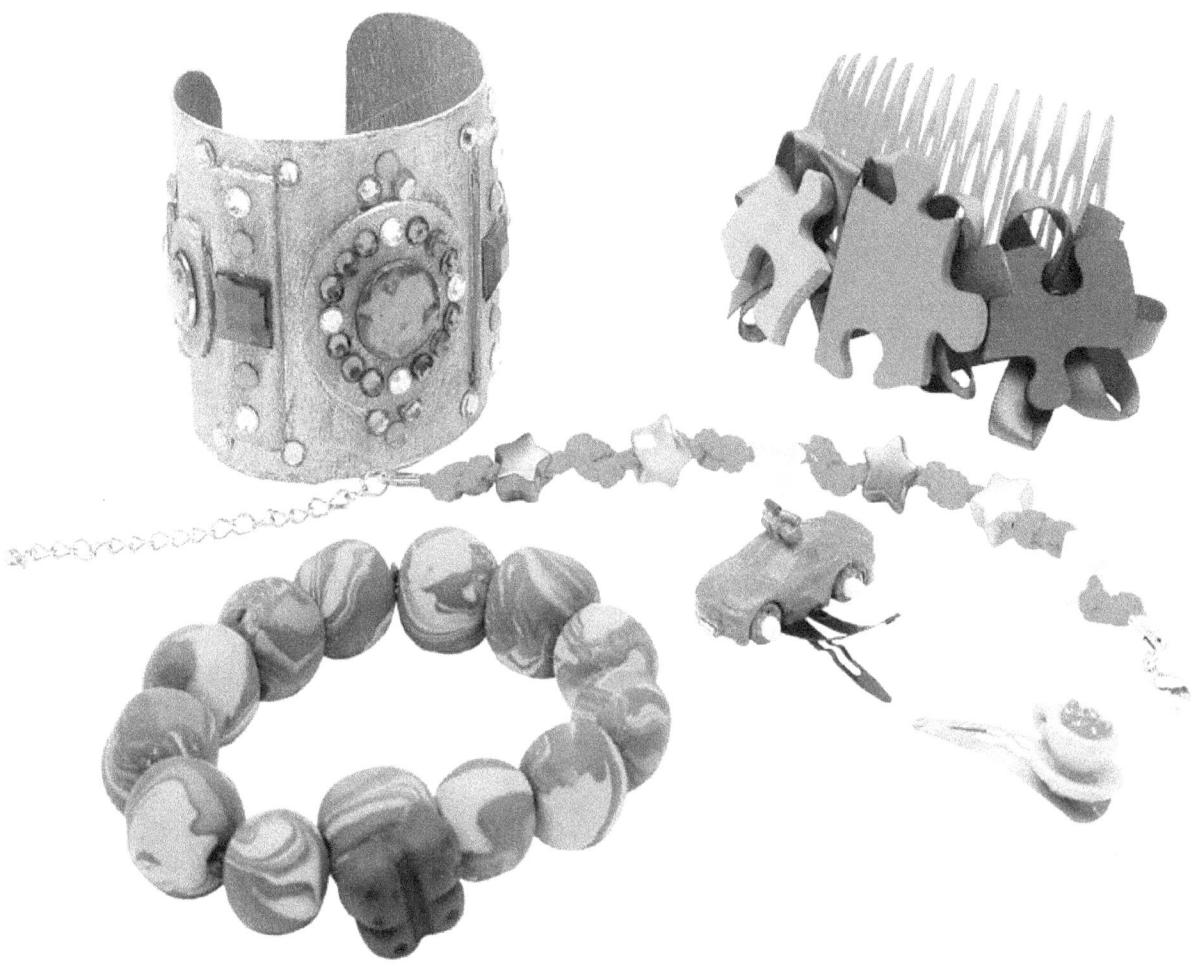

You'll always stand out from the crowd with handmade jewellery and accessories. All the projects in this chapter are easy to follow, but that doesn't mean that the final pieces won't make a big impact. You can look a million dollars, while saving a fortune!

Everyday Treasures

You don't have to rush down to your local craft shop before getting started. First have a look around at what you already have. You might have odd buttons from old clothes that you could use, a broken bead necklace that could be recycled or a spare ribbon.

Shop Around

There are lots of places where you can find materials for your jewellery. Try looking in hardware stores for round washers, rings or hooks. Second-hand shops will have lots of cheap jewellery that you can reuse the clasps and fastenings from.

Keep It Clean!

If you buy second-hand earrings, it's important that you clean them thoroughly before wearing them. Ask an adult to help you with this.

First, leave them to soak in boiling water for a few minutes. Then remove them, dry them and wipe them with some surgical spirit.

JEWELLERY TOOLKIT

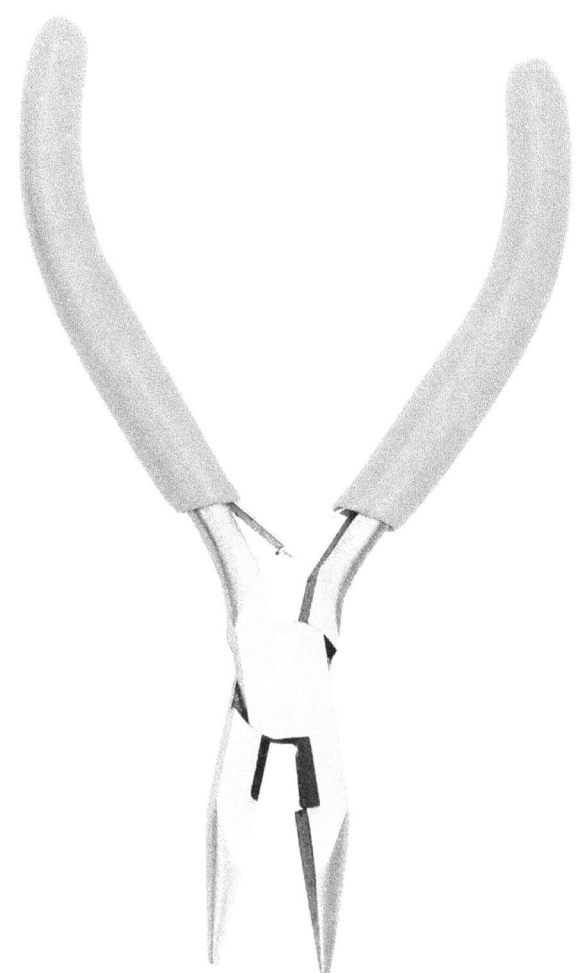

Jewellery Wire and Wire Cutters

Jewellery wire is very flexible, easy to cut and comes in different thicknesses and colours. To cut it, you will a piece of specialist equipment called wire cutters – but always ask an adult for help.

Cloth Tape Measure

You don't always need to be precise when making jewellery, but it's good to have a tape measure to hand in case you want two pieces to be identical.

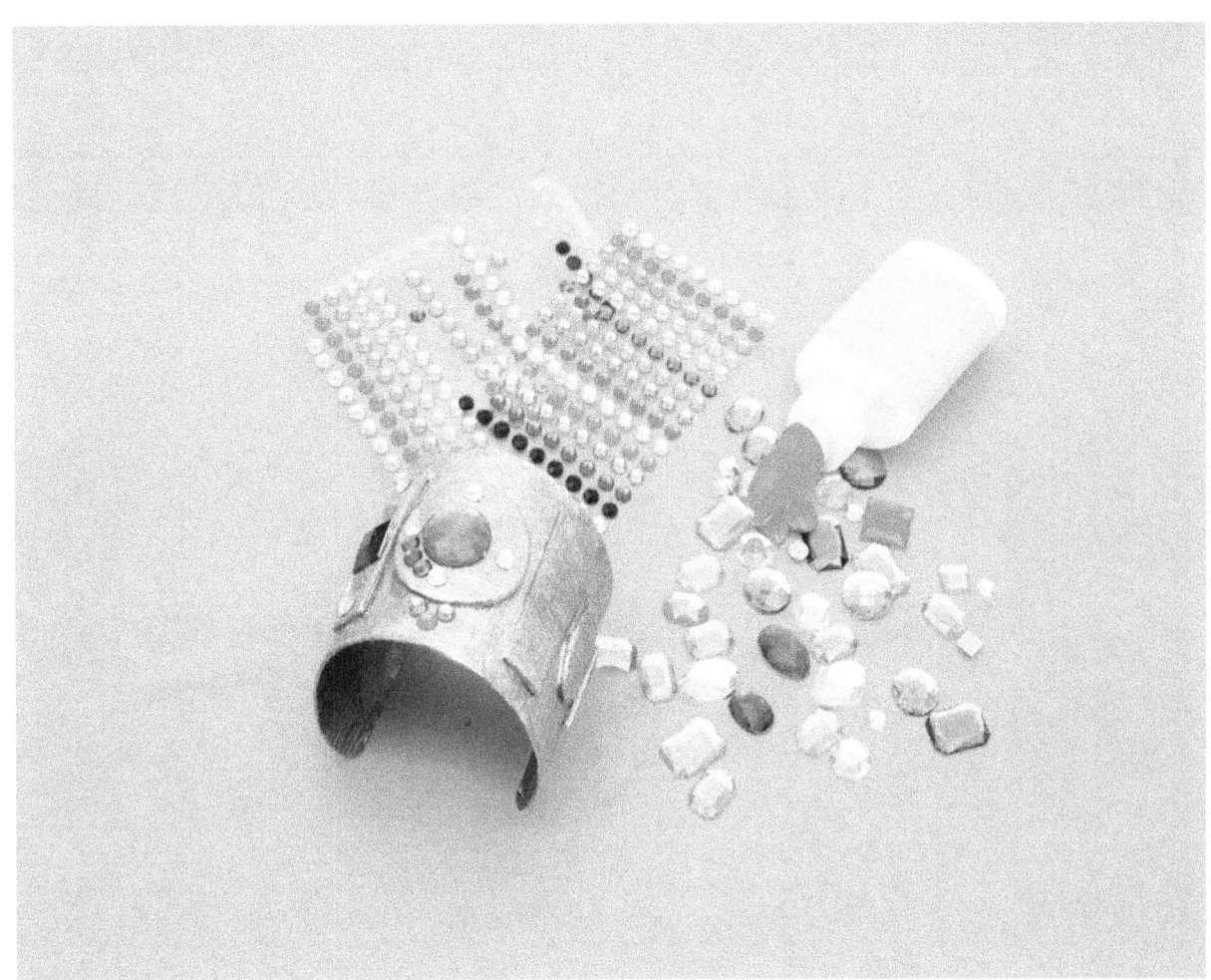

Clasps and Fastenings

Jewellery fastenings normally come in two parts and help you to take your jewellery on and off easily. You can buy them new from craft shops, or you may decide you want to recycle some old jewellery.

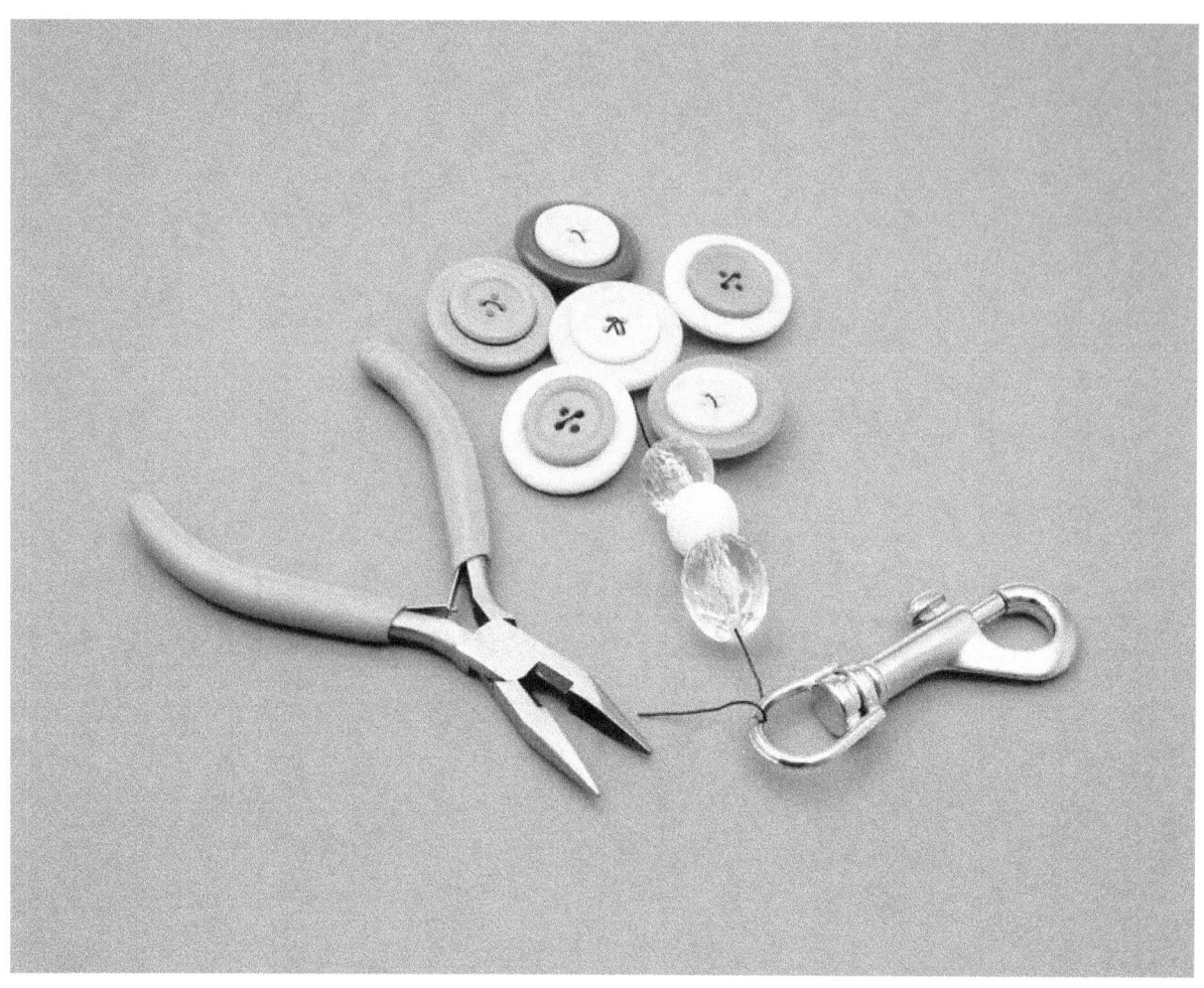

Superglue

This is a very strong kind of glue, and should only be used with adult supervision.

PENDANT NECKLACE

Pendants are jewels or other trinkets that hang from a chain. They can be made from many different objects. Believe it or not, this pendant is made from metal washers!

Pendants can also be used on earrings. You could make a matching set!

You will need

Embroidery thread

Metal washers (3 small, 1 medium and 1 large)

An old chain

Scissors

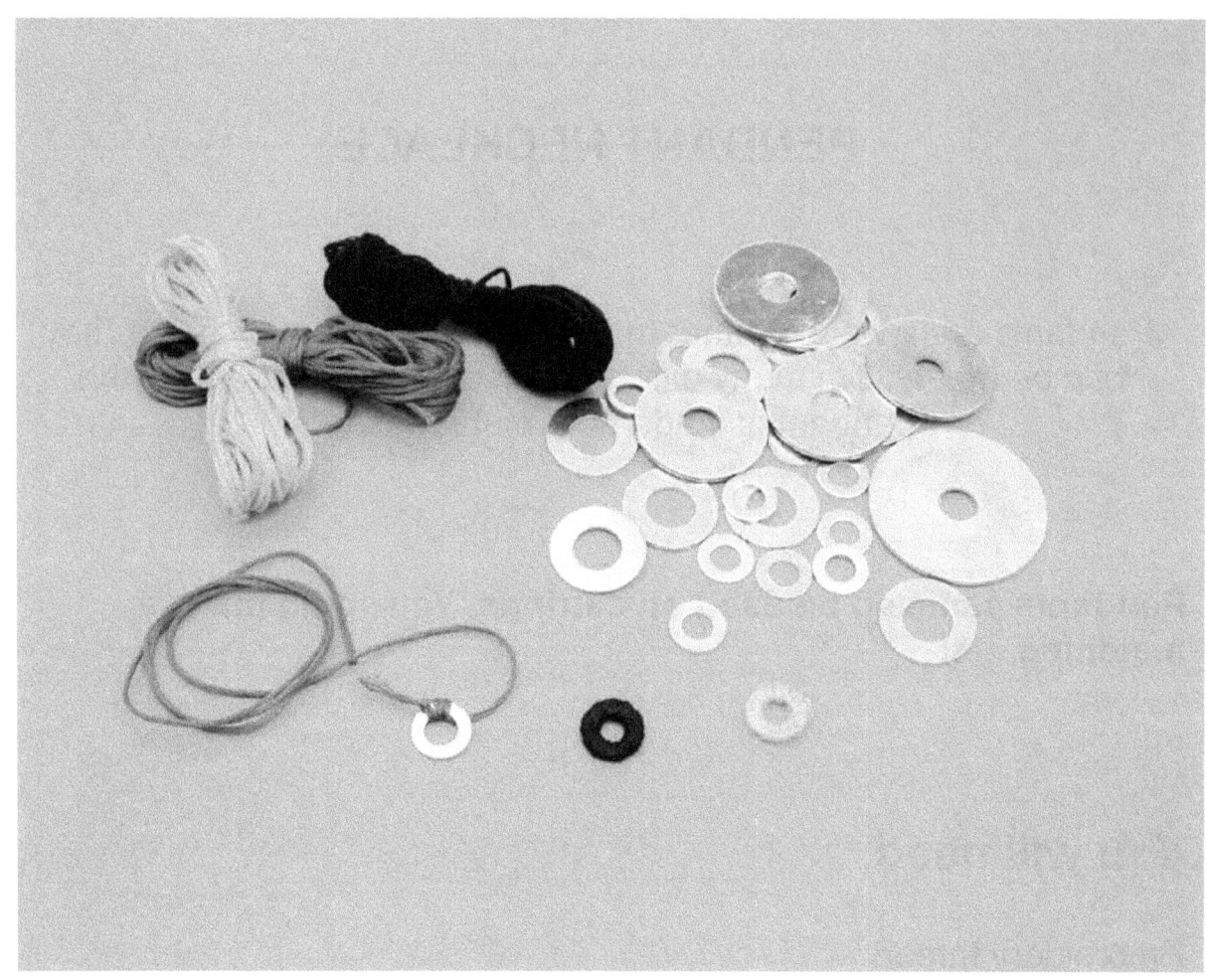

1. Tie a piece of embroidery thread to a small metal washer and start wrapping the thread round and round. Keep wrapping until you have covered the whole washer. Then repeat this twice more with other small washers.

2. Tie the three small washers together with embroidery thread of a different colour, so that they form a small triangle.

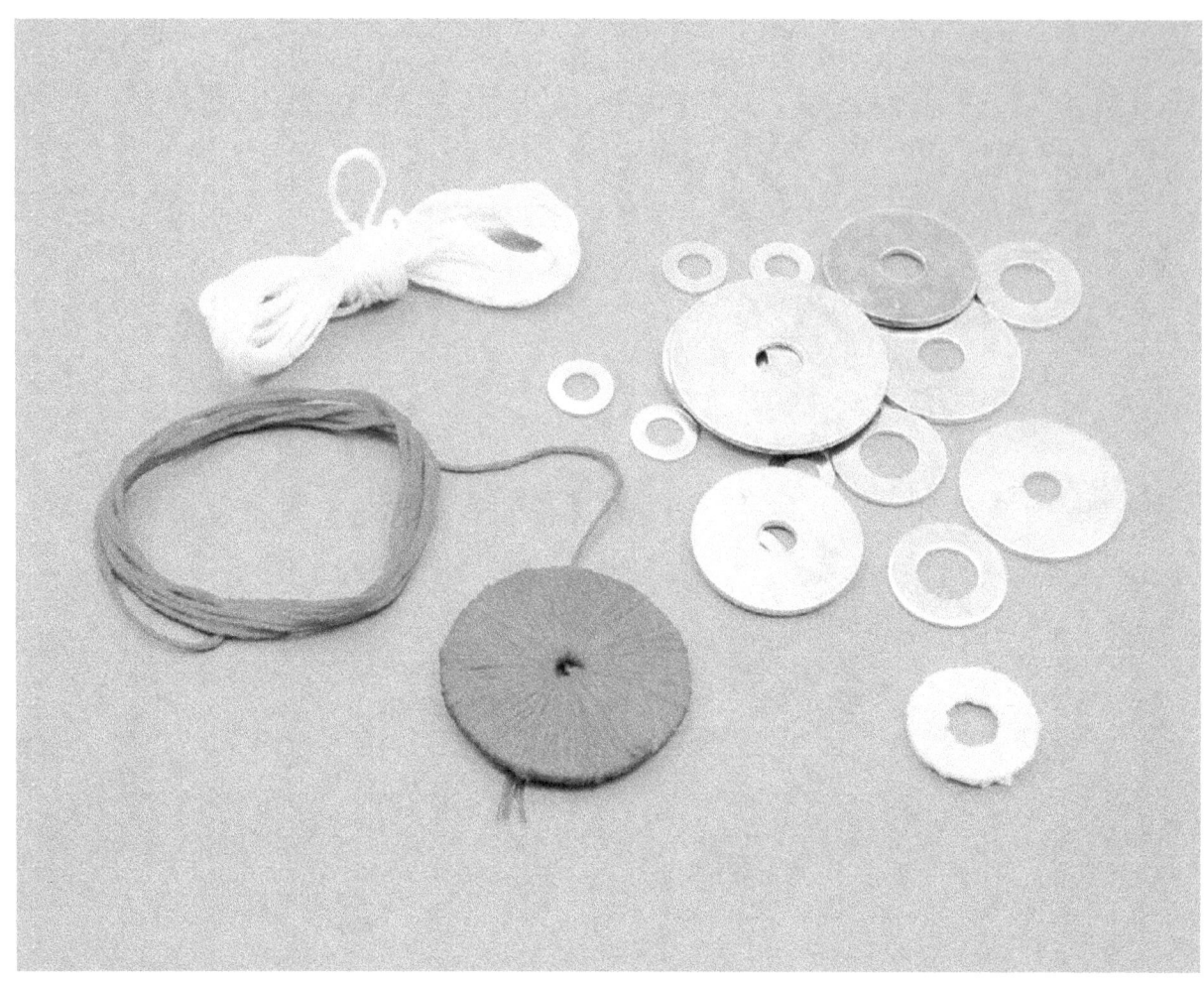

3. Now wrap some thread around a large washer and a medium-sized washer.

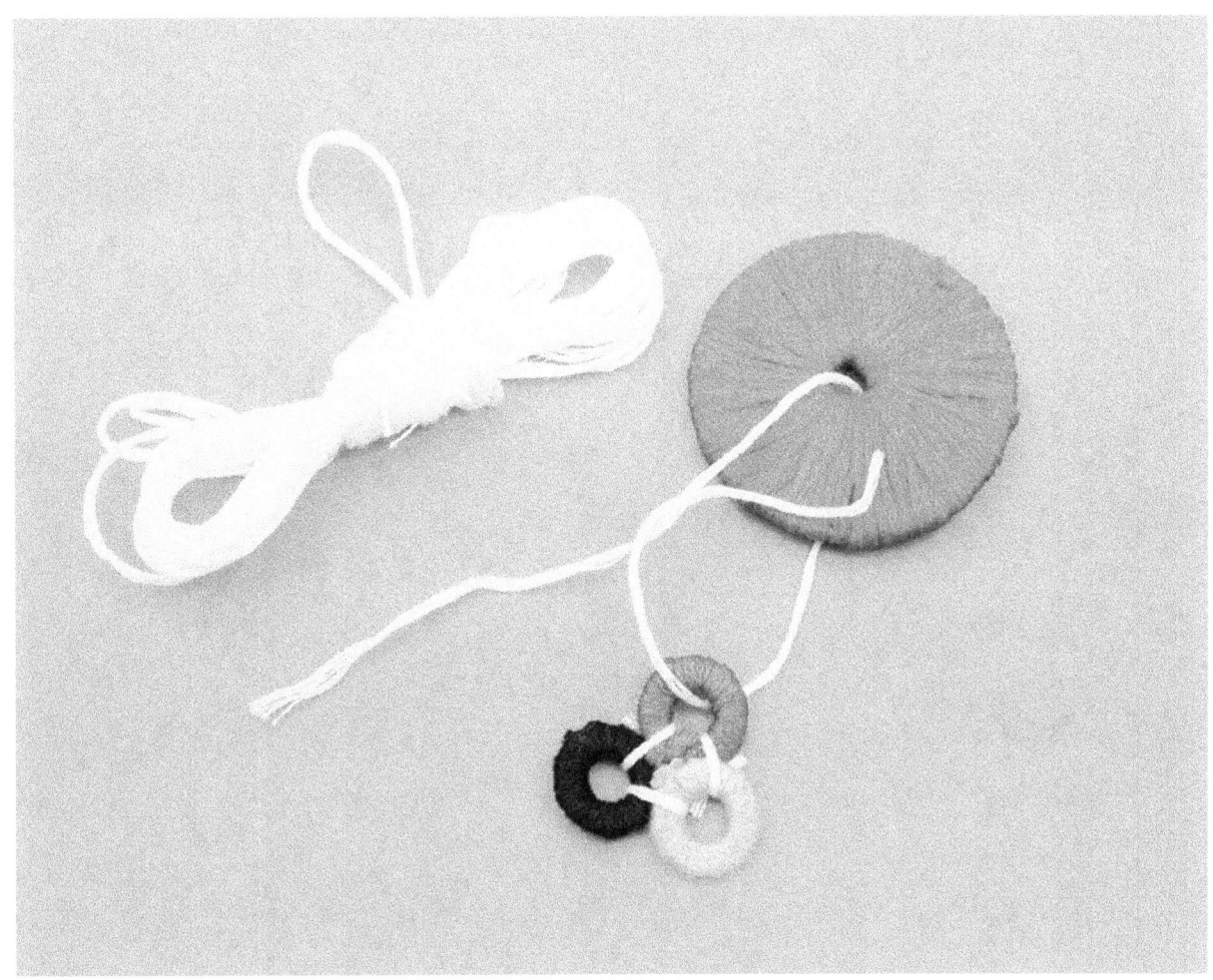

4. Attach the triangle of small washers to the large washer using more embroidery thread. Then attach the medium-sized washer to the other side.

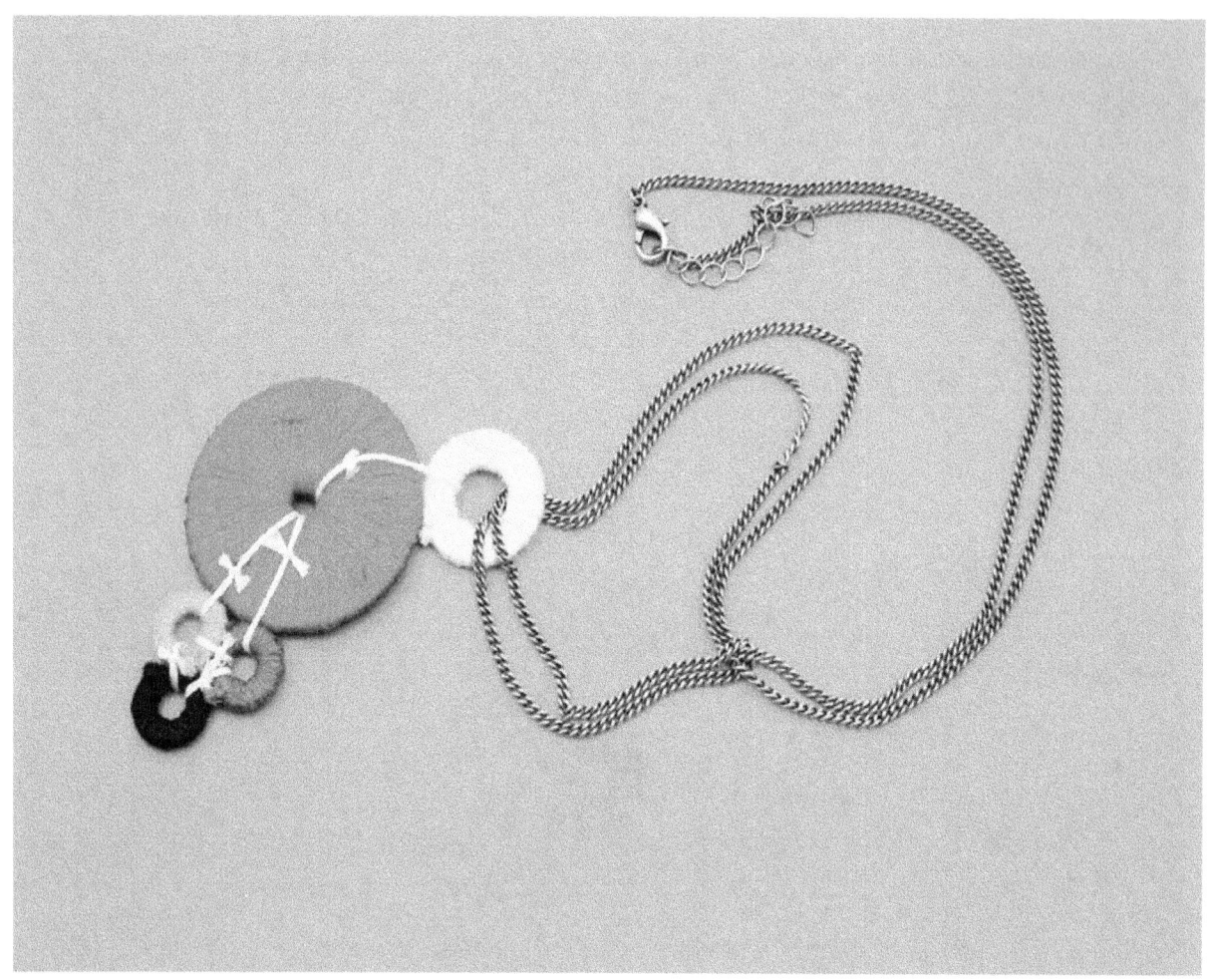

5. Thread your chain through the hole in the medium-sized washer.

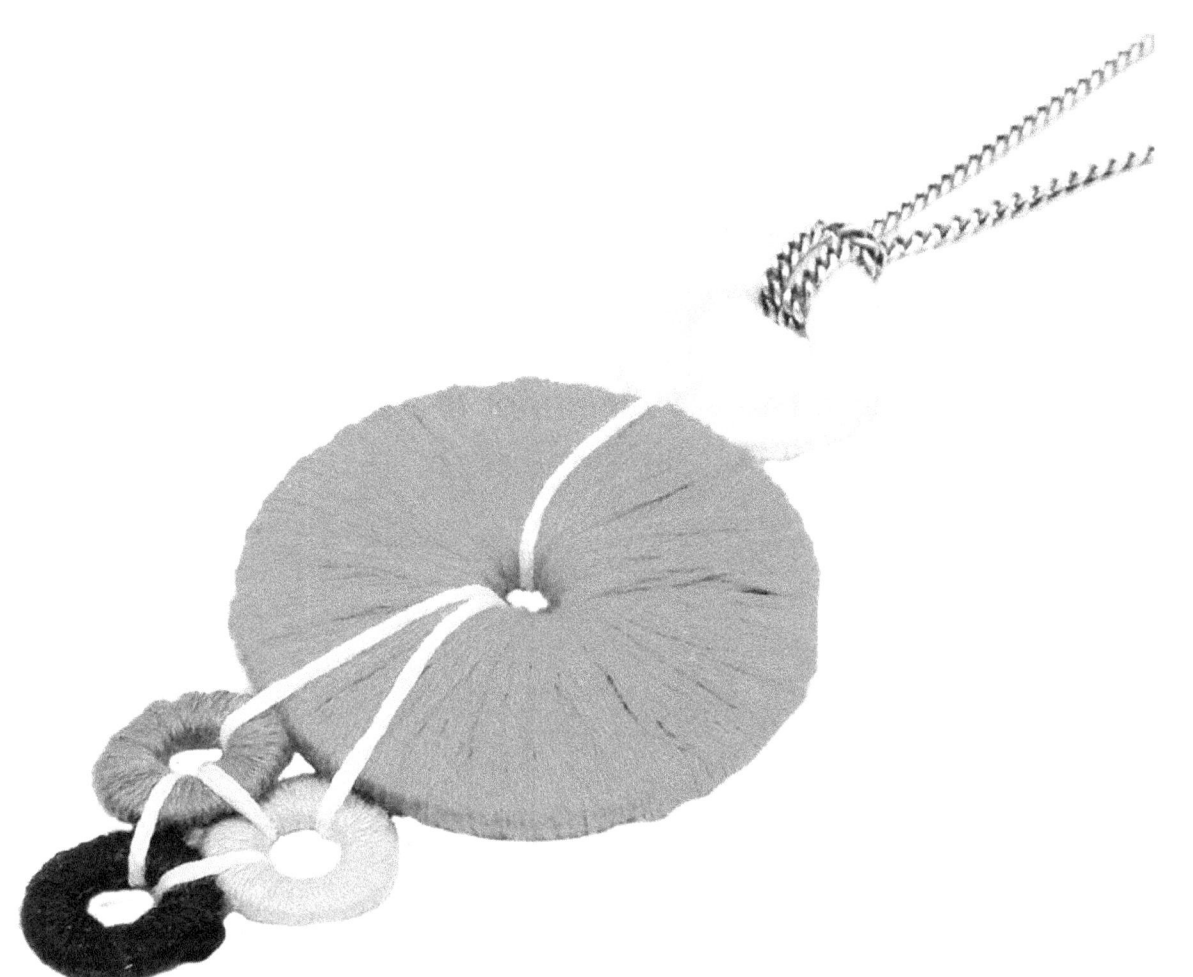

LUCKY RABBIT EARRINGS

Aren't these bunny earrings cute? You can make them for pierced or unpierced ears. Remember to ask an adult to help you when using wire cutters.

You will need

Jewellery wire

Wire cutters

Small, medium and large beads

Small pom-pom

Scissors

Felt and fabric glue

Earring hooks or clips

Tape measure

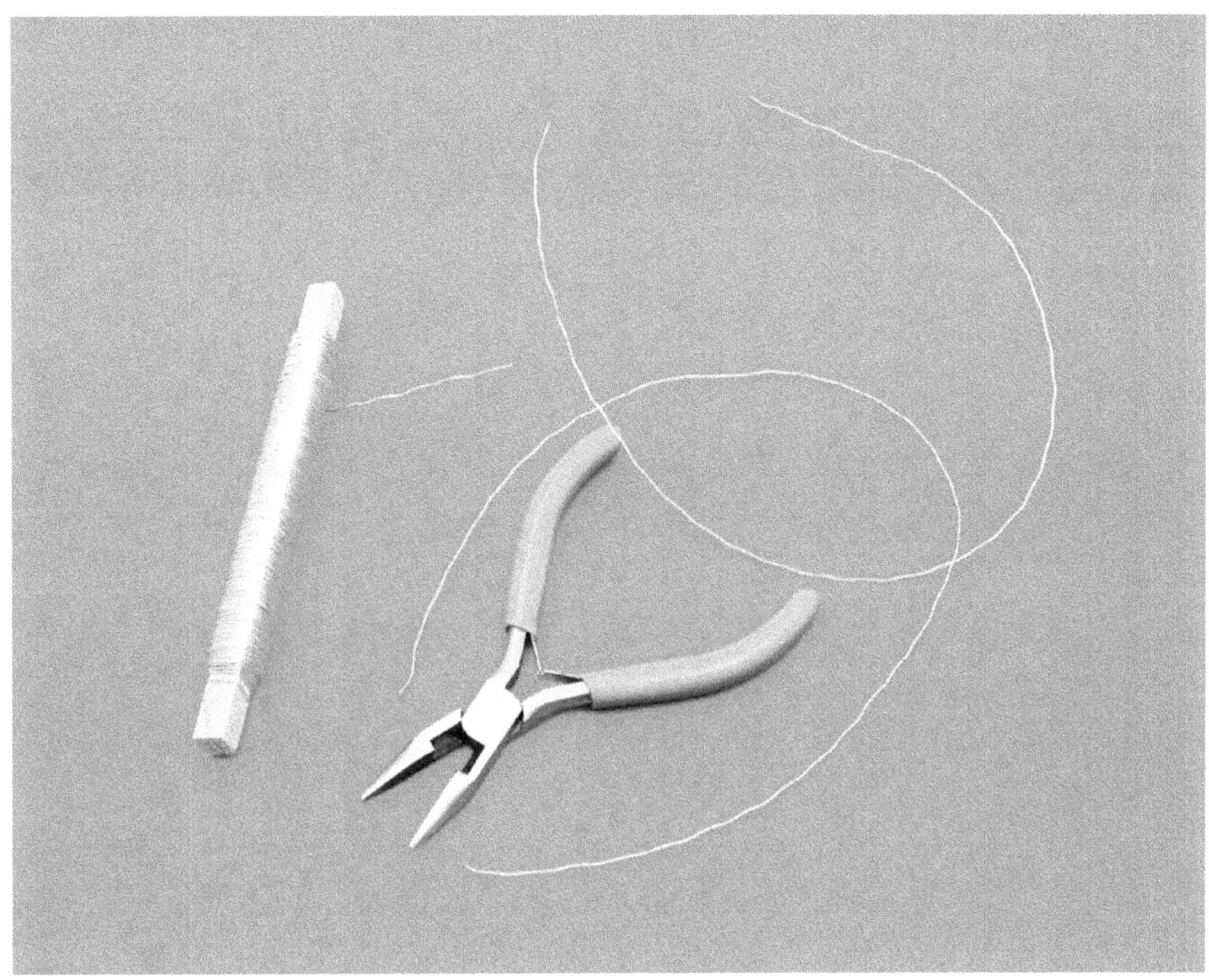

1. Cut two lengths of jewellery wire 40 cm (15 in) long, using wire cutters.

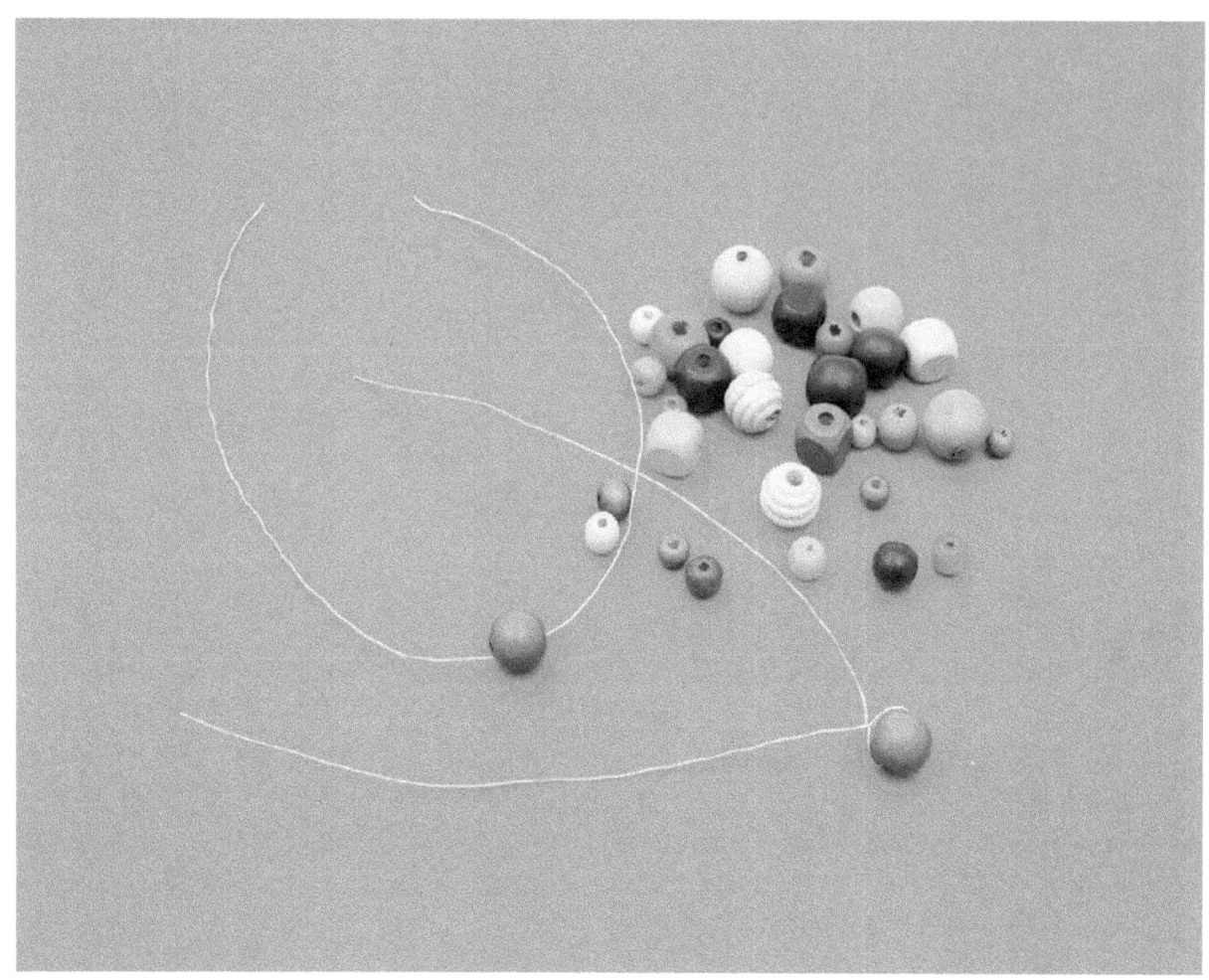

2. Thread one medium-sized bead to the middle of each wire and twist the wire to hold it in place. This will be the rabbit's head.

3. Thread a small bead onto both ends of each wire. Slide the beads down. Twist the ends of the wire together just above them. Push both ends of the wire through a large bead (the body). Then slide down two more small beads and twist again.

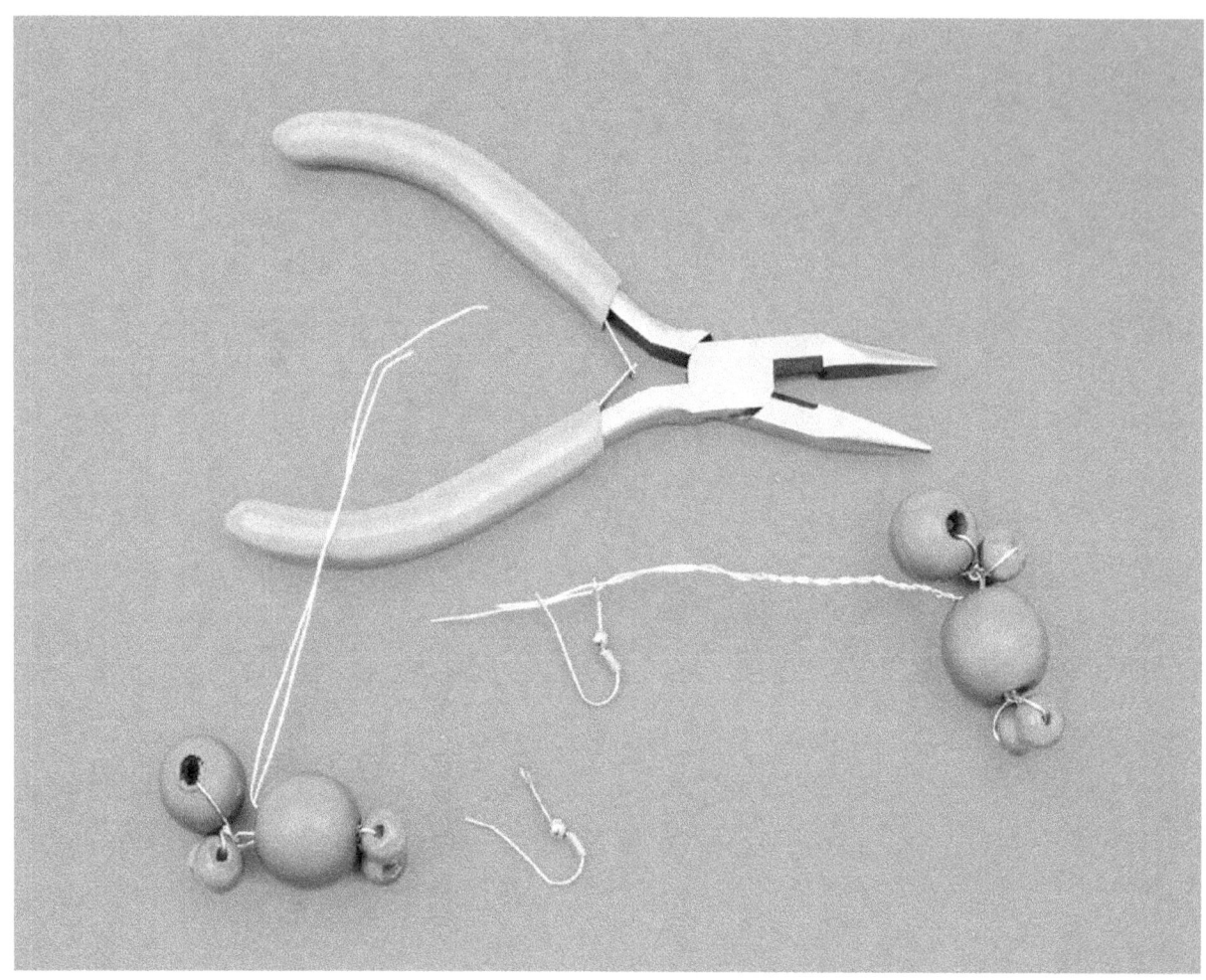

4. Poke the wires back through the bead body. Attach the earring hook or clip to the wire, and snip off any spare wire.

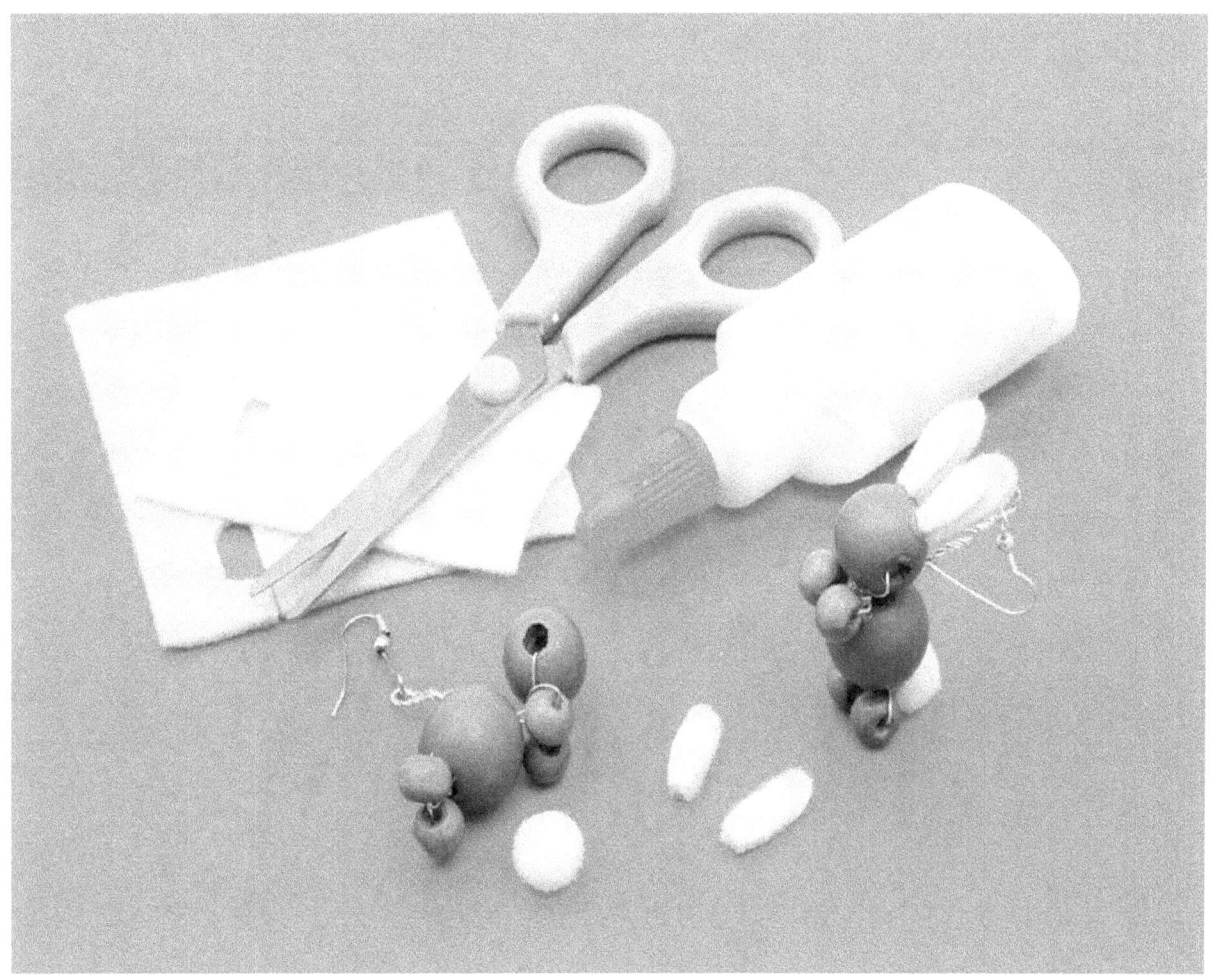

5. Cut out four small felt ears. Use fabric glue to stick them to the rabbits' heads. Finally, glue a small pom-pom to the back of each earring. This is the tail!

It was once believed that a rabbit's foot could bring you luck. Now that you're wearing eight, you should be especially lucky!

KNOTTED BRACELET

Sailors' knots are very useful to know if you are sailing the open seas. But did you ever think about using them to make a fashion bracelet? Take your time with the figure-eight knots – don't get yourself in a tangle!

You will need

String or shoelace 40 cm (15 in) long

Jewellery clasps

Wire cutters

Beads

Scissors

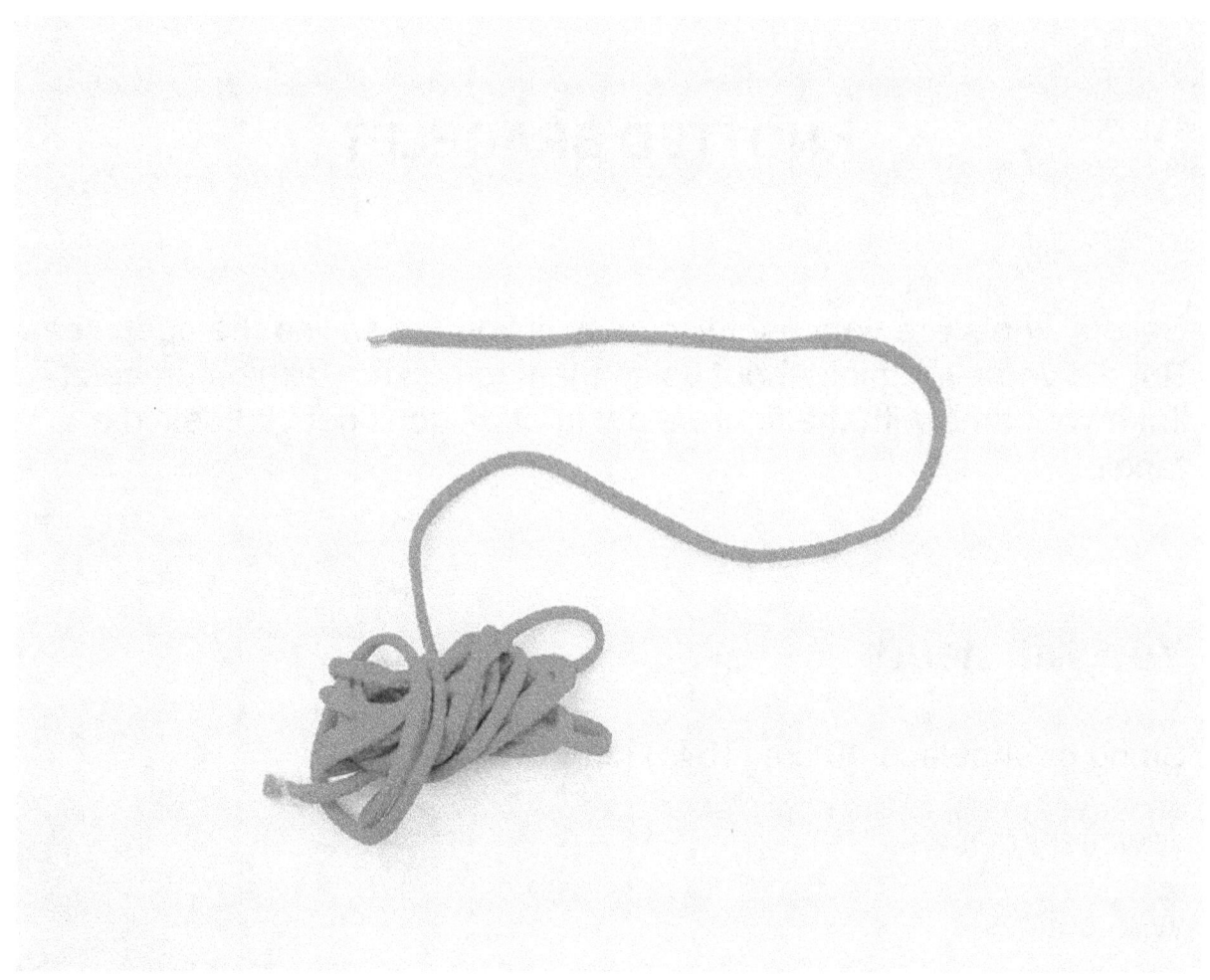

1. Half the string should be free, and half bundled up. Holding the bundled end, loop the free string into a backwards 'c'.

2. Keeping hold of the bundled end, lead the string up and over itself to make a 'b'.

3. Bring the string back downwards but this time lead it under the straight line. This will make a figure '8' shape.

4. Pass the string through the bottom loop of the '8': first over, then under. Pull it tight.

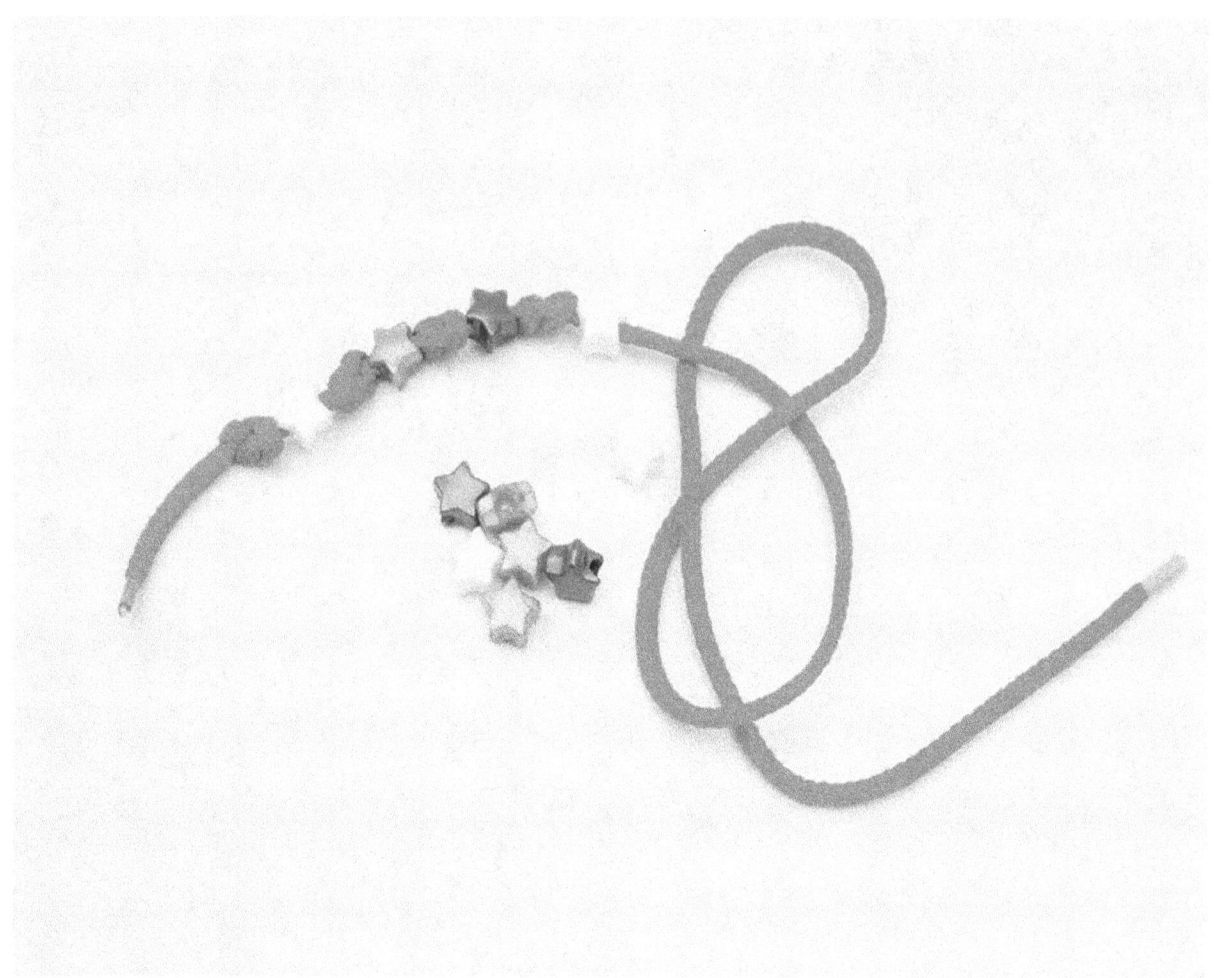

5. Repeat steps 1–4 to make more knots. Slide a bead onto the string at the bottom of each new knot. Do this all along the string. Tighten the knots carefully, pulling at either end to make sure they are in the right place.

6. Measure the knotted string against your wrist and trim it down if necessary. Then ask an adult to help you use wire cutters to attach some clasps to each end.

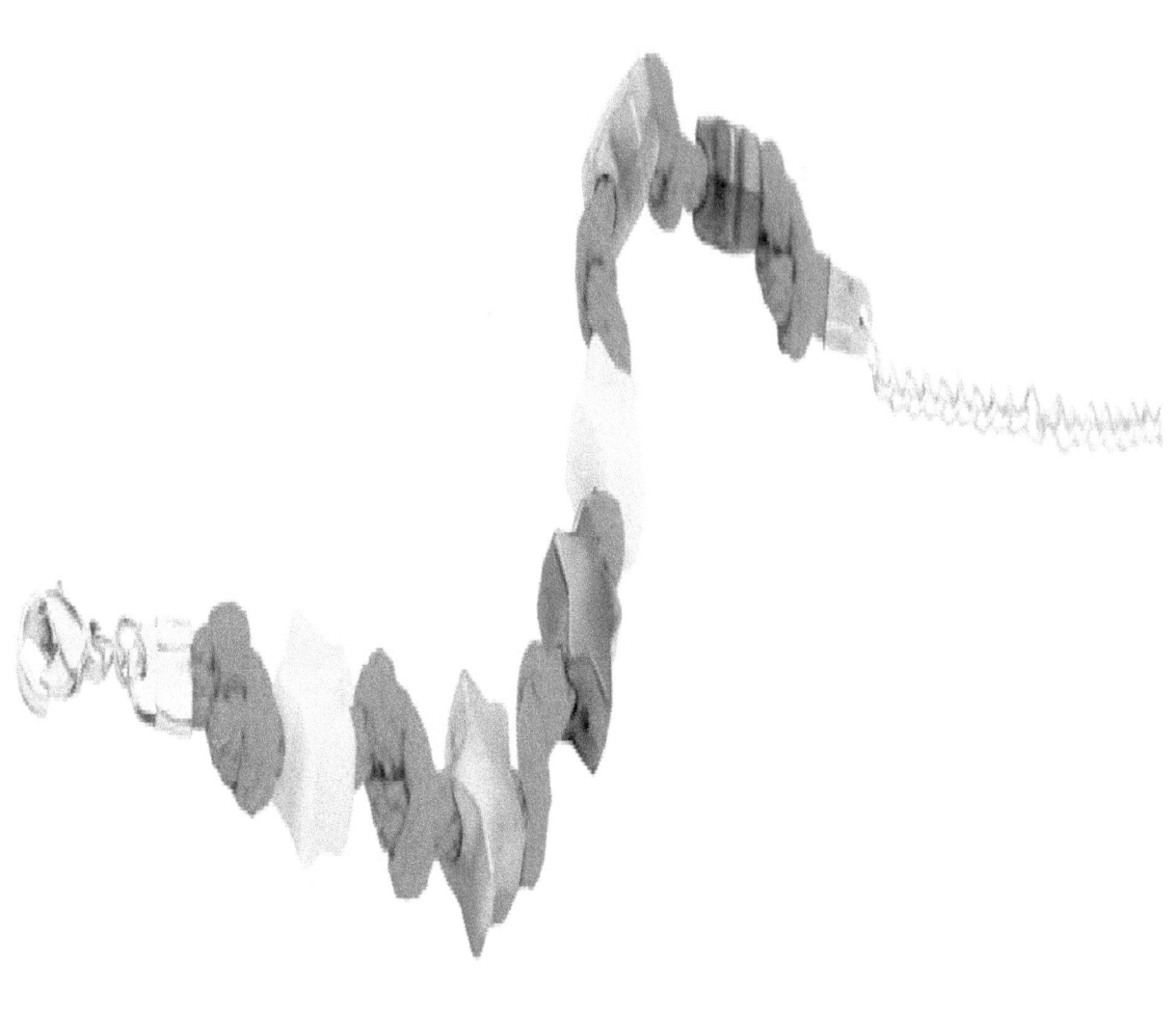

FABRIC FLOWER RING

A large, colourful ring can really transform an outfit. Why not make several fabric rings in different colours to match different outfit choices, or to give to friends?

You will need

Felt

Scissors

Old ring

Needle and thread

Craft glue

Fabric glue

Button

1. Cut out five petal shapes from felt, about 3 cm (1 in) long. Then cut out five smaller petal shapes in a different colour.

2. Pinch together the bottom of each petal. Ask an adult to help you sew a few stitches into each petal so that it stays pinched.

3. Ask your adult assistant to help you stitch the five large petals together in the centre. Do the same with the smaller petals.

4. Glue the two sets of petals together in the centre with fabric glue. Leave to dry.

5. Use the craft glue to fix a big button to the middle of the flower. Leave to dry. With adult help, sew the flower to your old ring.

You could attach these cute fabric flowers to other things, such as bags, tops, hats or brooch pins.

FUNKY TOY HAIR CLIPS

Do you have any old, unwanted plastic toys hiding at the back of your bedroom cupboards? Here's a fun way to turn them into cute and quirky jewellery. You won't be able to find hair clips like these in the shops!

You will need

Broken jewellery or toys

PVA glue

Small beads

Plain hair clip

Superglue

Acrylic paint

Paintbrush

1. Collect together some items you want to attach to your clips and clean them so they are free of dirt and dust.

2. When they are completely dry, paint each one a different colour using acrylic paint.

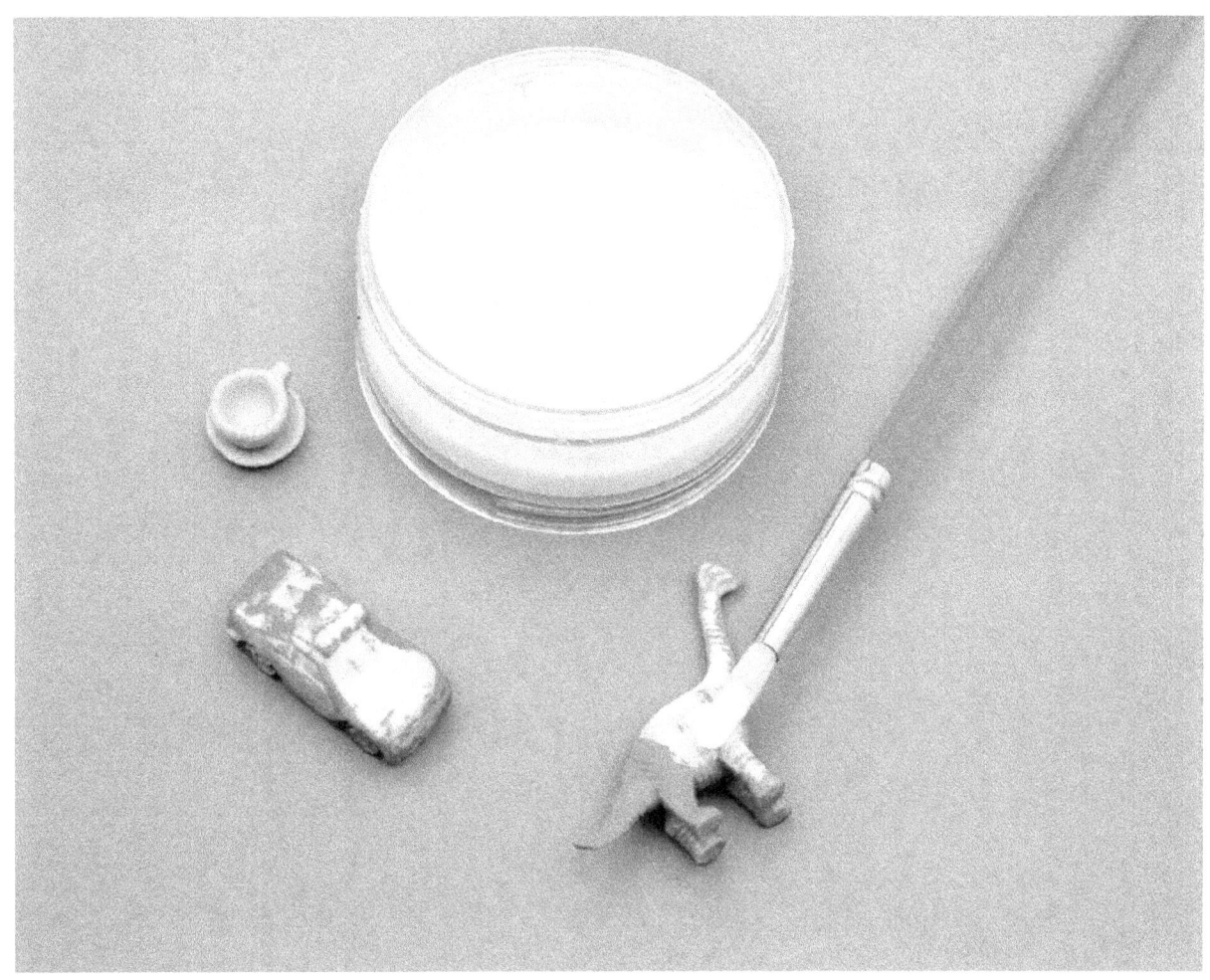

3. When the paint has dried, cover the toys with a thin layer of PVA glue. This will give them a shiny finish.

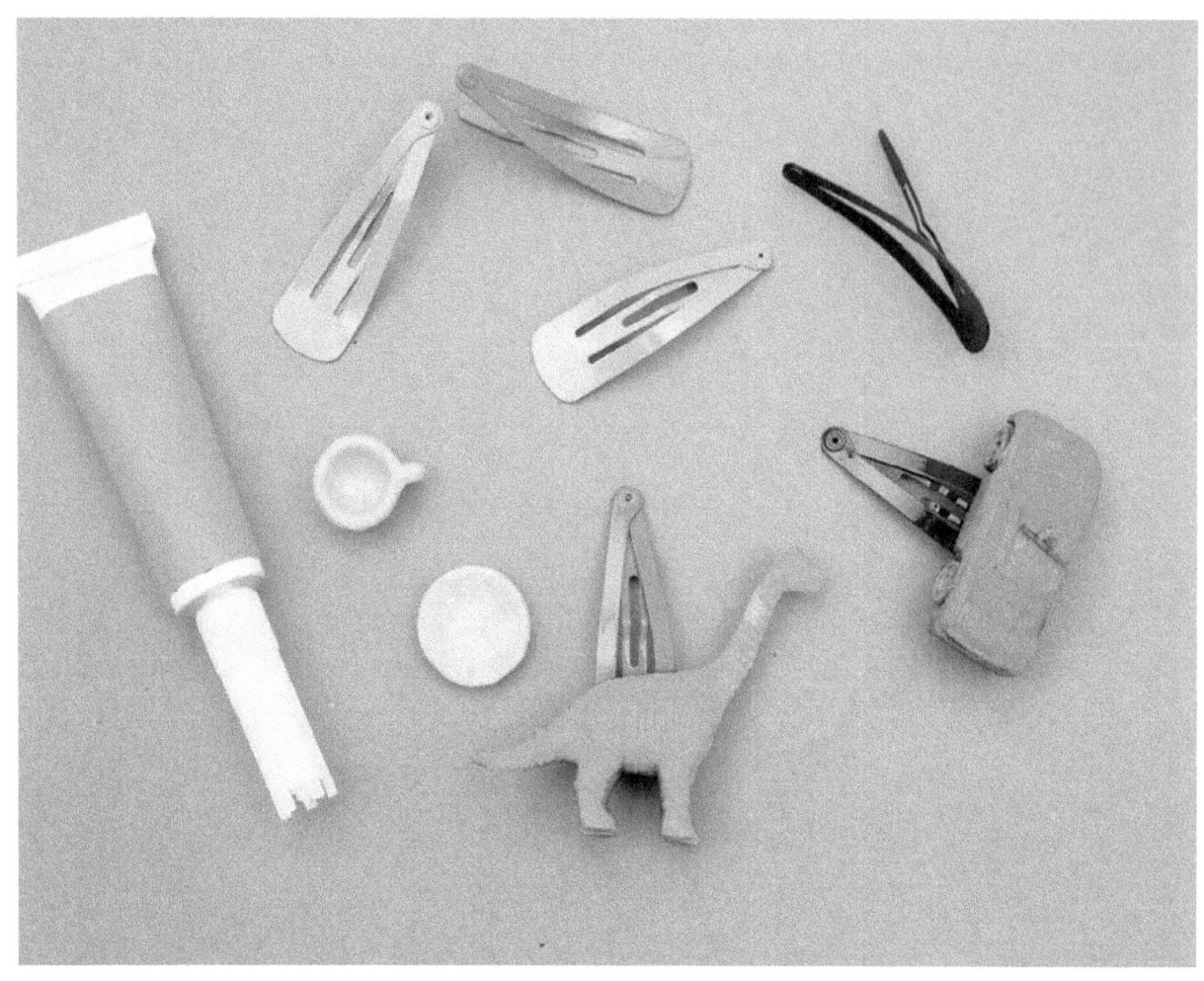

4. Ask an adult to superglue each toy to a clip. Leave the glue to set.

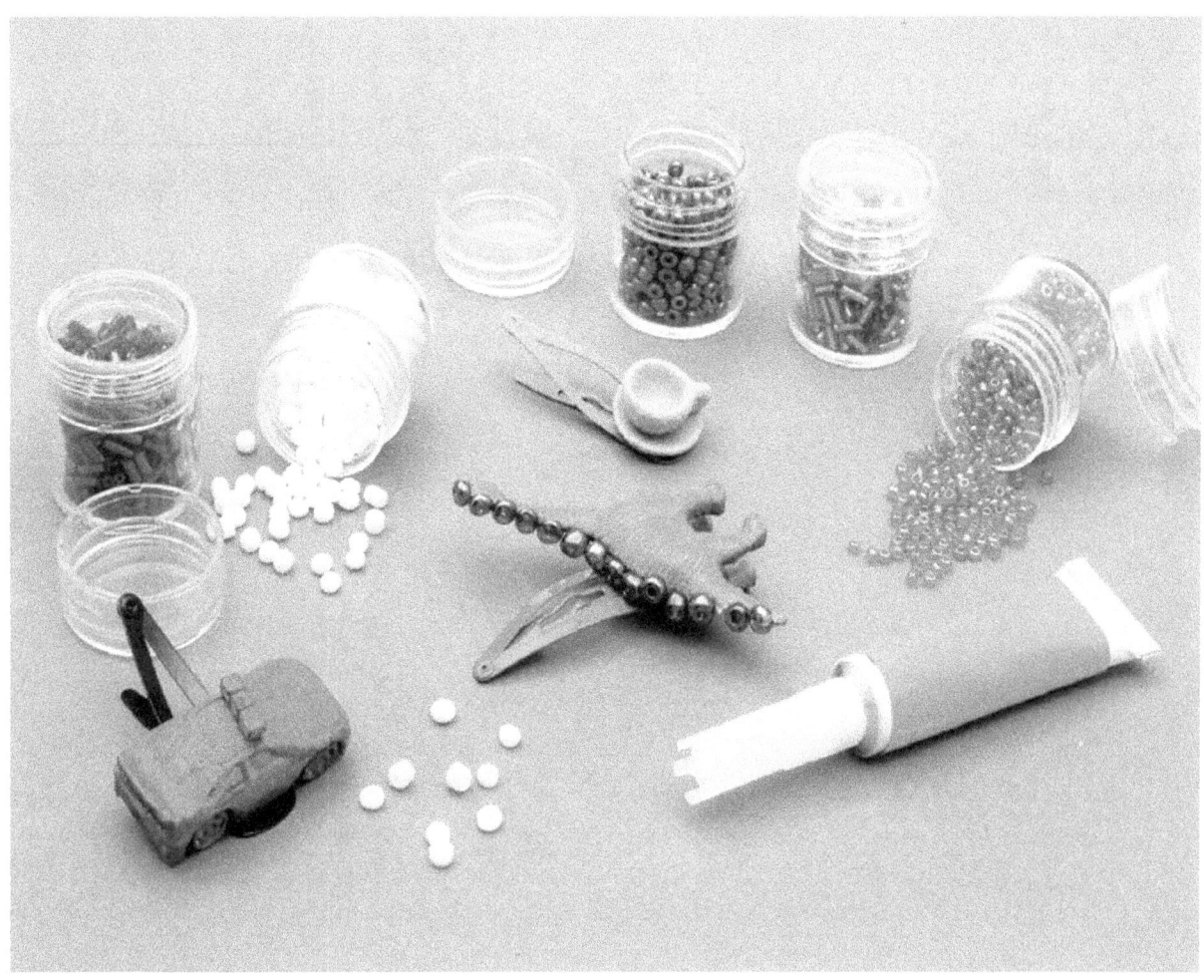

5. Use PVA glue to attach some small beads onto the toys.

JEWELLED CUFF

Cuffs are much wider than normal bracelets. This means that you have a nice large space to fill with colours and patterns! You could use a cuff like this as part of an outfit for a fancy dress party.

You will need

Cardboard tube

Craft foam shapes

Stick-on gems

PVA glue

Metallic paint

Scissors

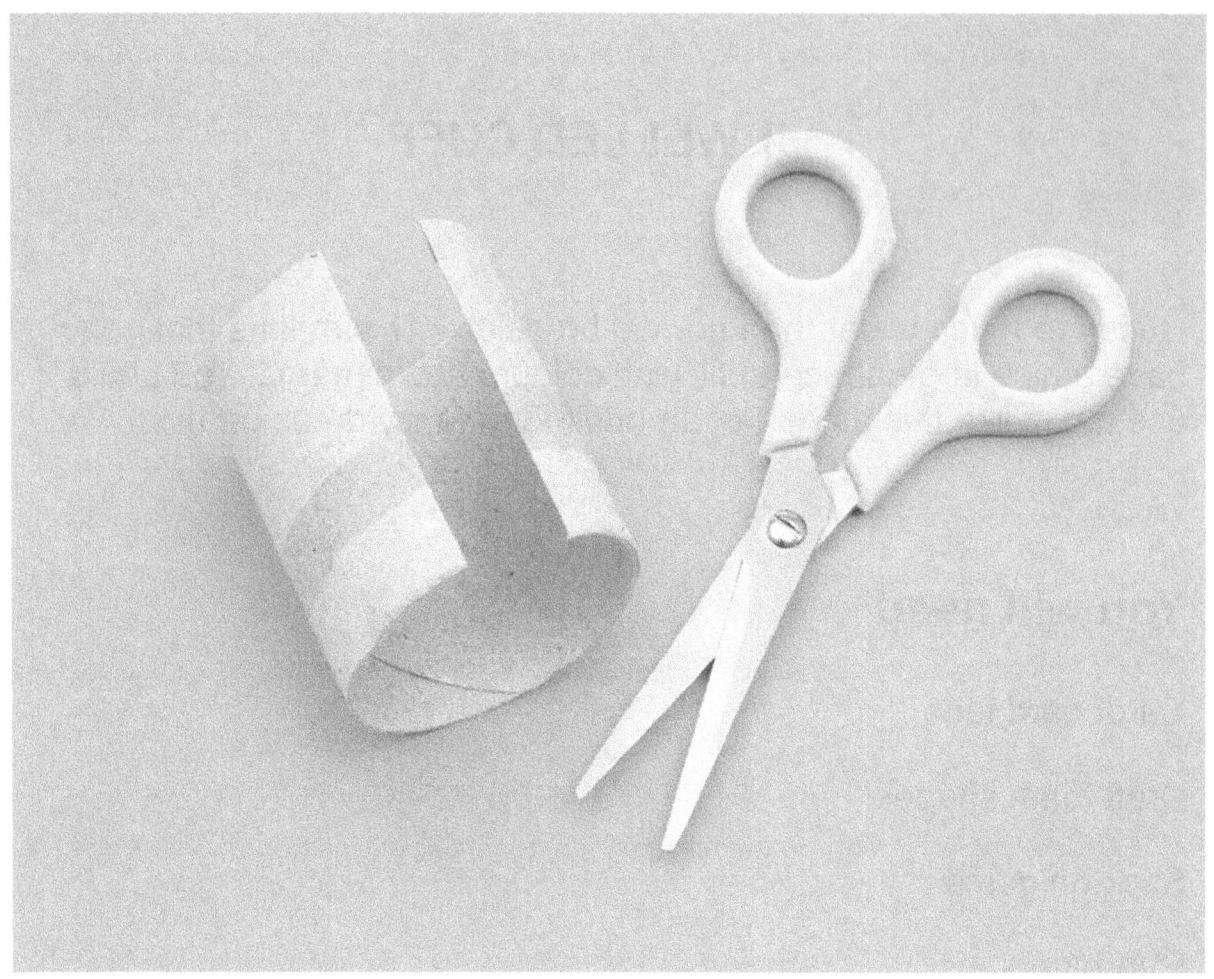

1. Cut a 6 cm (2 in) section from your cardboard tube with scissors. Snip down the length of the section so that you can get the cuff on and off your wrist.

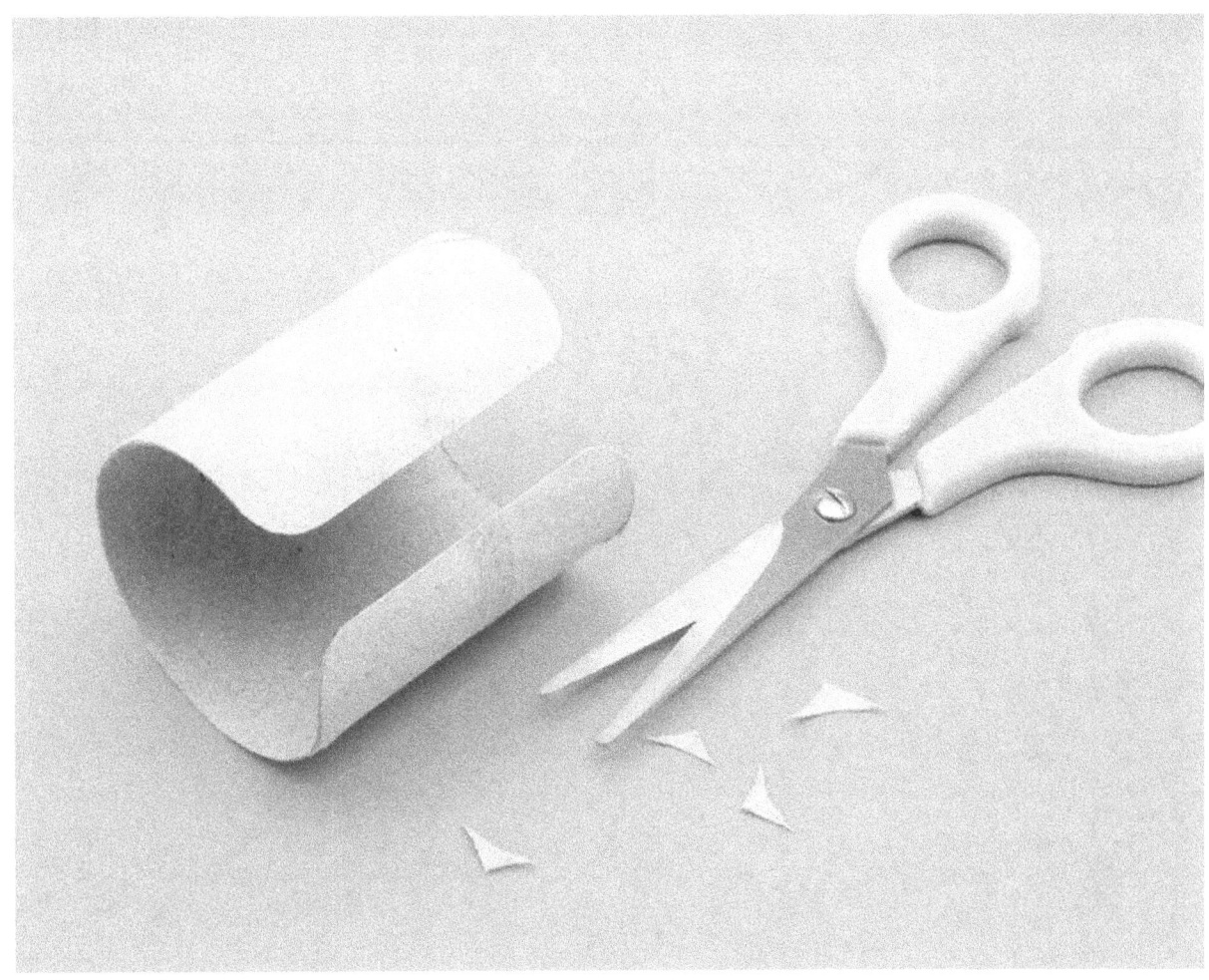

2. Cut around the edges of each corner using your scissors.

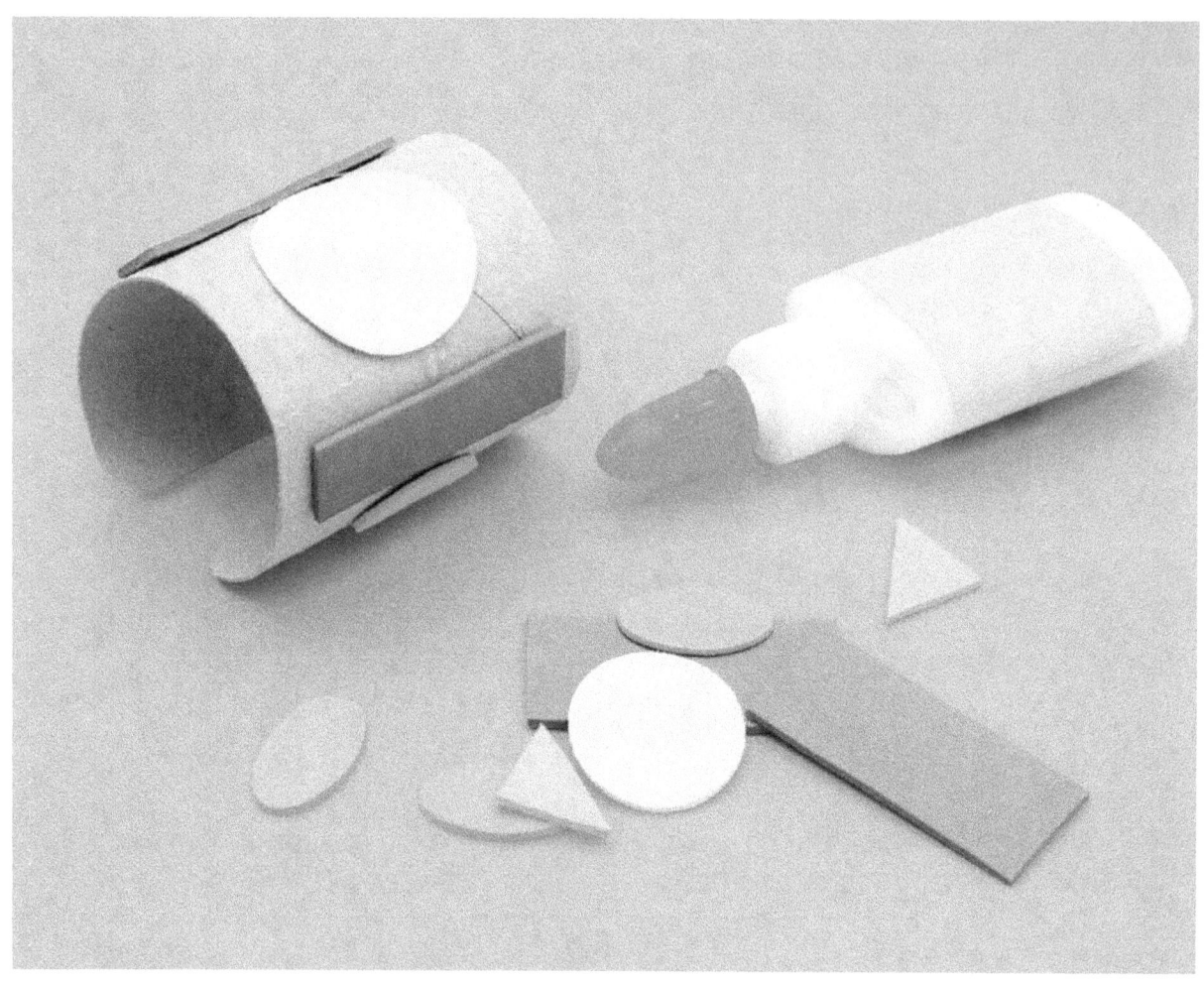

3. Use PVA glue to decorate the cuff with craft foam shapes.

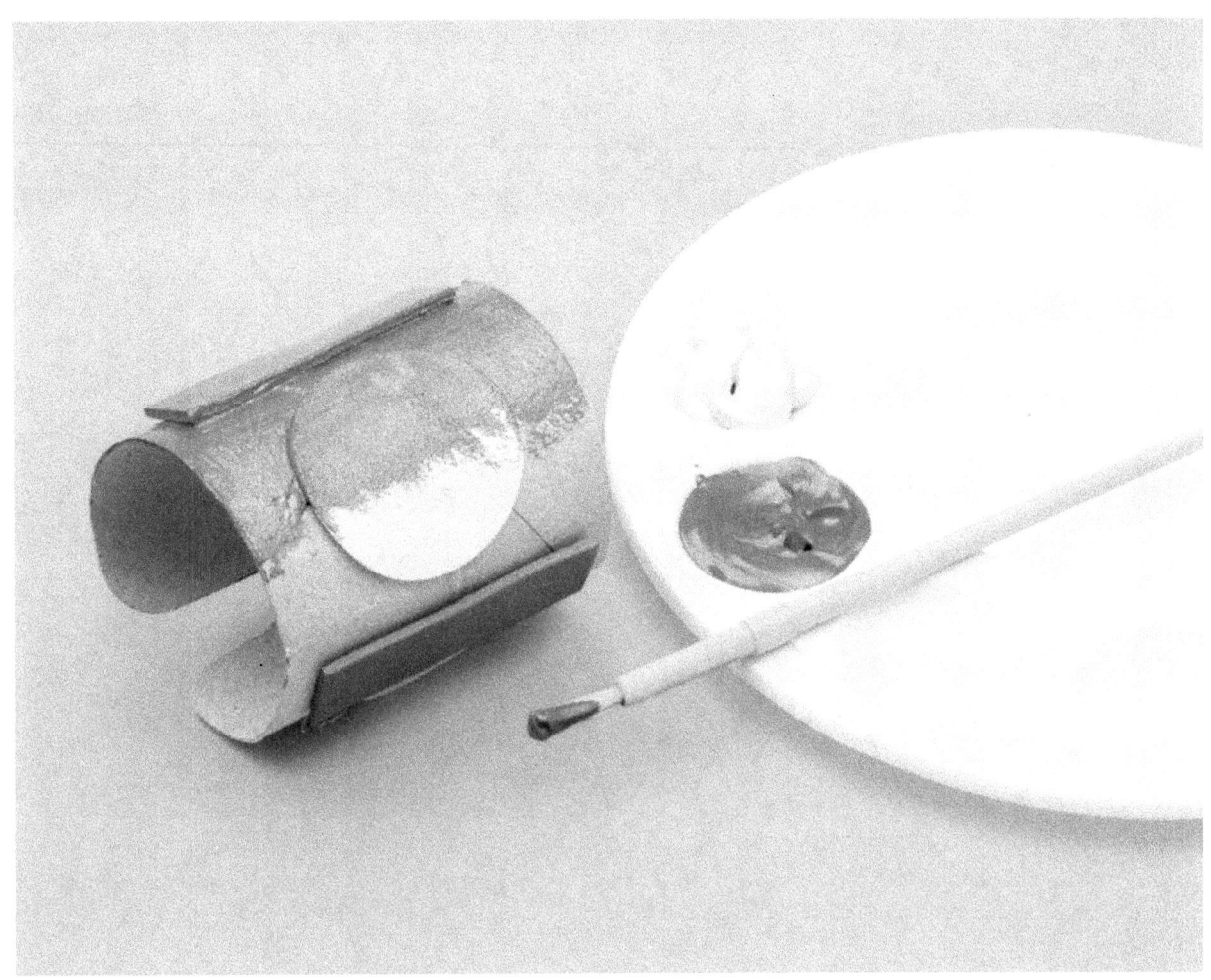

4. Paint the whole cuff with metallic paint and leave it to dry.

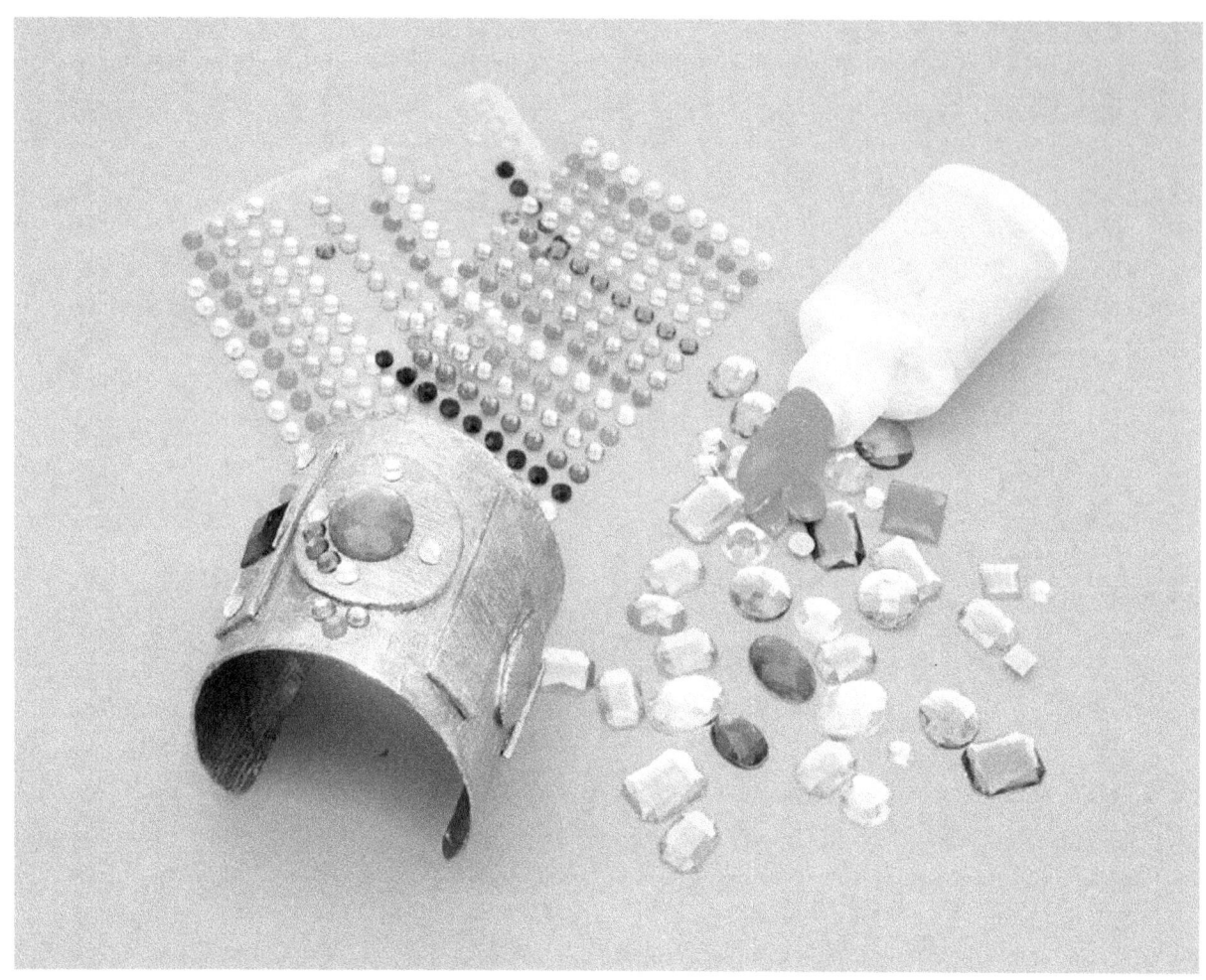

5. Decorate your cuff with some stick-on gems.

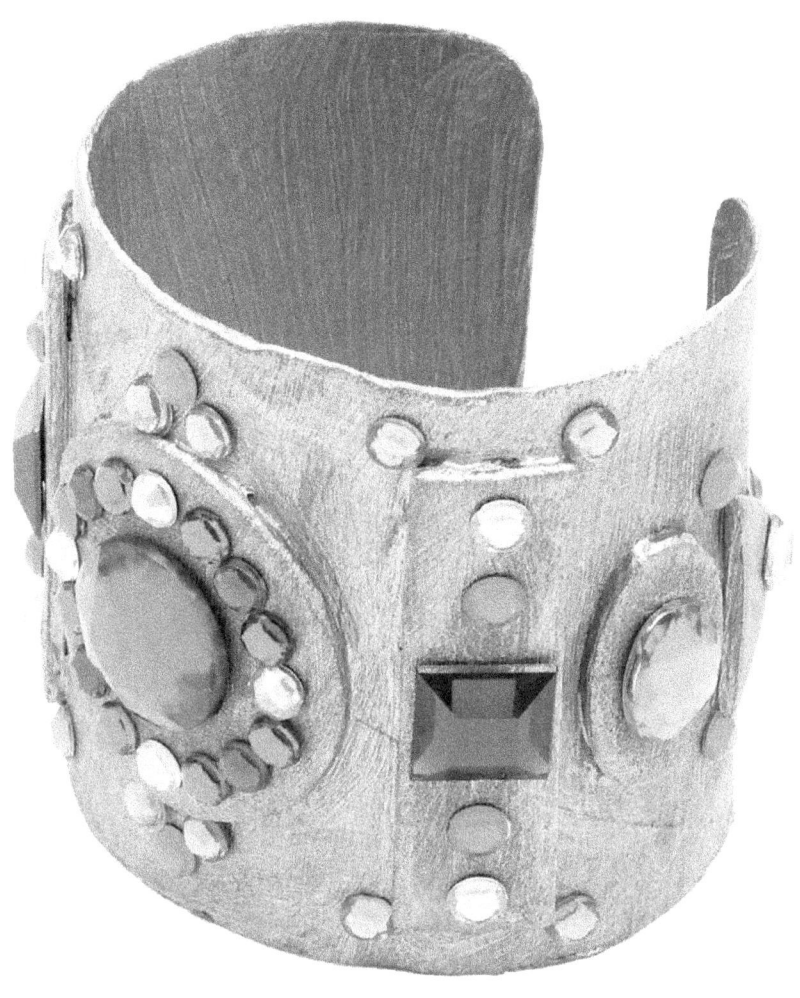

Alternatively, you could decorate your cuff with a collage.

PUZZLE PIECE HAIR COMB

Hair combs look great in long or short hair, and they can brighten up any outfit! These hair combs may look puzzling, but all your friends will love them.

You will need

Old puzzle pieces

Acrylic paint

Needle and thread

Paintbrush

Plain hair comb

Ribbon

PVA glue

Scissors

Tape measure

1. Choose three pieces from an old puzzle. Make sure that nobody wants to use it again!

2. Paint each piece in a different colour, using your acrylic paint.

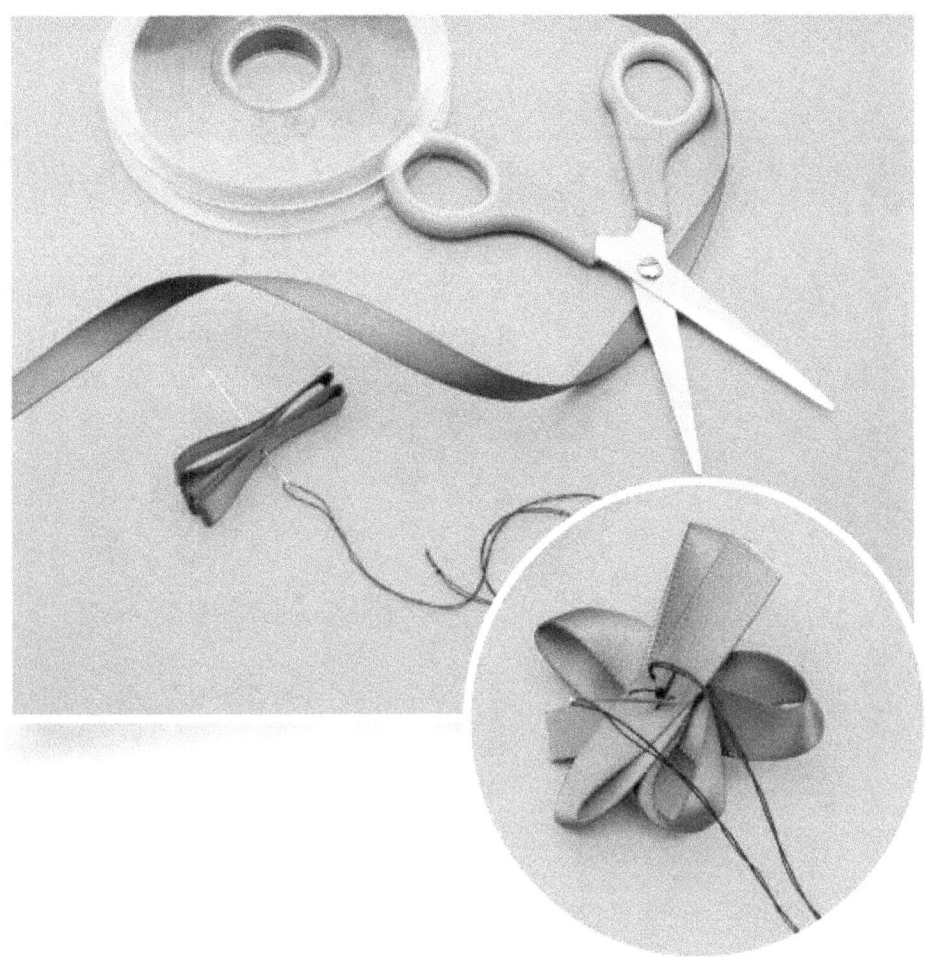

3. Cut a length of ribbon 30 cm (12 in) long. Fold it back and forth into a concertina. Ask an adult to pass a needle through the middle of the ribbon, then fan it out like a flower. Fix it in place with a few stitches.

4. Make two more ribbon 'flowers'. Use PVA glue to stick the puzzle pieces to them.

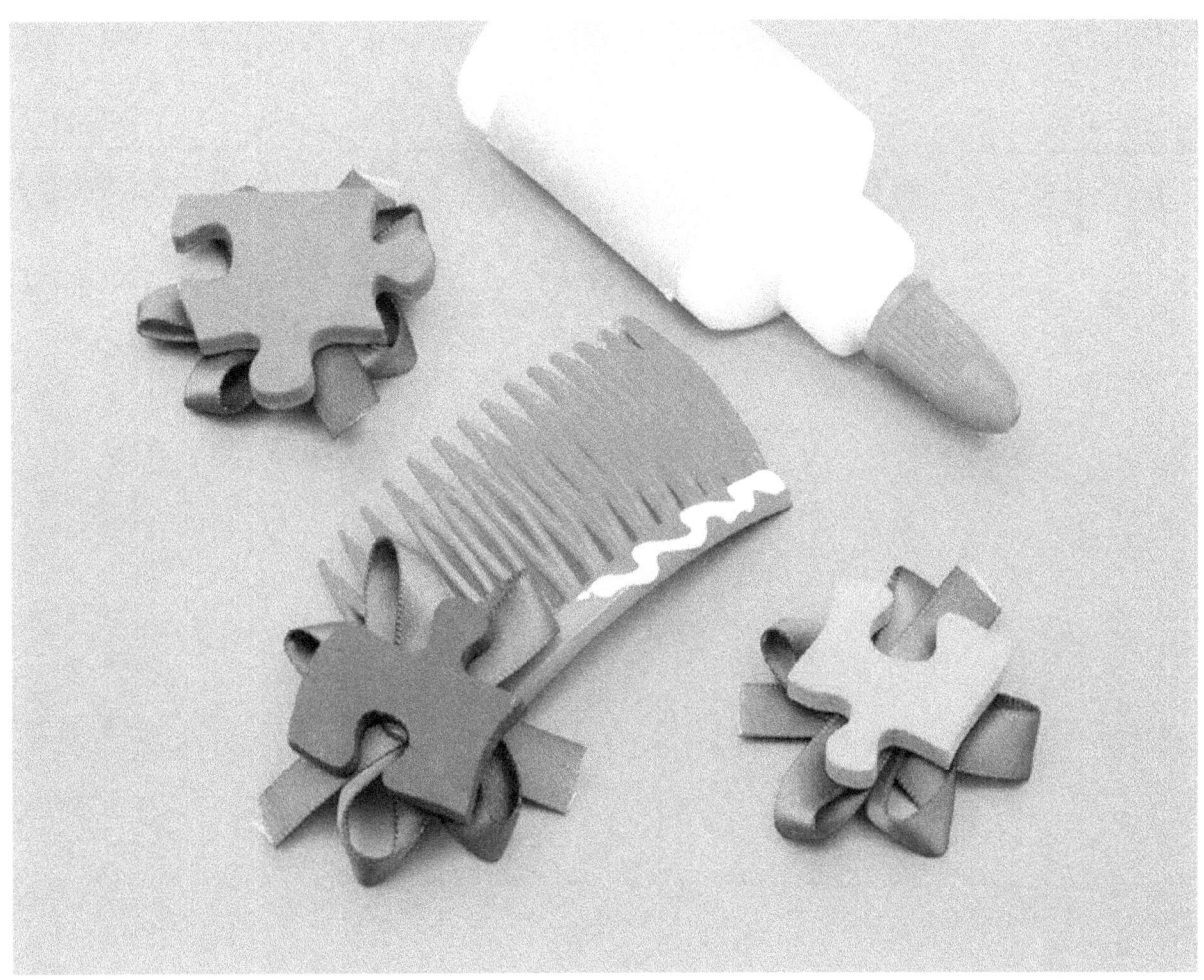

5. Fix the puzzle pieces and ribbon onto the hair comb with the craft glue. Leave to dry.

BUTTON BAG CHARM

Your favourite bag can be made even more stylish with a colourful charm. This can be attached anywhere: for example on zips, handles, or loops. You could make one for each of your bags.

You will need

Beads

Small and large buttons

Wire

Wire cutters

Key ring clasp

Tape measure

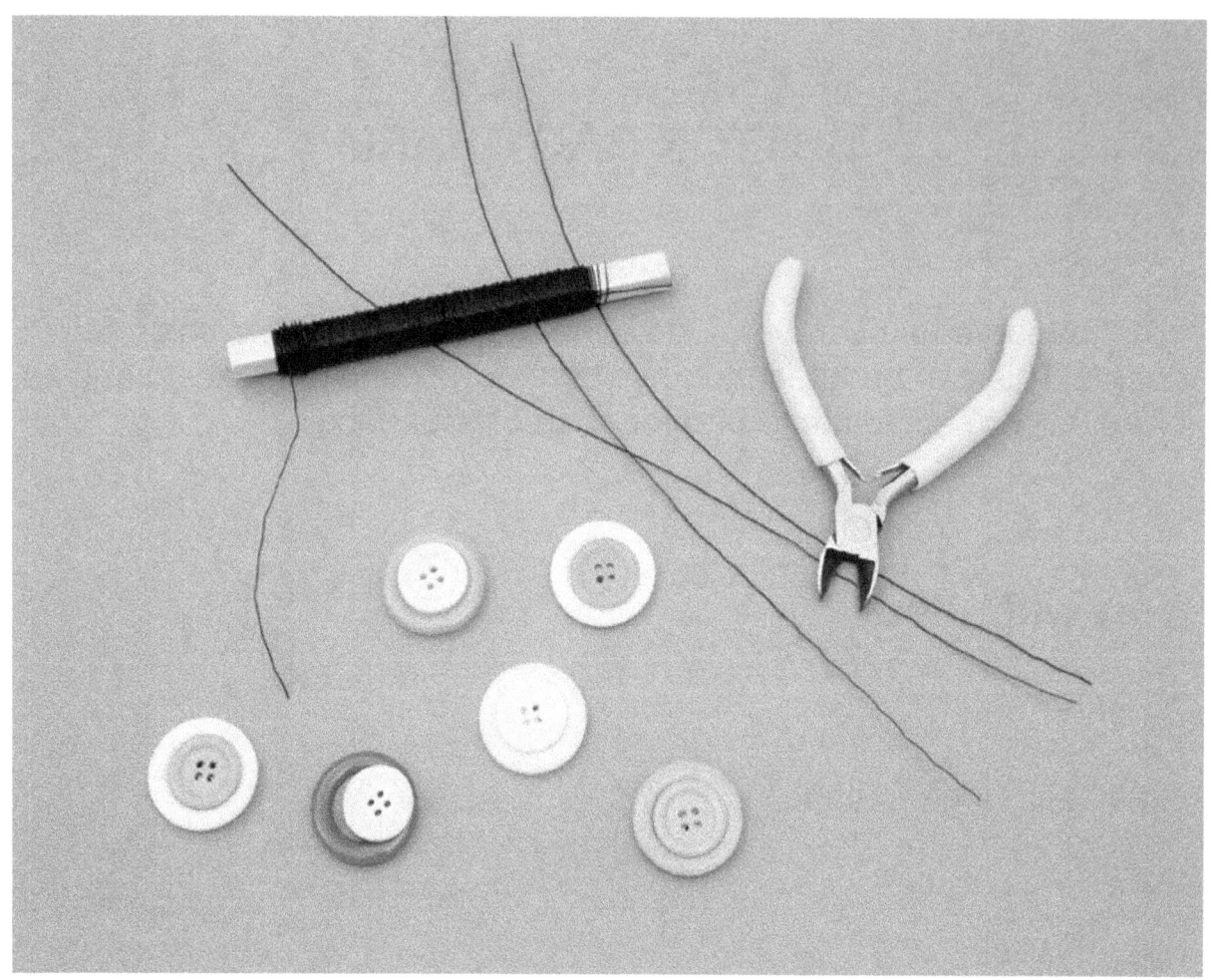

1. Place six small buttons onto six large buttons, making sure that the holes line up. Cut three pieces of wire 30 cm (12 in) long.

2. Thread a wire through one of the button stacks from underneath, into one hole and out of another. It will hold the buttons together. Thread two wires together in and out of the other two buttonholes.

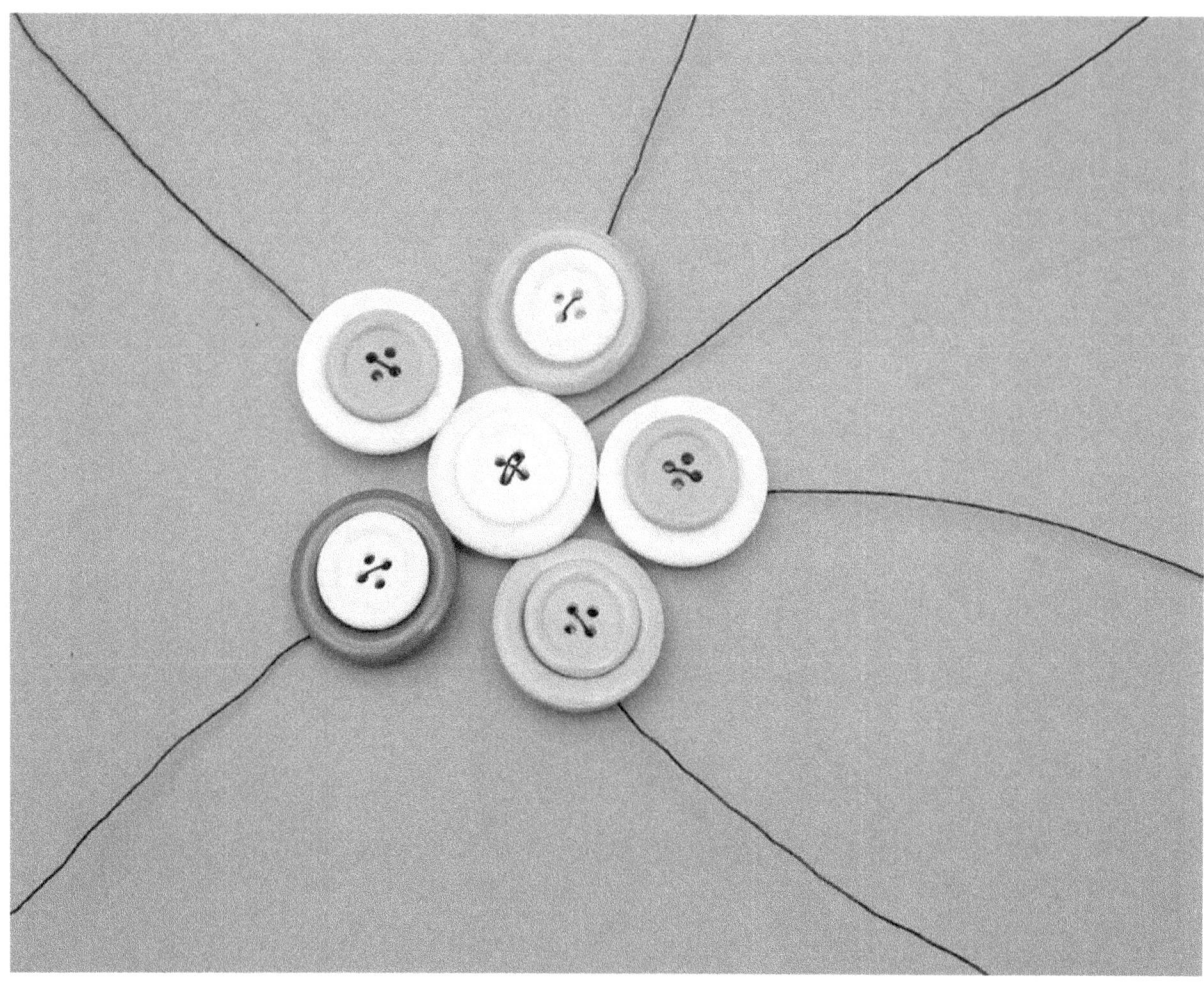

3. Thread the other five button stacks onto five of the wires attached to the first button. One wire should be left free.

4. Curl the wires behind the buttons so that they are fixed firmly in place. Thread some chunky beads onto the last remaining free wire.

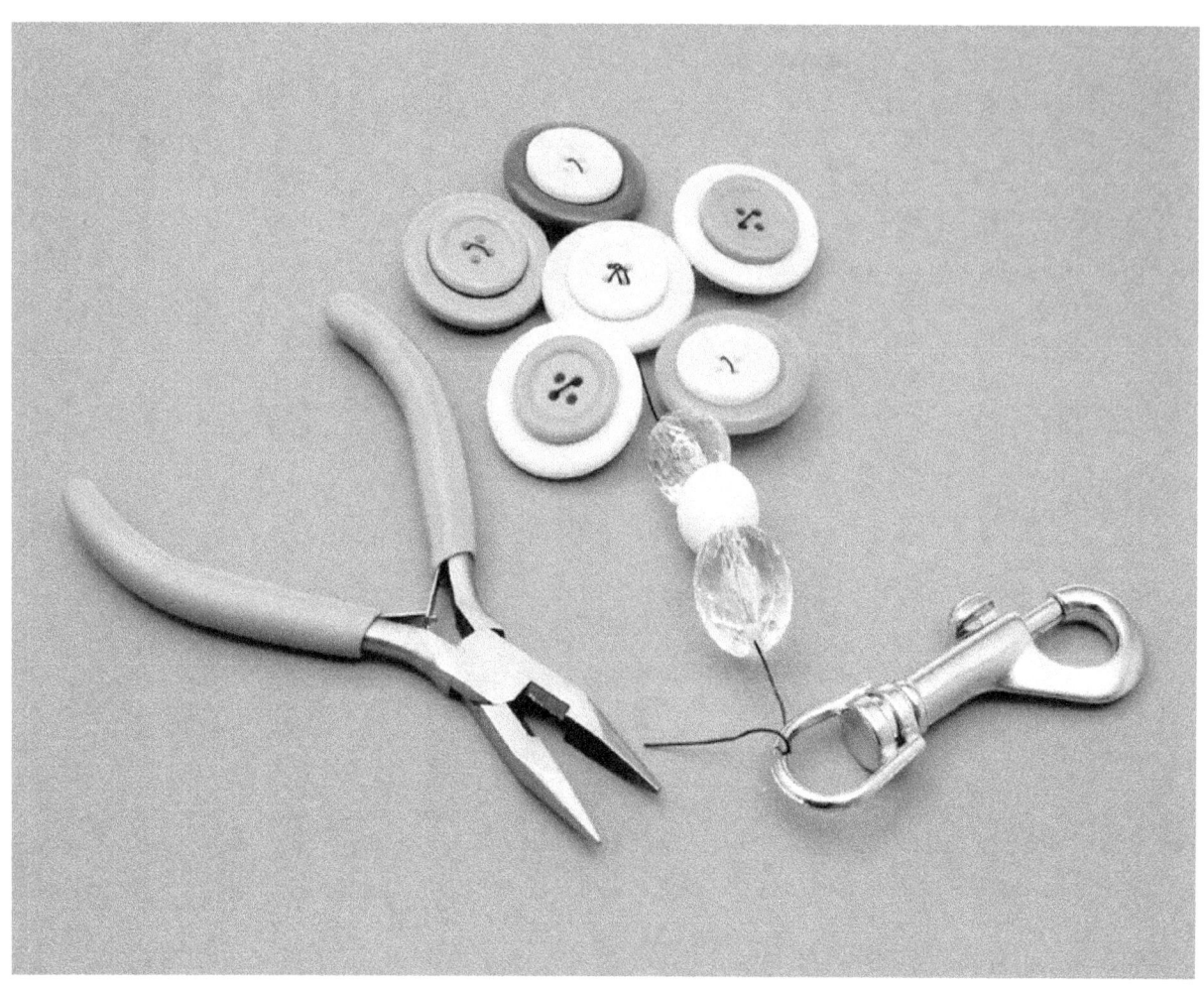

5. Attach the key ring clasp to the wire loop.

JEWELLERY TREE

Now that you have made all this awesome jewellery, you will want somewhere to display it! That's where this nifty tree comes in...

You will need

Gardening wire

Acrylic paint

Cardboard

Paintbrush

Wire cutters

Masking tape

Scissors

Pen or pencil

Ruler

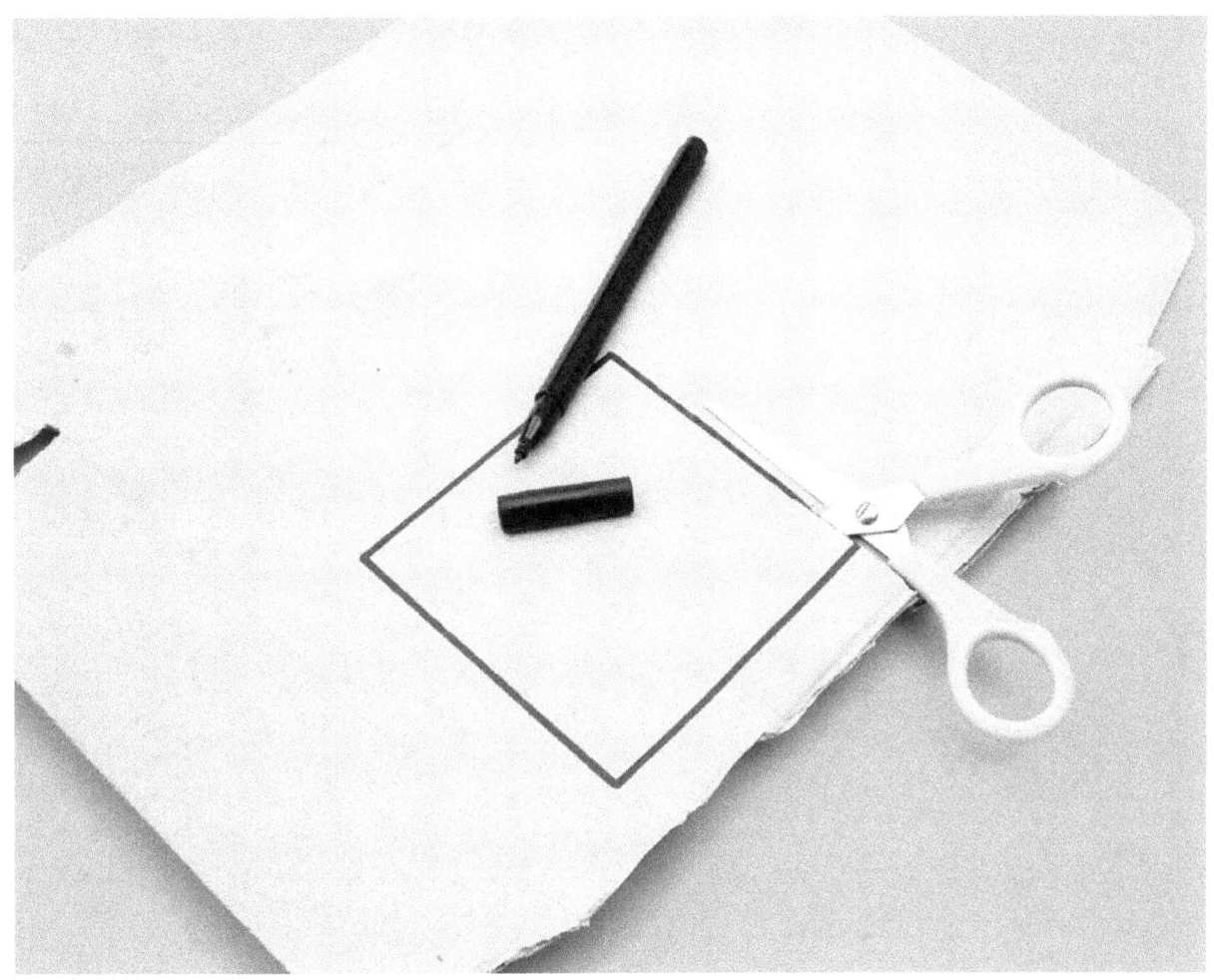

1. Cut a 10 x 10 cm (4 x 4 in) base from cardboard, using scissors.

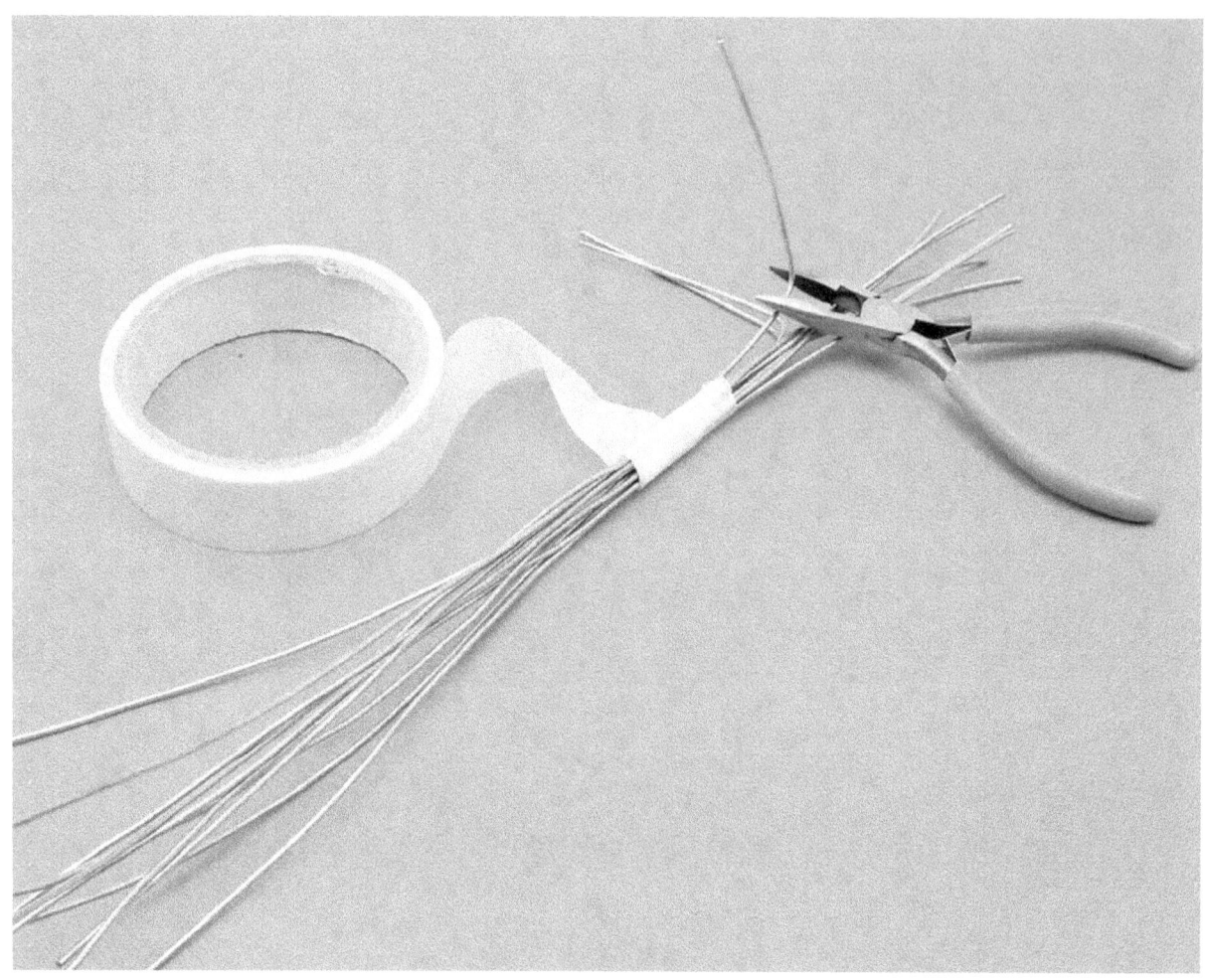

2. Ask an adult to help you cut ten 30-cm (12-in) lengths of wire, using wire cutters. Ask the adult to gather the wire together in a bunch and secure it in place about 6 cm (2.5 in) from one end with some masking tape.

3. Spread out the wires at the shorter end and secure them to the base with masking tape. Spread out the free ends of the wires to make branches. Ask an adult to help you curl the very ends with wire cutters.

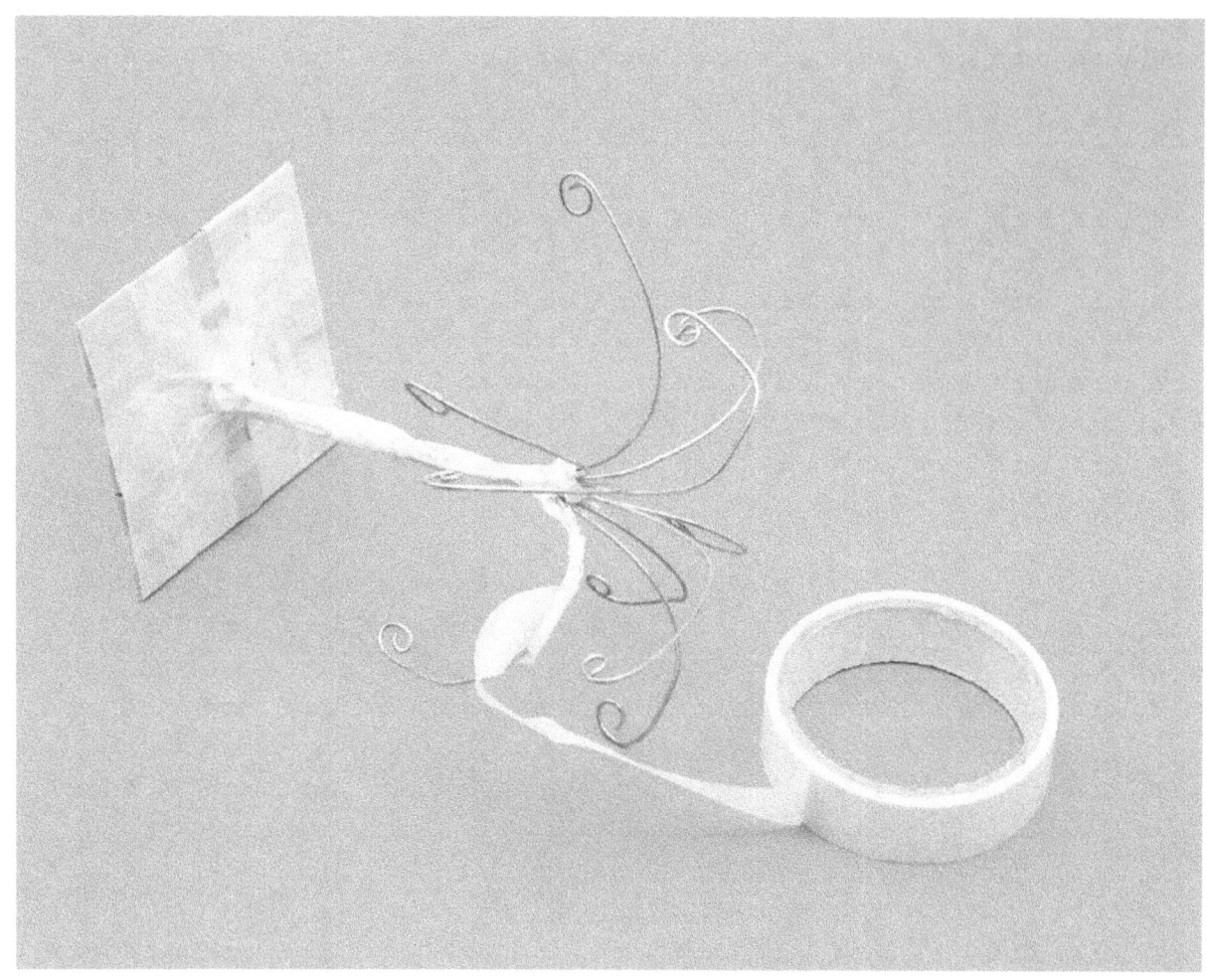

4. Cover the whole tree with masking tape, including the base.

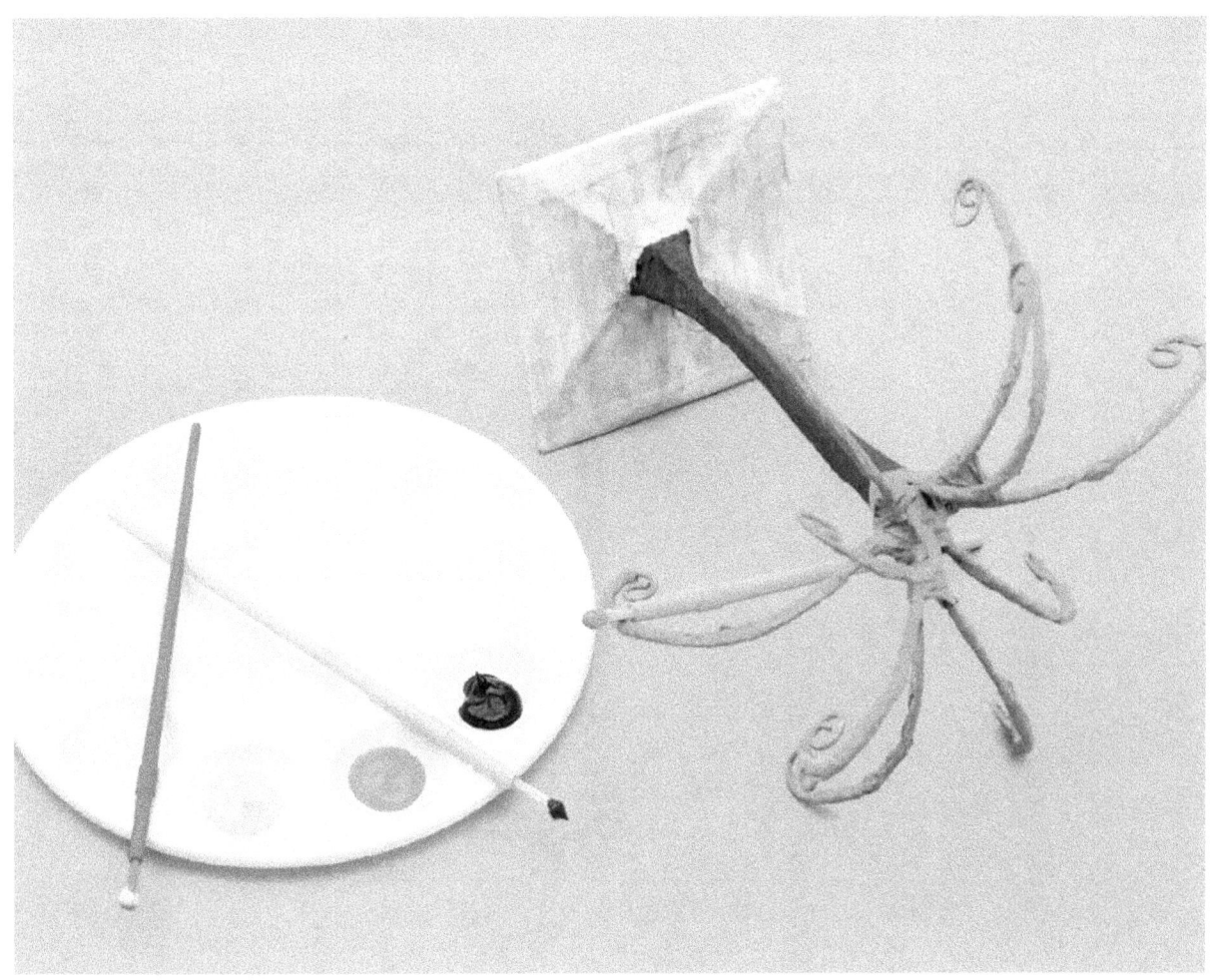

5. Paint the jewellery tree in acrylic paint and leave it to dry. When it has dried, you can hang your jewellery on the tree!

MAKE YOUR OWN PAPER CRAFTS

What do you think when you see a piece of paper? Do you just see a blank surface for you to write on? Well, look again. In this chapter, you will discover that paper can be the perfect material for cool craft projects.

Paper, Paper, Everywhere!

You don't have to rush out and buy packs of new paper to make the projects in this book. Just look around you and think about how you could re-use old wrapping paper, newspaper, magazines or even paper plates left over from a birthday party.

Other Bits and Bobs

Once you've found some paper, you can hunt around for fun materials to make your projects extra special. Use glitter or brightly coloured ribbons to make your creations sparkle and stand out. Cut up spare photographs (remembering to ask an adult first!) to give a project the personal touch.

Keep It Clean!

If you are painting or using a messy technique, make sure you cover the surface you are working on with newspaper or a piece of plastic.

PAPER TOOLKIT

Pencils and Pens

Several of these projects will require you to use pencils and pens. When creating a design, it's often a good idea to sketch it out lightly in pencil first. Then, when you're sure you've got it just how you want it, go over it in ink.

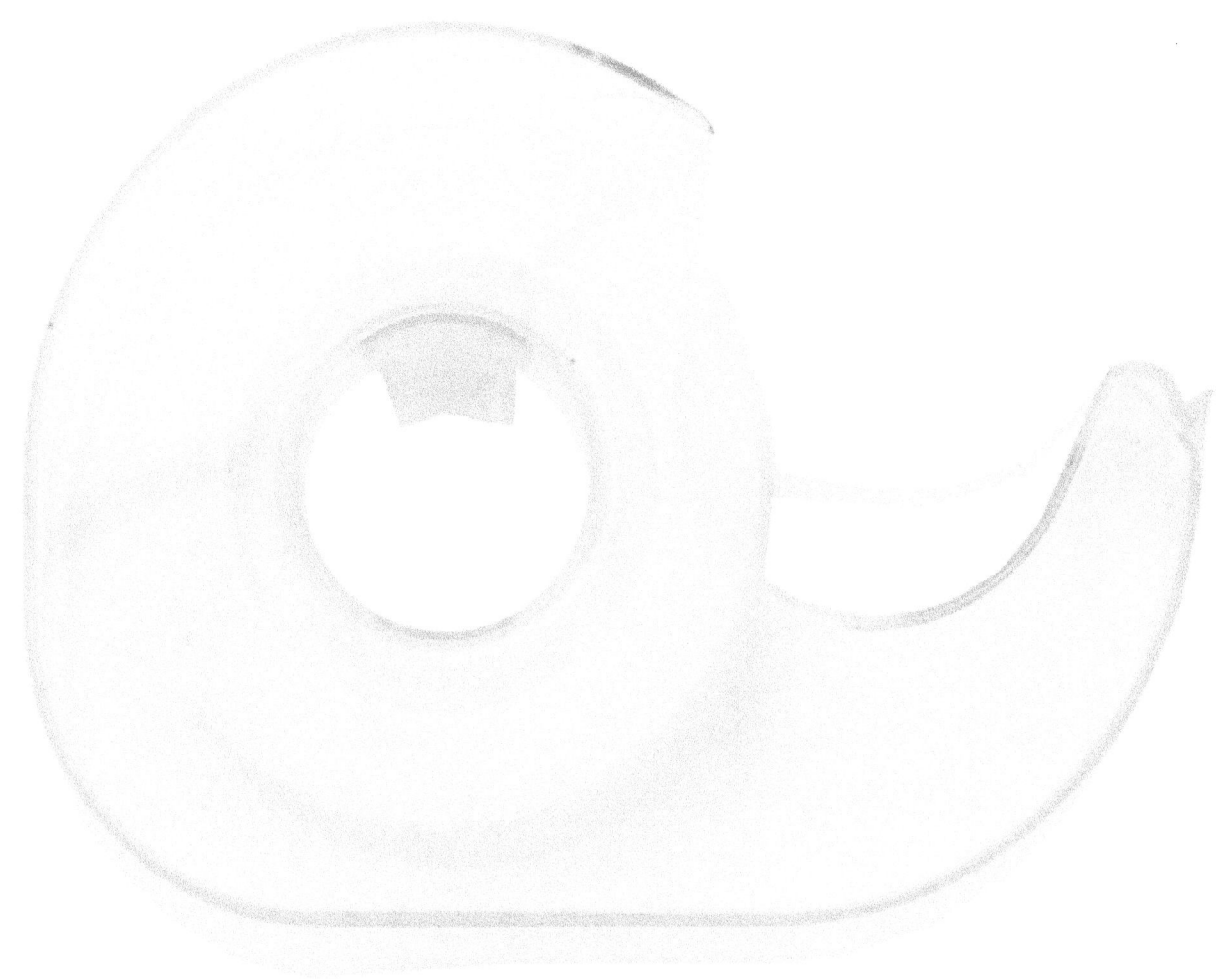

Coloured Paper and Tissue Paper

Many of these projects can be made with plain old white paper. But to really bring your creations to life, try using pieces of paper that have different shades and textures.

Sticky Tape

Single-sided sticky tape is brilliant for sticking together paper, card or other light objects.

CUBE PUZZLE

Decorate your paper boxes with a pattern, then jumble them up. How quickly can you put them back together in the right order?

You will need

Card

Ruler

Paper

Pencil

Scissors

Sticky tape

Coloured paper

Glue stick

1. Measure a 5 x 5 cm (2 in x 2 in) square of card. This is your template. Use scissors to cut it out, then draw around the square six times on a piece of paper to make a 'T' shape.

2. Use your scissors to cut out the 'T' shape and then fold along each line, pressing firmly to make a crisp fold.

3. Fold the sides of the 'T' up to make a cube. Fix everything in place using sticky tape. Make another eight cubes, so that there are nine cubes in total.

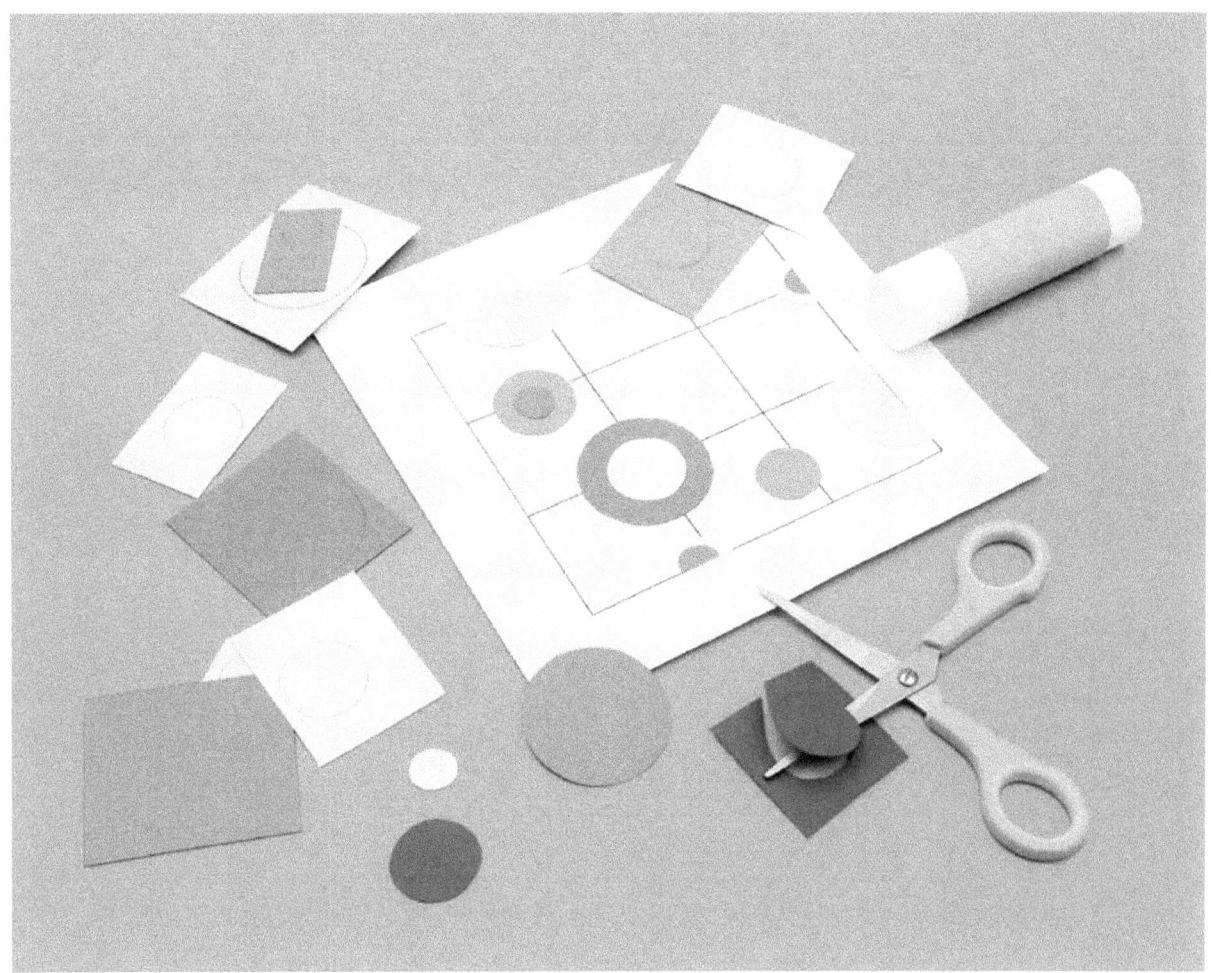

4. Tracing around your template again, draw a large square made up of nine smaller squares. Cut out circles of coloured card and glue them on in a pattern. Each circle should overlap at least two squares.

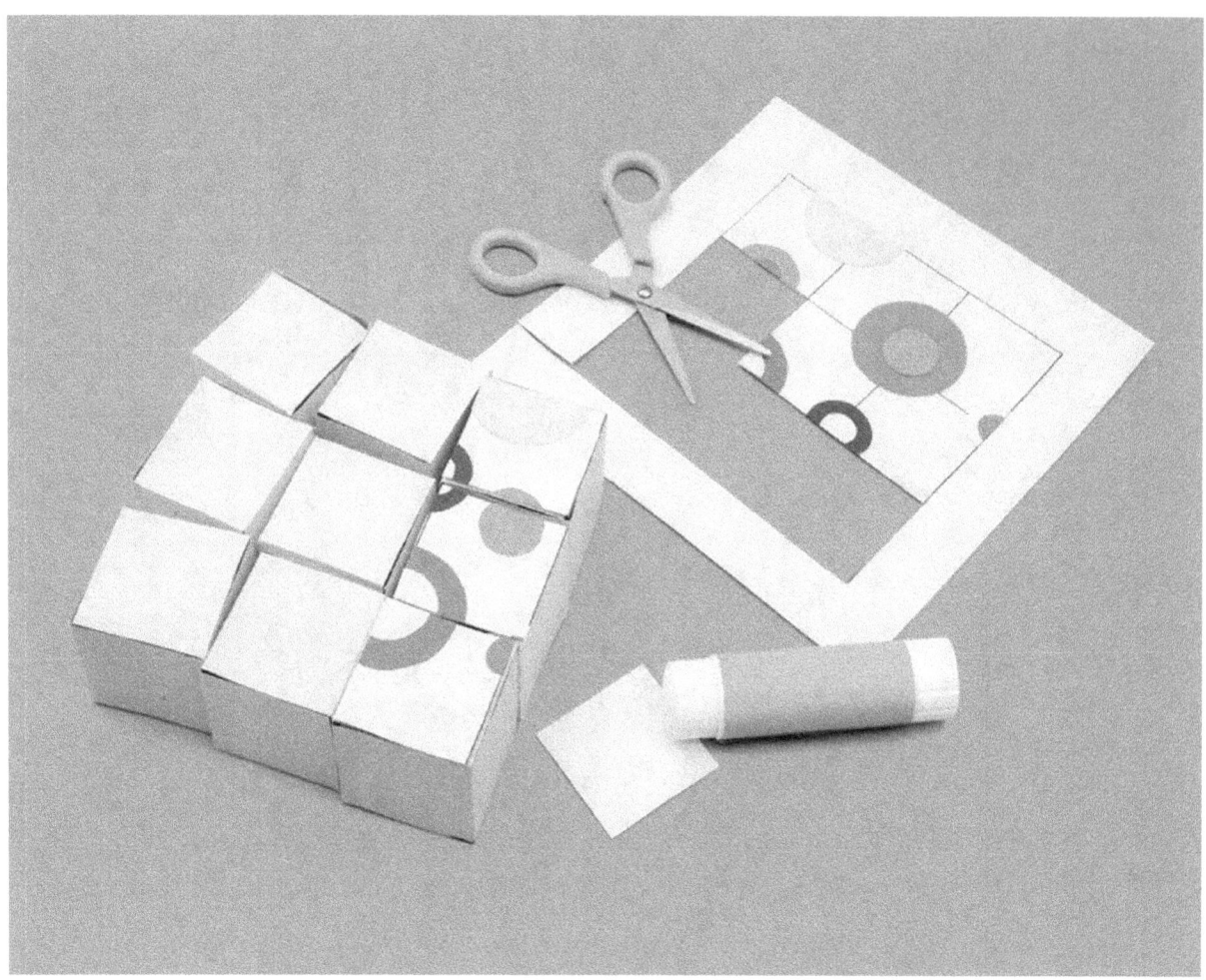

5. One by one, cut out the patterned squares and stick them onto the face of your cubes using a glue stick. If you would like to make the puzzle extra hard, you could repeat steps 4 and 5 so that your cubes have part of a different pattern on each side.

PAPER PULP MONSTERS

Paper pulp is great, messy fun. You can shape and mould the pulp into crazy shapes and creatures... such as these monsters!

You will need

Coloured tissue paper

PVA glue

Googly eyes

Plastic sheet

Water

Plastic pot

Wooden stirring stick

1. Half-fill a plastic pot with water. Tear some tissue paper into small pieces and put it in the pot. Leave to soak for a few hours.

2. Remove the tissue paper and squeeze out the excess water.
Empty any water from the pot and put the tissue back inside.

3. Pour in some PVA glue and mix together well with the stirrer to make the paper pulp.

4. Cover your work surface with a plastic sheet. Mould the paper pulp mixture into the shape of a monster. Then make some more in other colours!

5. Press googly eyes onto your monsters and leave them to dry in a warm place.

MAKE YOUR OWN NOTEBOOK

Keep your notes, scribbles and doodles in one place with this handy, handmade hardback book.

You will need

10 pieces of A4 paper

A piece of stiff card that is slightly bigger than A4

A piece of wrapping paper that is slightly larger than the stiff card

Coloured ribbon

Coloured paper

Stapler

Glue stick

Sticky tape

1. Fold the 10 pieces of A4 paper in half and secure them in place by using one staple in the middle of the folded edge.

2. Cover one side of the stiff card with wrapping paper. Fold the paper around the edges of the card, and stick it down with tape.

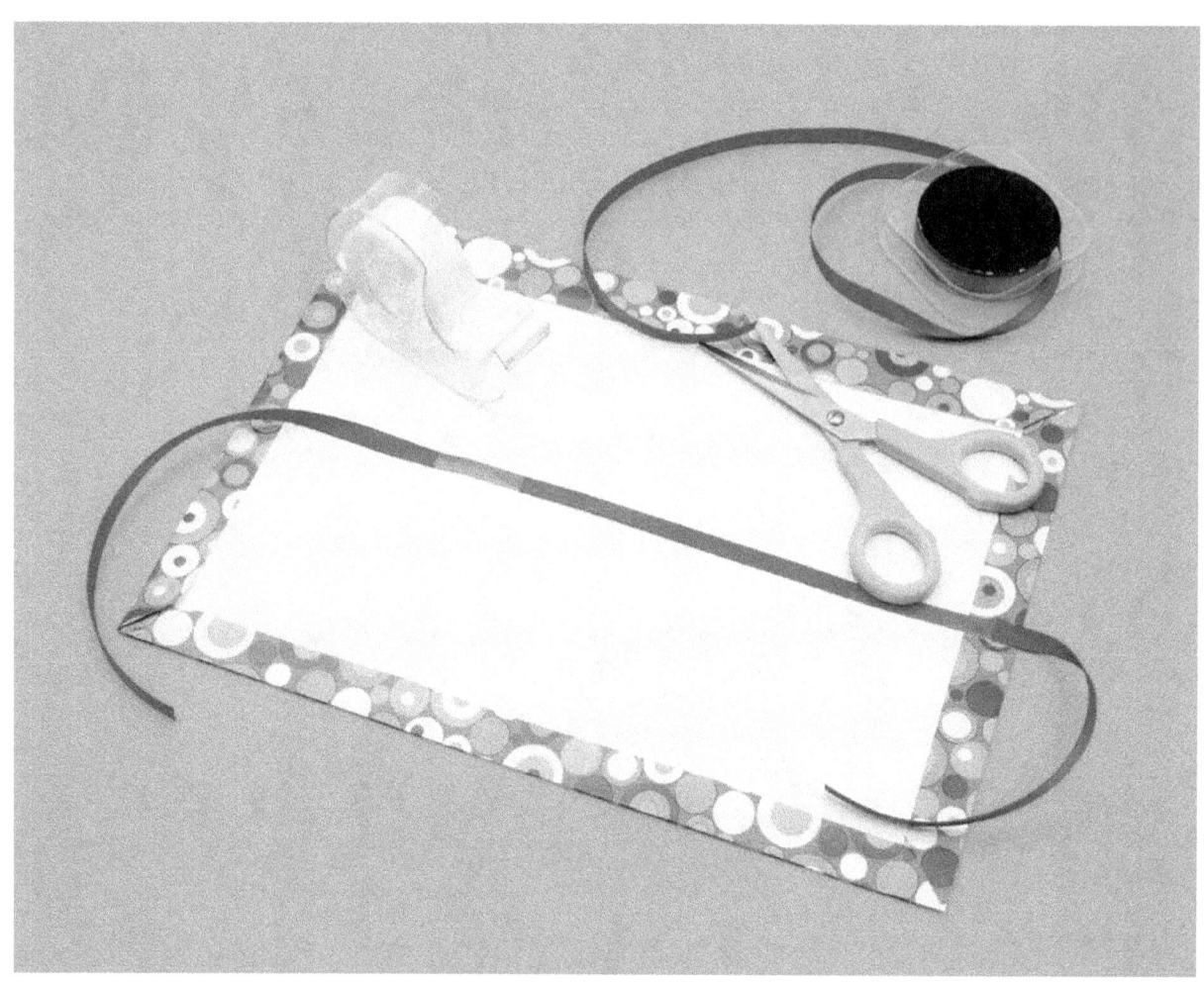

3. Lay a length of ribbon onto the card and fix it in place with sticky tape.

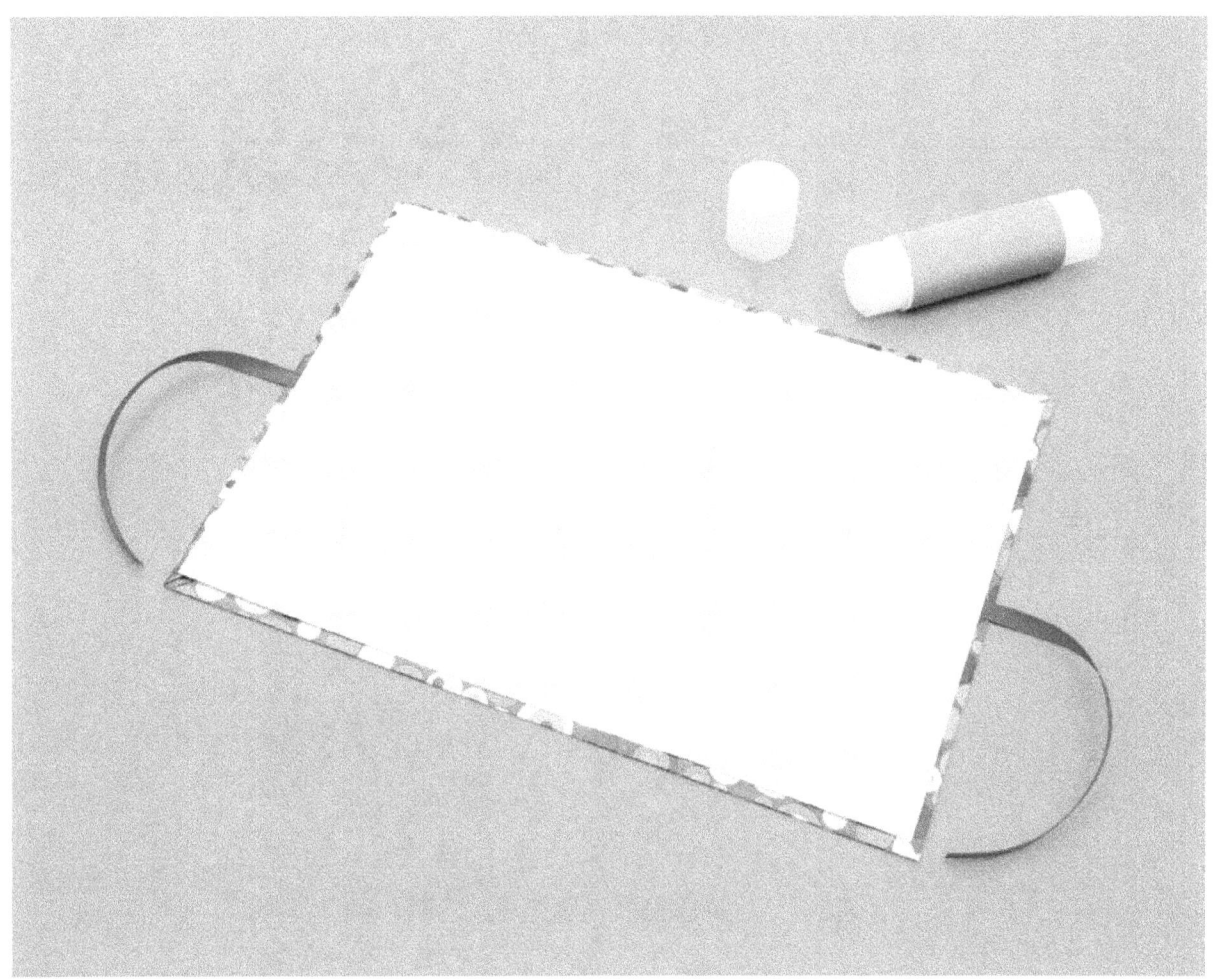

4. Cover the ribbon with a piece of coloured paper that is slightly smaller than the card and fix it in place with a glue stick.

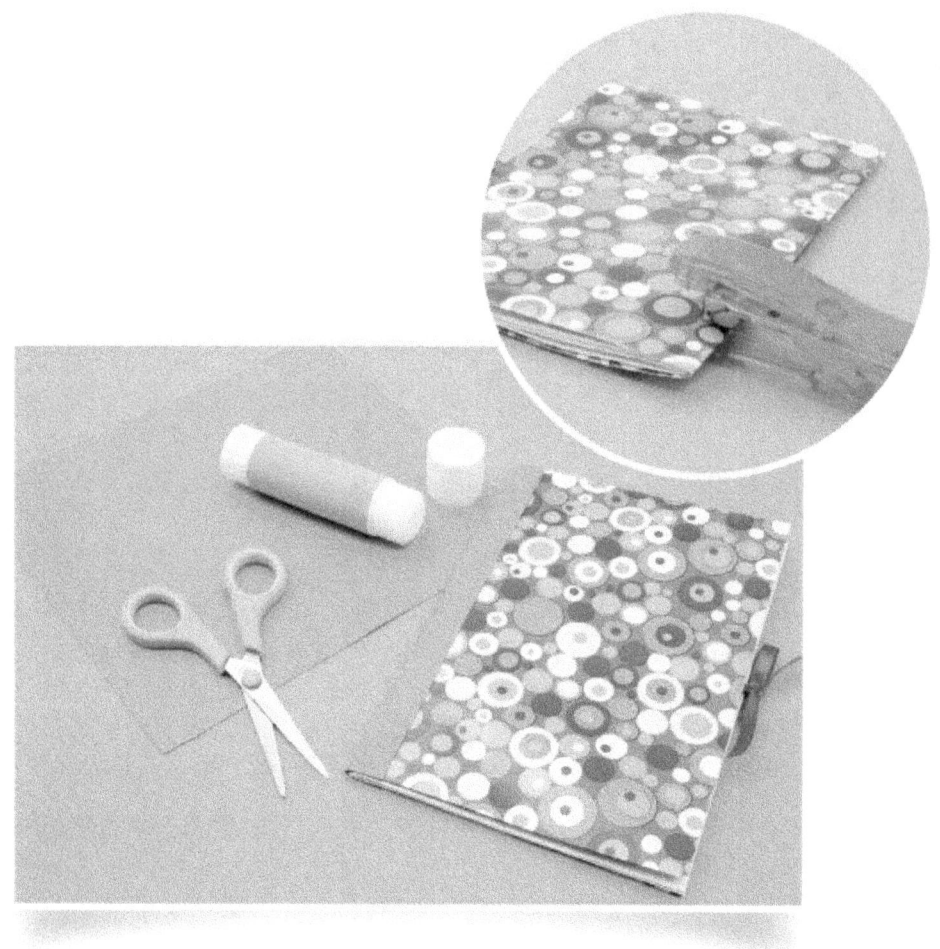

5. Fold the card in half and sandwich the paper pages inside. Secure everything in place using two staples at the top and bottom of the spine.

6. Glue a strip of coloured paper on the spine with a glue stick to hide the staples.

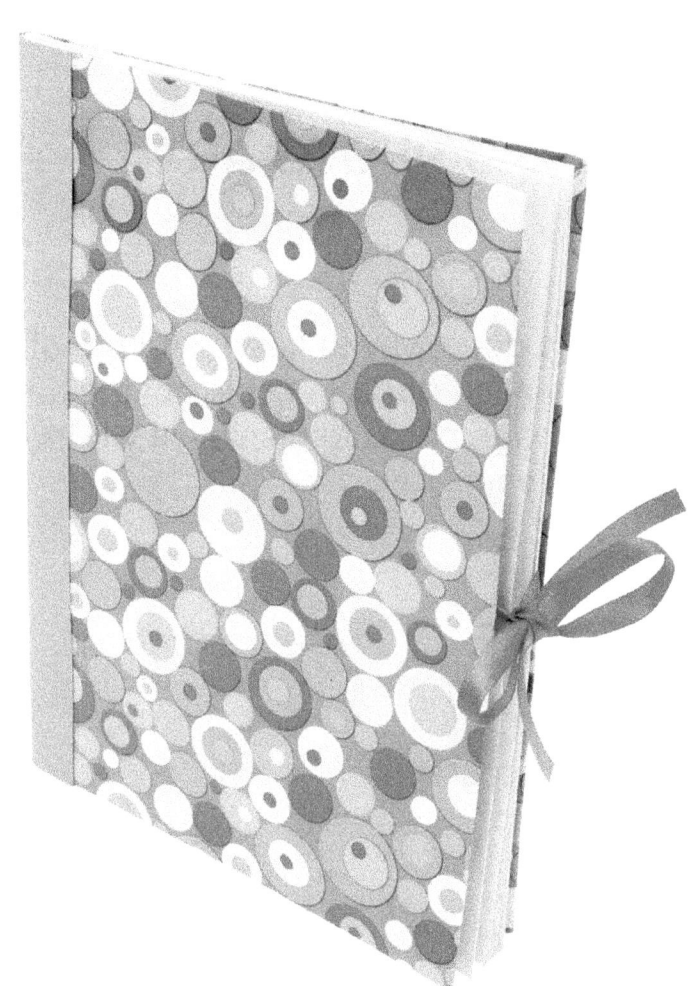

3-D PHOTO ART

Taking photographs is a good way to keep a record of all the fun times you've had. By printing multiple copies of the same photo, you can make a 3-D découpage photo to display. It will look like the picture is leaping out at you!

You will need

4 copies of the same photograph

Scissors

Sticky foam pads

Card

Glue stick

1. Cut a piece of card to the same size as your photographs. Glue one of the photographs onto the card using a glue stick.

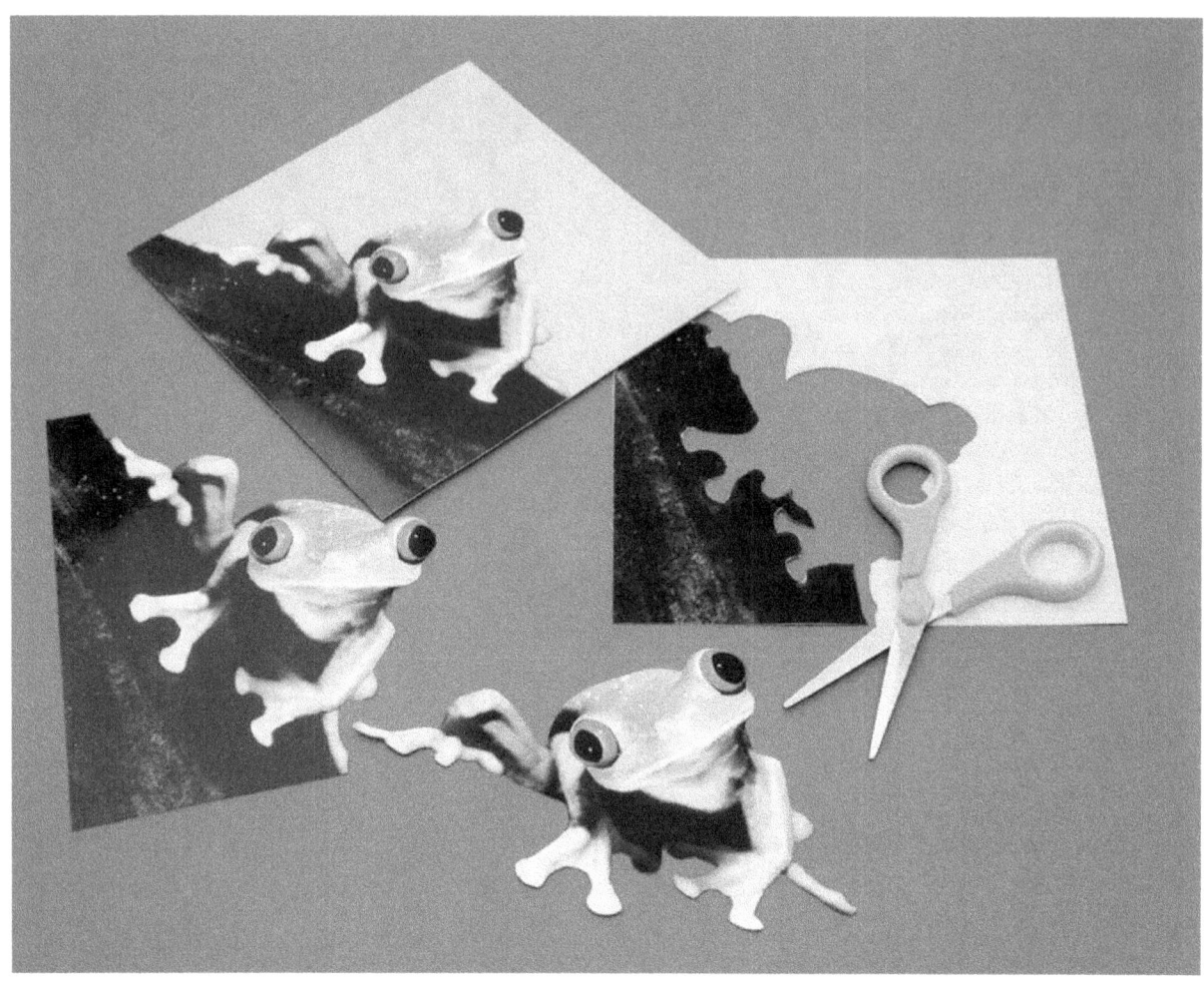

2. Take another copy of the photograph and cut out the whole foreground, using scissors. Then, take the third copy of the photograph and cut out a smaller part of the foreground.

3. Stick foam pads to the back of the cut-out pieces of the photographs.

4. Stick the cut-out pieces on top of the original photograph.

5. Cut out tiny details from the fourth photograph. These might be parts like the eyes or the hands. Stick these to the cardboard using more sticky foam pads.

QUILLING CARDS

Quilling is a way of folding or curling paper to create amazing patterns. These cards are pretty to look at and easy to make. All you need is a steady hand!

You will need

Coloured paper

A shredder or scissors

Card

Glue stick

Pen

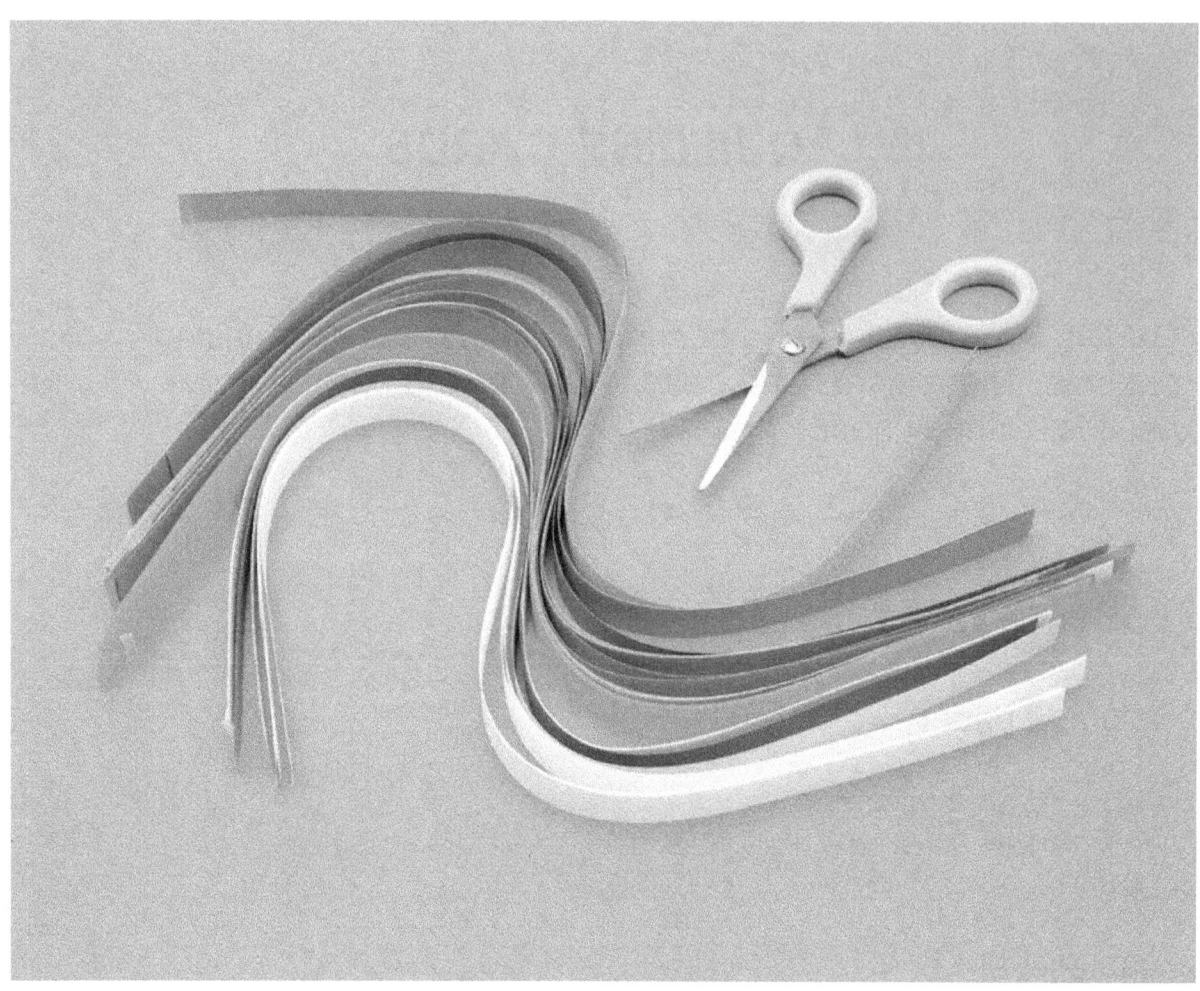

1. Use a shredder to cut the coloured paper into strips. If you don't have a shredder you can always cut it by hand using scissors, but make sure the strips are as even as possible.

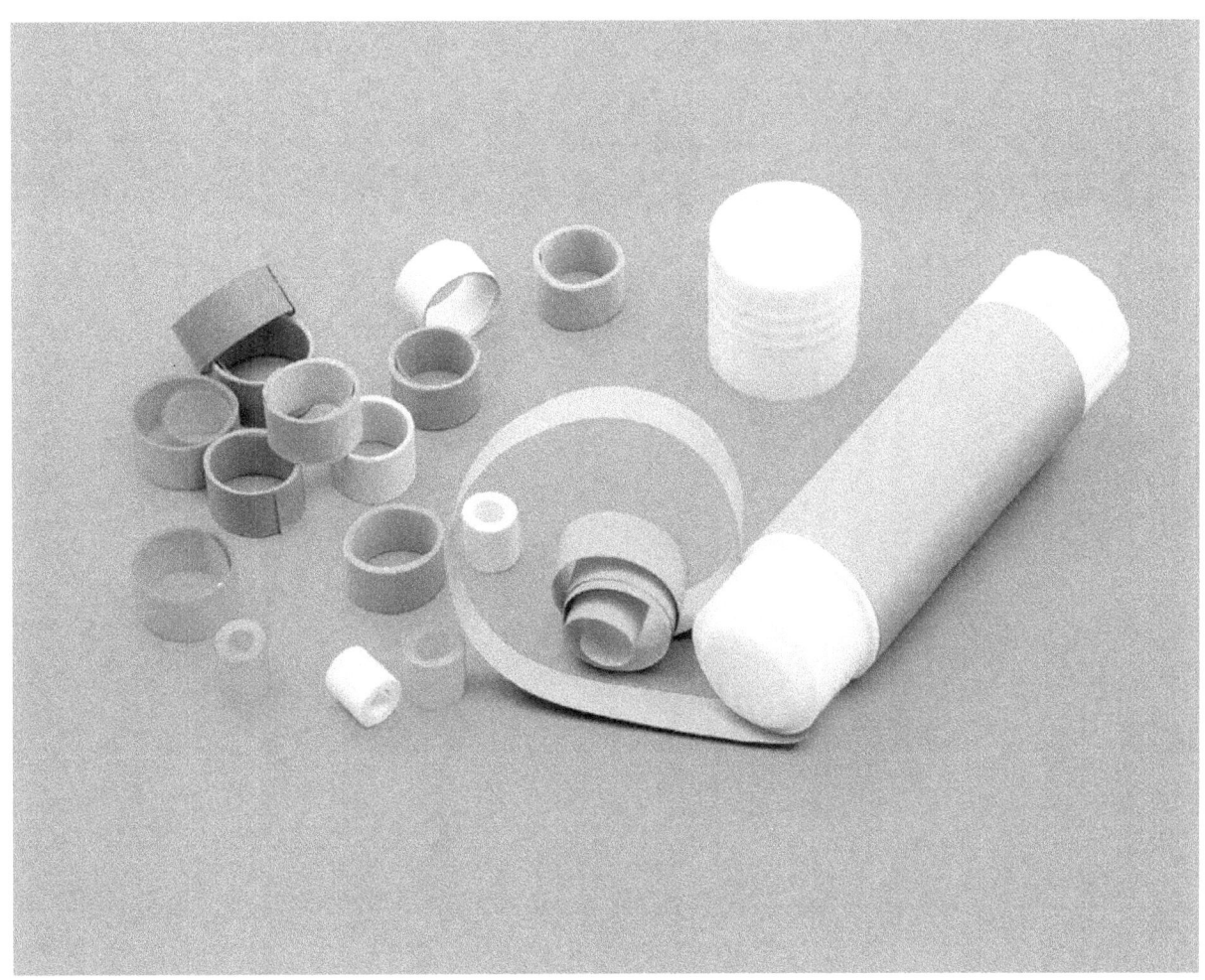

2. Coil each strip of paper into a tight circle and fix it in place using a glue stick.

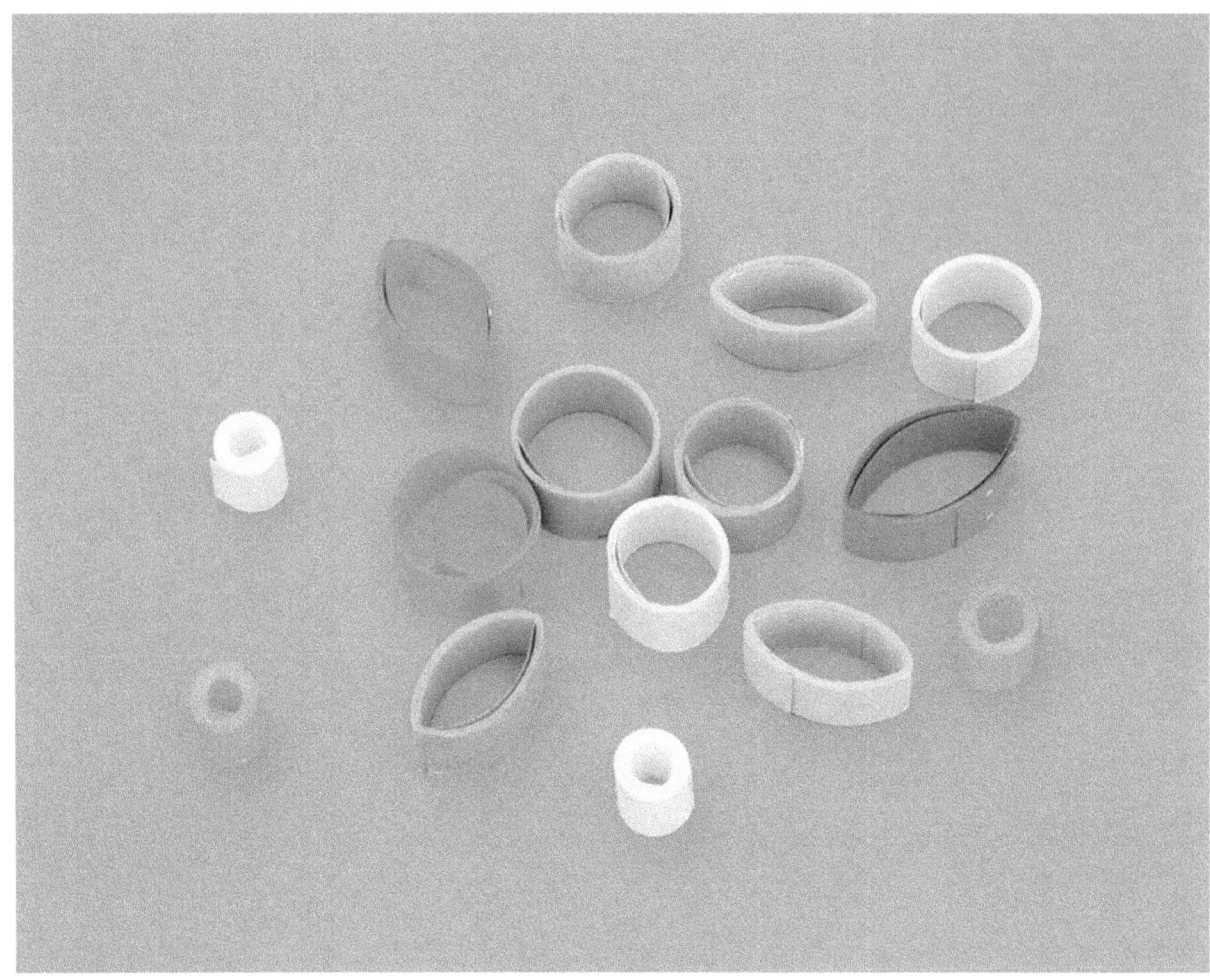

3. Make some of the circles big and some of them small. Squash some of the circles so that they turn into ellipse shapes.

4. Fold a piece of card in two. Using a pen, draw a big star shape on one side.

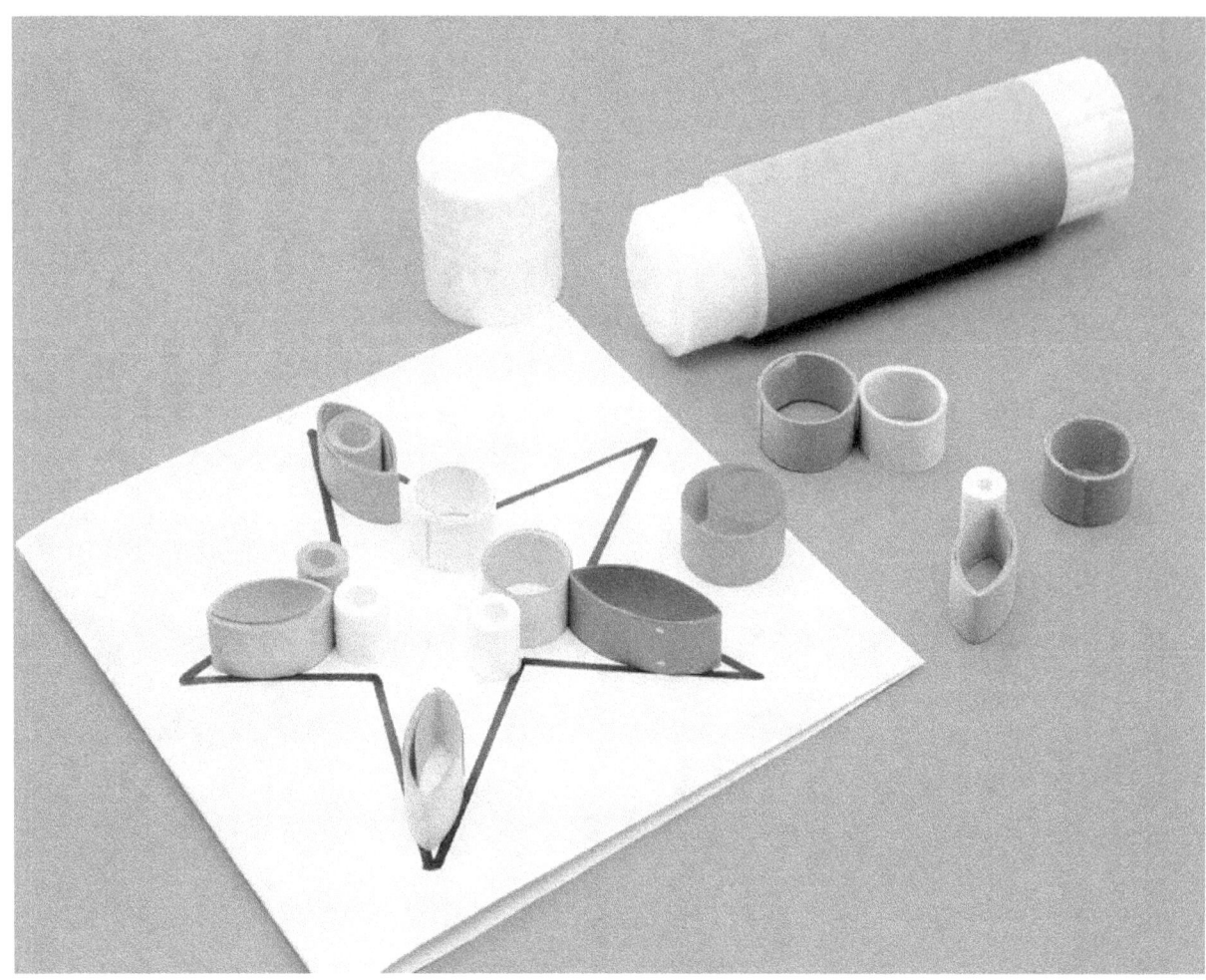

5. Cover the inside of the star shape with some glue stick and press the shapes into the glue. Fill the whole shape with the quilled coils of paper. Leave to dry.

GIANT CRAYONS

These crazy crayons make for a fun bedroom decoration. They look just like the real thing – only 10 times bigger!

You will need

White and coloured paper

Acrylic or poster paint

Paintbrushes

Polystyrene cups

Black marker pen

Glue stick

PVA glue

Masking tape

Sticky tape

Scissors

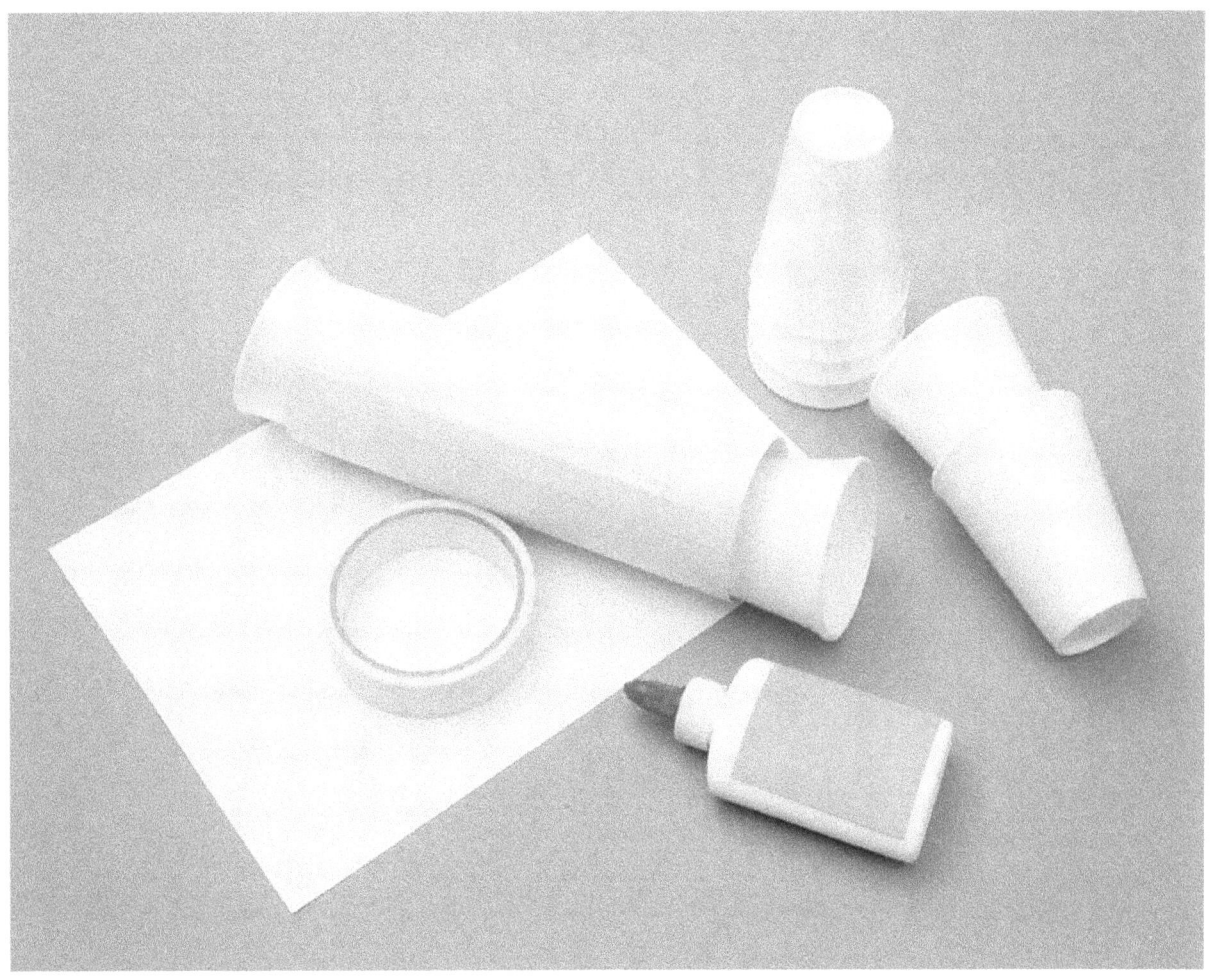

1. Roll a piece of paper into a tube just big enough to fit a polystyrene cup inside. Hold the tube together with masking tape.

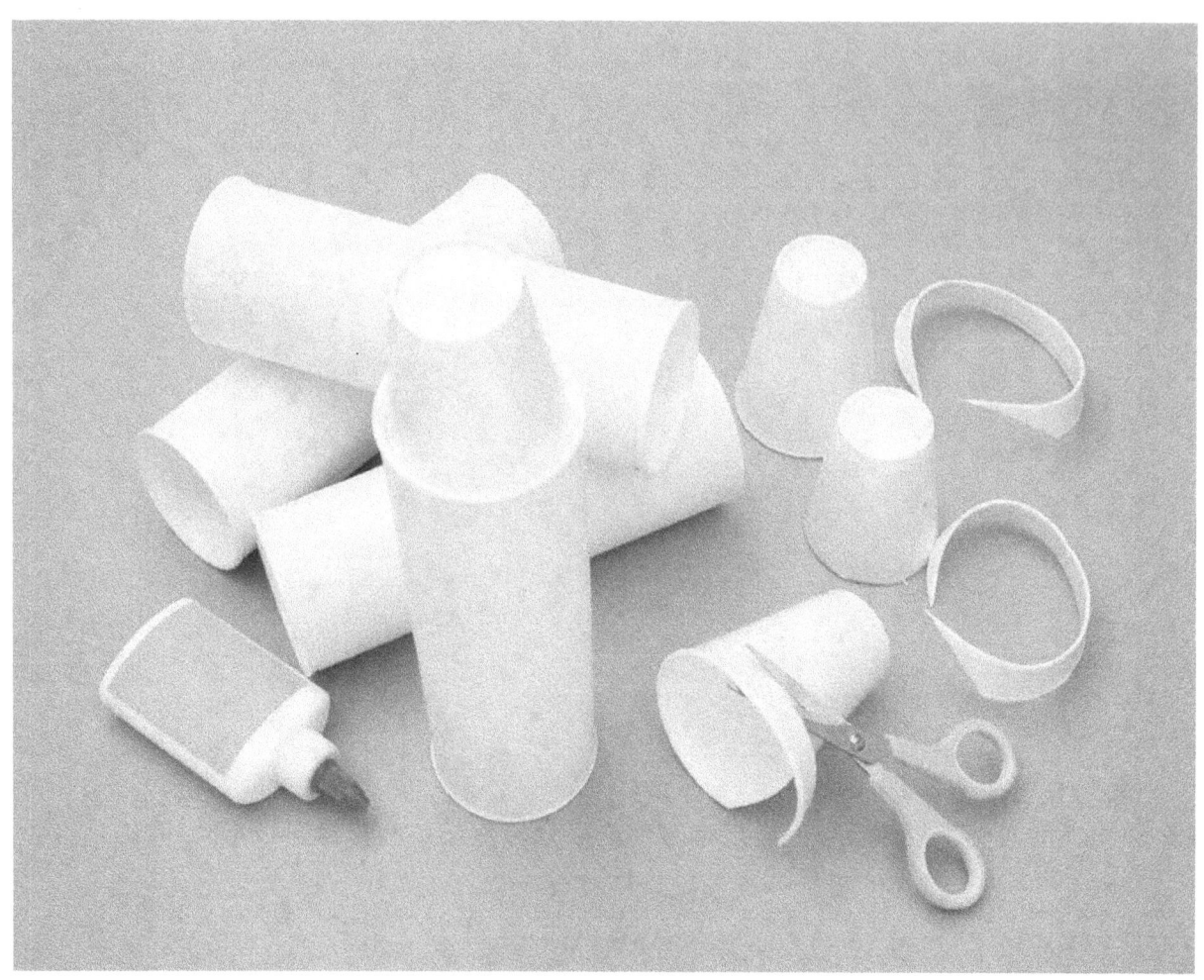

2. Use scissors to cut off the rim of a cup. Stick it to the top of the tube with glue to make the crayon. Then make three more!

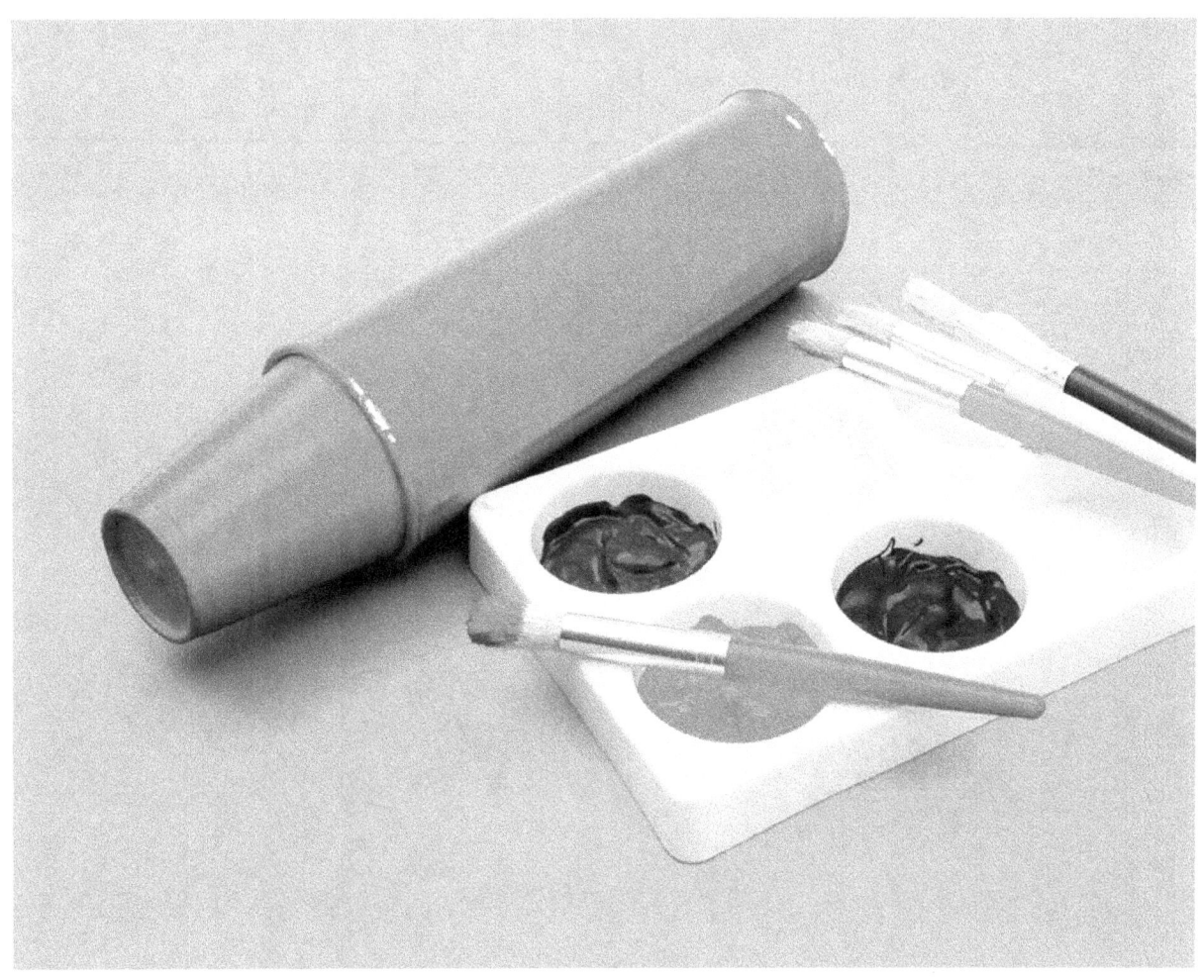

3. Paint each giant crayon in a bright colour with acrylic paints and leave to dry.

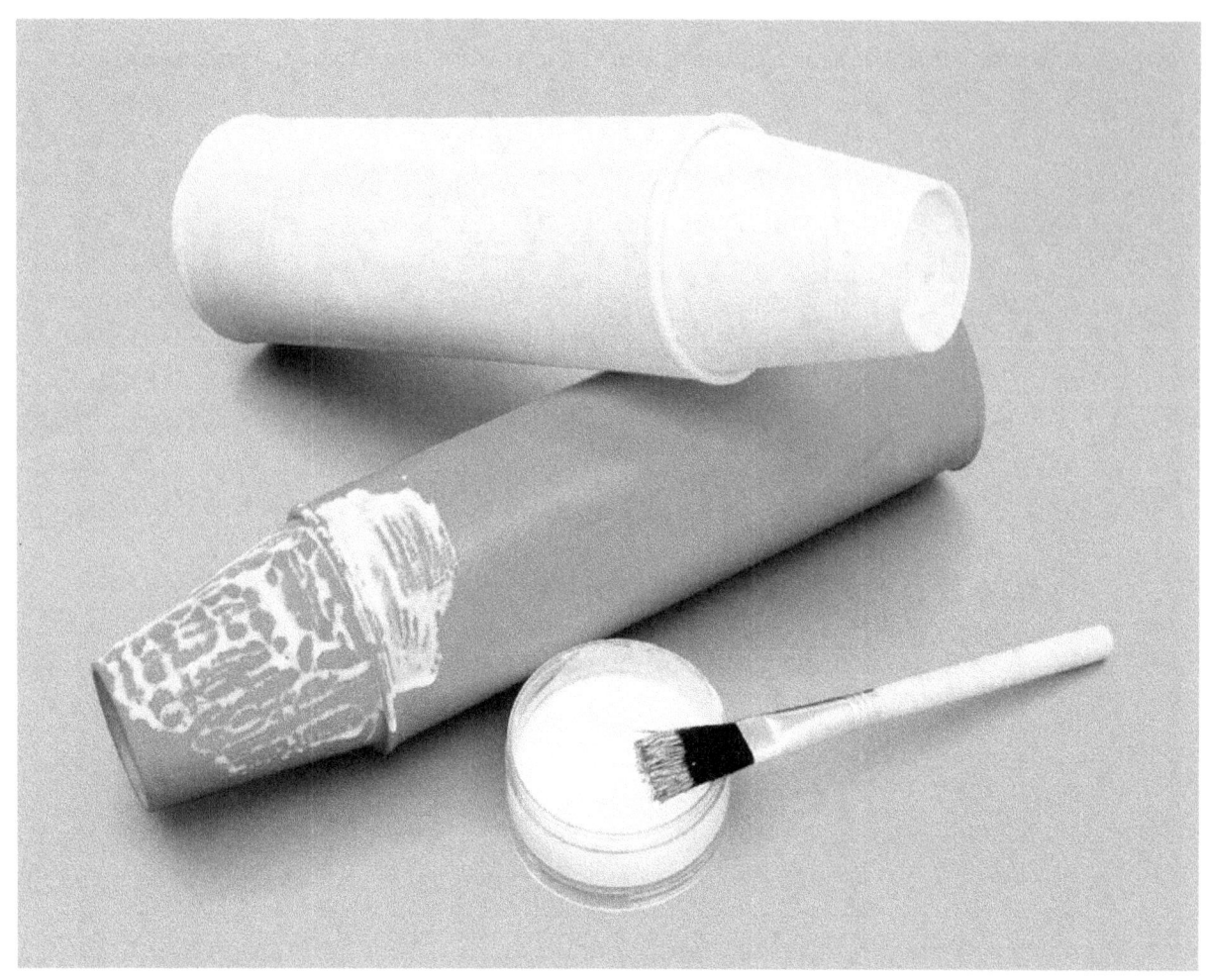

4. Give each crayon a coat of PVA glue. It will dry see-through and make your crayon look waxy and shiny.

5. With a marker, draw details onto pieces of paper that match the colours of the crayons.

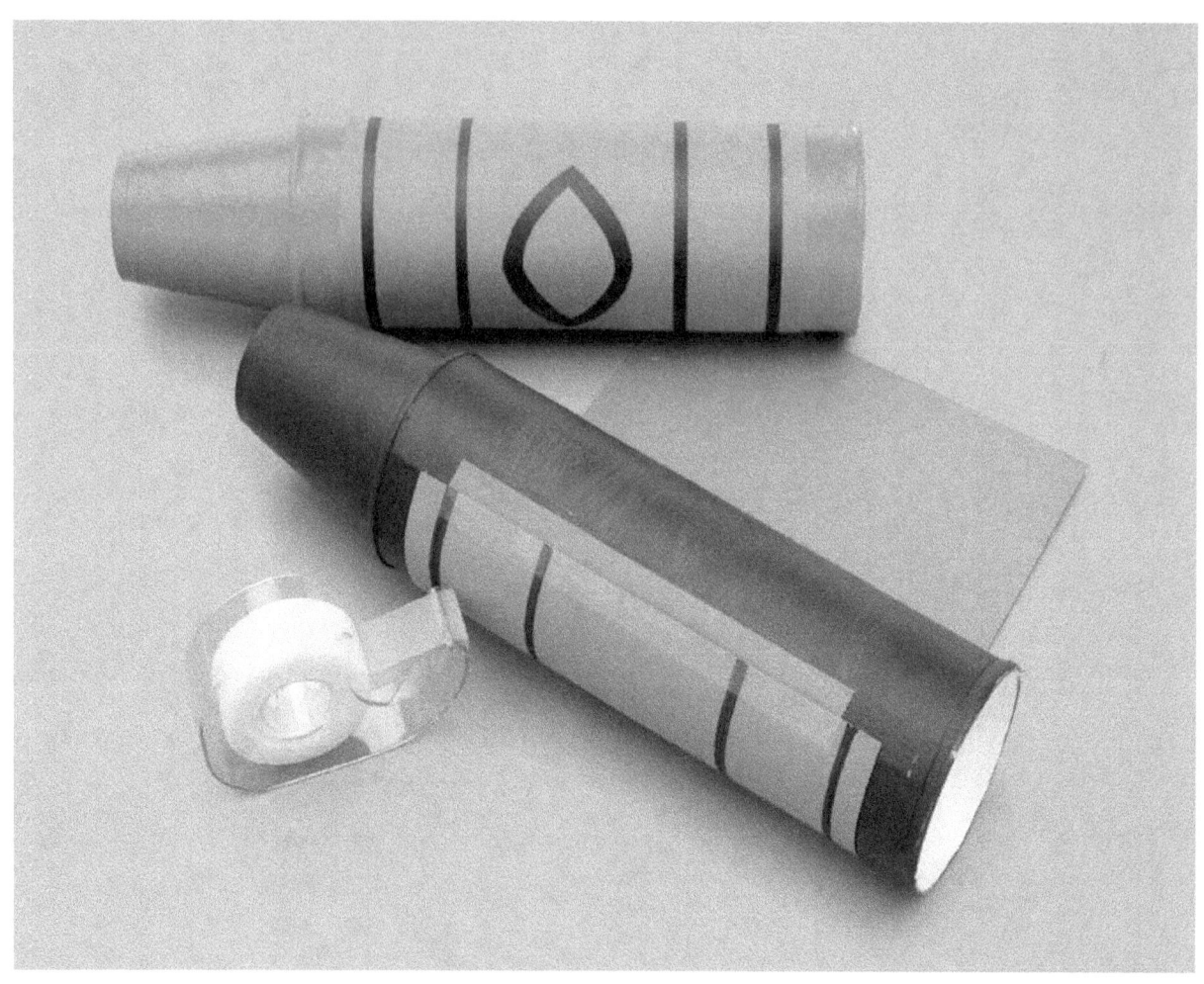

6. Stick the pieces of paper onto the crayons and fix them in place with sticky tape.

PAPER GLOBE LAMPSHADE

Brighten up your room by decorating a plain paper globe lampshade with cute cartoon pictures.

You will need

A paper globe lampshade

Coloured tissue paper

PVA glue

Scissors

Pen

Paper

1. Draw a design onto a piece of paper. This pattern will be repeated around your lampshade three times.

2. Trace your design three times onto pieces of tissue paper. Copy different elements onto different coloured paper.

3. Cut all your pieces out using scissors and arrange them in order so they match your design.

4. Paint a thin layer of PVA glue onto the whole of the lampshade. Start sticking on your tissue paper designs, one piece at a time.

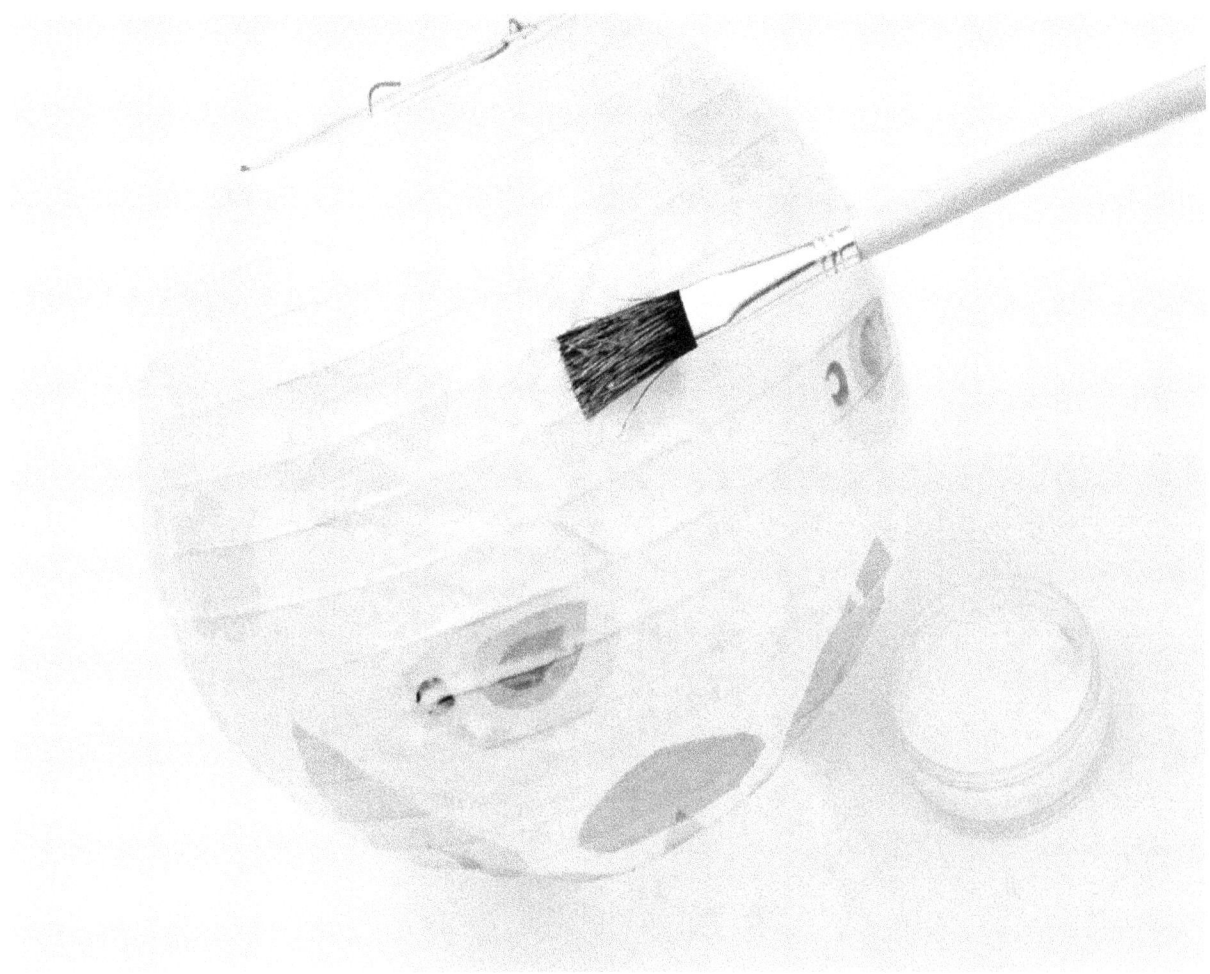

5. Coat the whole lampshade in another thin layer of PVA glue to seal the tissue paper in place. Leave it to dry.

ENVELOPES AND NOTEPAPER

Personalised stationery looks really cool. People will love to receive customised letters from you! They'll look even better in handmade envelopes.

You will need

Wrapping paper

Plain paper

White label stickers

Glue stick

Scissors

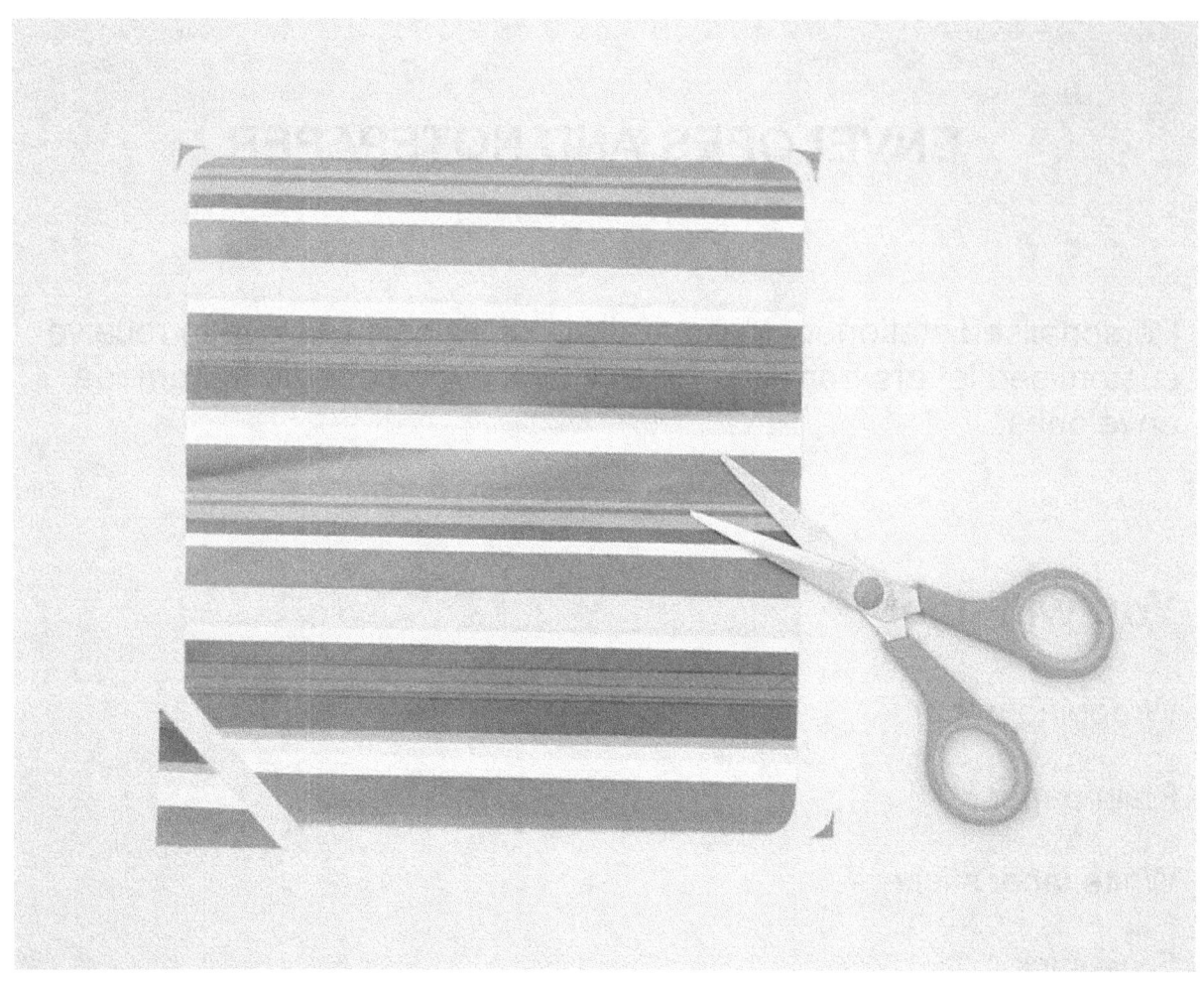

1. Cut a piece of wrapping paper into a square 20 cm x 20 cm (8 in x 8 in). Cut around three of the edges to make them round. Snip a triangle off the other corner.

2. Fold the flat corner into the middle on the other side of the paper. Press it firmly to make a crisp crease.

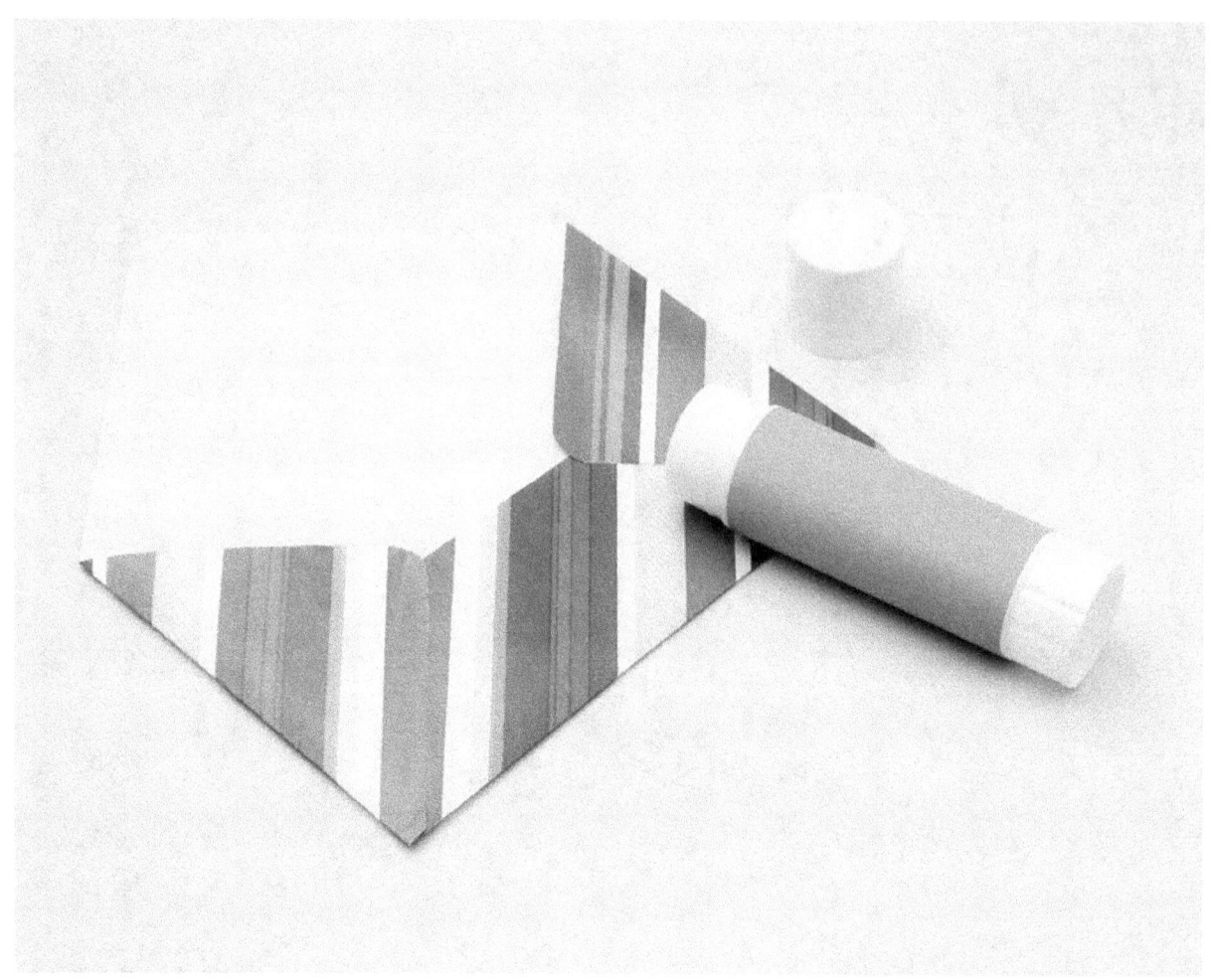

3. Fold in the two rounded corners on either side. Glue them in place with glue stick.

4. Fold the last rounded corner in but do not stick it down.

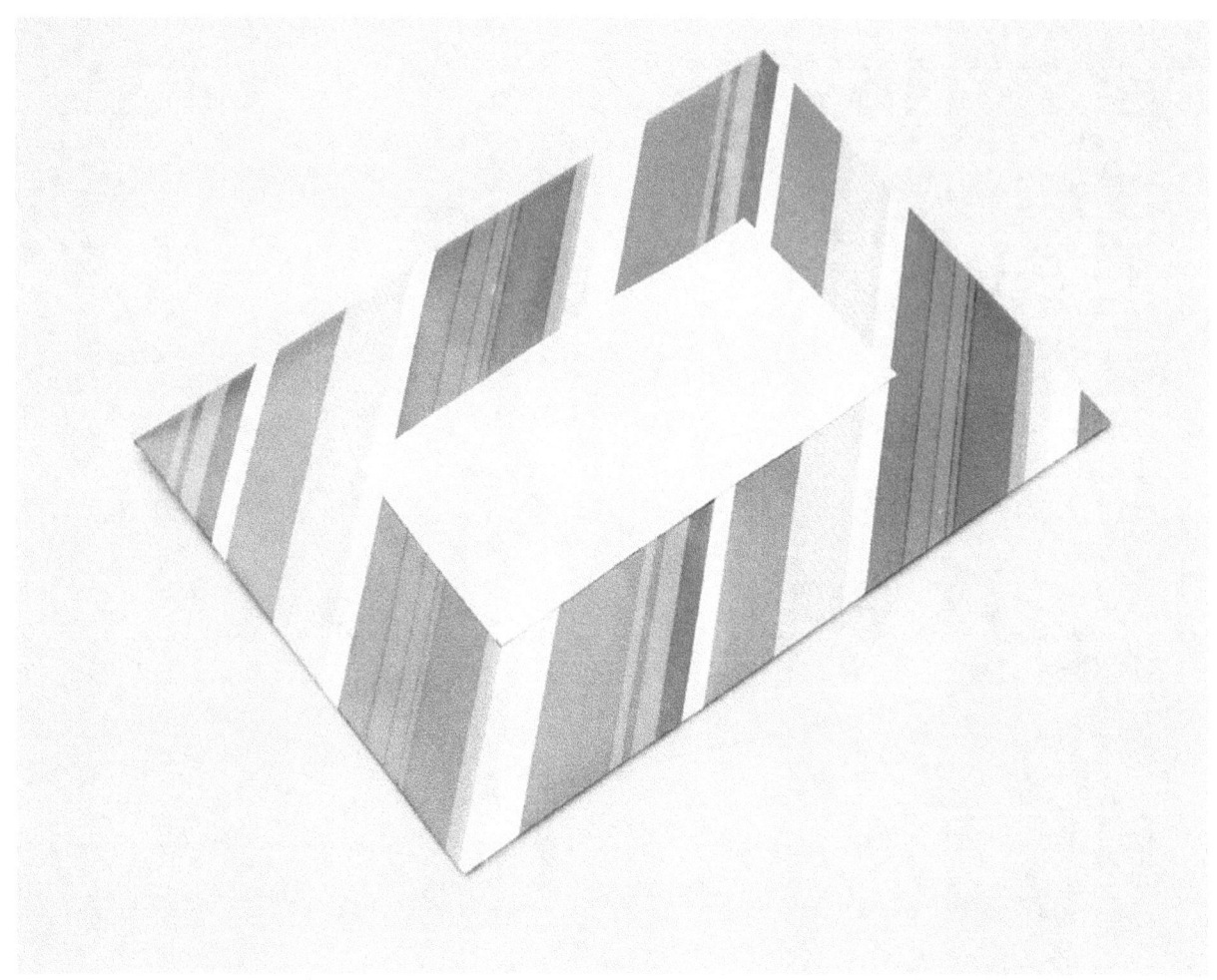

5. Turn over the envelope and stick a white label onto it.

6. For your letter, decorate a piece of plain paper with patterns cut from the wrapping paper you used to make the envelope.

PAPER BOUQUET

The art of making paper flowers is centuries old and is still popular today. Give your bouquet to a teacher to say thank you, or to a friend or family member as a gift.

You will need

A4 coloured paper

Double-sided sticky tape

Scissors

Black marker pen

Green garden canes

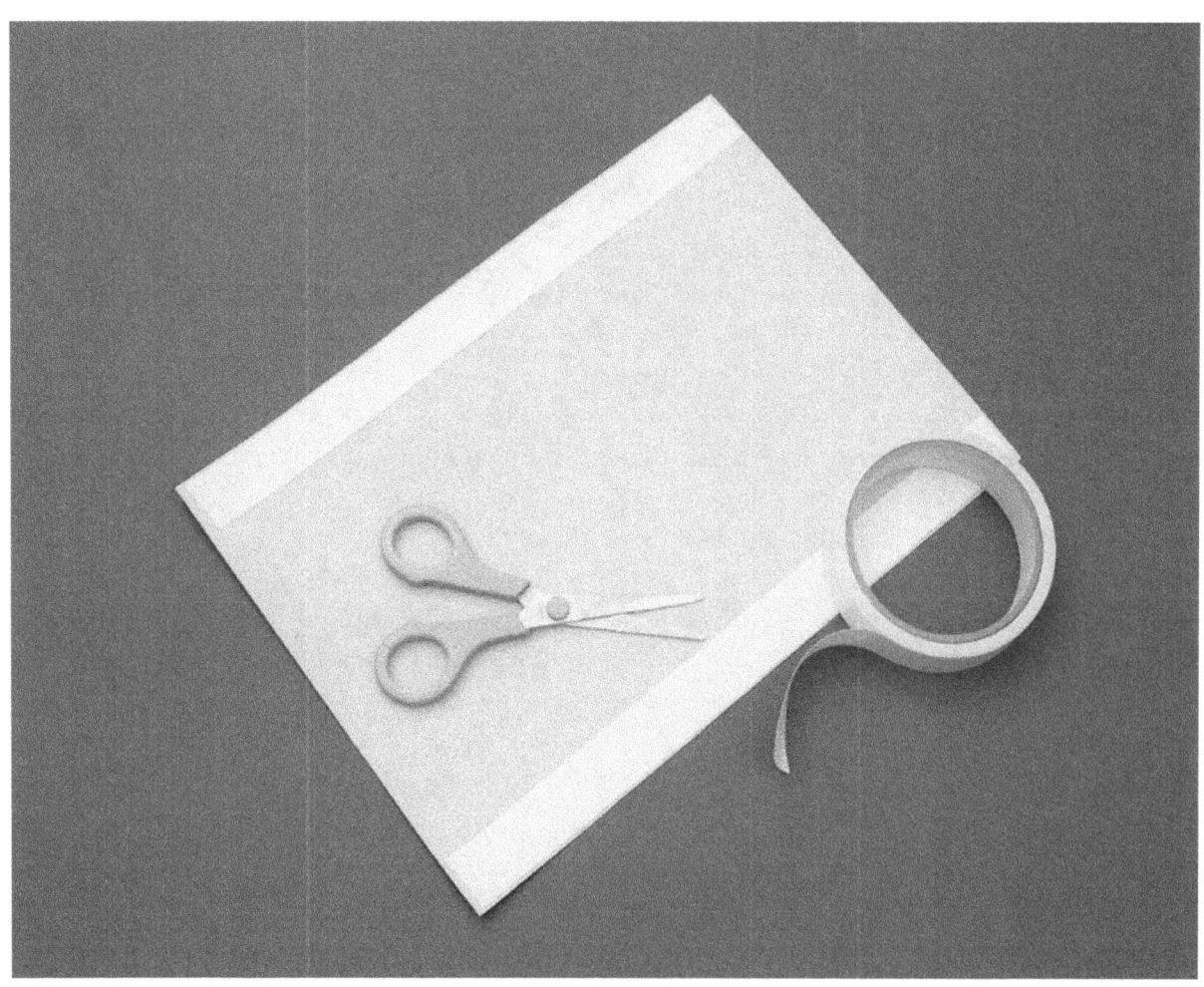

1. Put a strip of double-sided sticky tape along both sides of the long edge of the coloured paper. Do not remove the paper backing from the tape yet!

2. Fold the paper in half lengthways so that the two strips of tape meet. Then fold it in half widthways.

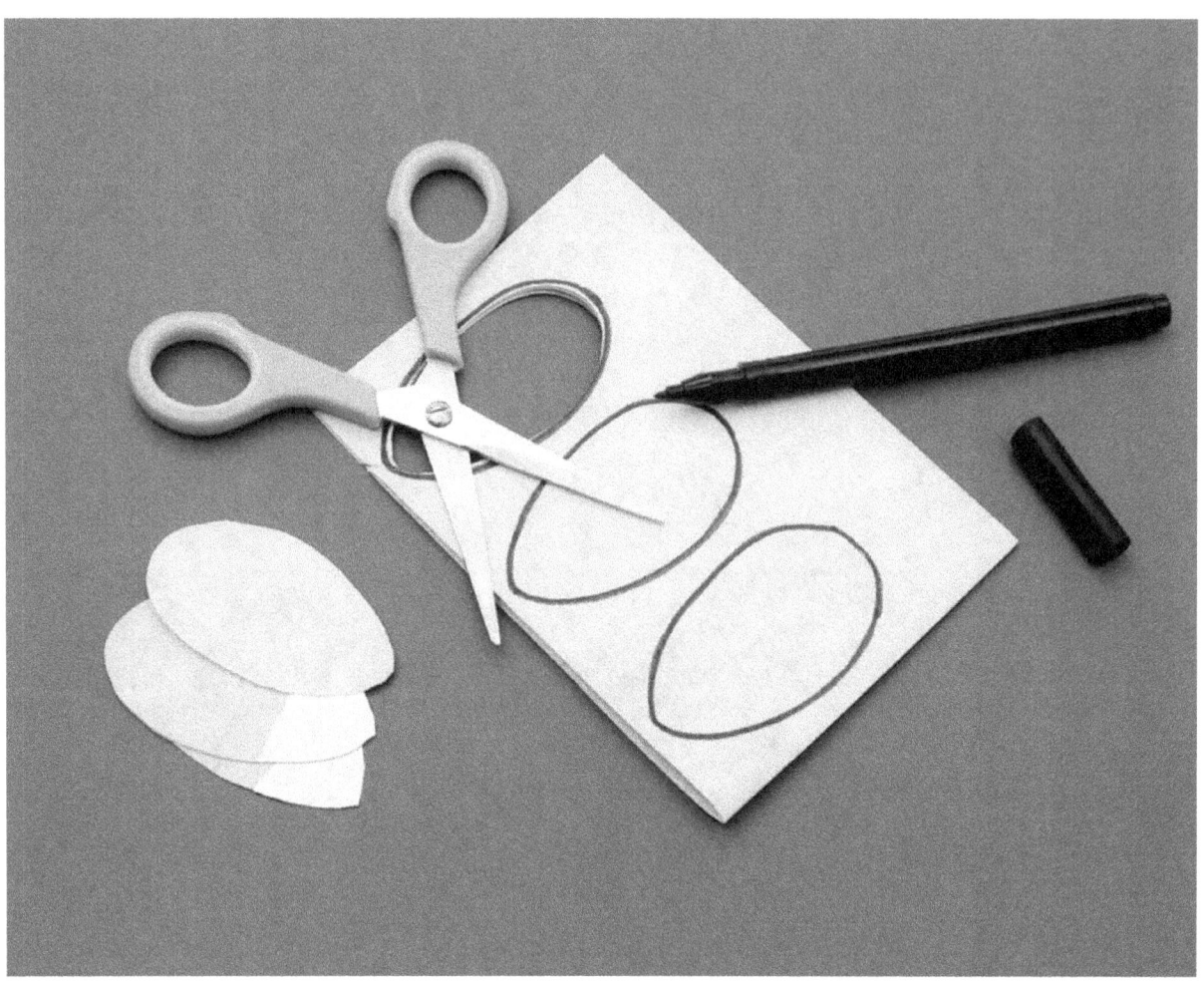

3. Draw three petal shapes onto the paper, making sure that one end of each petal is over the sticky tape. Cut them out with scissors.

4. Peel off the paper from the tape on one petal. Stick the petal around the top of a green garden cane.

5. Repeat this, going around the cane until you have used all the petals.

6. Repeat steps 1–5 with different-coloured paper until you have enough flower stems to make a bouquet! Peel back the petals to make the flowers look like they are in bloom.

MAKE YOUR OWN RECYCLING CRAFTS

You don't have to go shopping to fill your home with cool new decorations and handy objects. You can transform unwanted old stuff into all kinds of amazing craft items! All you need is a little imagination.

Going Global

Always remember to 'reduce, re-use and recycle'. By turning old things into useful craft objects, you will be keeping them from going to landfill and helping our planet!

What a Load of Rubbish!

Your home is sure to be full of unwanted objects that could be used in craft projects. Plastic containers are always handy. Scrap paper can be used in many different ways. You could cut up old clothes for textile crafts. Your friends and family will be amazed when you tell them your new craft projects are mostly made from 'junk'!

RECYCLING TOOLKIT

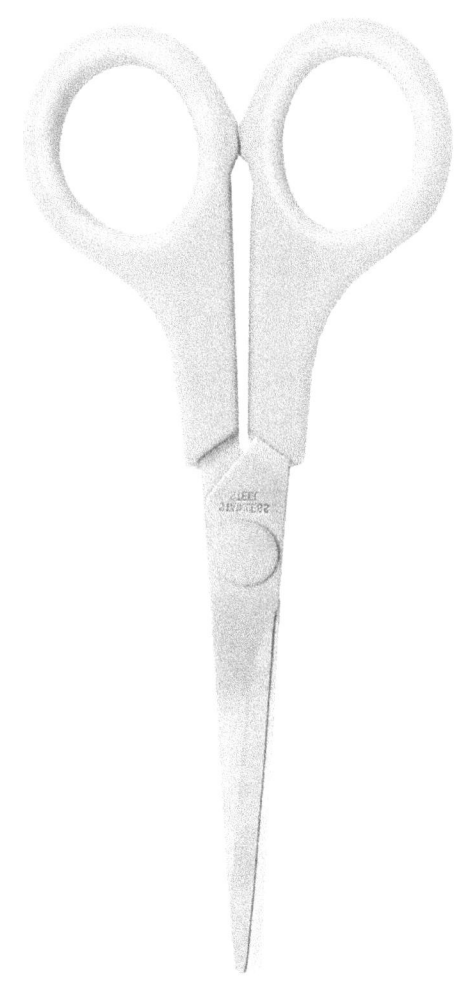

Scissors

You'll need a good pair of scissors to cut your pieces of recycled material down to the right size. Always ask an adult to help you.

Glue Stick

This is very easy to use, and great for sticking together pieces of paper or other small items

String and Wool

Old bits of string and wool can be more handy than you might think. They can be used to hold pieces of jewellery together, or even to add colourful finishing touches to your creations.

BOTTLE TOPS IN BLOOM

This fun project will turn plastic bottle tops into flowers that you can use to decorate your room. The best part is that you don't need to water them to keep them looking pretty!

You will need

Bottle tops

Craft foam

Craft glue

Garden canes

Paper

Pen

Scissors

Vase or plastic bottle

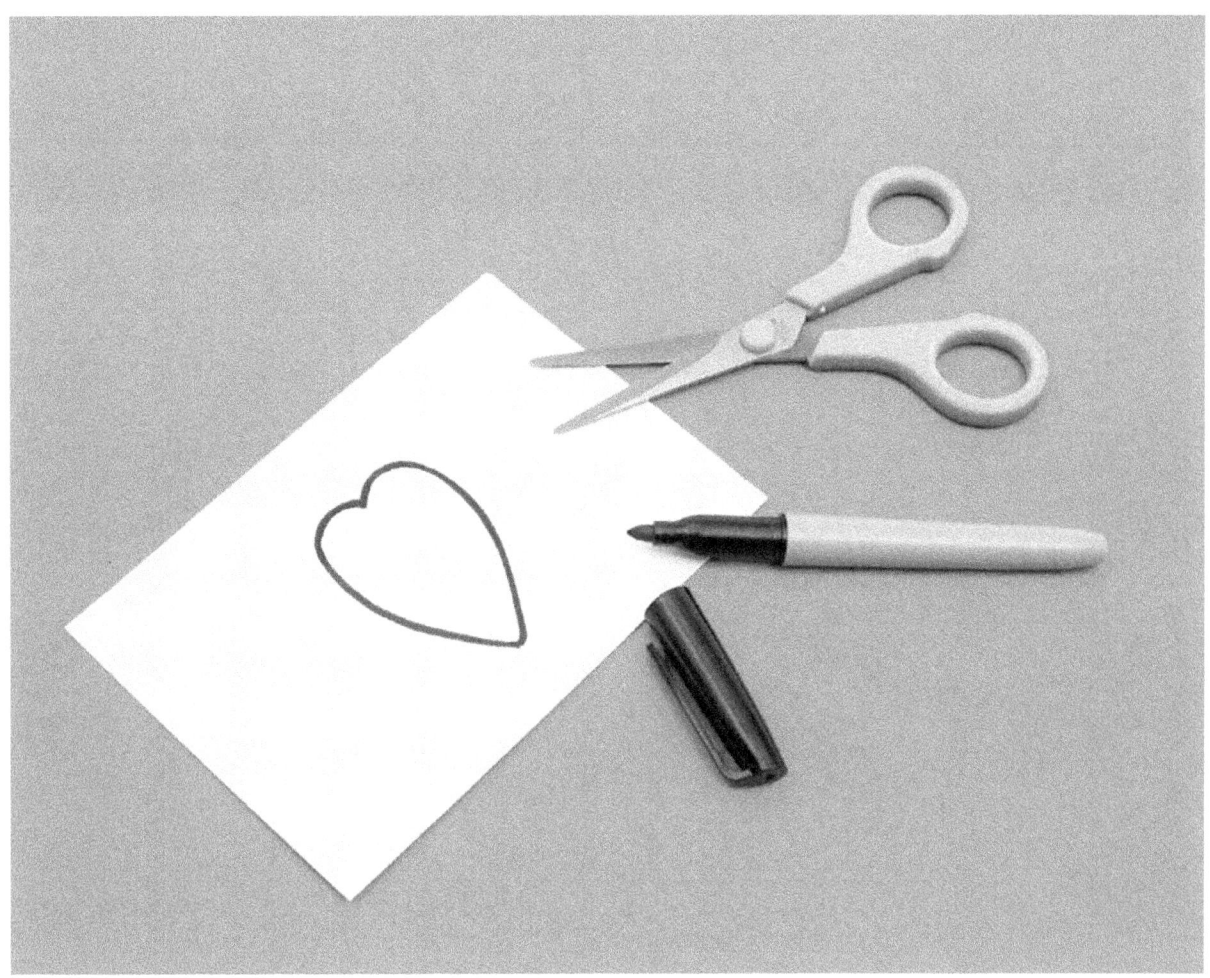

1. Draw a petal shape onto a piece of paper with a pen. Cut it out to make a template.

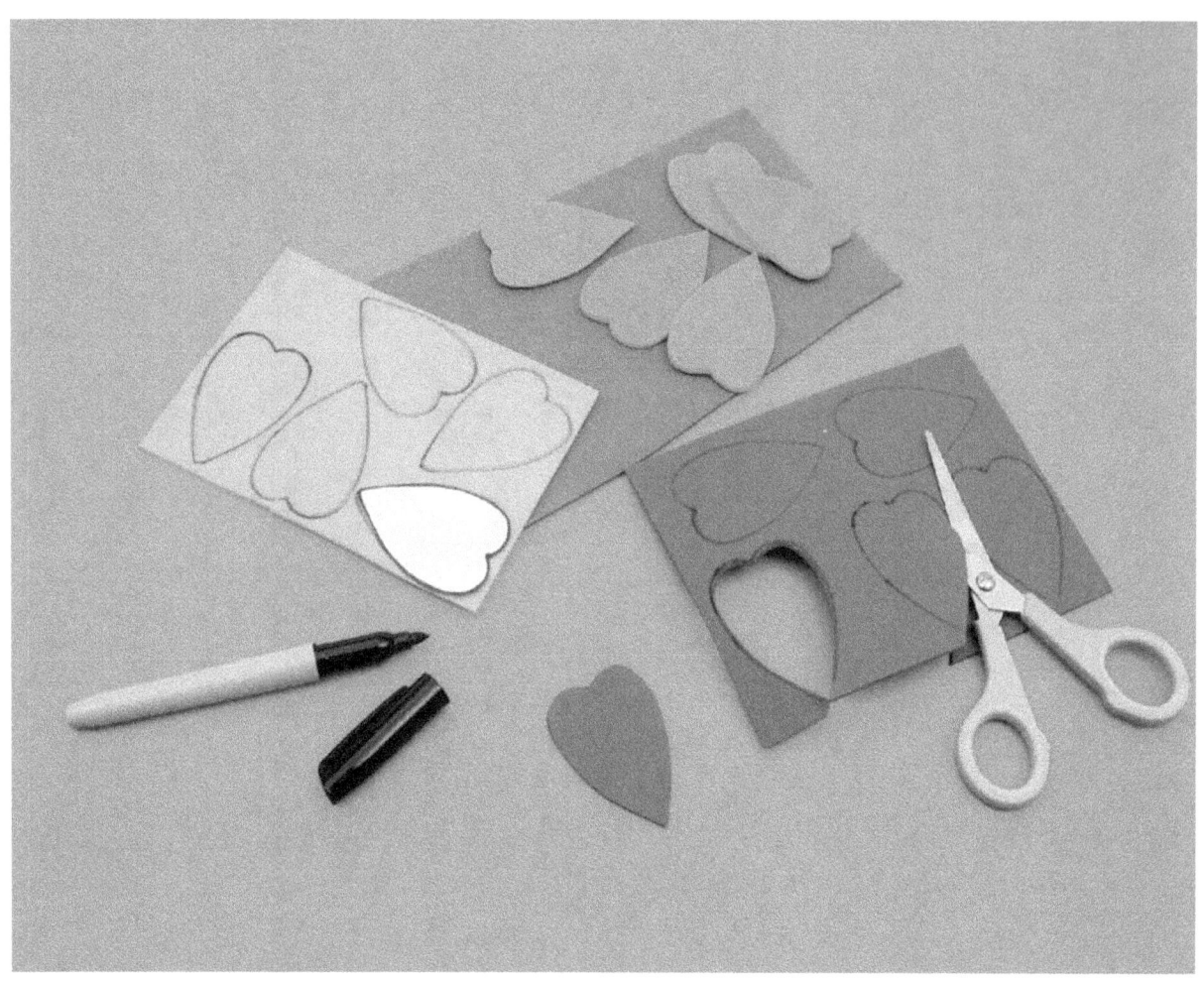

2. Trace around your template onto craft foam of different colours. Cut out the petals. You will need five petals for each flower.

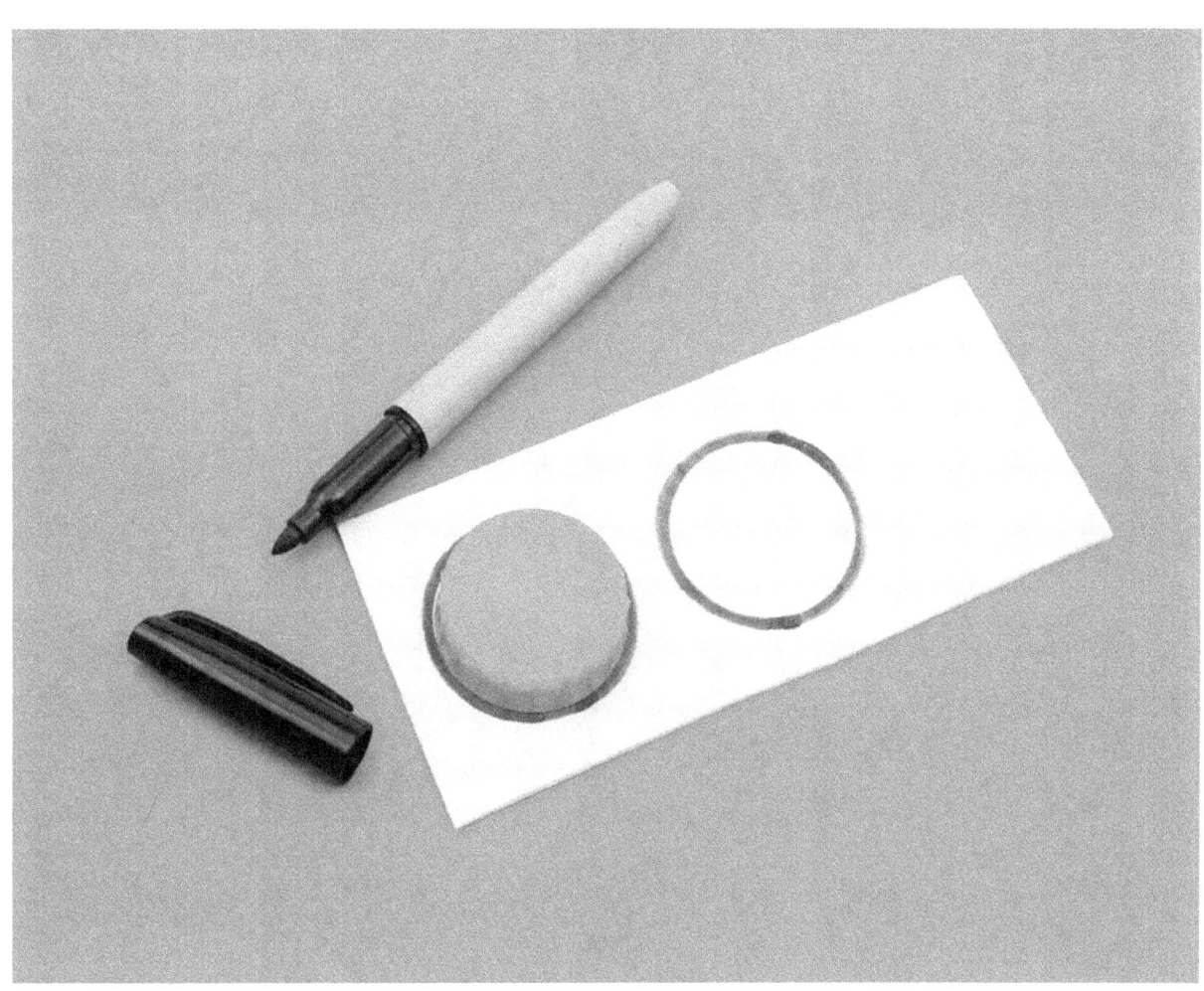

3. Draw around your bottle top twice onto craft foam and cut it out. You will need two circles for each flower you make.

4. Glue your petals onto the flat part of the bottle top and leave them to dry.

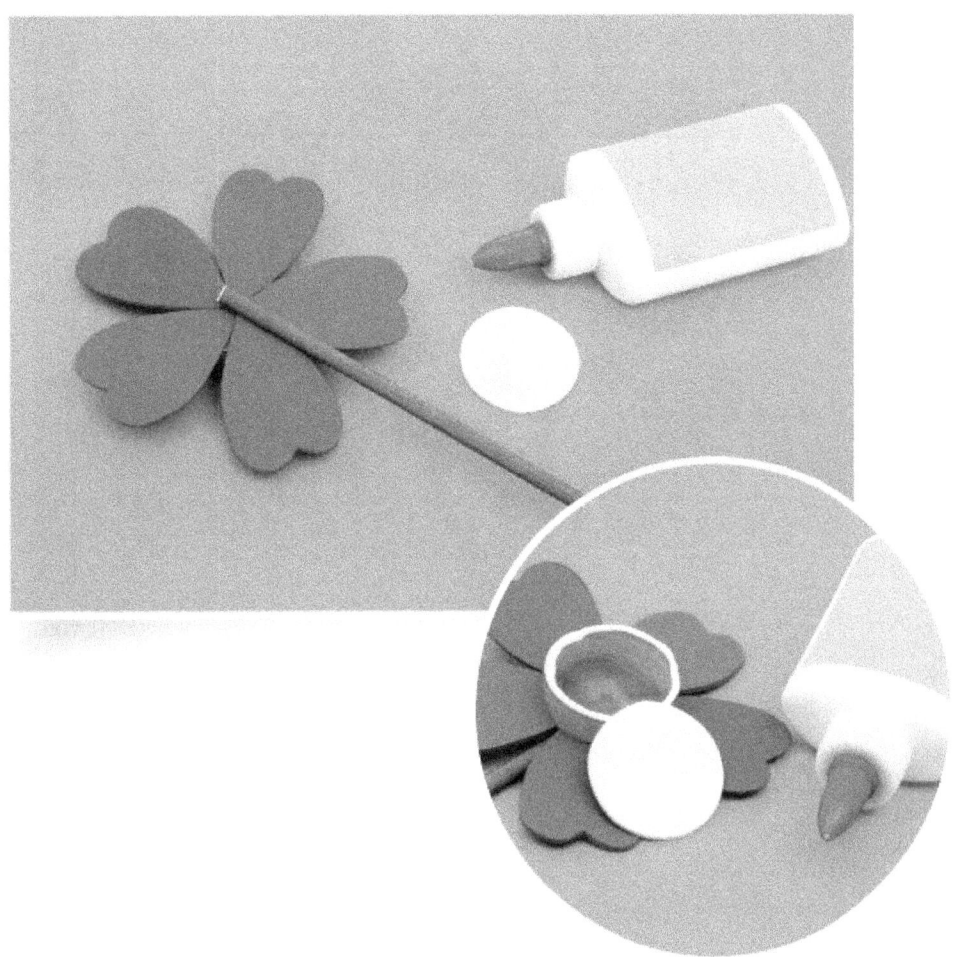

5. Place a garden cane onto the back of the flower and cover it with one of the foam circles, gluing it in place with the craft glue. Turn the flower over and cover the bottle cap with the other foam circle, gluing it down with the craft glue. Repeat steps 3–5 to make more flowers. Leave them to dry, then arrange them in a vase or plastic bottle.

STACKABLE ROCKET BOXES

These space-themed boxes are made from empty food containers. You can use them to store little objects or hide secret stuff!

You will need

Cardboard packaging tubes with lids

Pencil

Coloured paper

Glue stick

Sticky tape

Scissors and ruler

Black marker pen

1. Find four tube-shaped containers that will fit neatly inside each other.

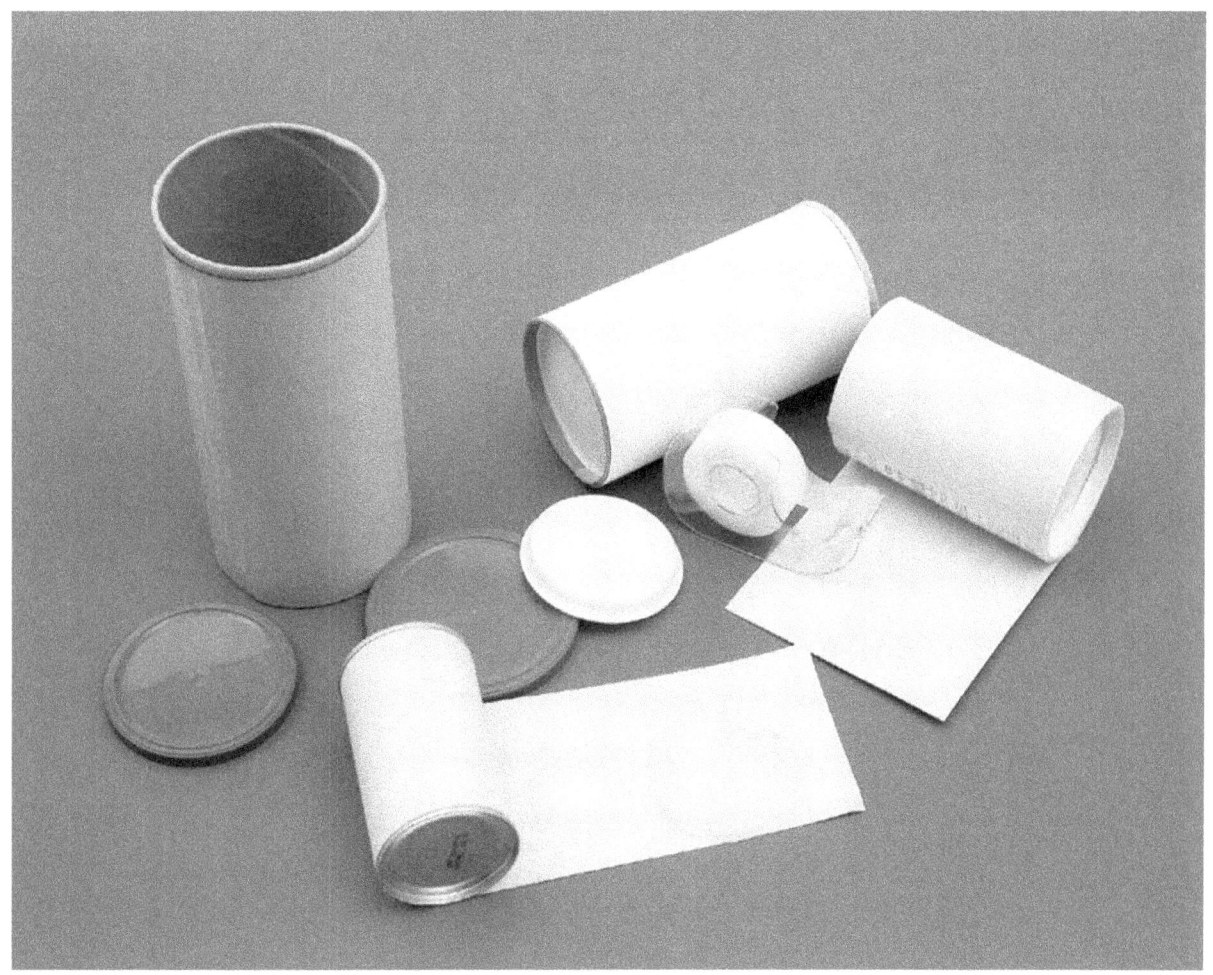

2. Measure the height of each tube, and cut a piece of paper to that height. Wrap paper around the tubes and tape it in place.

3. Draw the shapes that make up a rocket, an astronaut, a robot and a spotty space alien onto coloured paper. Cut out the paper shapes with scissors.

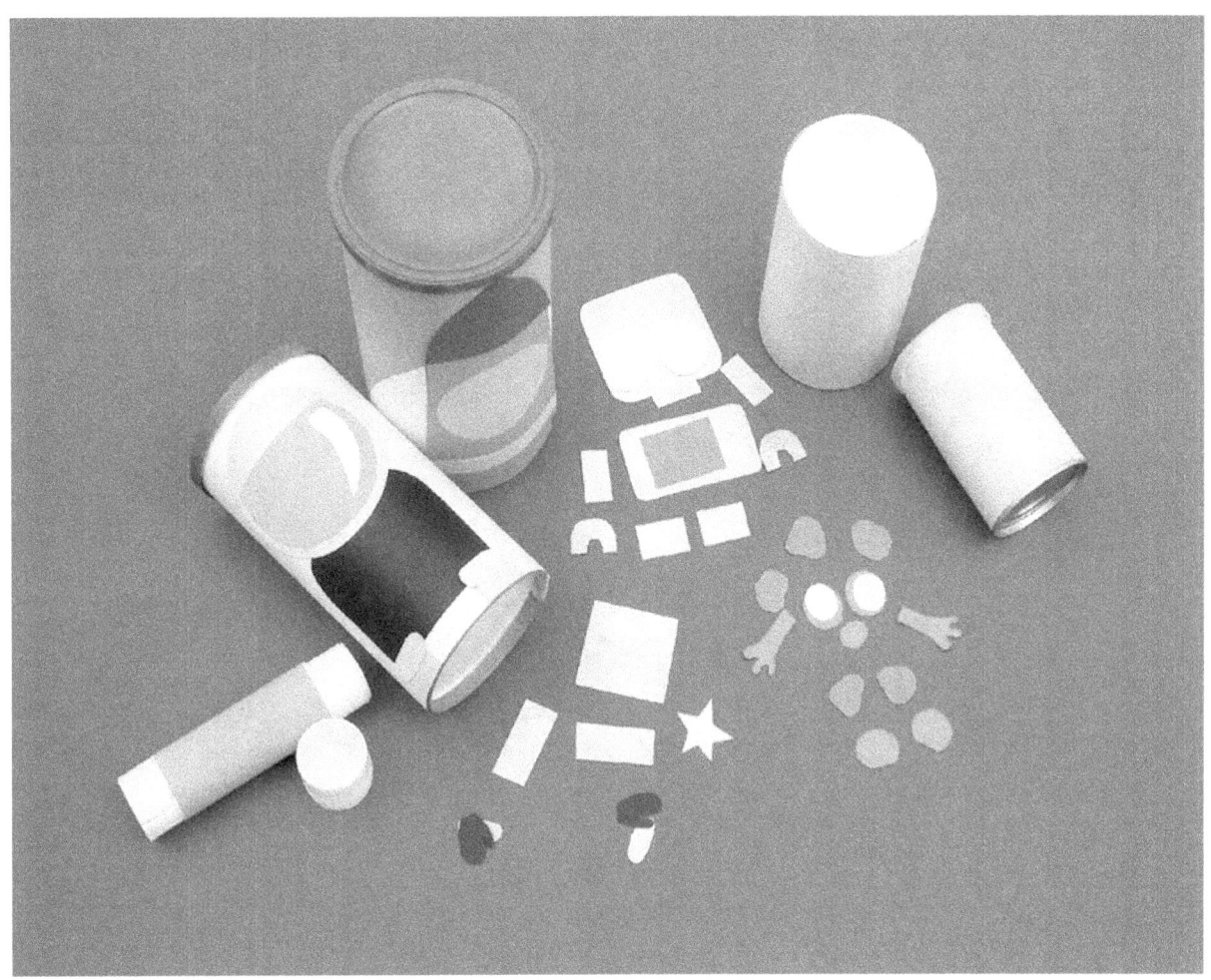

4. Glue all the paper shapes onto your containers with a glue stick.

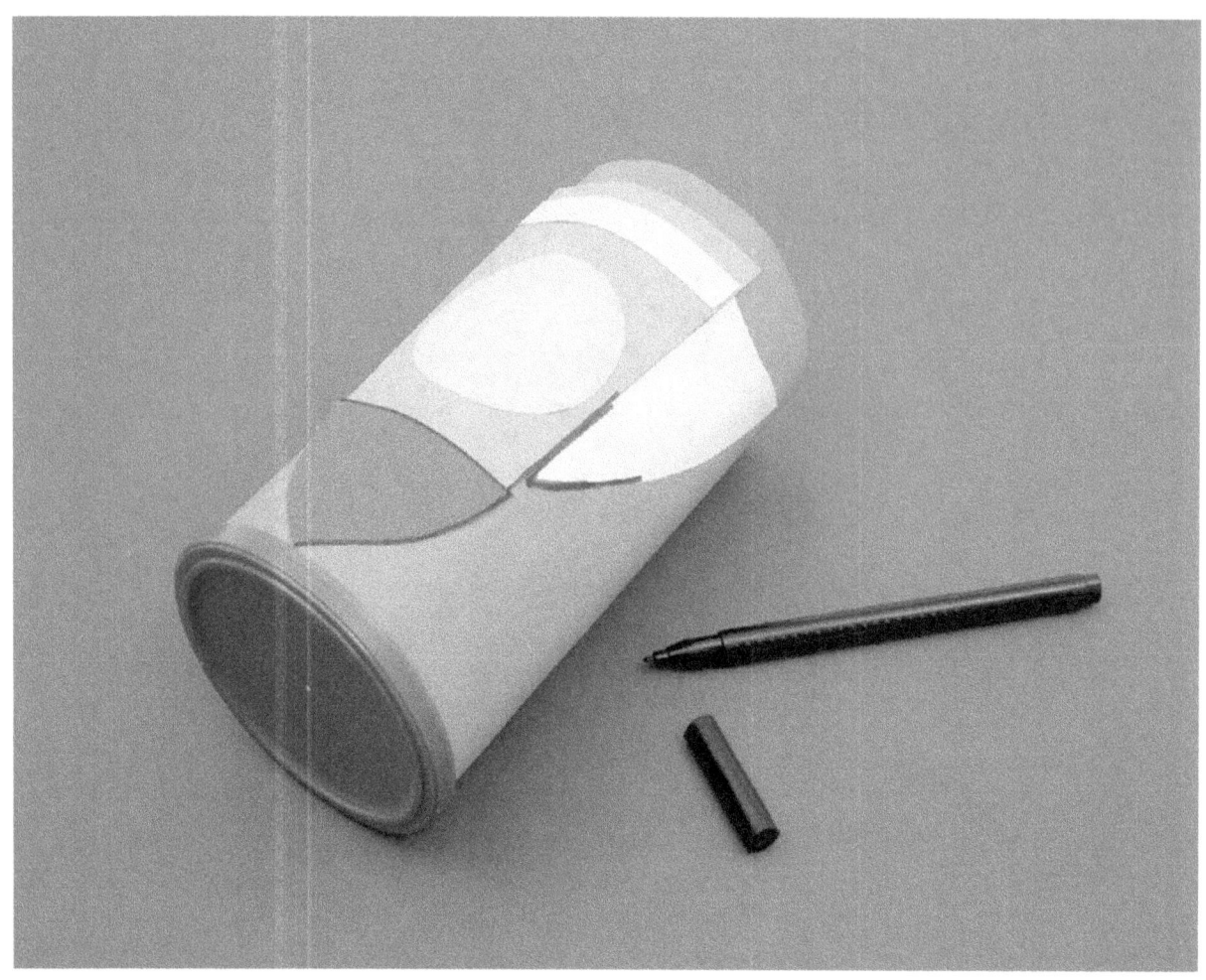

5. Outline the decorations with a black marker pen to add some detailing.

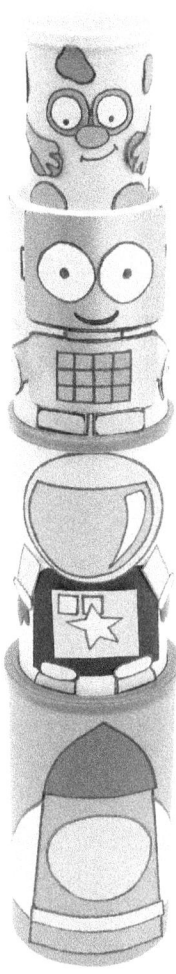

Your stackable containers don't need to have a space theme. They can be anything you want them to be.

BEACH HUT PEN POTS

Spending time at the beach is a great thing to do in the summer. With this craft you can still be reminded of those sunny days even when it starts to pour with rain.

You will need

2 kitchen roll tubes

Cardboard

Patterned paper

Coloured card

Sandpaper

Black marker pen

PVA glue

Scissors and ruler

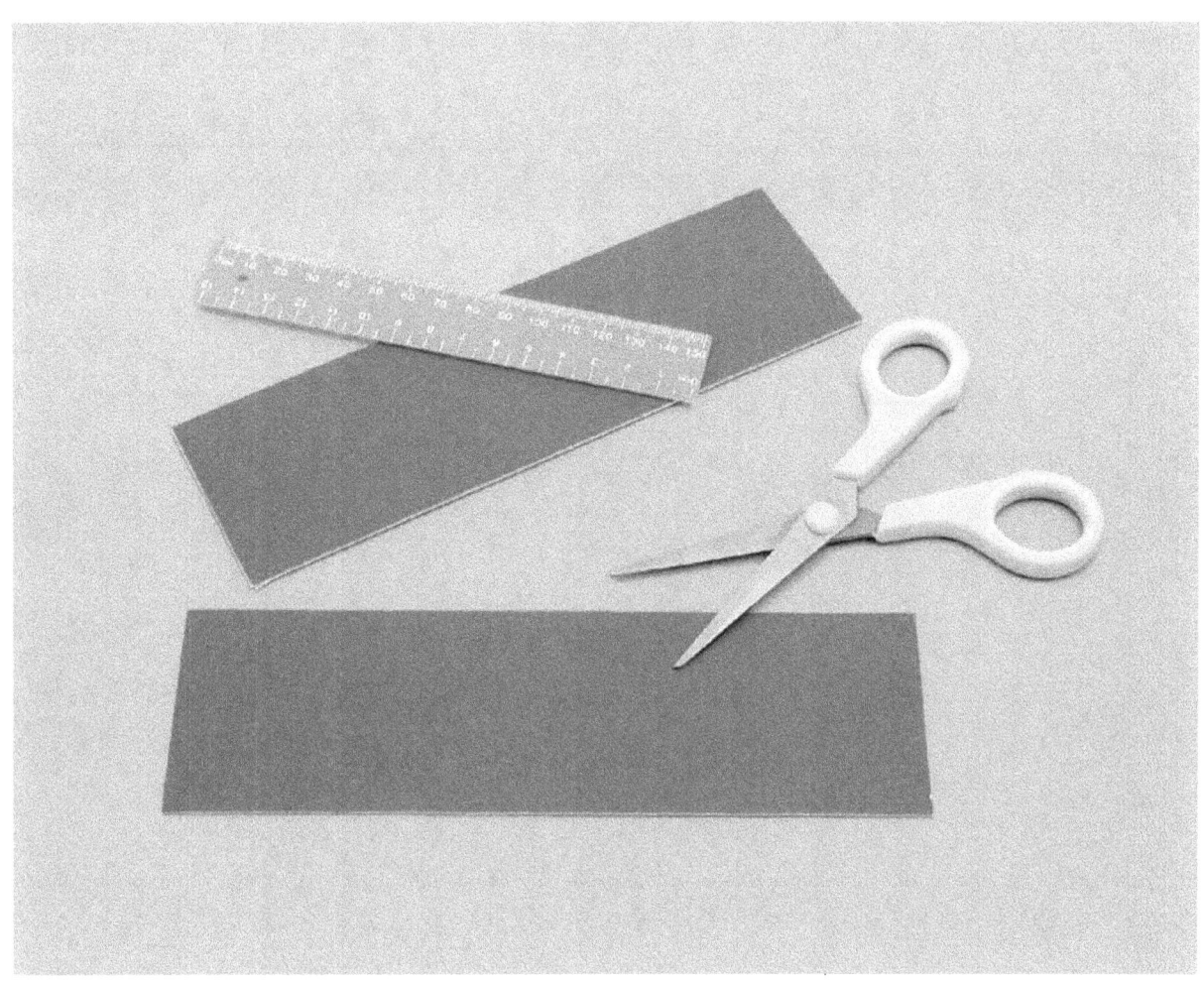

1. Cut a piece of cardboard that measures 6 x 20 cm (2.5 x 8 in).

2. Cut some sandpaper to the same size as your cardboard. Use PVA glue to stick it to the cardboard.

3. Cut each kitchen roll tube in half, to make four tubes. Measure their height and cut four pieces of patterned paper to that height. Wrap the patterned paper around the tubes. Then stick it in place with PVA glue.

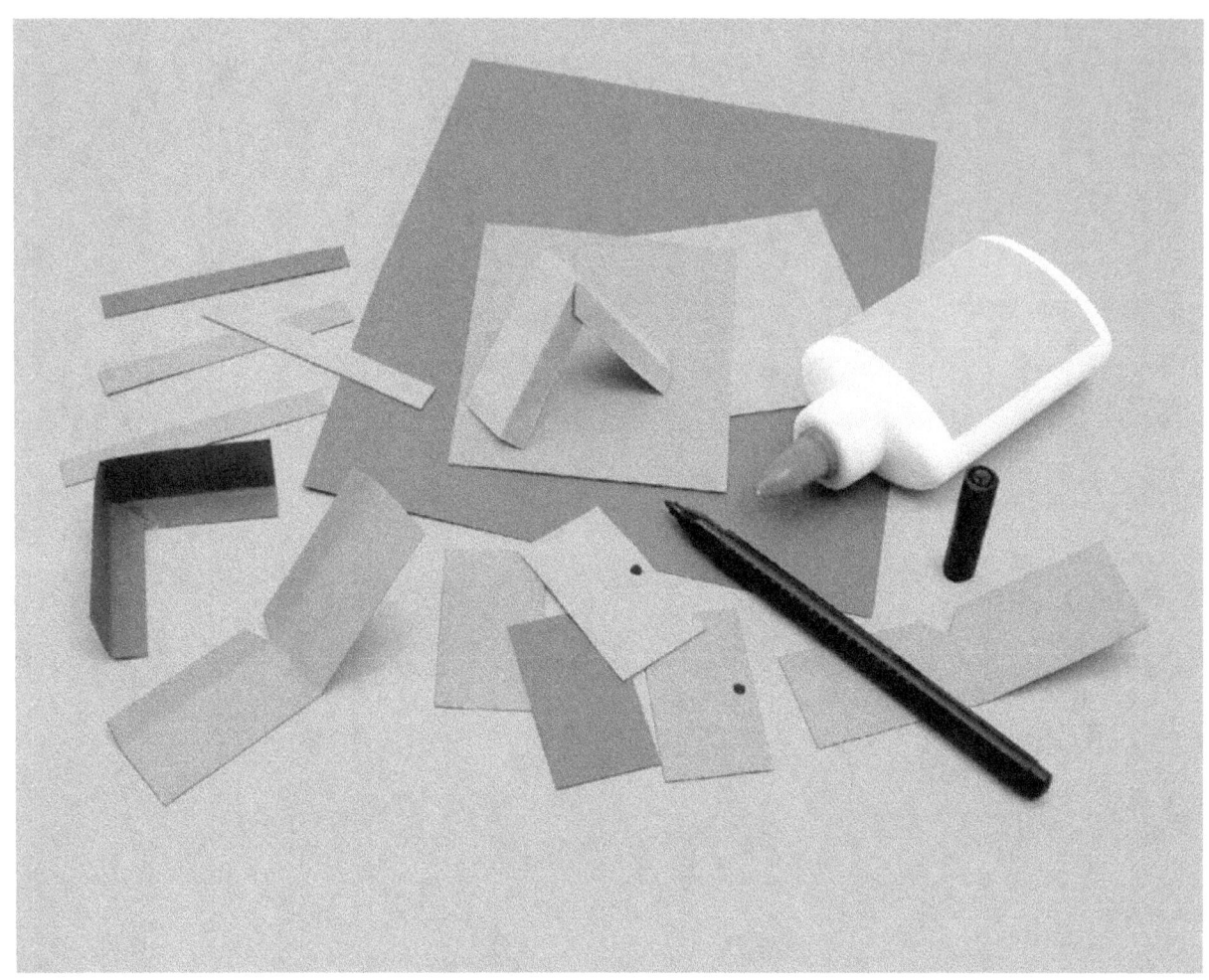

4. Cut out four rectangles of card measuring 8 x 3 cm (3 x 1 in). Fold them down the middle, and cut a small notch into that fold. Then fold the edge of the card to the same depth as the notch. Cut four smaller 8 x 6-cm (3 x 2-in) rectangles. Draw on a dot.

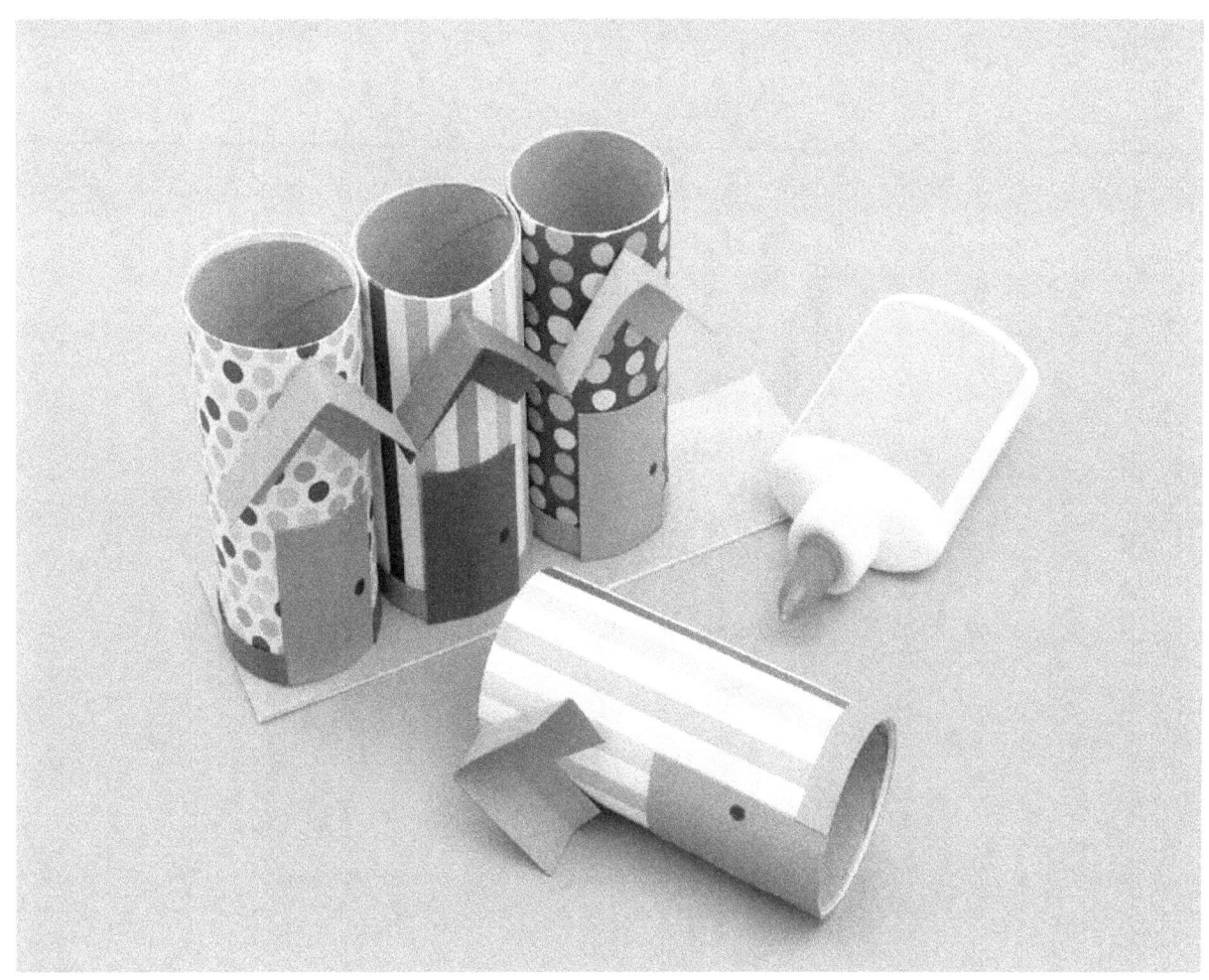

5. Glue the card shapes to your tubes with PVA, as shown above. The pointed shapes are roofs, and the rectangles are doors. Glue the beach huts in a row on top of your sandpaper. Leave everything to dry.

BEDROOM PINBOARD

Are you always losing little notes, photos and cards? Then what you need is a personalised pinboard, to keep them all in one place! It's simple to make but looks great.

You will need

Cardboard and paper

Marker pen or pencil

Fabric

Ribbon and buttons

Fabric glue

Large plate Scissors

1. Draw around a large plate onto your cardboard. Then cut out the circle.

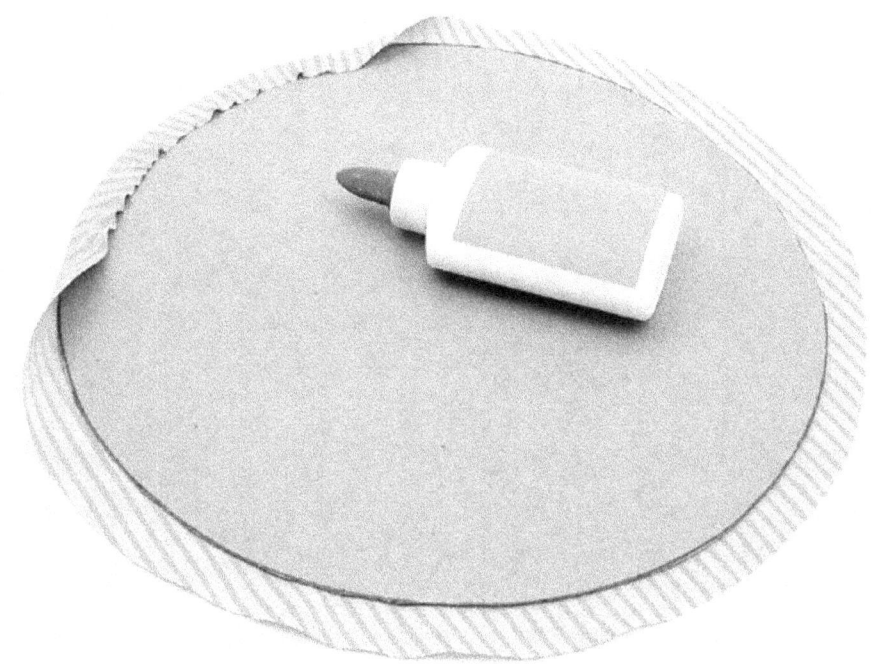

2. Cover the cardboard circle with some fabric. Cut the fabric into a circle a little larger than the plate. Fold over the edge of the fabric and stick it down with fabric glue.

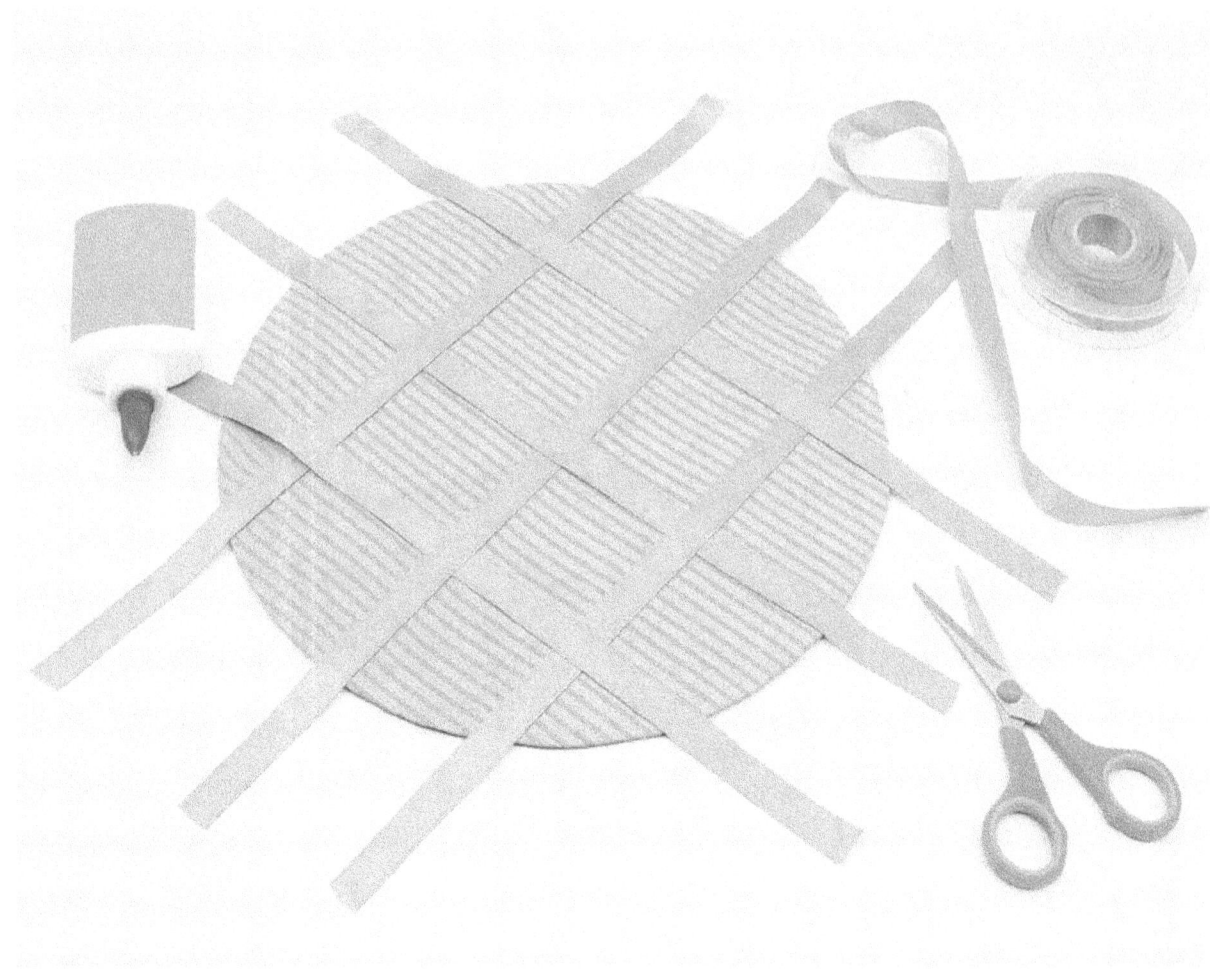

3. Cut six lengths of ribbon at least 5 cm (2 in) longer than your circle's diameter. Lay them over the fabric in a criss-cross pattern. Turn over the circle, and glue them in place.

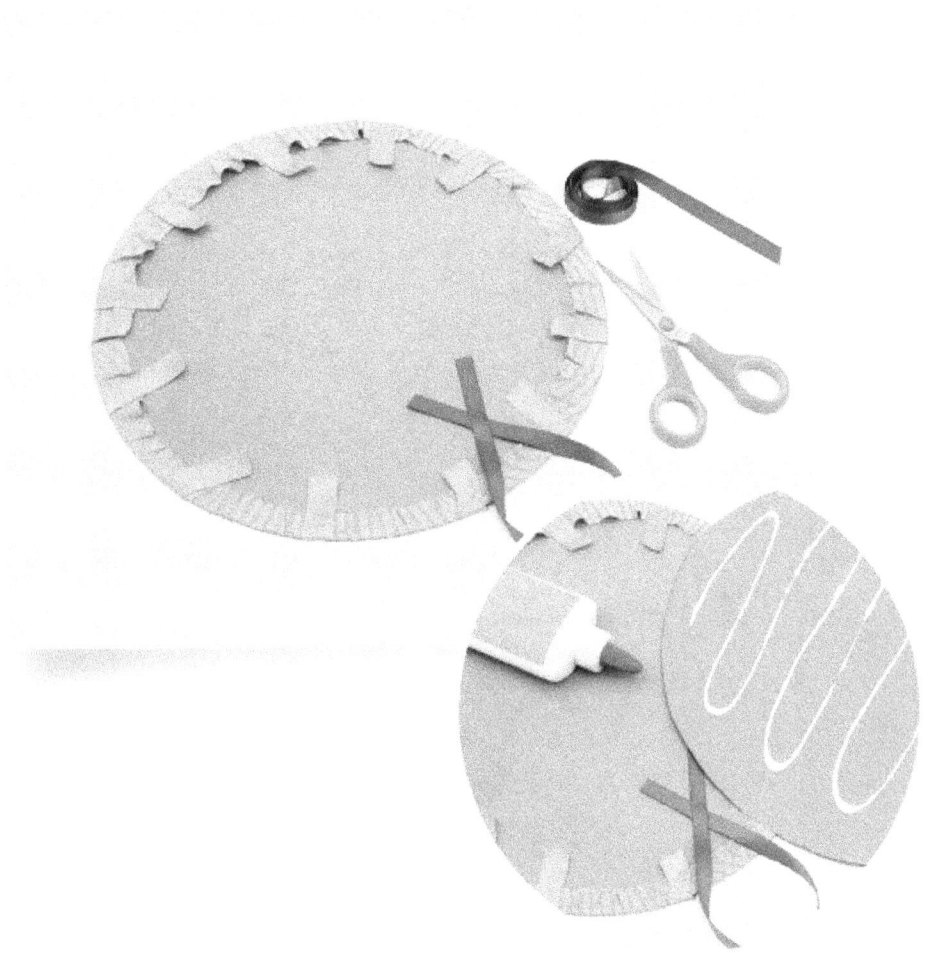

4. Make a loop of ribbon and glue it to the edge of the cardboard. Then draw around your plate onto a piece of paper and cut out the circle. Glue the paper onto the back of your board.

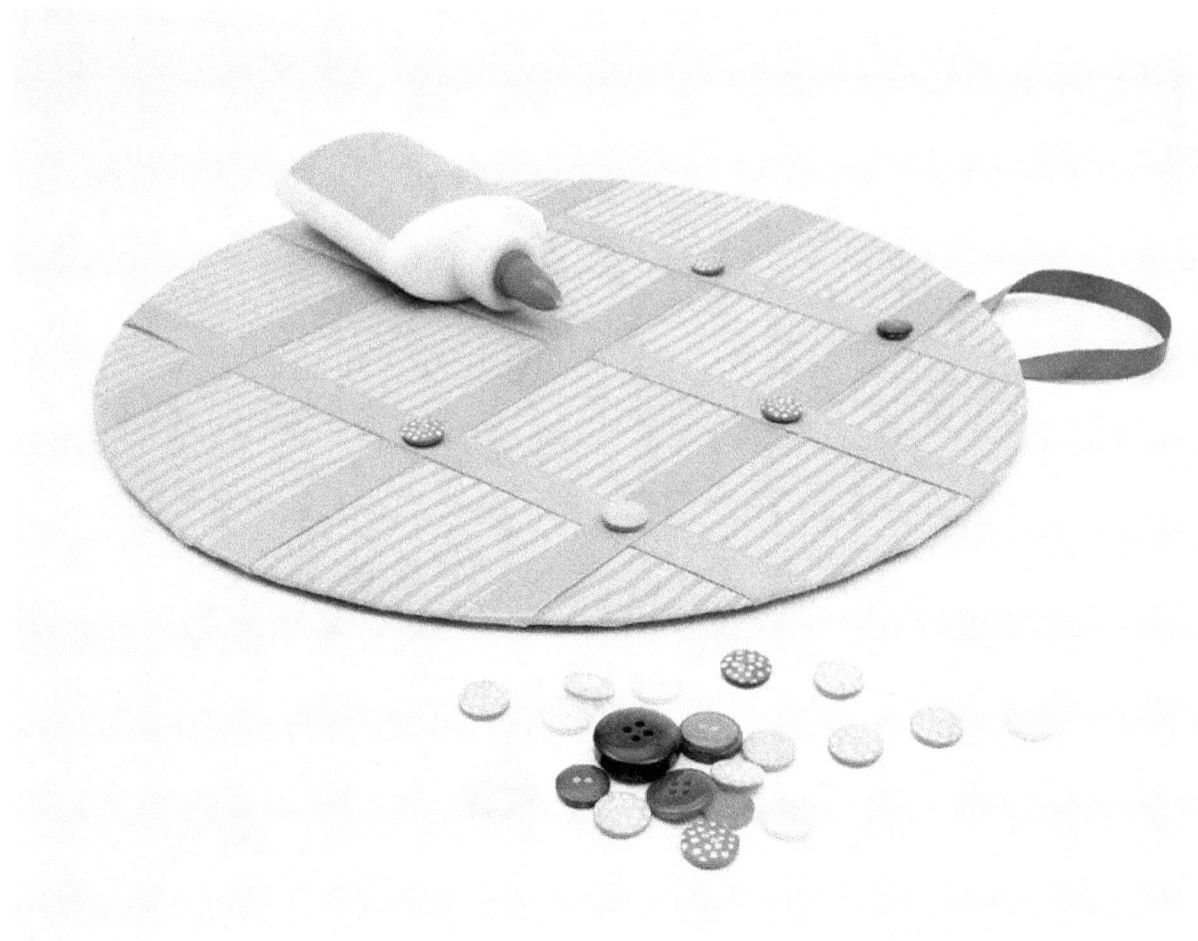

5. Glue some buttons to the front of your board where the ribbons cross over.

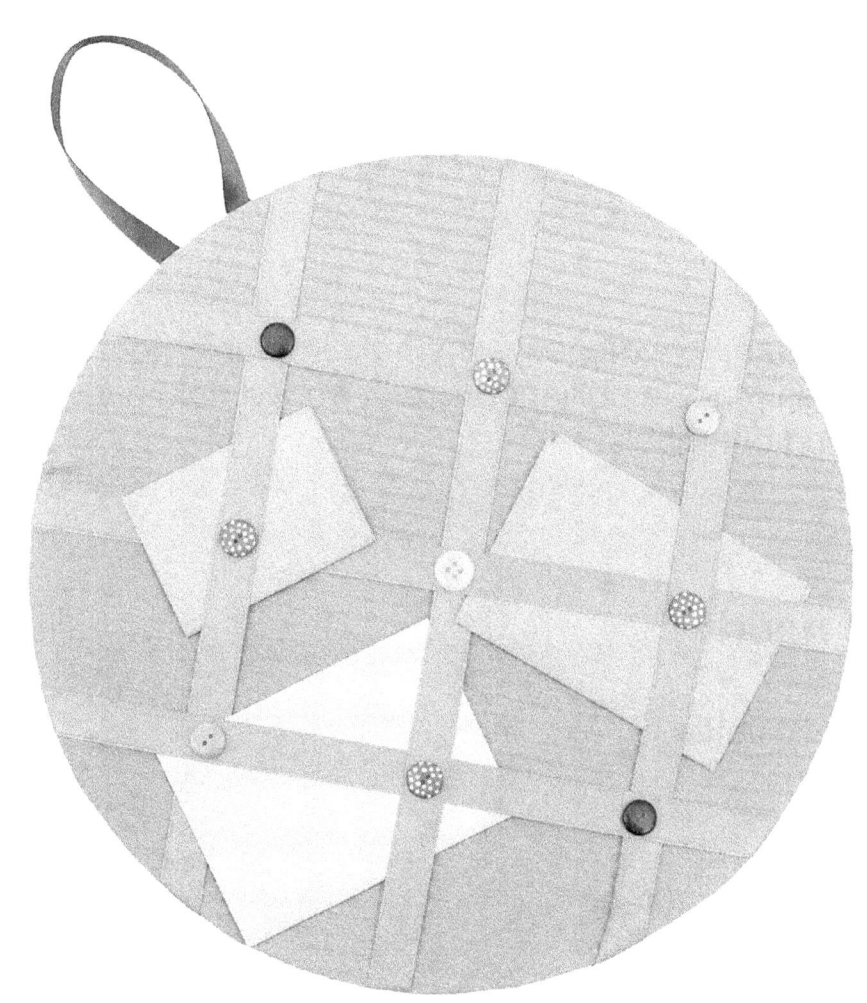

WATER BOTTLE BRACELETS

You wouldn't want to wear jewellery made of junk, right? Wrong! Here is how you can make a brilliant bracelet from an old plastic bottle. It looks anything but rubbish!

You will need

A 2-litre plastic bottle

Wool

Metallic embroidery thread

Sticky tape

Scissors

Black marker pen

Ruler

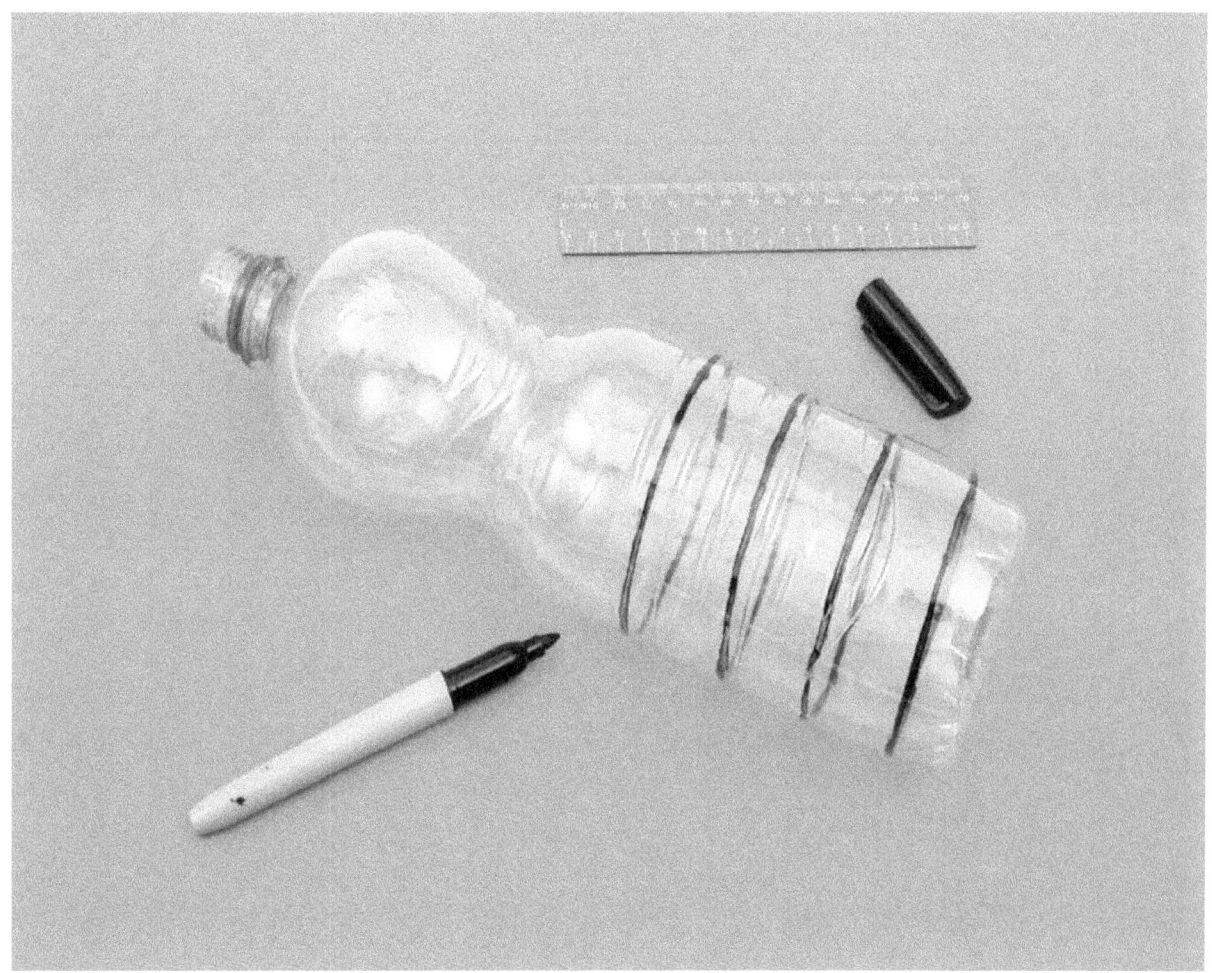

1. Draw lines around a plastic bottle with a marker pen. Use a ruler to measure them – they should be about 3 cm (1 in) apart.

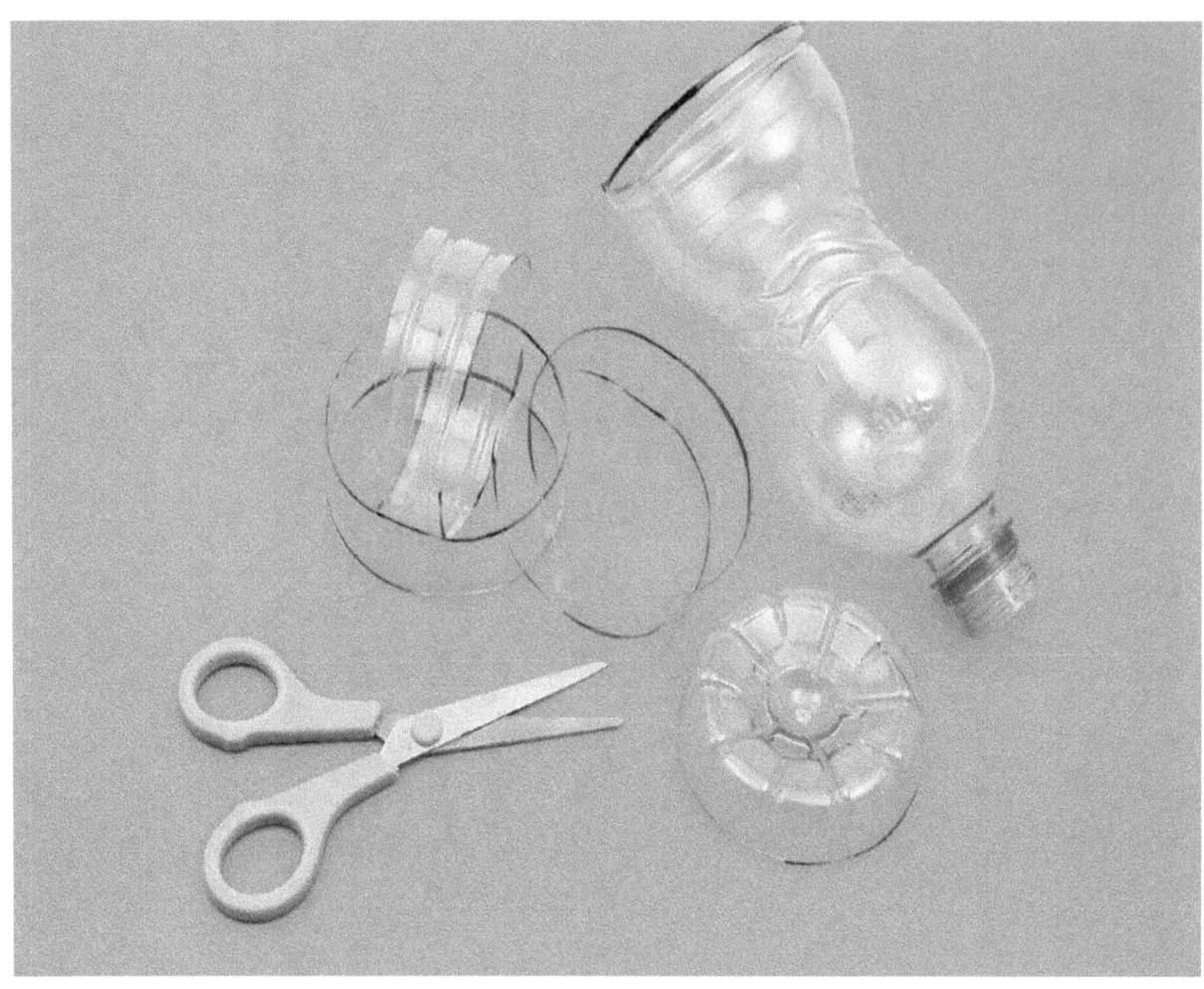

2. Cut along the lines to make plastic rings. These will be your bracelets!

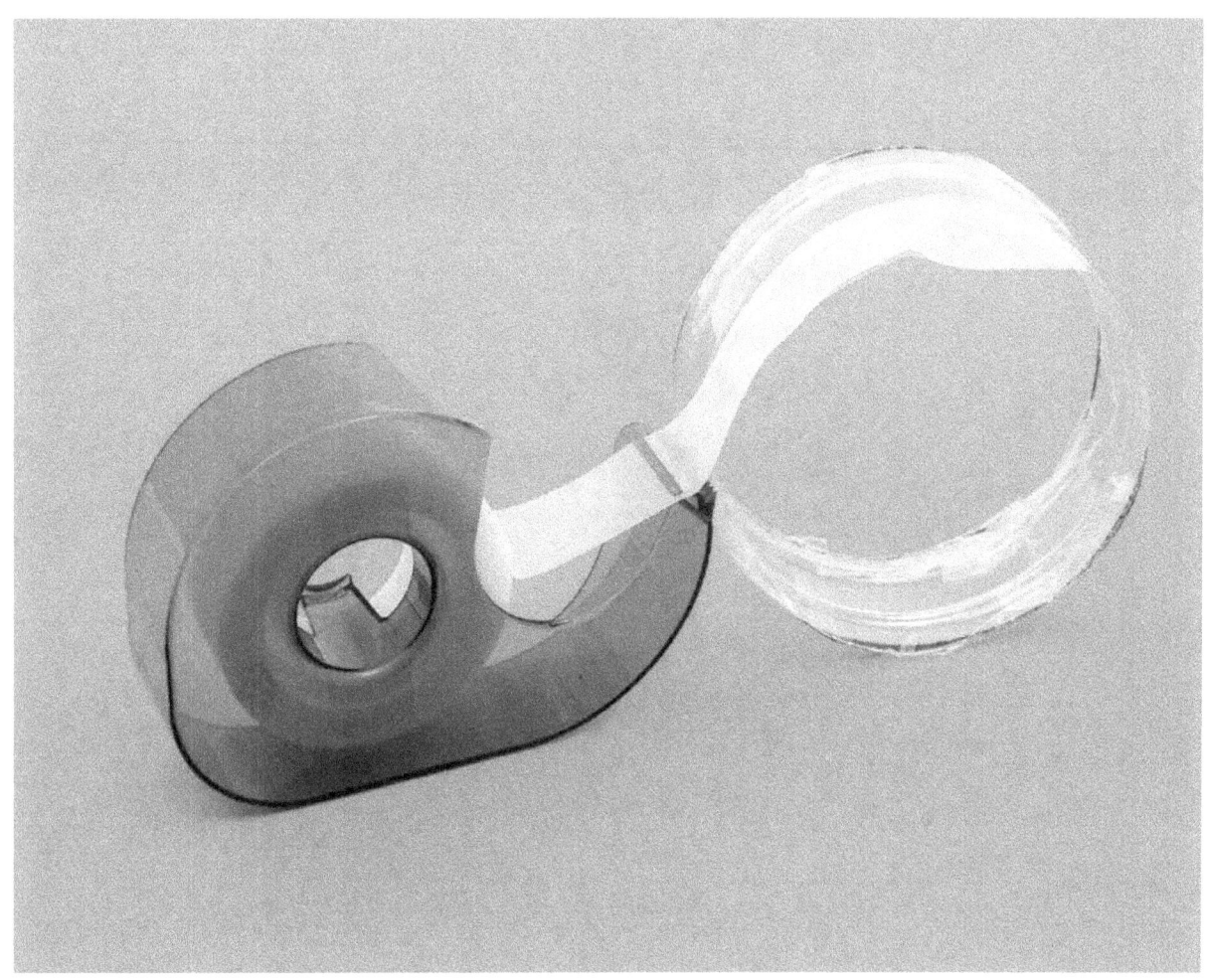

3. Tape over the edges of each bracelet with some sticky tape, so they are not sharp.

4. Wrap wool round and round each plastic bracelet. Change colours to make stripes. When you're done, make a knot.

5. As a finishing touch, wind some metallic embroidery thread around each bracelet in a zig-zag.

You could also make some smaller rings from a smaller plastic bottle and attach them to a necklace or earring clips!

SCRAP PAPER DAISY CHAIN

Rescue some paper from the bin or recycling box, and you can make a daisy chain that lasts forever! If you don't have a shredder, just use scissors.

You will need

Shredder or scissors, ruler and pen

Scrap paper

PVA glue

Green string or wool

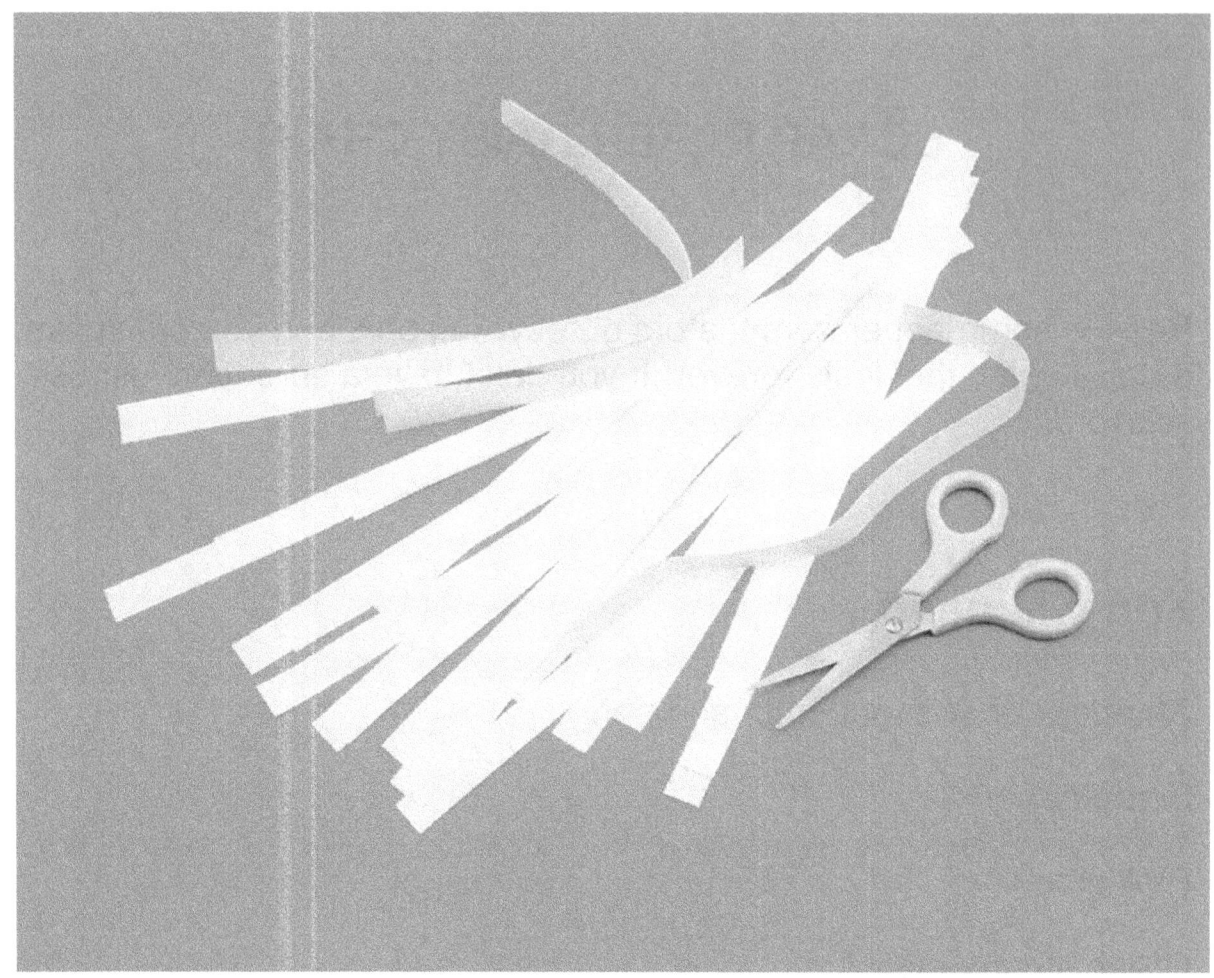

1. Either shred some white and yellow paper, or use a ruler, pen and scissors to cut it into long, straight strips. You will need 10 strips of yellow paper and 60 strips of white paper.

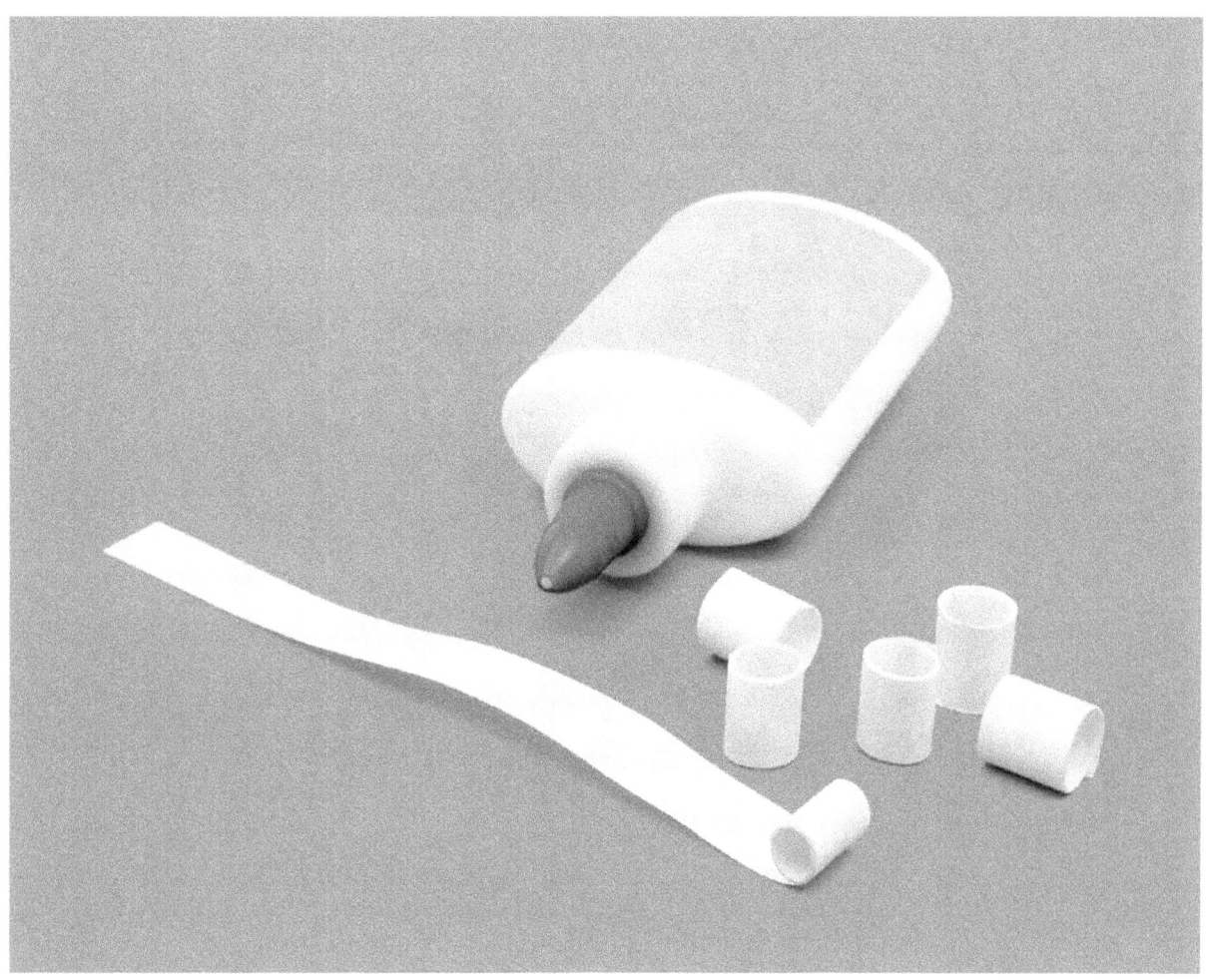

2. Coil the yellow paper into tight rings. Fix the ends in place with some PVA glue. These rings will be the centres of your daisies.

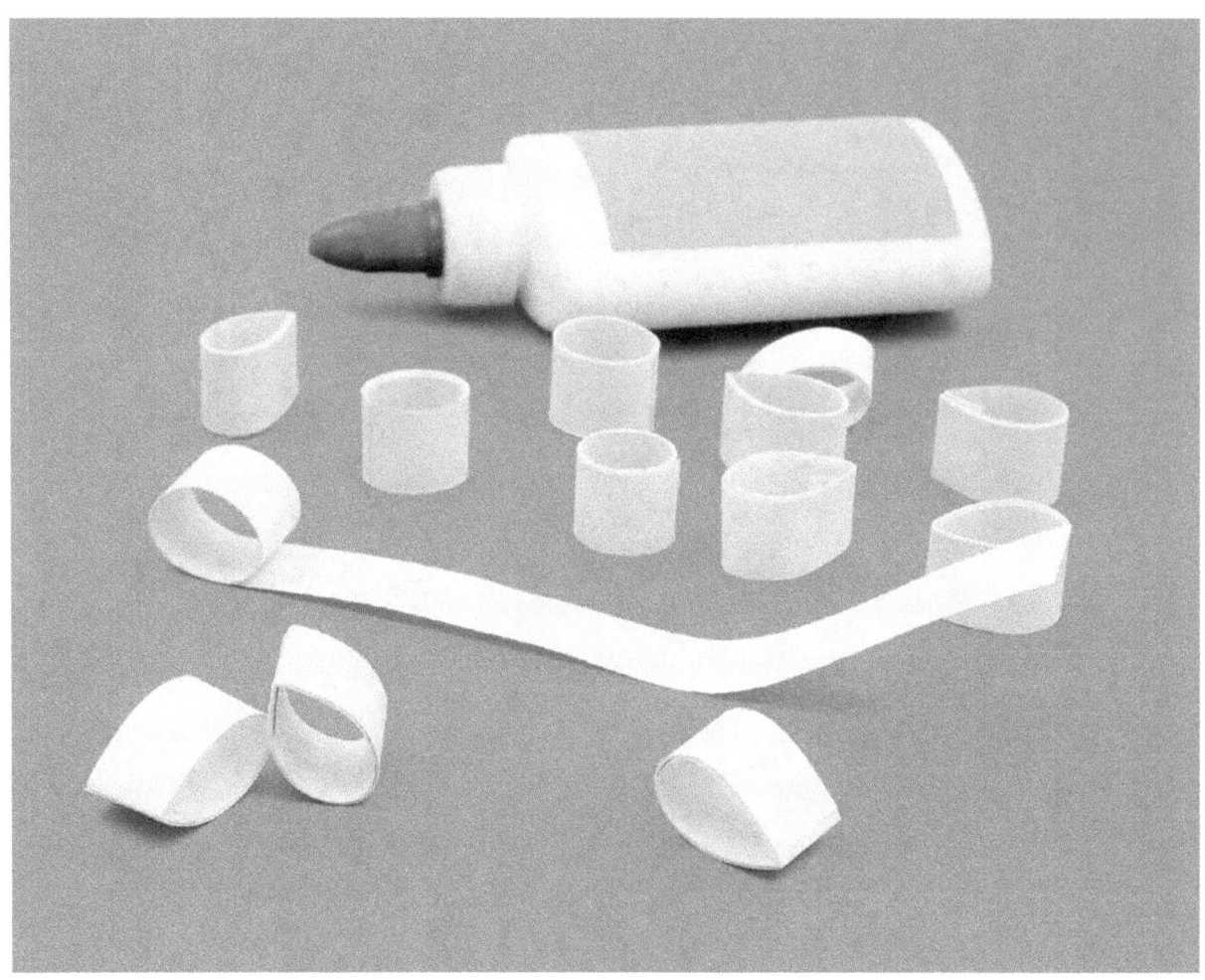

3. Now coil up the white paper into slightly larger rings. Fix the ends in place with some glue. Pinch one end of each white ring to make a point. These will make your petals.

4. Fix six white petals to each yellow ring with PVA glue. Leave them to dry on a protected surface.

5. Peel off the flowers and thread them onto a length of green string or wool.

Make lots of different coloured flowers using shredded magazines. You can use them to decorate picture frames, blank cards or even a keepsake box.

PEACOCK BOOKENDS

You'll be as proud as a peacock when you show everyone this fun craft. You can use these bird-brained buddies to prop up your books, or as a decoration.

If you enjoy making these peacocks, you could also try decorating bookends as lighthouses, moon rockets or the turrets of a castle.

You will need

2 crisp tubes with lids

Double-sided sticky tape

Sticky tape

Scissors and ruler

PVA glue

Sand

Coloured card

Felt-tip pens

Googly eyes

Glitter glue

1. Fill two crisp tubes with sand to make them heavy. Replace the lids and fix them in place with sticky tape.

2. Measure the height of your tubes. Cut two pieces of blue card to that height. Wrap them around the tubes and tape them in place with double-sided tape.

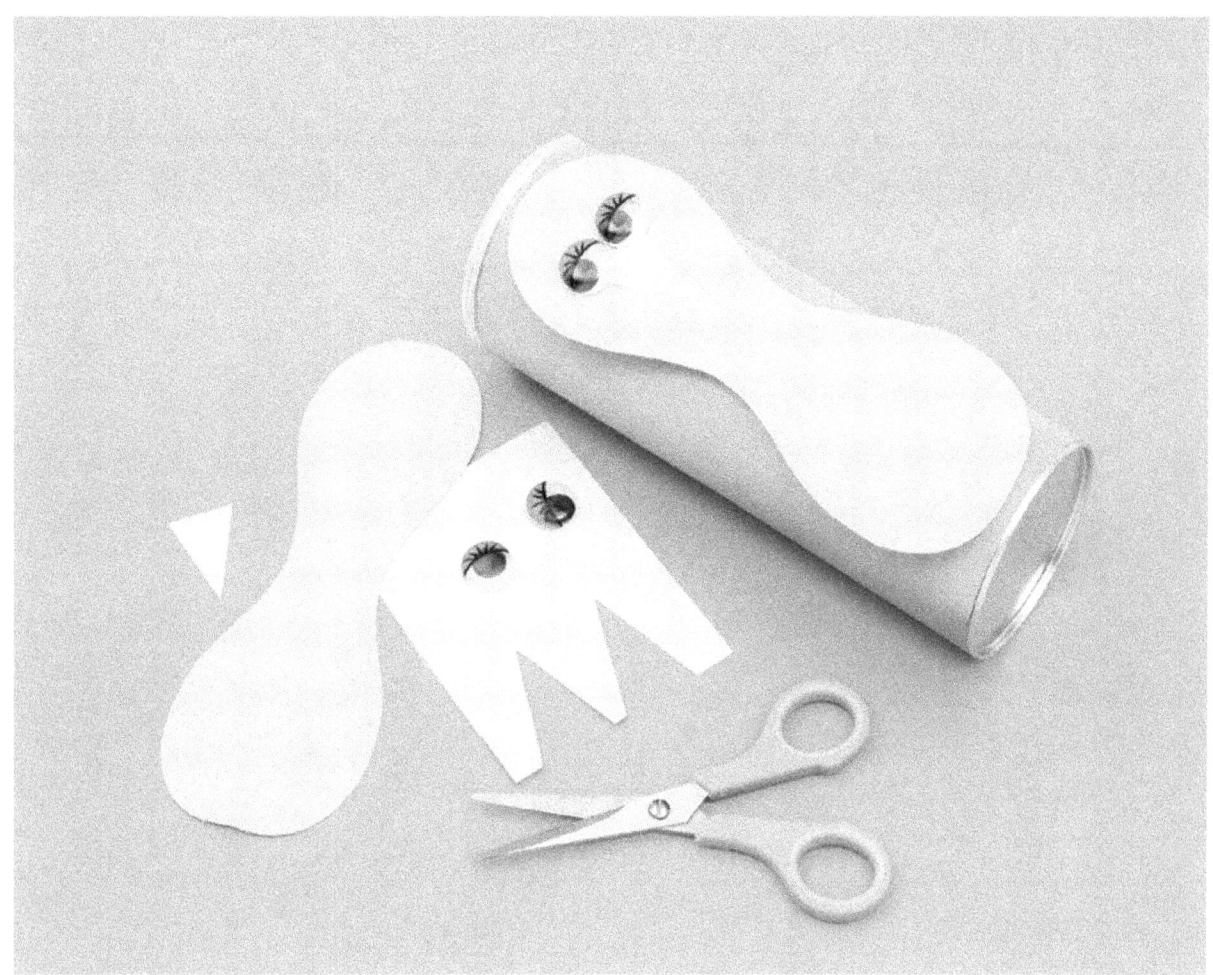

3. Draw two body shapes like pinched ovals onto blue card, and triangular beaks onto yellow card. Cut them out and fix them to the tubes with double-sided sticky tape. Then stick on googly eyes with PVA glue.

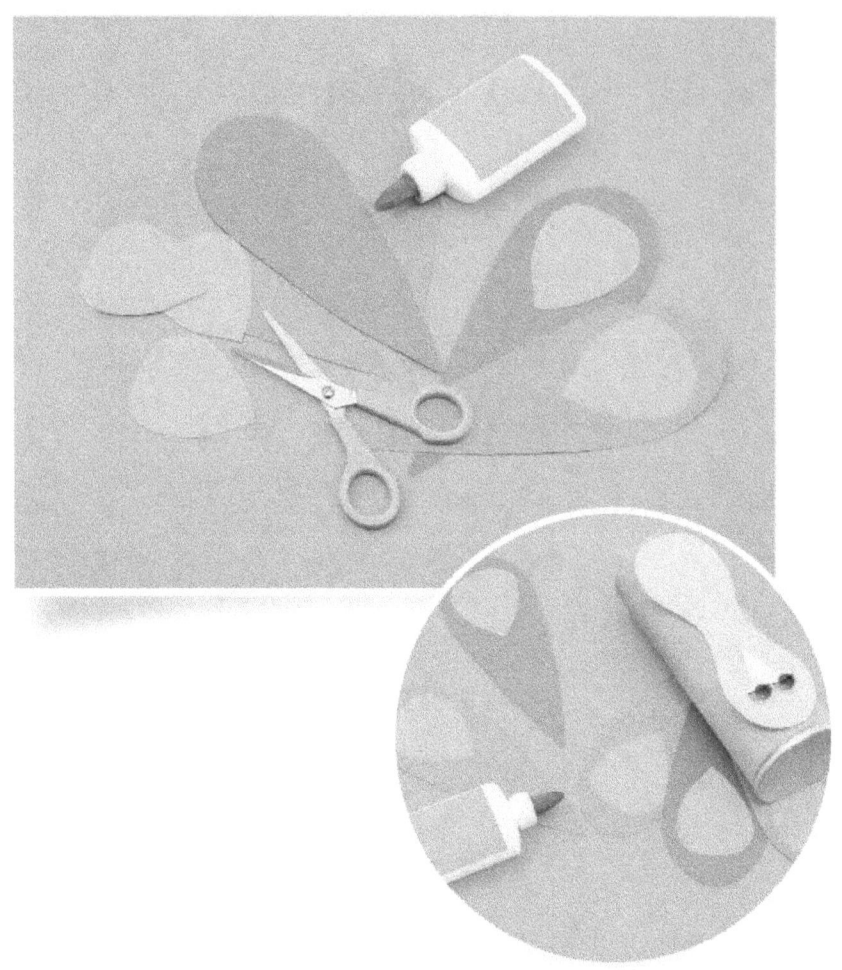

4. Cut out feather shapes from green, blue and purple card. Stick the feathers to your tube in a fan shape.

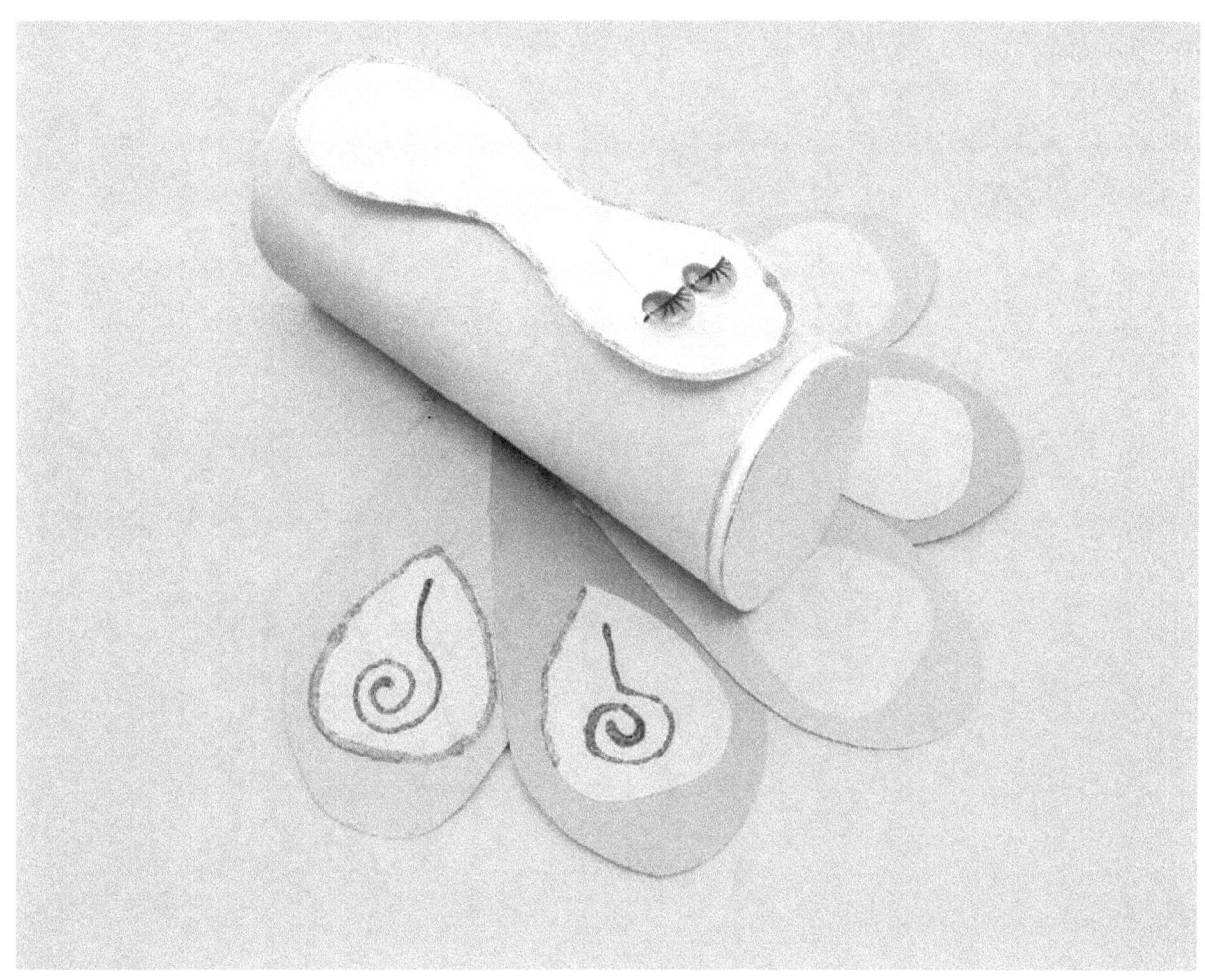

5. Add detail to your peacocks' bodies and feathers with felt-tip pens and glitter glue.

SUNNY DAYS CLOCK

You should always make time for craft... and now you can use craft to make a timepiece! The rays of this cheery sunburst clock are made from scrap paper – or you could use newspaper.

You will need

A clock kit (from a craft shop)

Scrap paper

Knitting needles

Pencil and paintbrush

PVA glue

Cardboard

Acrylic paint

Coloured card

Scissors

Large cup

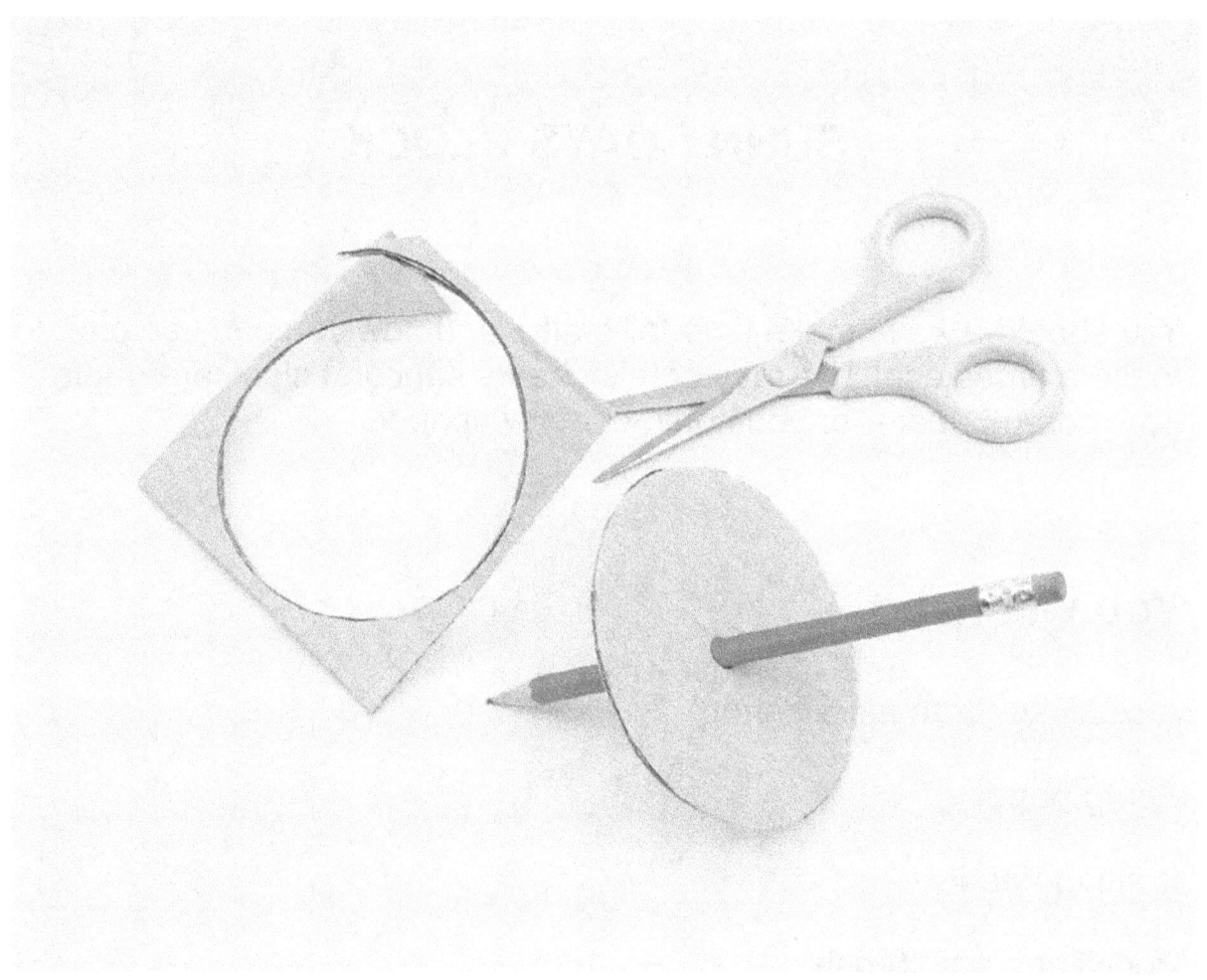

1. Draw around a large cup onto cardboard. Make a hole in the middle with a pencil so that your clock pieces can fit through.

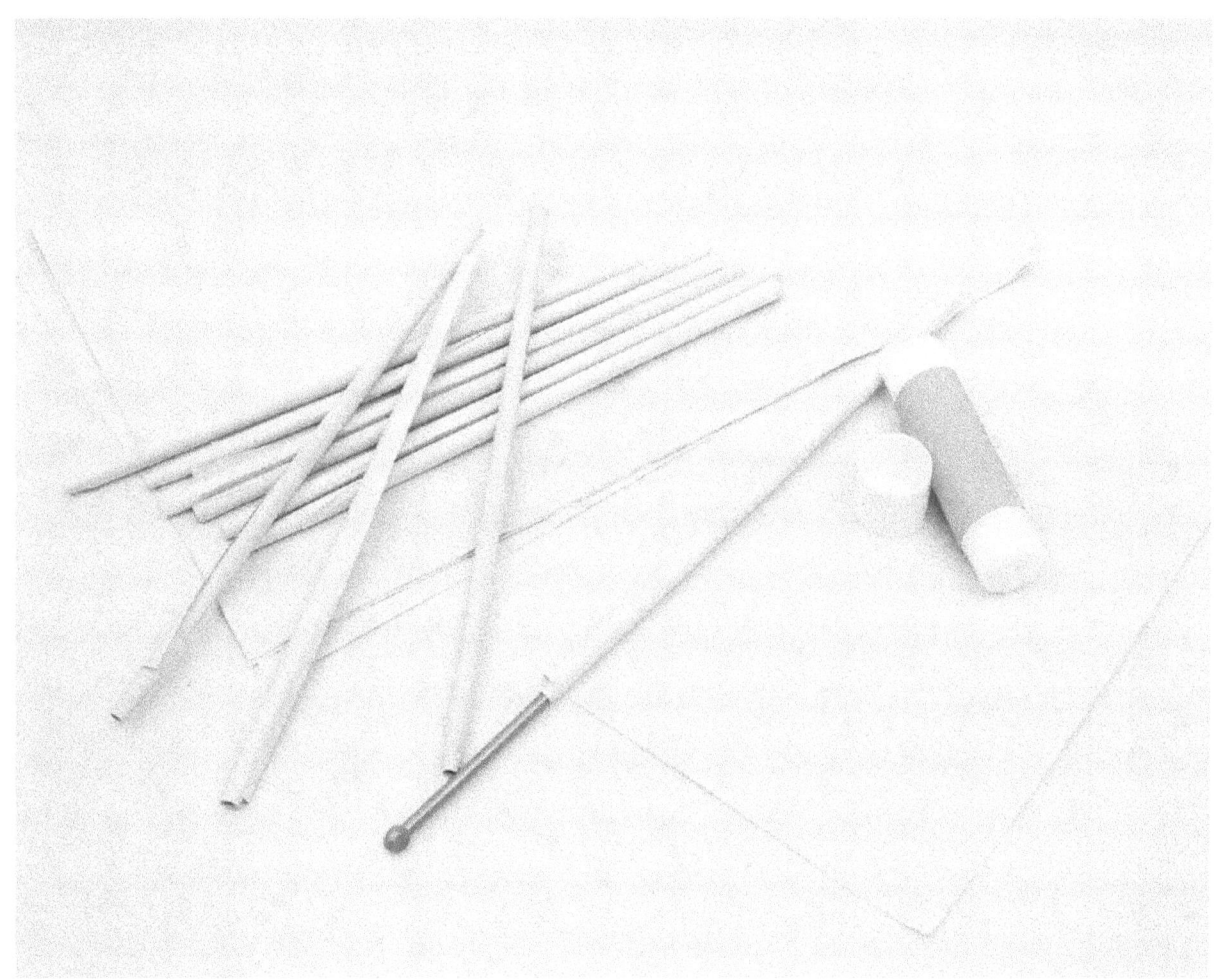

2. Spread some glue down one of the short edges of a piece of paper. Place your knitting needle at the opposite end and start rolling it up into a tube. Fix it in place with more glue. Repeat this 11 times.

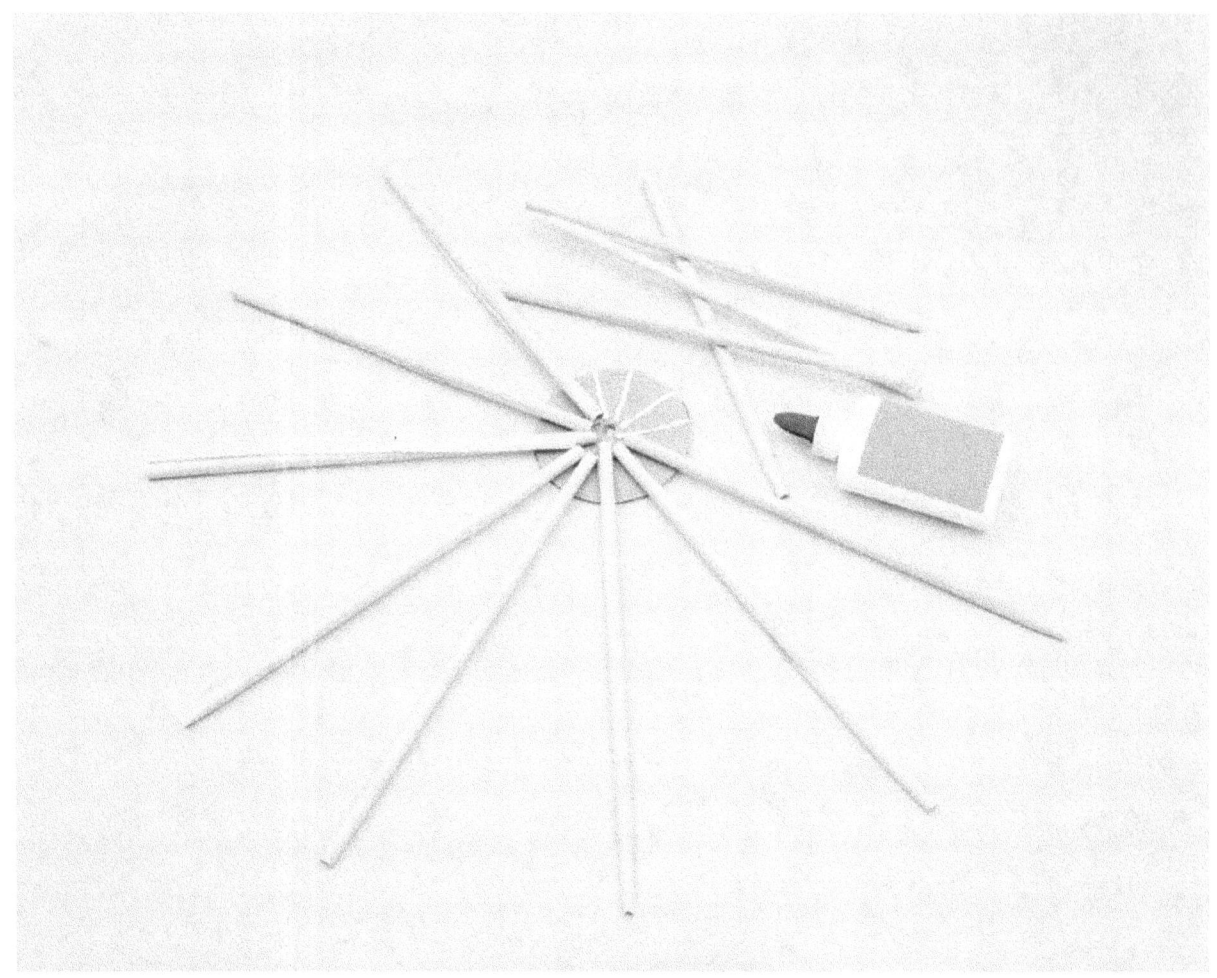

3. Cover your cardboard circle with PVA glue, then place your paper tubes so they make a starburst pattern. Be careful not to cover over the hole you made in the middle of the cardboard.

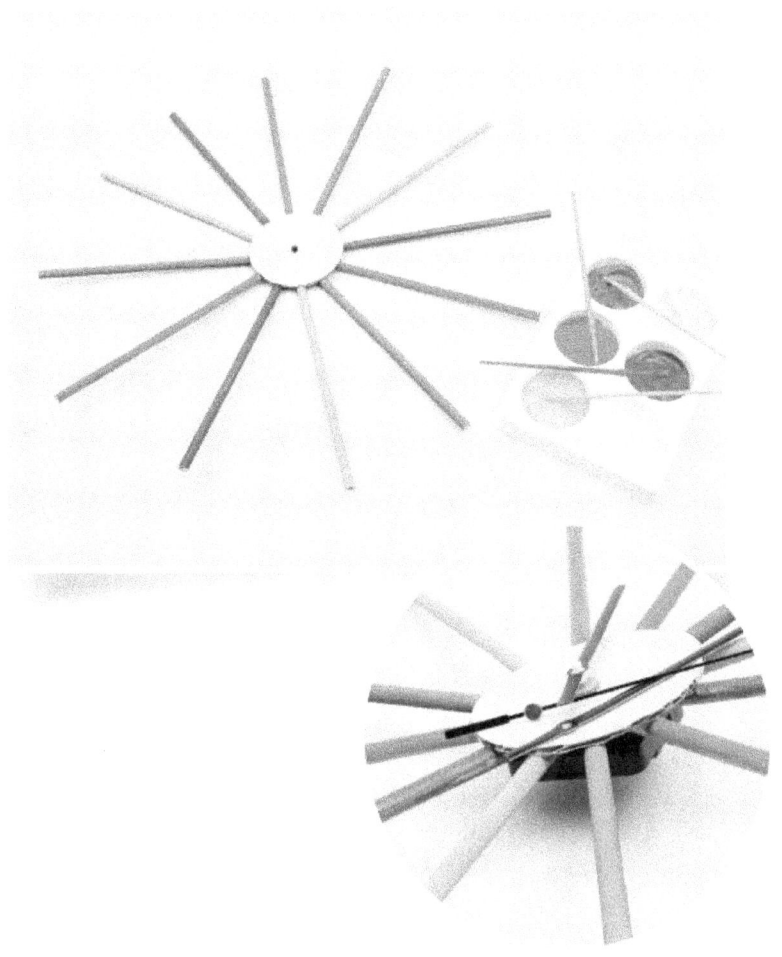

4. Paint the tubes in bright colours using your acrylic paint. Then insert the clock mechanism, following the kit's instructions.

5. Cut out triangle shapes from coloured card and stick one on the end of each paper tube.

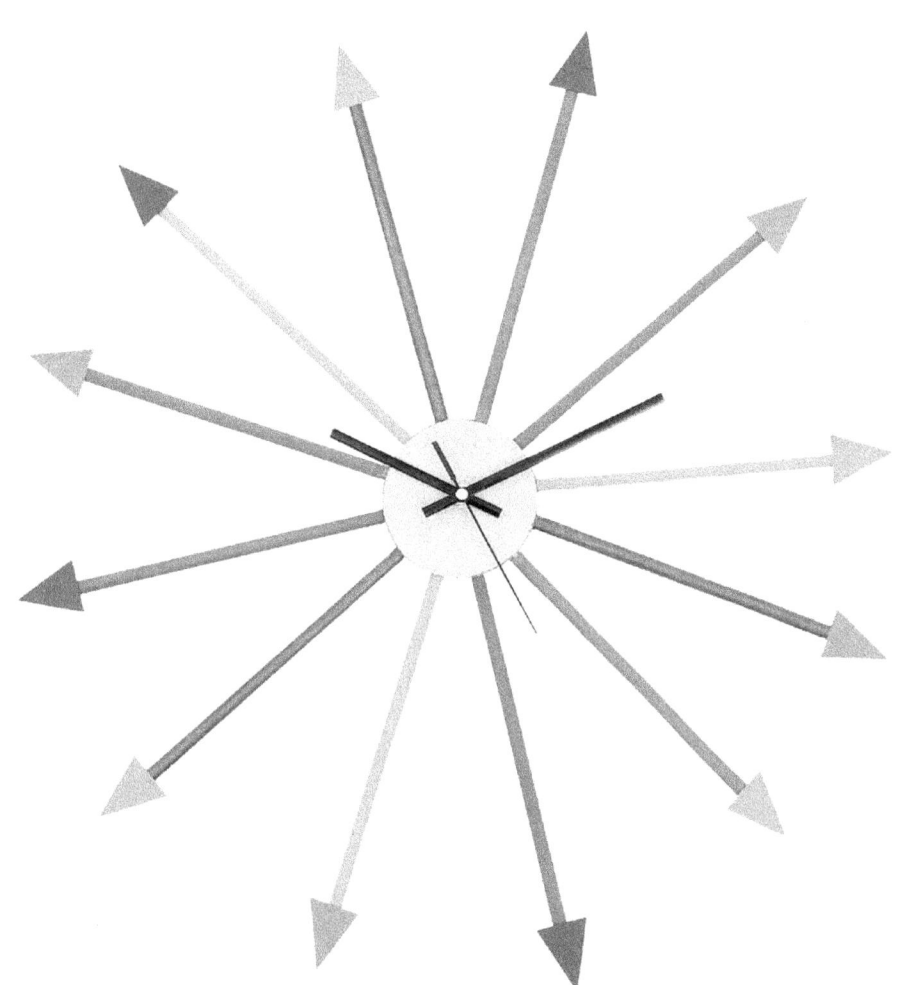

PLASTIC BAG WEAVING

Every household seems to have a drawer or cupboard bursting with plastic bags – they get everywhere! By weaving several bags together, you can make this cute, colourful pencil case.

You will need

Plastic bags

Sticky tape

Cardboard

Scissors

Ruler

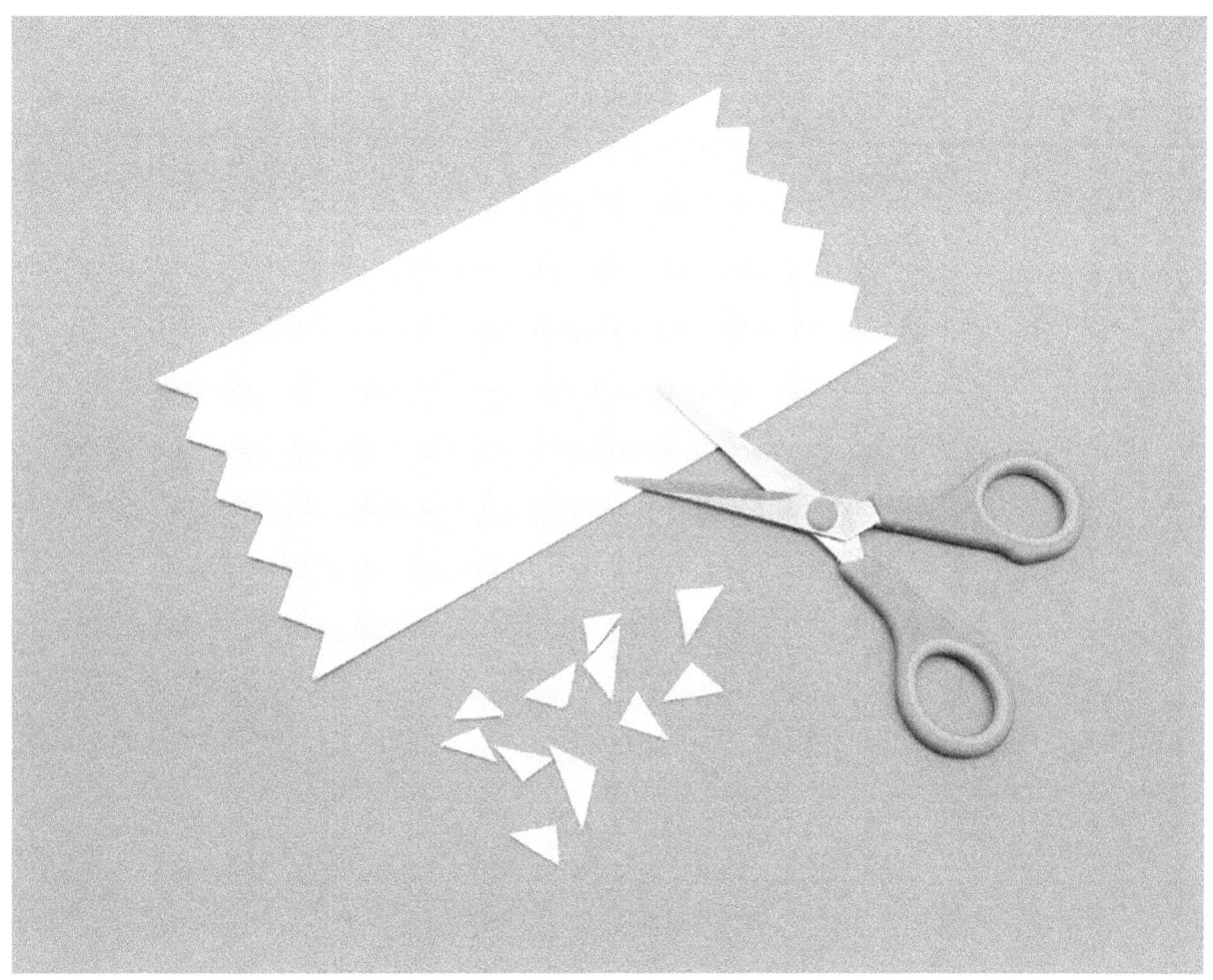

1. Cut a piece of cardboard into a rectangle that measures 10 x 20 cm (4 x 8 in). Snip five small triangles into each of the short sides.

2. Cut the plastic bags into pieces that are 1 cm (0.4 in) wide, so you have strips ready to weave with.

3. Wind strips around the grooves in the card so that you make lines of colour. Fix them in place with sticky tape.

4. Use different coloured strips of plastic bag to weave in and out of the longer pieces. You will end up with a colourful checkerboard effect.

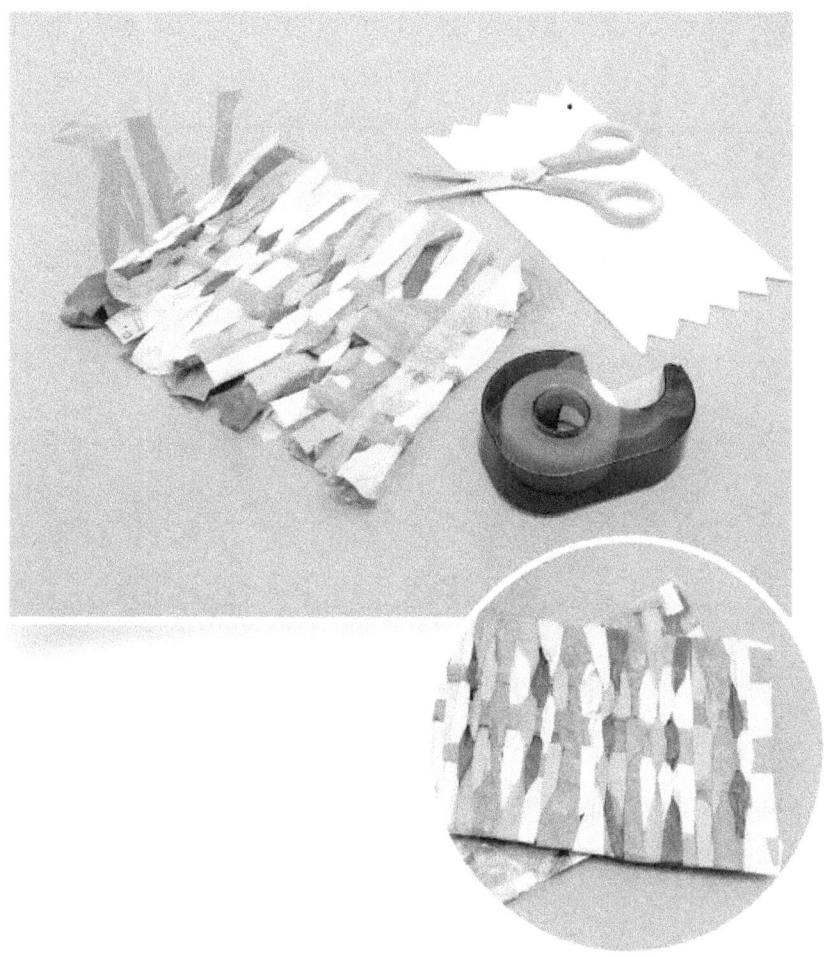

5. Cut the weaving off the board, making sure it doesn't unravel. Fold over the loose edges to make a rectangle and fix it in place with your sticky tape. Repeat steps 2–5 so that you have two woven rectangles. Use more tape to attach the two pieces together on three sides. This will make your handy pencil case.

You could also make a pouch for your mobile phone or music player. Just change the size of the cardboard in step 1 to make the case smaller.

MAKE YOUR OWN TEXTILES CRAFTS

Making textile crafts is much easier than most people think... and it's also lots of fun! Please make sure you ask an adult to help you with your first few projects, and always remember to be careful with pins and needles.

SIMPLE STITCHES

Before you start you might need to learn a few basic stitches!

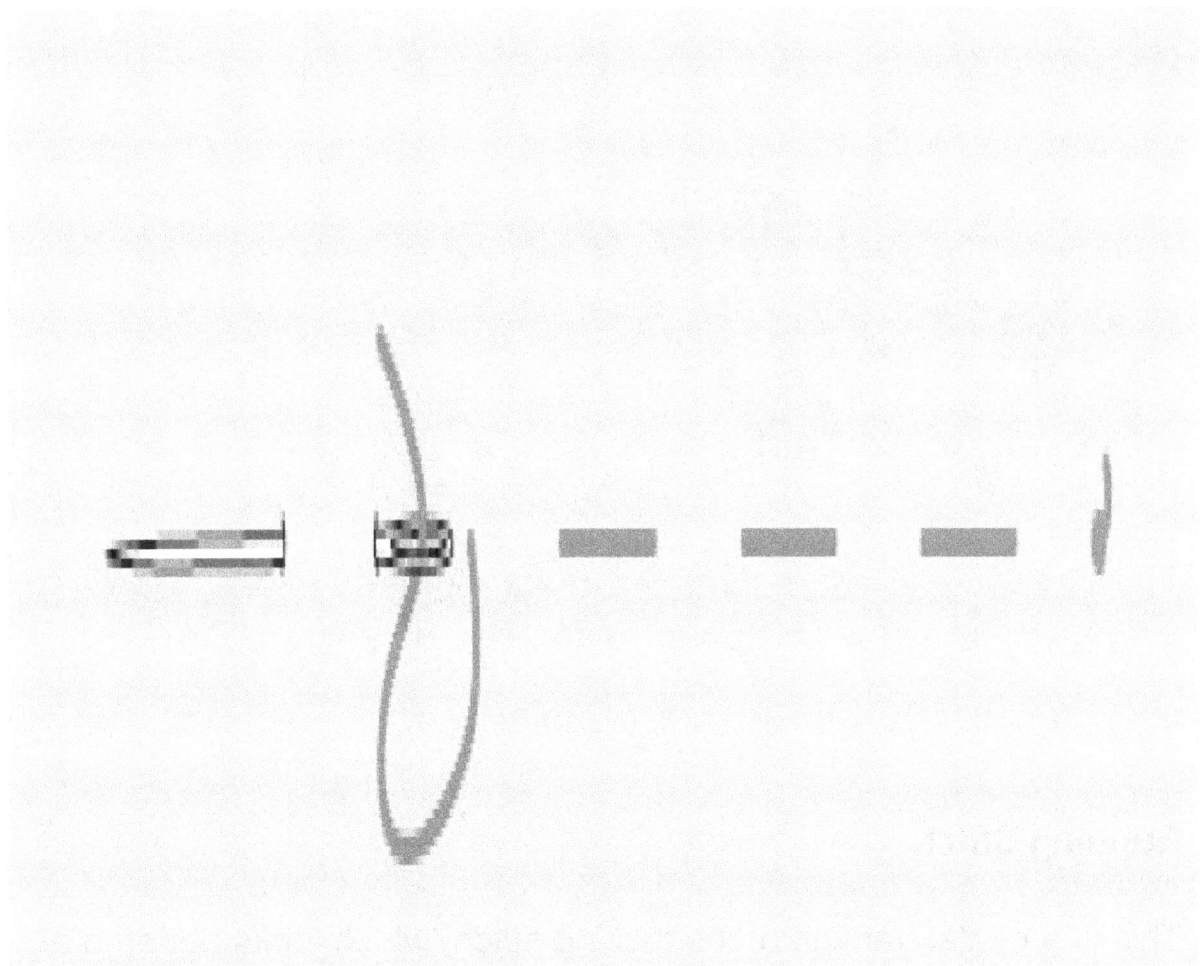

Tacking Stitch

This stitch is used to temporarily hold two pieces of fabric together. It is then removed when you have finished your neat stitches. Make sure you have put a knot in the thread and make long, loose stitches that go in and out of the fabric.

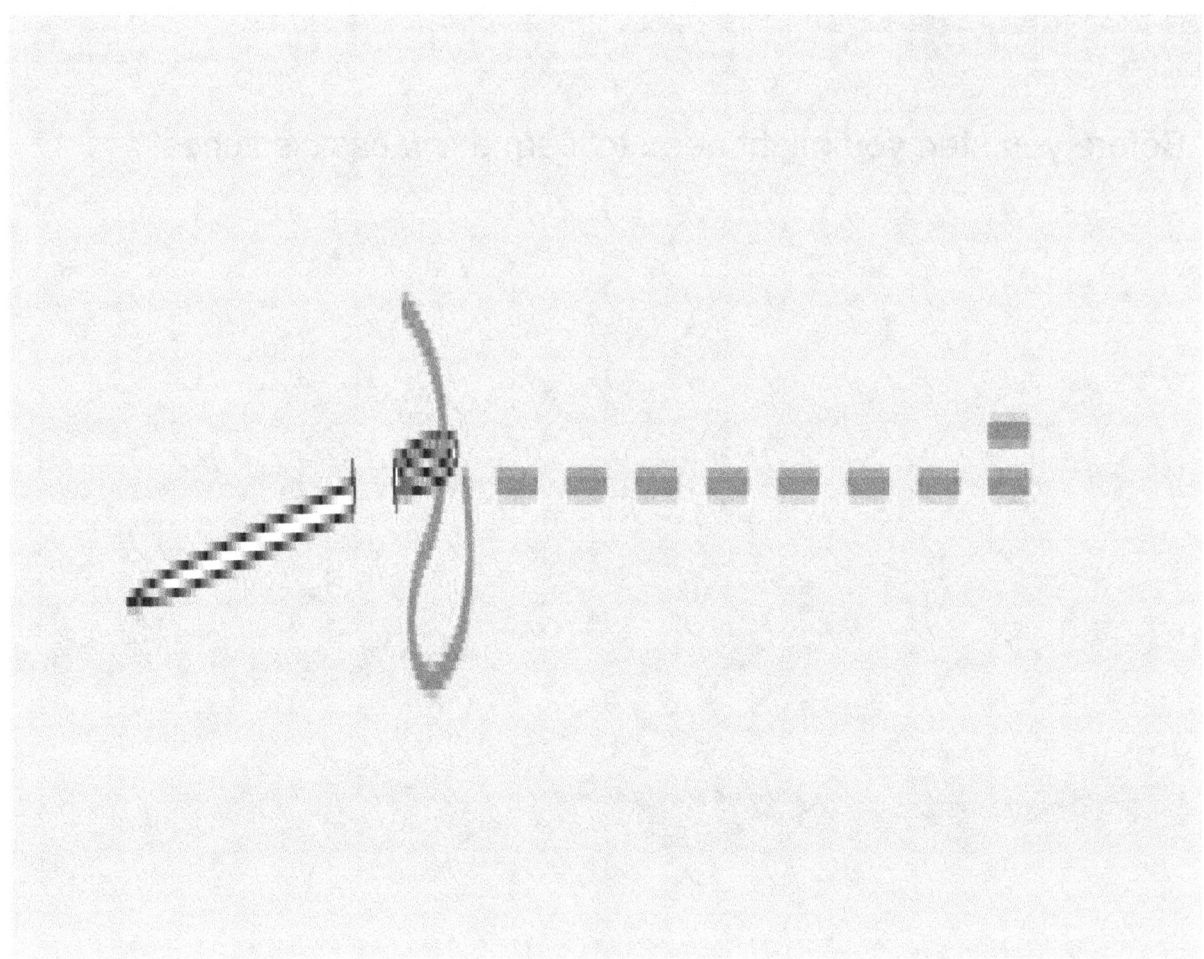

Running Stitch

This is a neater version of the tacking stitch, which looks better in a finished project and can be used for decoration. First tie a knot in your thread (you should do this for all permanent stitches), then sew two small stitches on top of each other. Push the needle in and out of the fabric, making sure that each stitch and the gap between the stitches are the same length. To finish, tie a knot in the thread at the back of the fabric before you cut off the unused part of the thread with scissors.

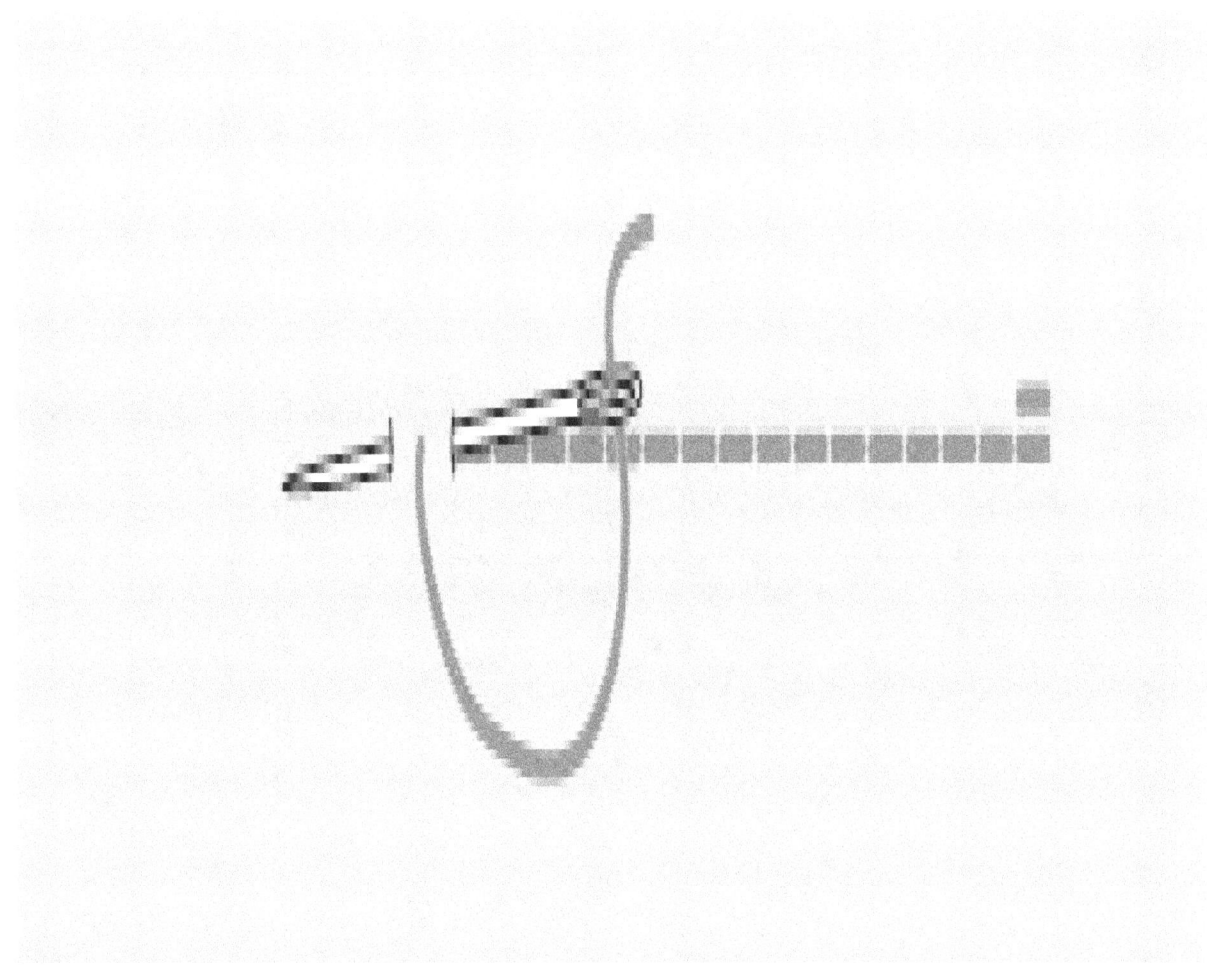

Back Stitch

Back stitch is similar to running stitch but without the gaps. Make your first stitch in the same way as you would with a running stitch. Then push the needle up through the fabric, but instead of moving it forwards to make the next stitch, push it back through the hole you made with the previous stitch and back up again in front of the stitch. Repeat this all along the fabric.

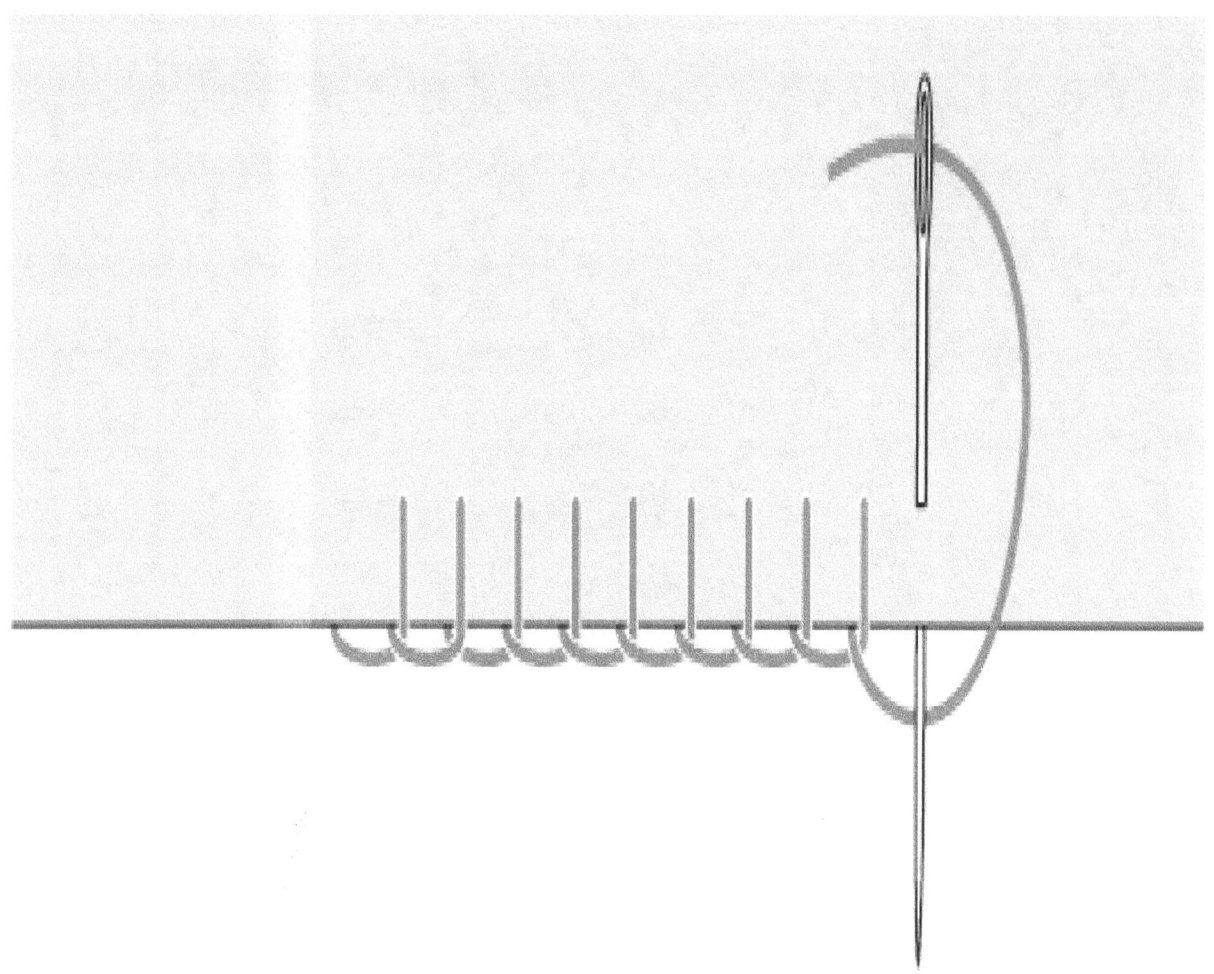

Blanket Stitch and Whip Stitch

These are used to attach two pieces of fabric together. A whip stitch is very simple – you just loop the thread around and around in a spiral, passing it through the fabric. A blanket stitch (shown left) is a little more advanced. Pass the needle up through the fabric, making sure that it is at least 1 cm (0.4 in) from the edge. Then pass the needle through the back of the fabric again 1 cm (0.4 in) along and and start to pull the needle and thread through the fabric. Stop when you have made a small loop and pass the needle through the loop you have just made.

TEXTILE TOOLKIT

Needle and Thread

These are essential items. You will need a sharp needle with a large enough eye for you to pass thread through. Ask an adult to help you the first time you use a needle, so that you don't prick yourself.

Felt and Fabric

The important difference between felt and fabric is that fabric frays and felt does not. Most of the time, you will want to avoid leaving a raw (unstitched) fabric edge, because if you do this your project will not last as long. Felt is easy to cut and you can either stick it together with fabric glue or sew it together with a needle and thread.

CUTE SOCK OWLS

Where do all those missing socks disappear to? You can make use of odd socks by turning them into lovable owls.

You will need

Socks

Cushion stuffing

Felt

Needle and thread

Buttons Scissors

Fabric glue

1. Choose a colourful sock and pack it with cushion stuffing until it is half full.

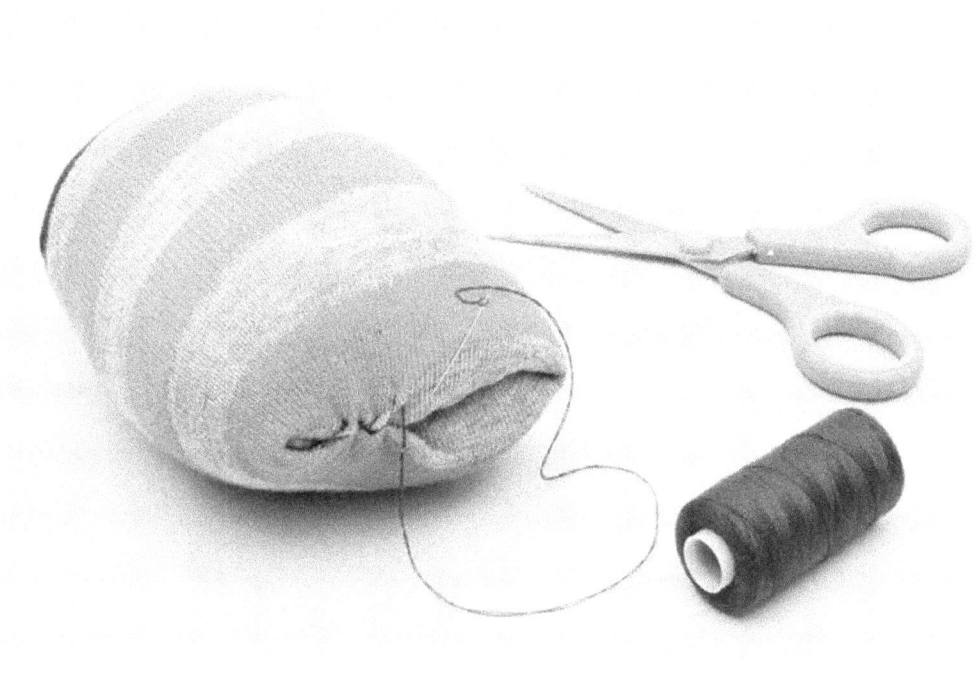

2. Tuck in the spare part of the sock and sew a few whip stitches to hold it in place. Tie a knot and snip off the loose end of the thread.

3. Using scissors, cut these shapes from felt: a large triangle for the face, two small triangles for the beak, two wings, two circles for eyes, two feet and two feather shapes.

4. Sew all the felt shapes – except the beak – to your sock with your needle and thread, using a whip stitch.

5. Sew on the two small triangles to form the beak. Only sew on the short end of each triangle, so that the beak stands out from the face.

6. Use fabric glue for the eyes. Glue a small button (the pupil) on top of a medium-sized button (the eye). Pinch the top of the owl together and sew together to make the ears.

ROCK STAR RAG DOLL

This punk rock rag doll may be made from scrap material, but he's got some real rock star attitude! You could try making a doll that looks like a cute mini-version of a real-life performer.

You will need

Felt

Brightly coloured fabric (use old bit of clothes or scraps from other projects)

Cushion stuffing

Coloured wool

Needle and thread

Scissors

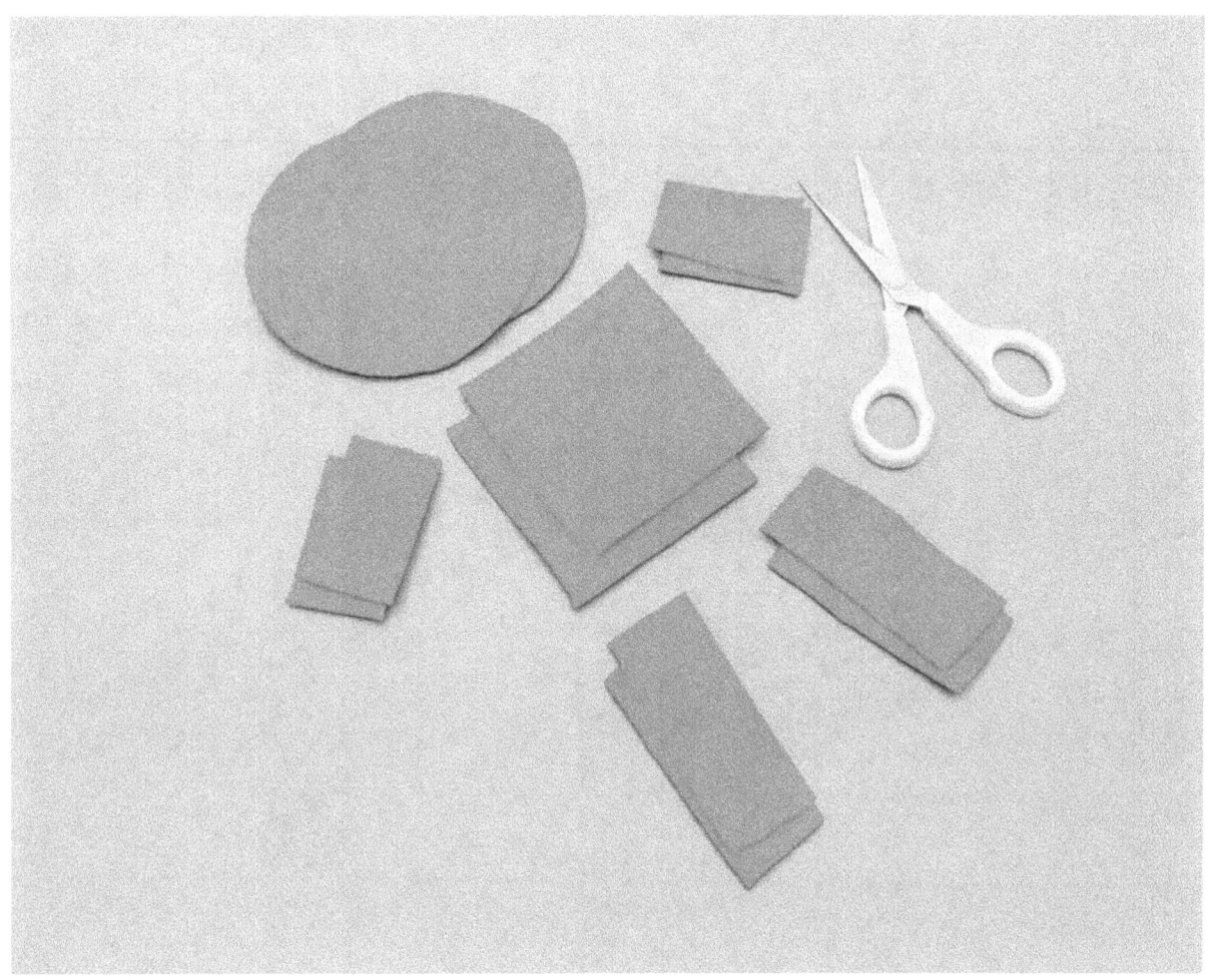

1. Cut out two circles, two squares, four long rectangles and four short rectangles from your scrap fabric.

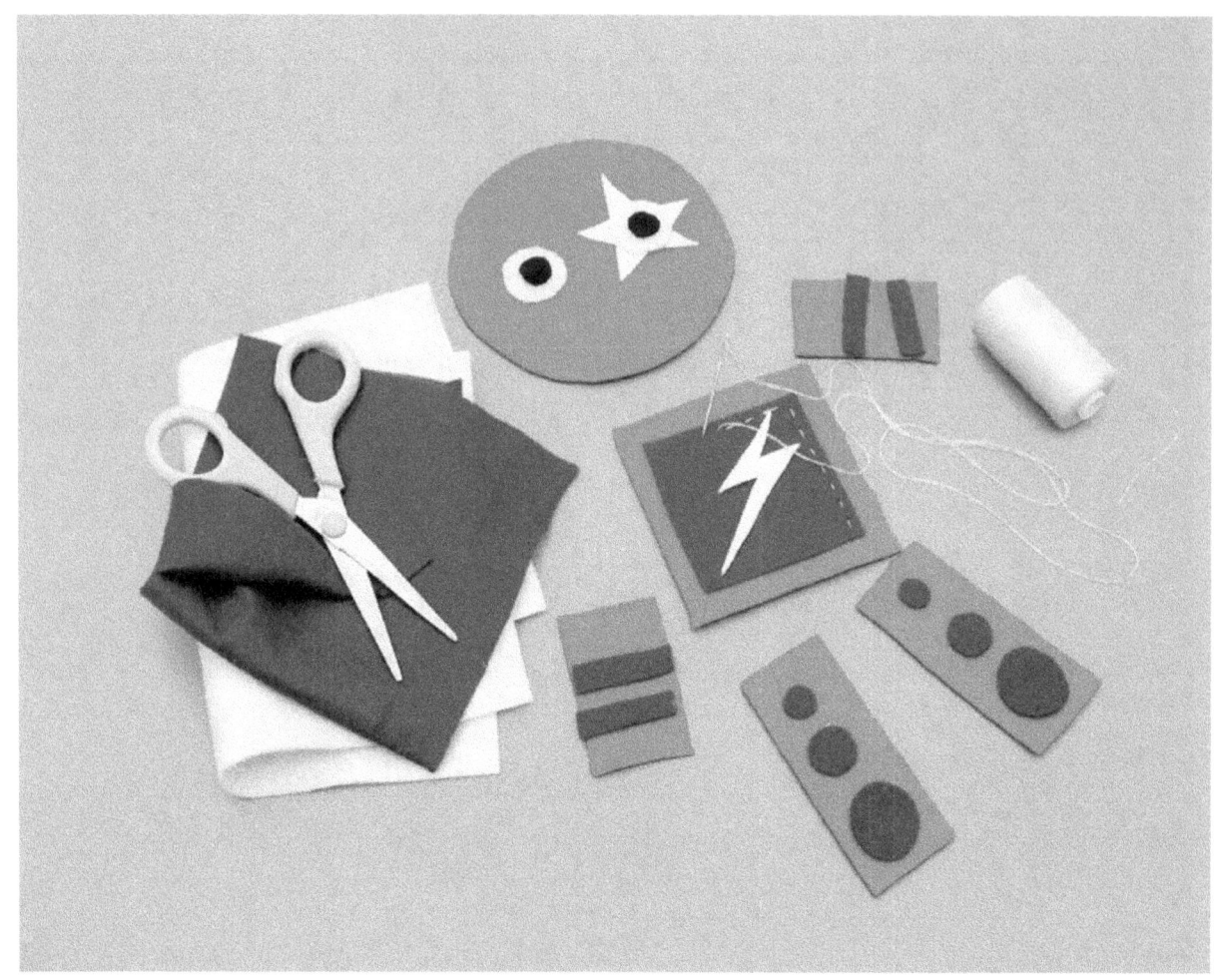

2. Now cut shapes out of felt to make details such as eyes and patterns on the clothing. Sew them on with a running stitch. You may want to use a brightly coloured thread.

3. Use a whip stitch to sew matching pairs of shapes together to make the head, body, arms and legs. Make sure that the right sides of the fabric are facing outwards. Leave a 5-cm (2-in) gap along one edge of each of your pairs. Stuff each of your body parts with cushion stuffing, then sew up the gap.

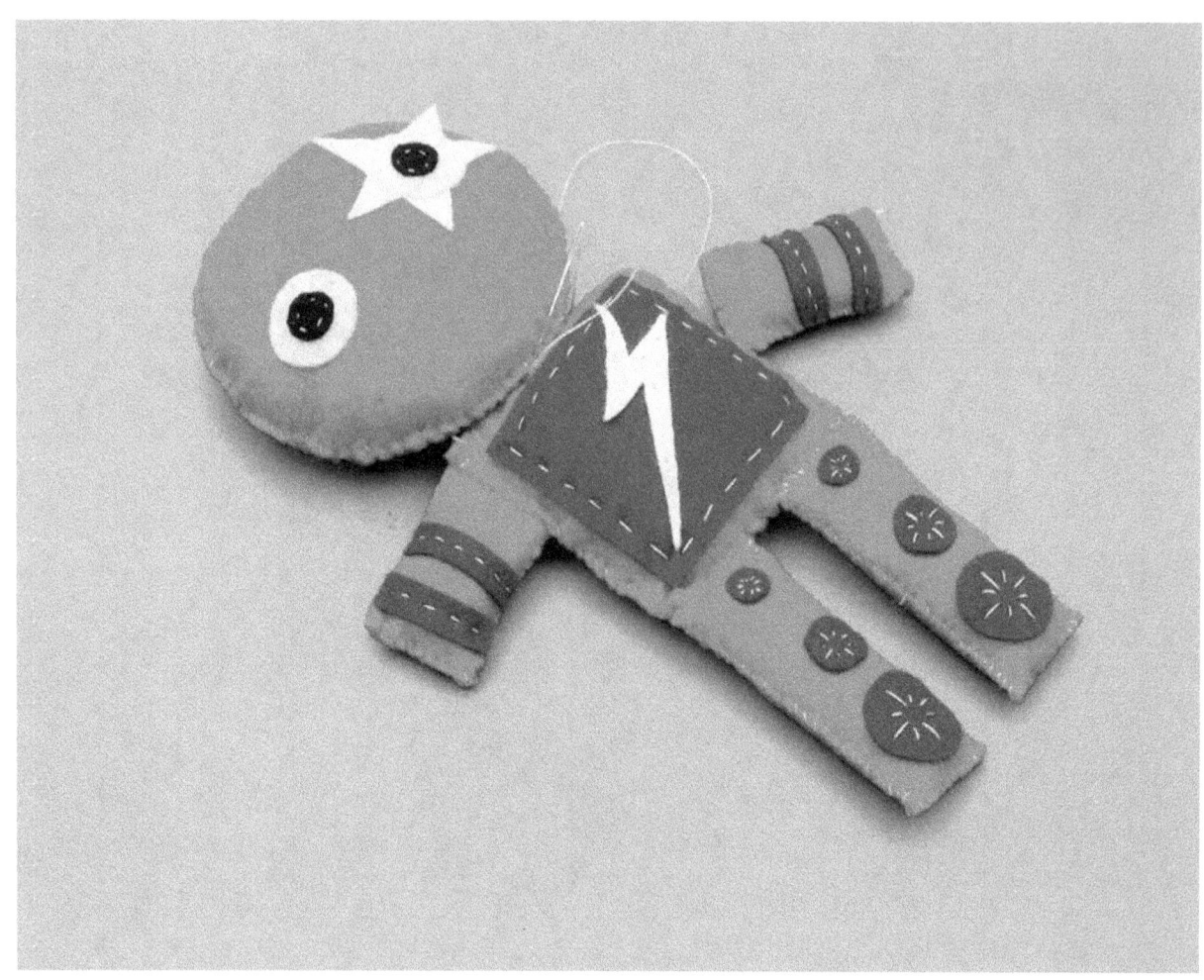

4. Use a whip stitch again to sew all the pieces together to make the body.

5. Cut a handful of wool to the same length and tie the pieces together in the middle. Sew them onto the head of your doll.

TOADSTOOL DOORSTOP

This bean bag creation will prop your door open... and add a little fun to your room. A toadstool doorstop, complete with fluttering butterfly, also makes a great gift!

You will need:

Red, white and green cotton fabric

Needle and thread

Sturdy corduroy

Large buttons

Dried chickpeas

Sturdy scissors

Tape measure

Pins

Felt

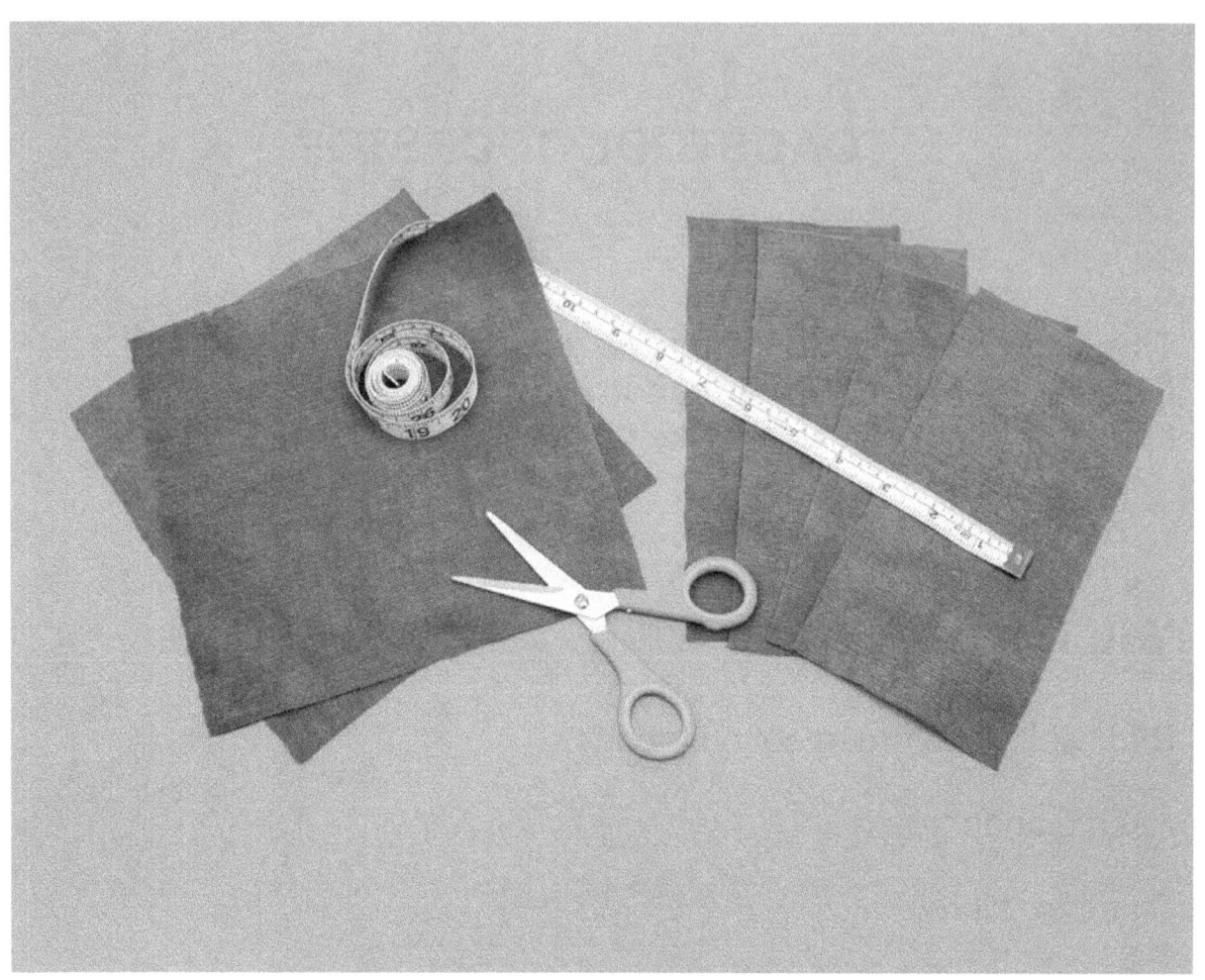

1. Cut two squares of corduroy fabric measuring 20 x 20 cm (8 x 8 in), and four rectangles measuring 10 x 20 cm (4 x 8 in). Use a sturdy pair of scissors for this.

2. Cut out a semicircle of red cotton fabric, a rectangle of white cotton and a zigzag shape from the green fabric for the grass. You don't need to measure the pieces, but they must fit on a corduroy square.

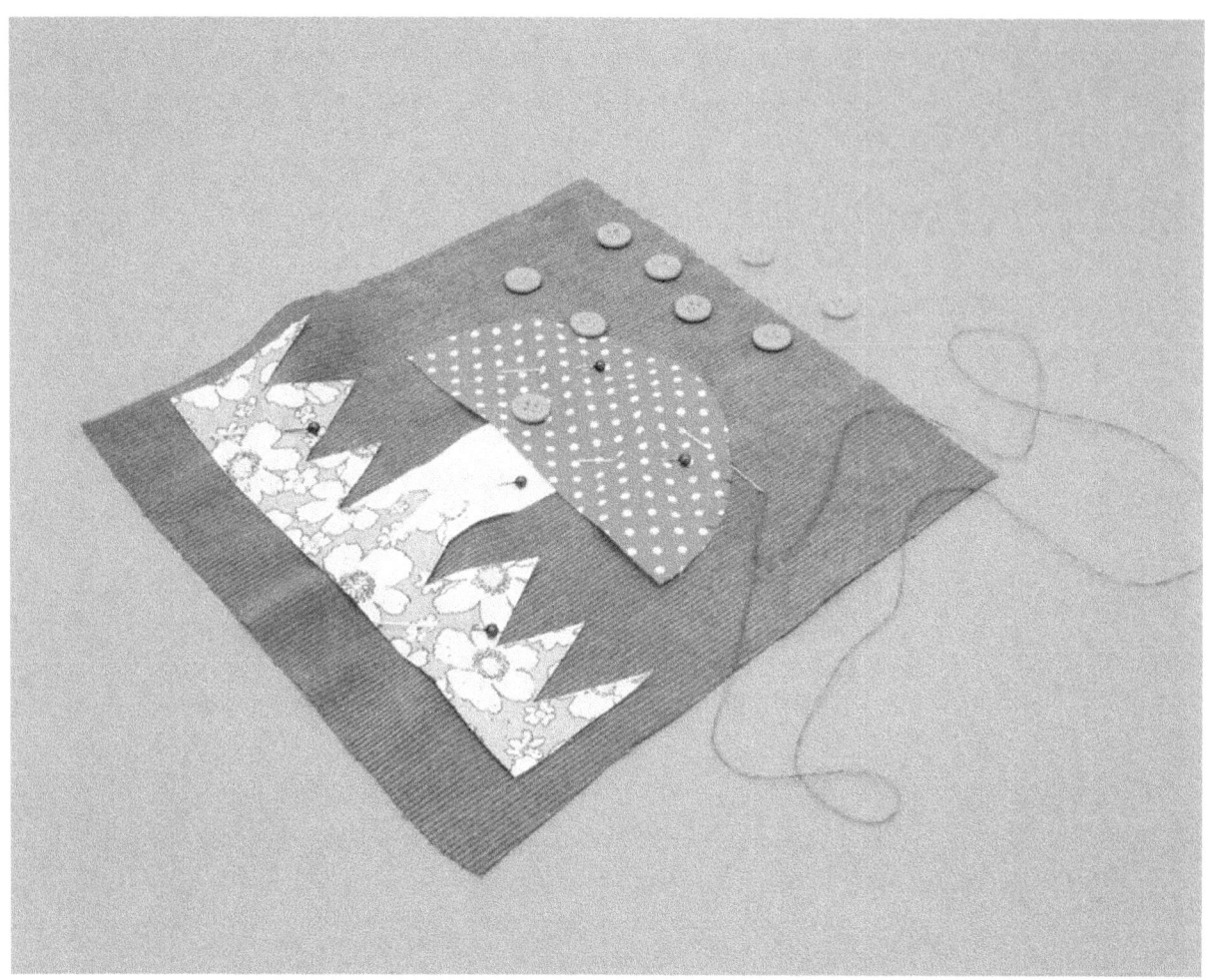

3. Use pins to fix the shapes in place on one of the corduroy squares. Then sew them on using a running or whip stitch. Sew on some large buttons for the toadstool's spots.

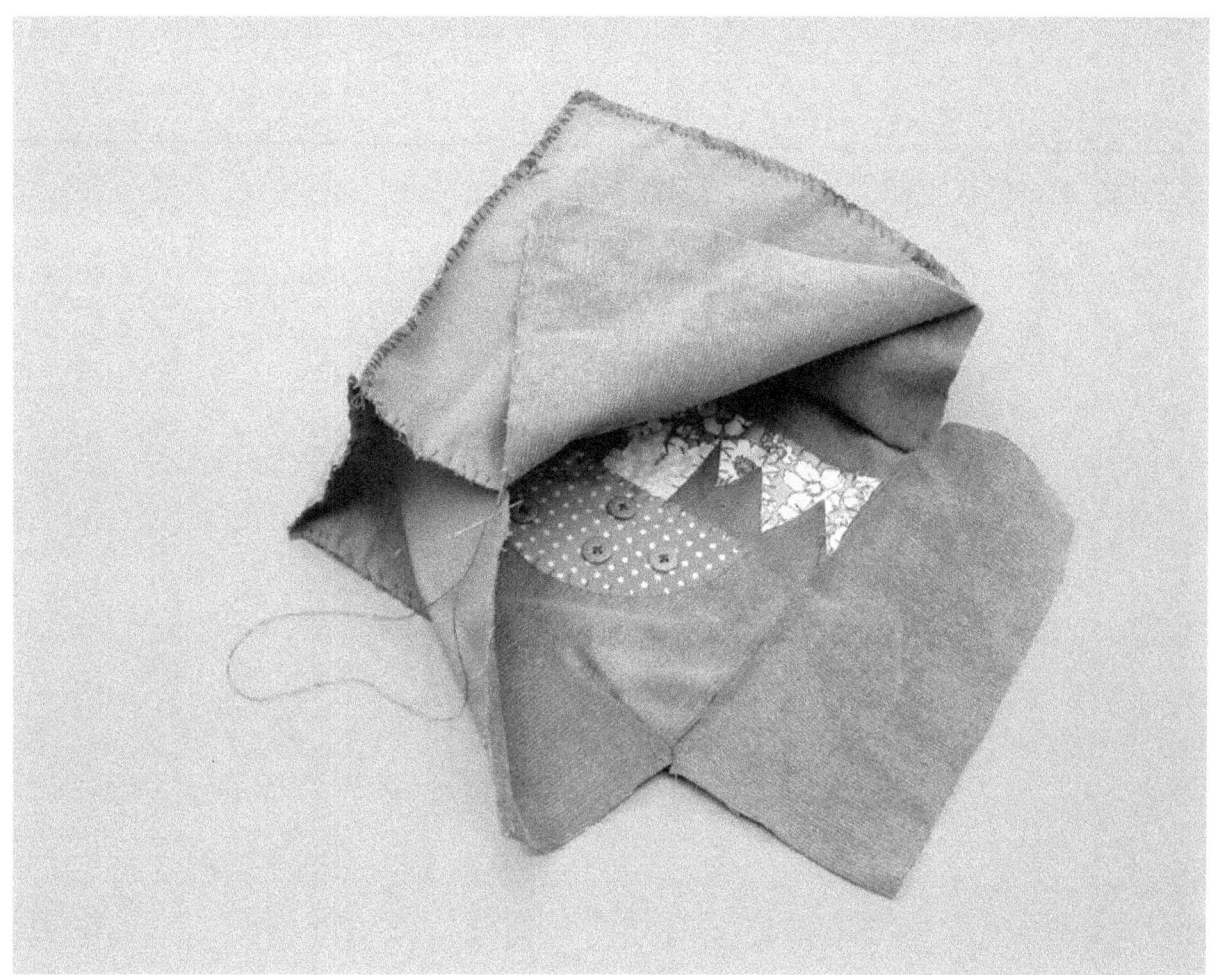

4. Sew the corduroy pieces together to make a box shape. It must be stitched together inside out, with the square sides facing each other. Remember to leave a 5-cm (2-in) gap in the stitching along one side.

5. Turn the doorstop right-side out and fill it with dried chickpeas. Sew up the gap in the stitching to keep all the filling in place. Cut a butterfly shape from felt and sew it onto the corner of the doorstop.

TOTALLY BRILLIANT TOTE

Appliqué is the craft of sewing decorations onto material. It can make something ordinary look unique and original. Decorate a canvas tote using this technique and you will really stand out from the crowd!

You will need:

Plain canvas bag

Fabric in several different colours

Needle and thread

Ribbon

Pins

Pen and paper

Scissors

Felt

1. Draw a tortoise shape onto a piece of paper using a marker pen, then cut it out with scissors. This is your template.

2. Pin your paper template onto your fabric and cut it out. Repeat this four more times using material of different colours.

3. Sew four fabric shapes onto the bottom of the bag using a needle and thread. A whip stitch will work nicely. Space them out as evenly as possible.

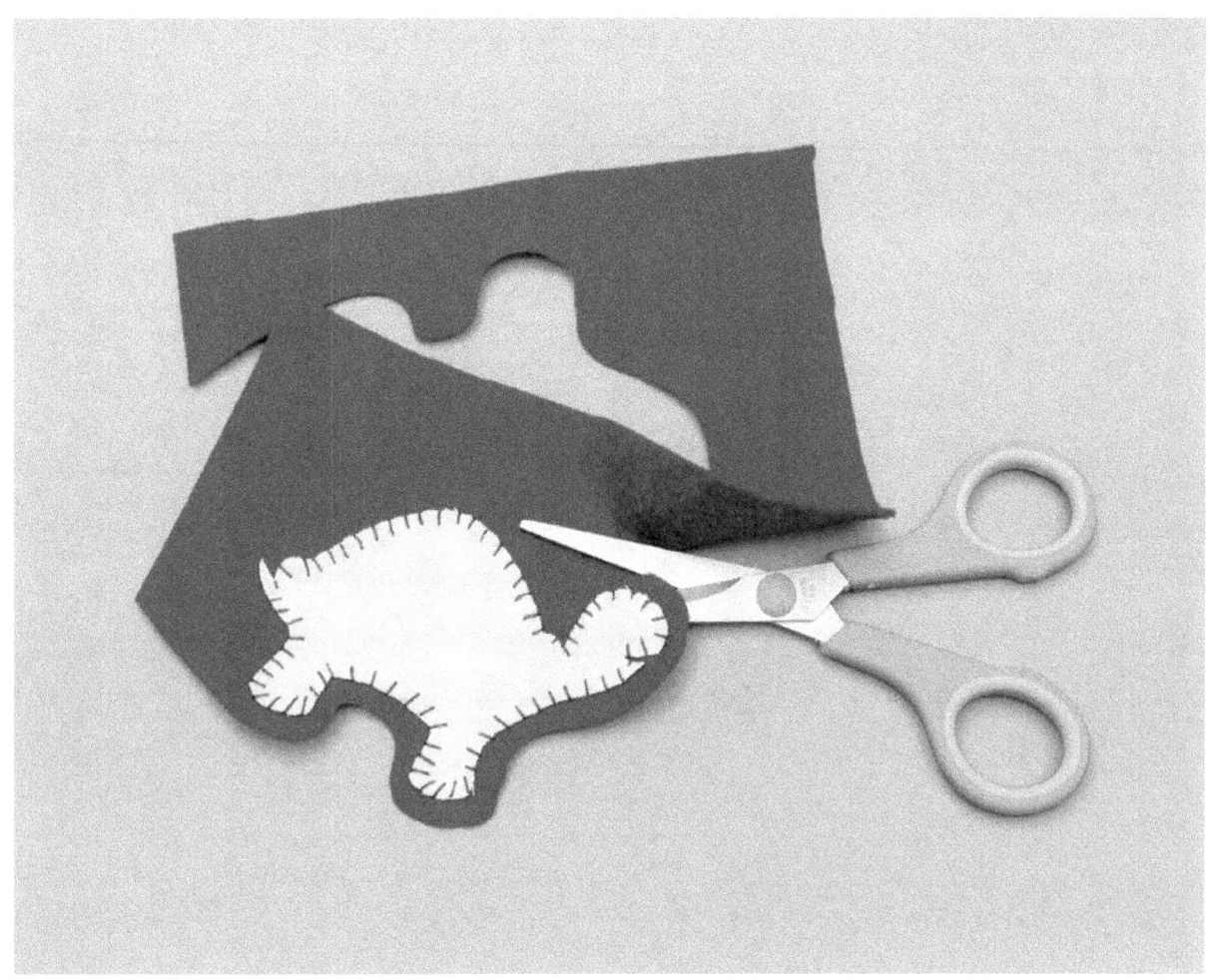

4. Sew the last fabric shape onto a piece of felt, again using a whip stitch. Cut around it, leaving a 1-cm (0.4-in) border of felt.

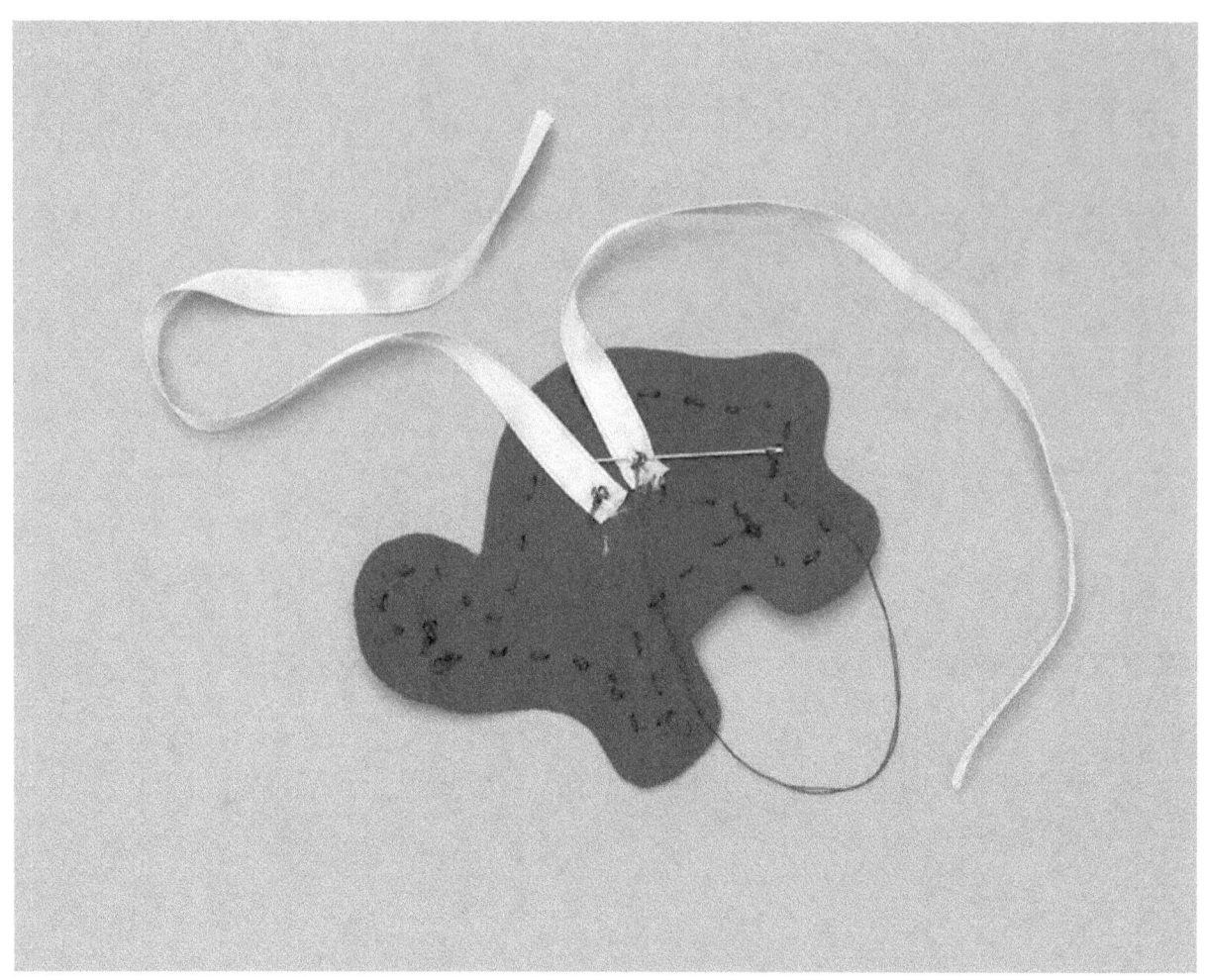

5. Sew two lengths of ribbon to the back of the felt shape. Tie it onto the handle of your canvas bag.

JEAN GENIUS DESK MASCOT

This super-smart mascot will cheer you on when you are studying or taking exams. He won't tell you the answers, though! He is made from an old pair of jeans.

You will need:

Denim from old jeans

Felt

Cushion filling

Pins

Needle and thread

Fabric glue

Wool

Scissors

Tape measure

1. Cut out two 15 x 15-cm (6 x 6-in) squares of denim, using scissors. Pin them together with the darker side facing inwards.

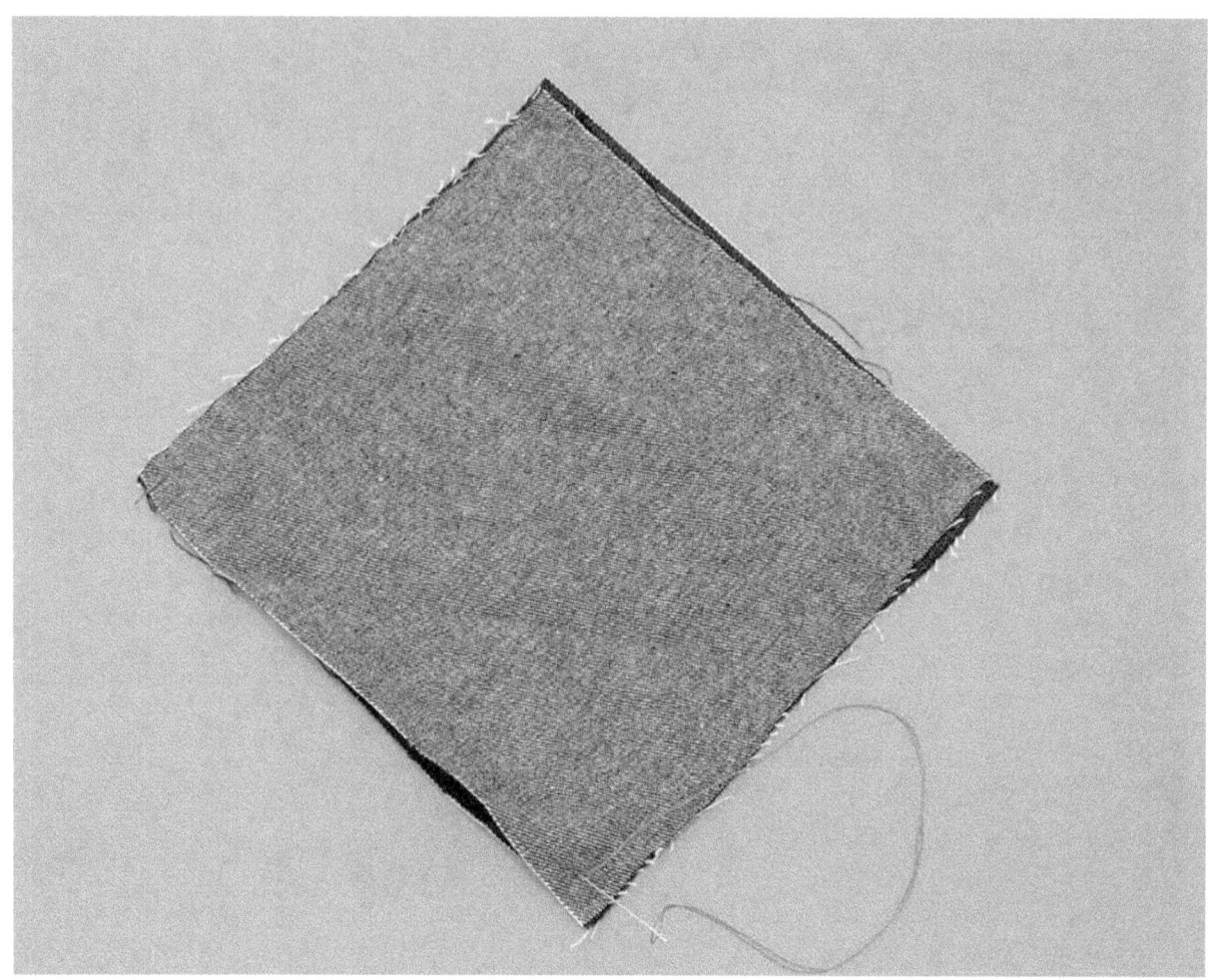

2. Sew three of the sides together using your needle and thread.

3. Turn the fabric right-side out. Fill it with cushion filling. Pinch the middle of the unstitched sides together to make a triangle. Sew along the edge with a running stitch.

4. Cut out different felt decorations for your mascot. You will need eyes, a mouth, a nose, glasses and a bow tie. Stick these to your mascot with fabric glue.

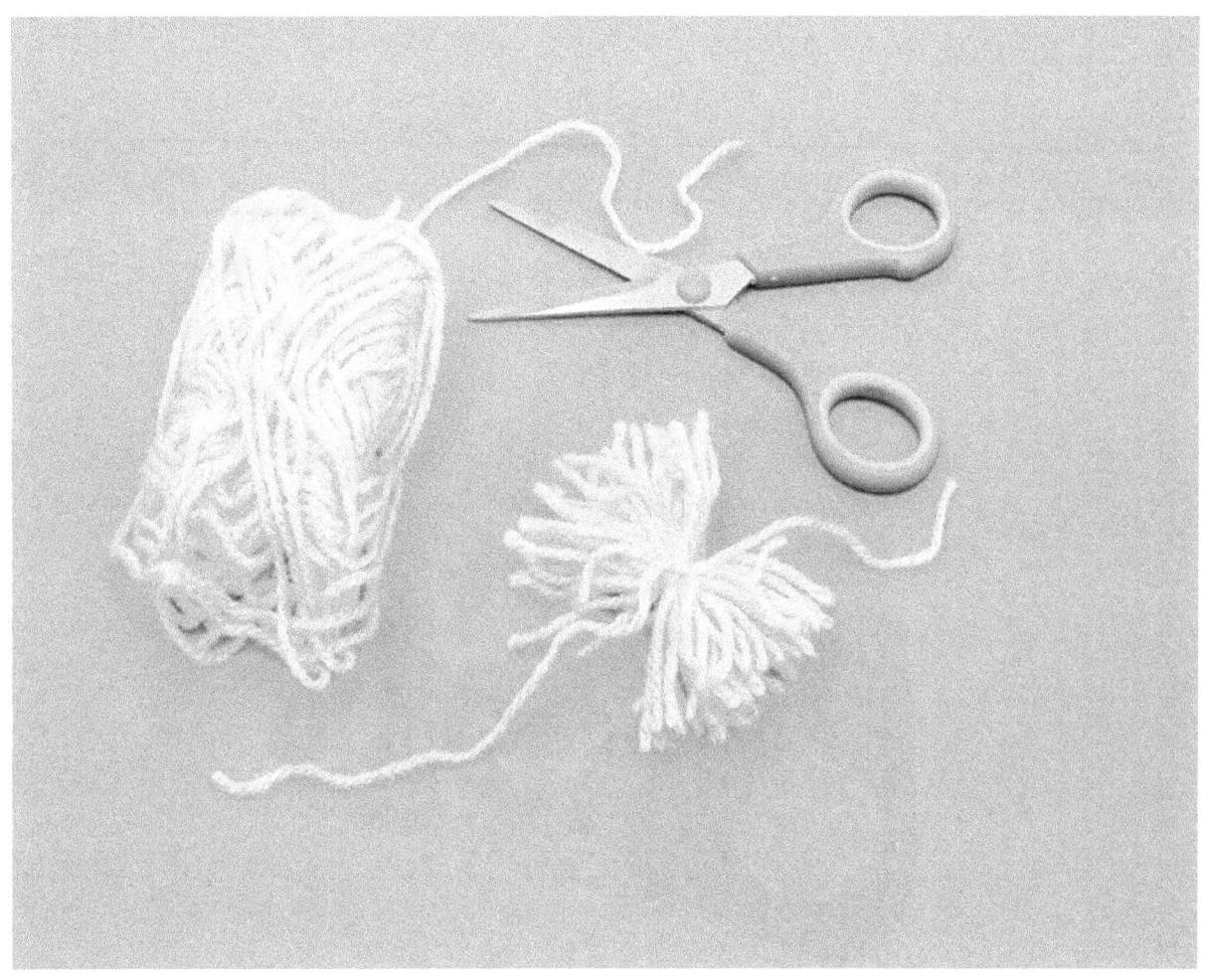

5. Cut a handful of wool to the same length, and tie it in the middle. Then stitch it onto the top of the mascot, for hair!

SECRET DIARY COVER

Make a customised cover for your most treasured book. It will look extra special, and the cover will also help protect it.

You will need:

Felt

Buttons

Ribbon

Fabric glue

Needle and thread

Hardback book

Tape measure

Scissors

Sequins

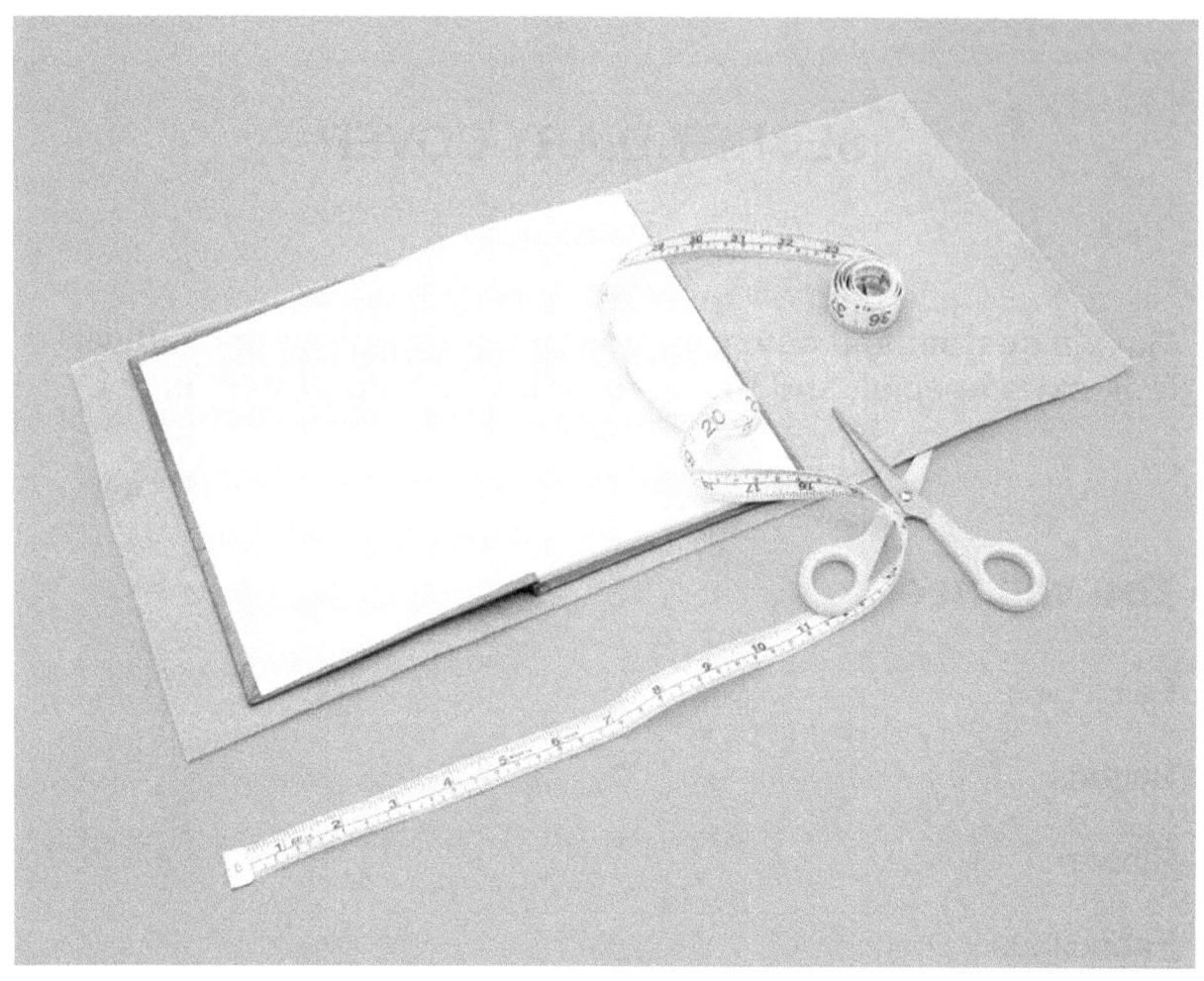

1. Open up your book and measure it. Cut a piece of felt 1 cm (0.4 in) taller and 6 cm (2.4 in) wider than the open book.

2. Cut out some felt shapes. You will need some orange strips, a pink circle, a yellow triangle, a blue wave, a brown rectangle and a red blobby shape (look at the picture!). Sew them in place with a running stitch.

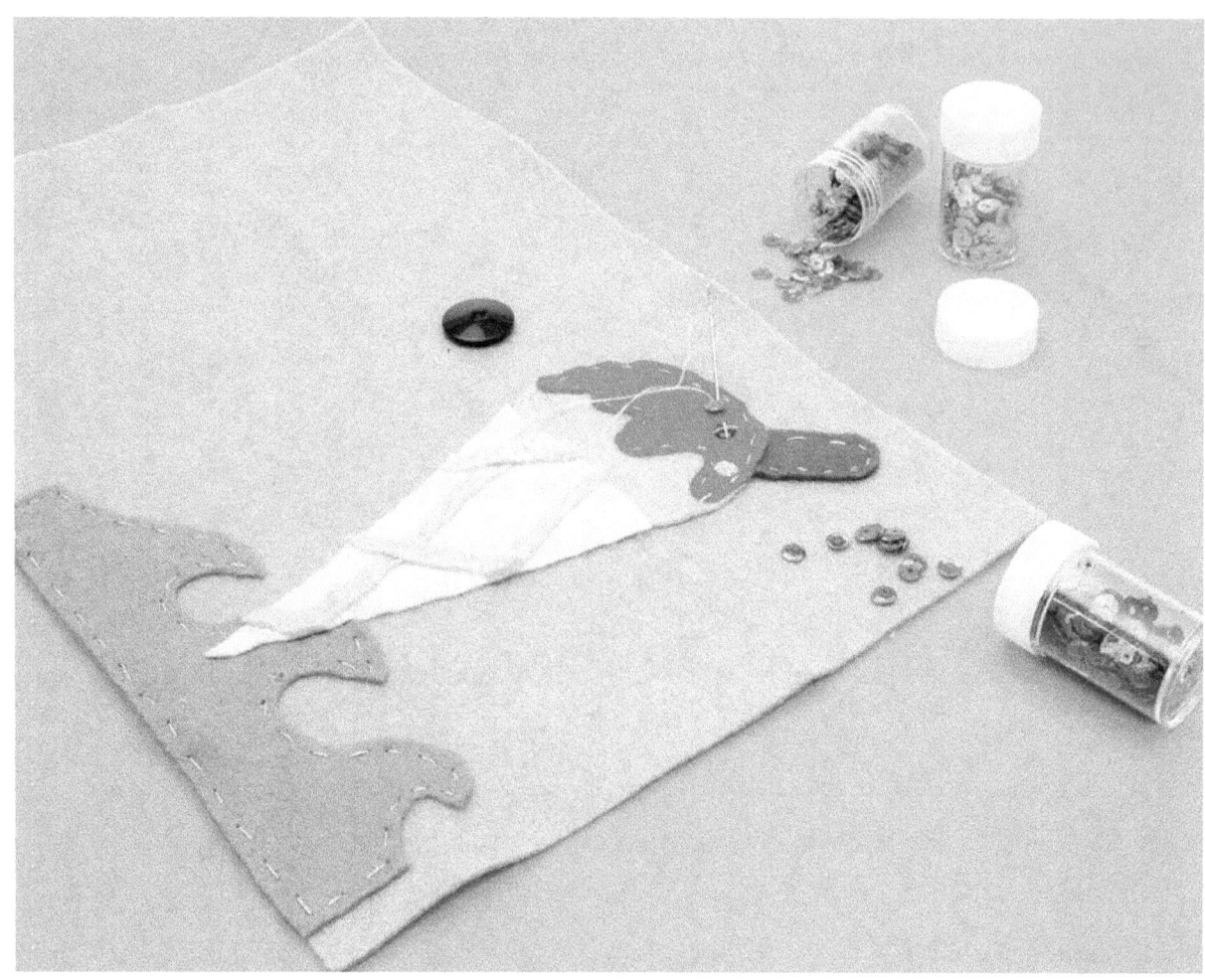

3. Sew on some sequins. Stitch a button about 6 cm (2.4 in) from the right-hand edge.

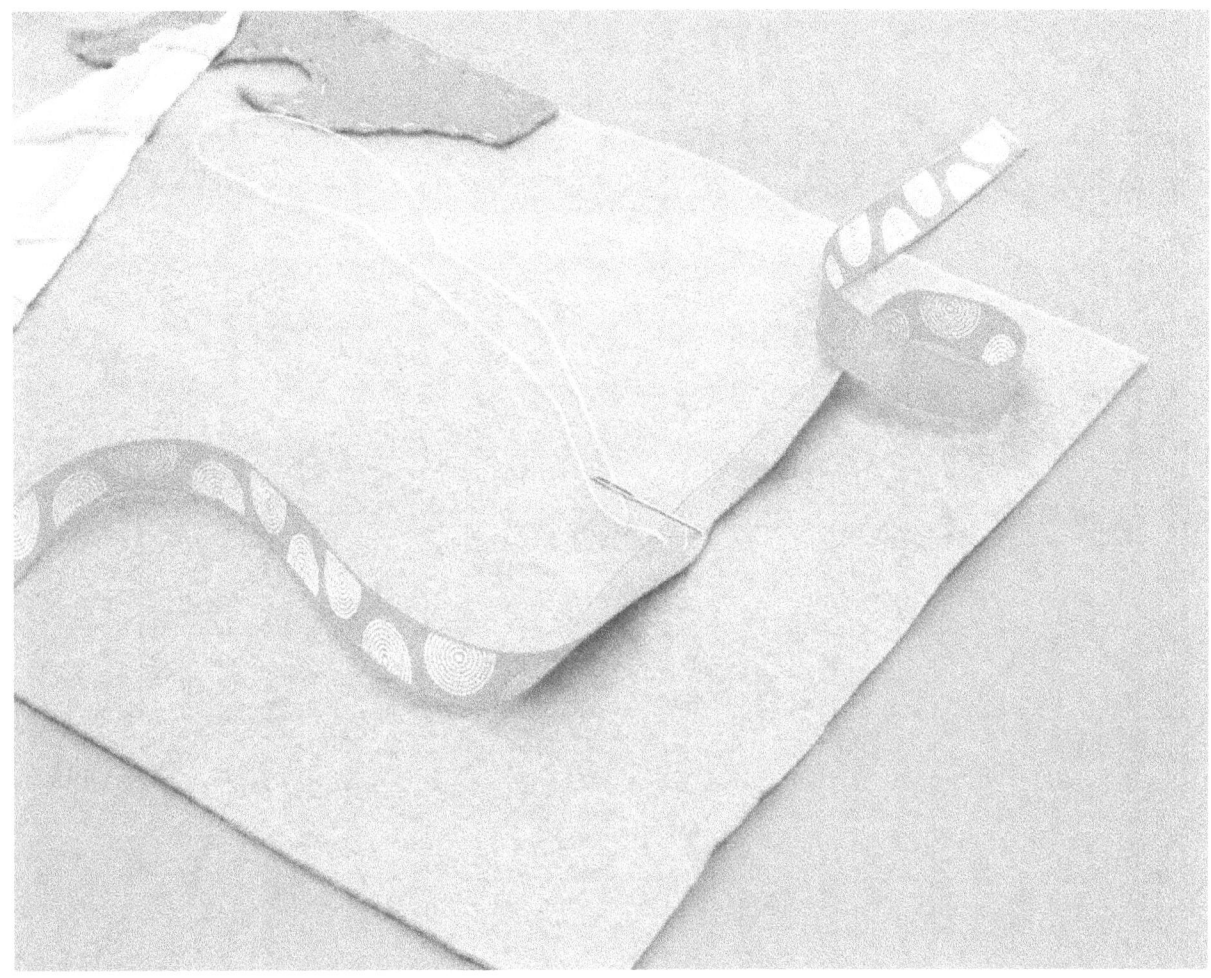

4. Cut a 20-cm (8-in) length of ribbon. Stitch it to the middle of the opposite side of the cover from the button, about 6 cm (2.4 in) from the edge. Attach it at the middle of the ribbon.

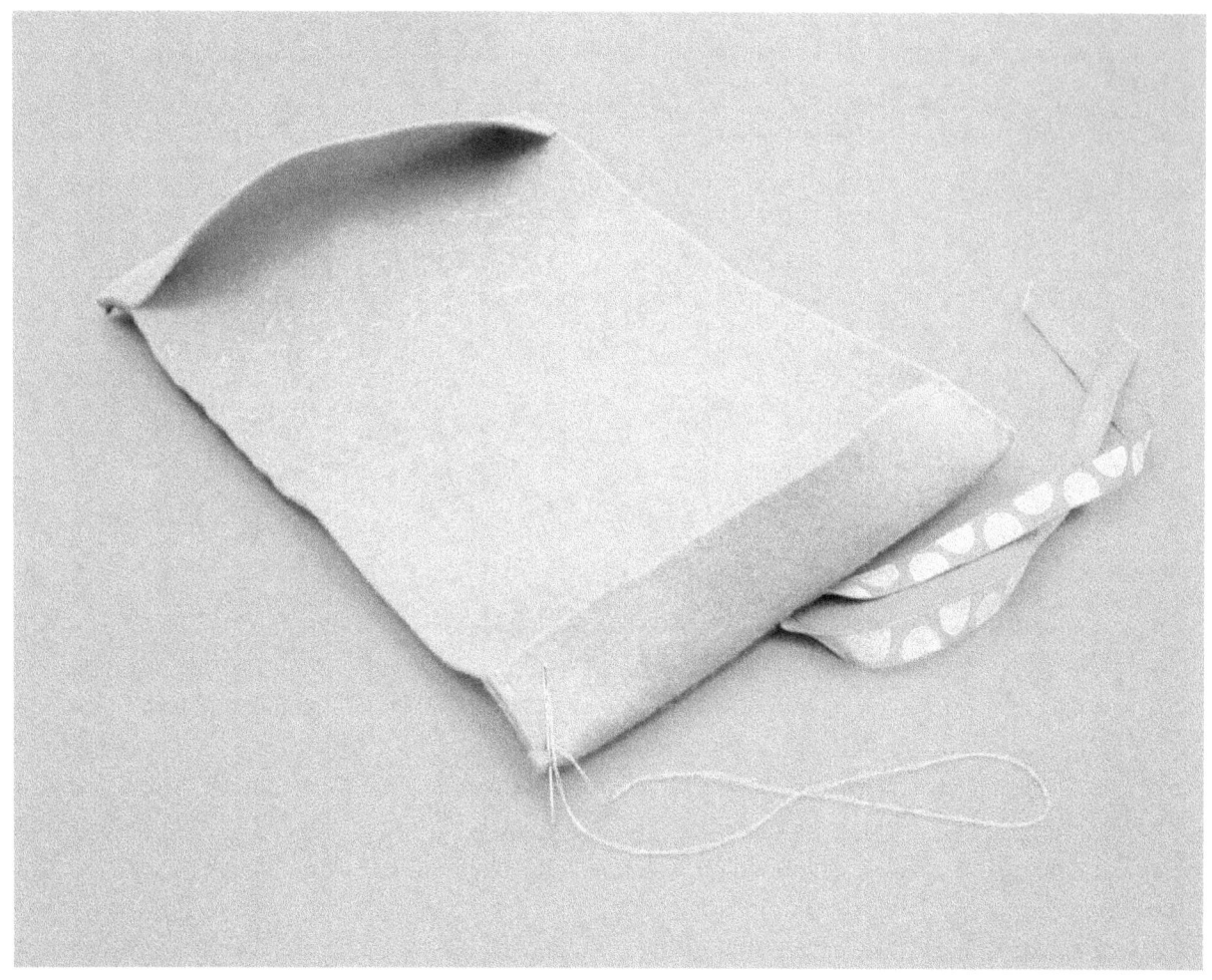

5. Fold over 3 cm (1 in) of each side. Sew a running stitch at the top and bottom of the folds.

6. Slip the book inside the cover. Tie the ribbon to secure the book.

MINI BAG ORGANISER

These little storage bags are very handy, and they will look great hanging on your bedroom wall. Now you will always know where your stuff is!

You will need:

Cotton fabric

Ribbon

Cardboard

Pegs

Fabric glue

Needle and thread

Scissors

Tape measure

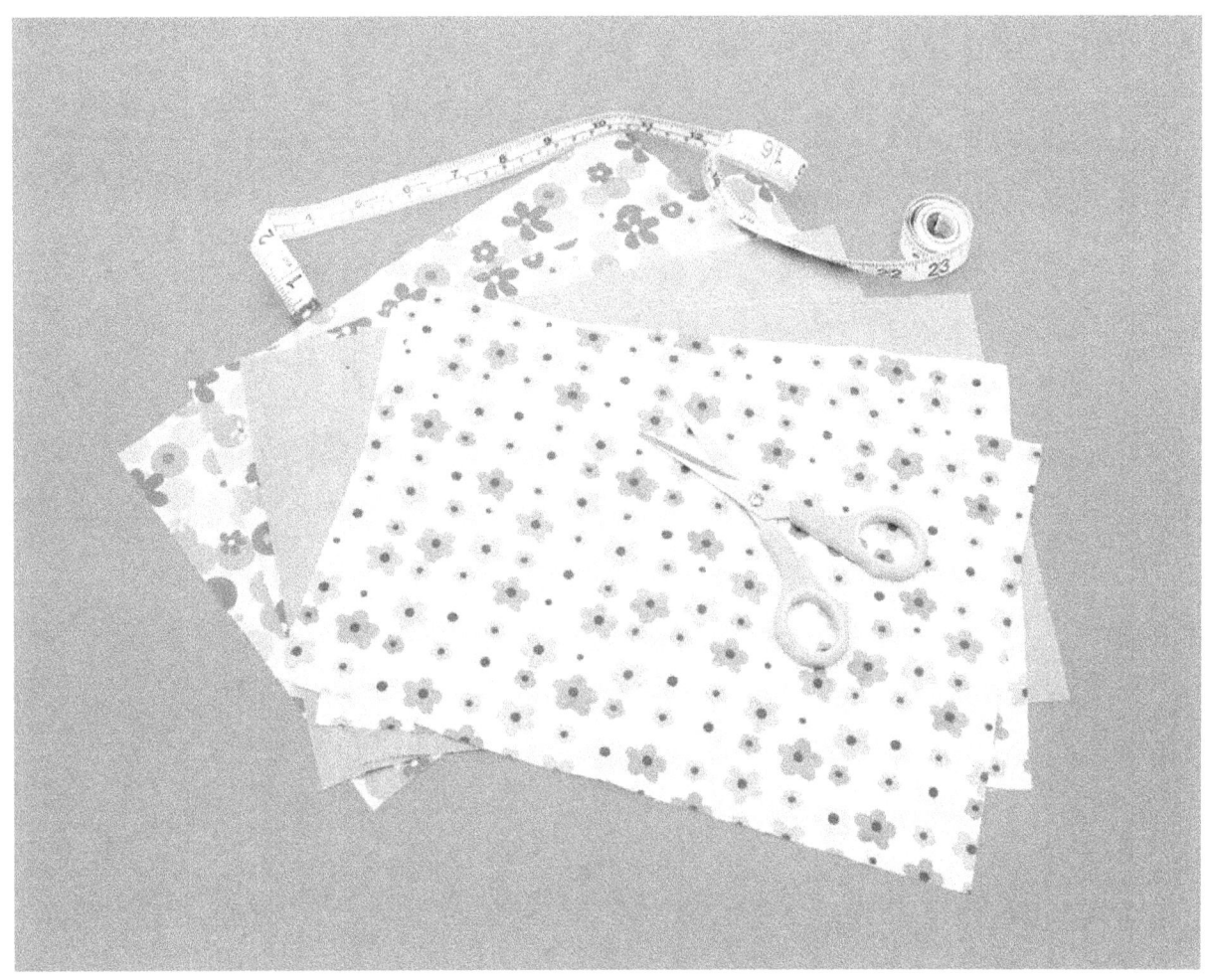

1. Cut six fabric rectangles measuring 20 x 30 cm (8 x 12 in).

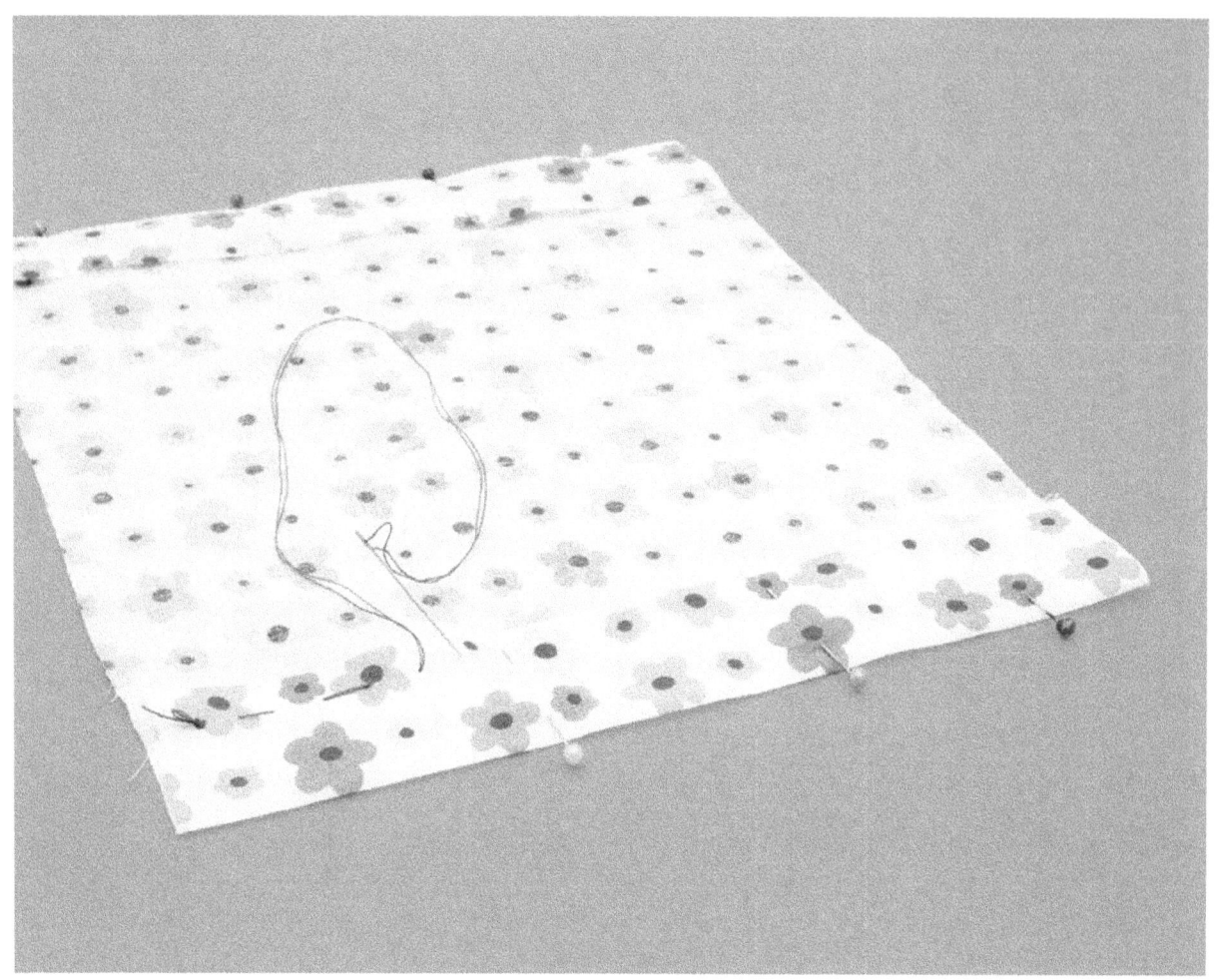

2. Fold the short sides of each rectangle over by 3 cm (1 in). Sew the folded edges in place with a back stitch.

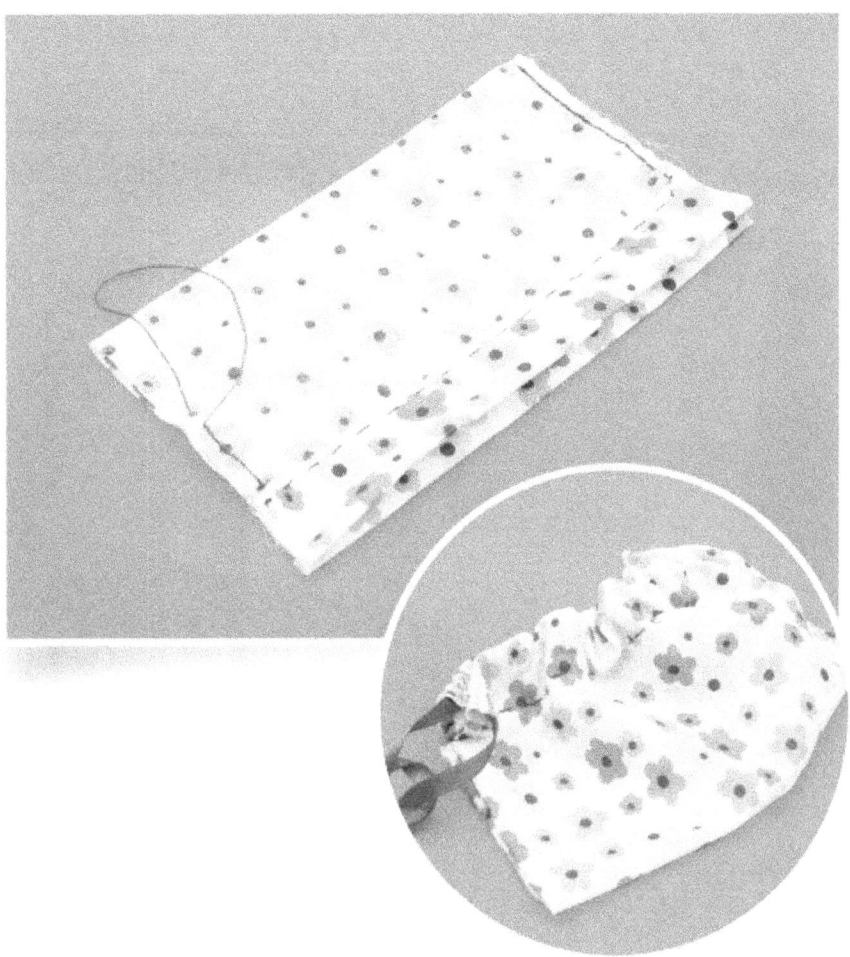

3. Fold each rectangle in half, with the outside of the cloth facing in. Sew up the two sides with a back stitch. Snip a 'V' shape on either side and pass your drawstring ribbon through the holes. Repeat this five times.

4. Cut out a rectangle of cardboard measuring 50 x 40 cm (20 x 16 in). Then cut out a rectangle of fabric measuring 60 x 50 cm (24 x 20 in). Fold the edges of the fabric around the card and glue them in place.

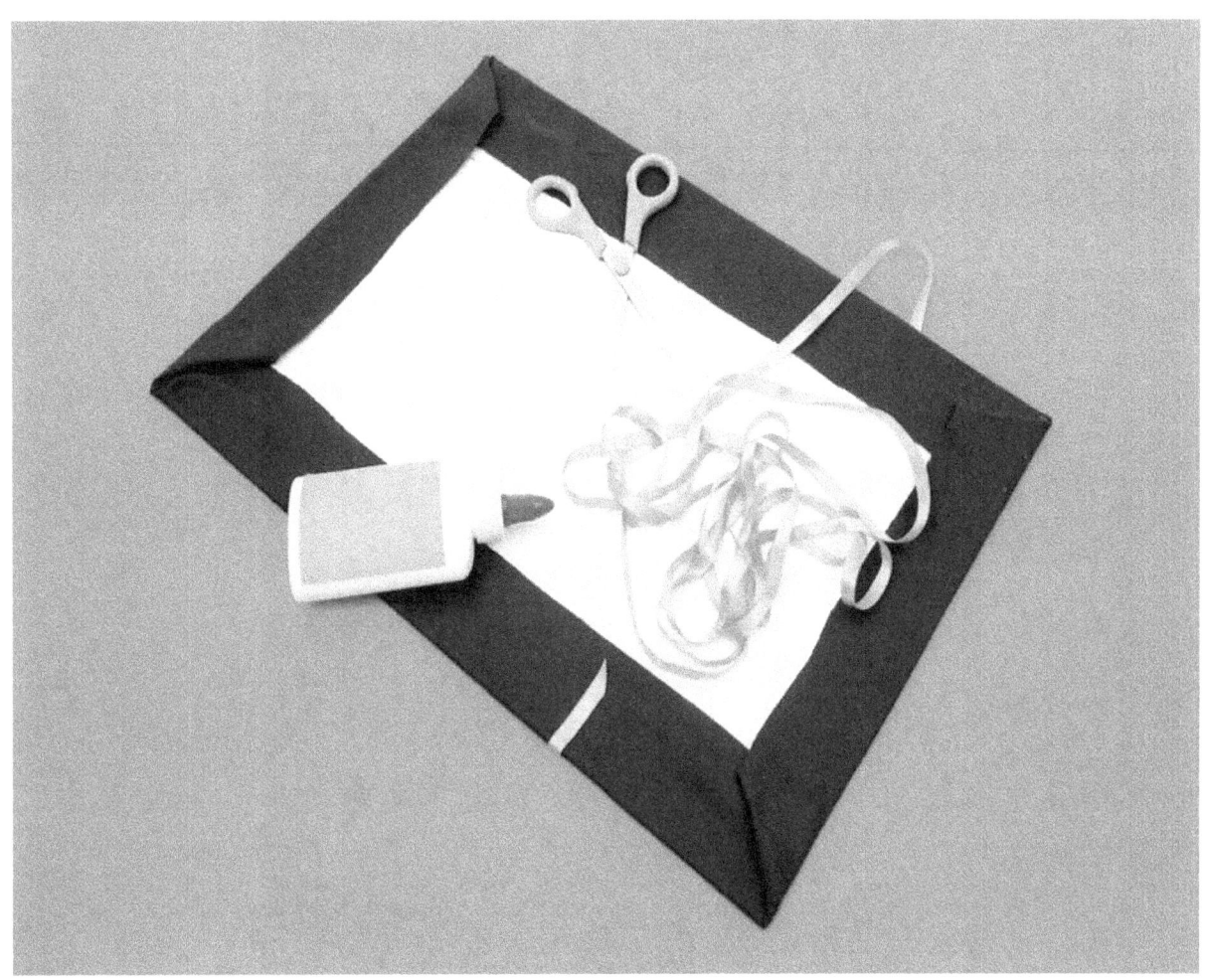

5. Cut two pieces of ribbon 50 cm (20 in) long. Wrap them around the cardboard and glue the ends down. Hang three pegs from each ribbon (see right).

CUPCAKE PINCUSHION

These cute cupcakes look good enough to eat! They are very handy for sticking pins in when you are sewing. But they also look great just as room decorations.

You will need:

Silicone cupcake case

Cushion filling

Felt

Shiny beads

Fabric glue

Needle and thread

Scissors

Ruler

Compass

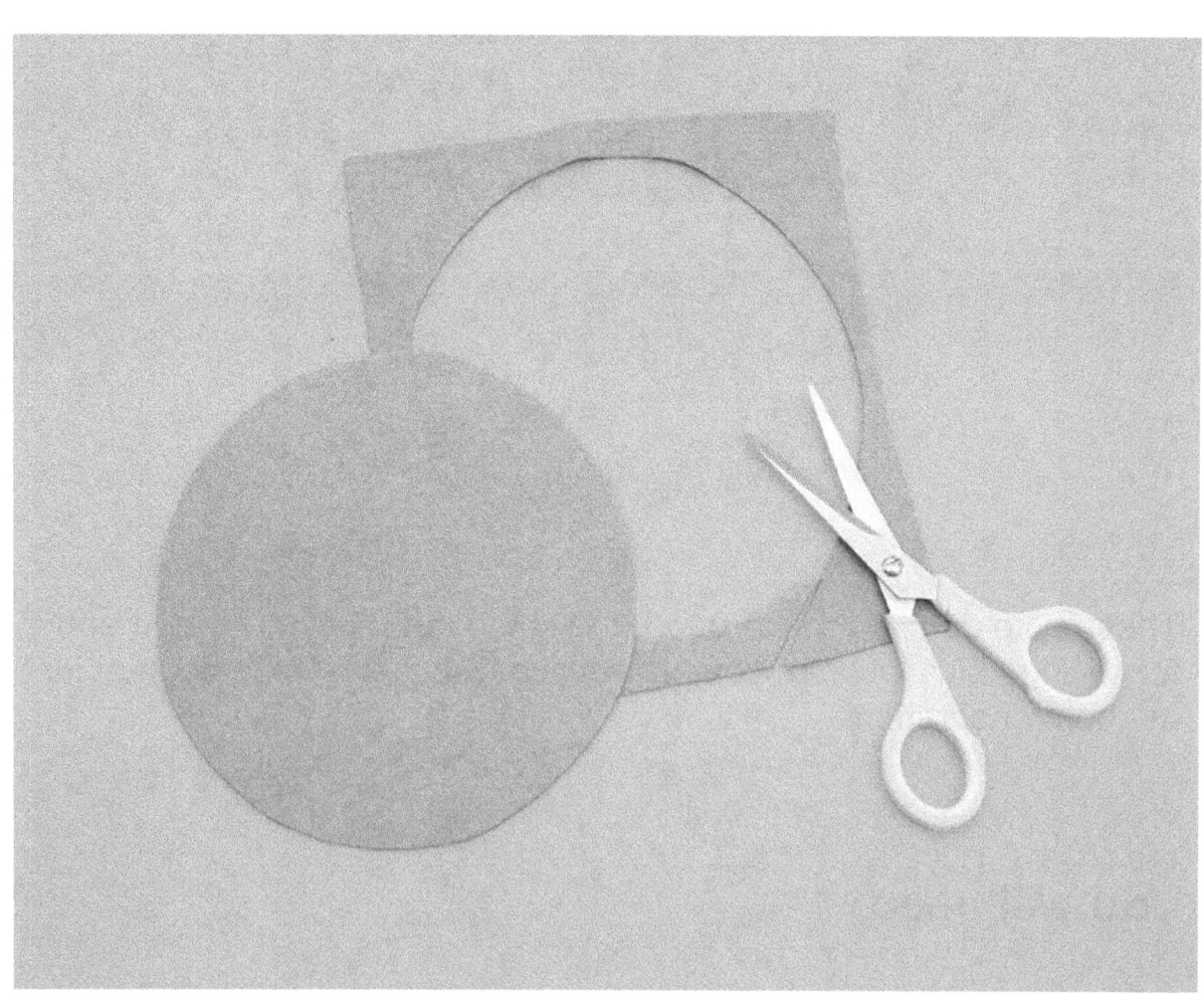

1. Cut out a circle of felt that is 15 cm (6 in) in diameter. You can measure the circle with a ruler and compass.

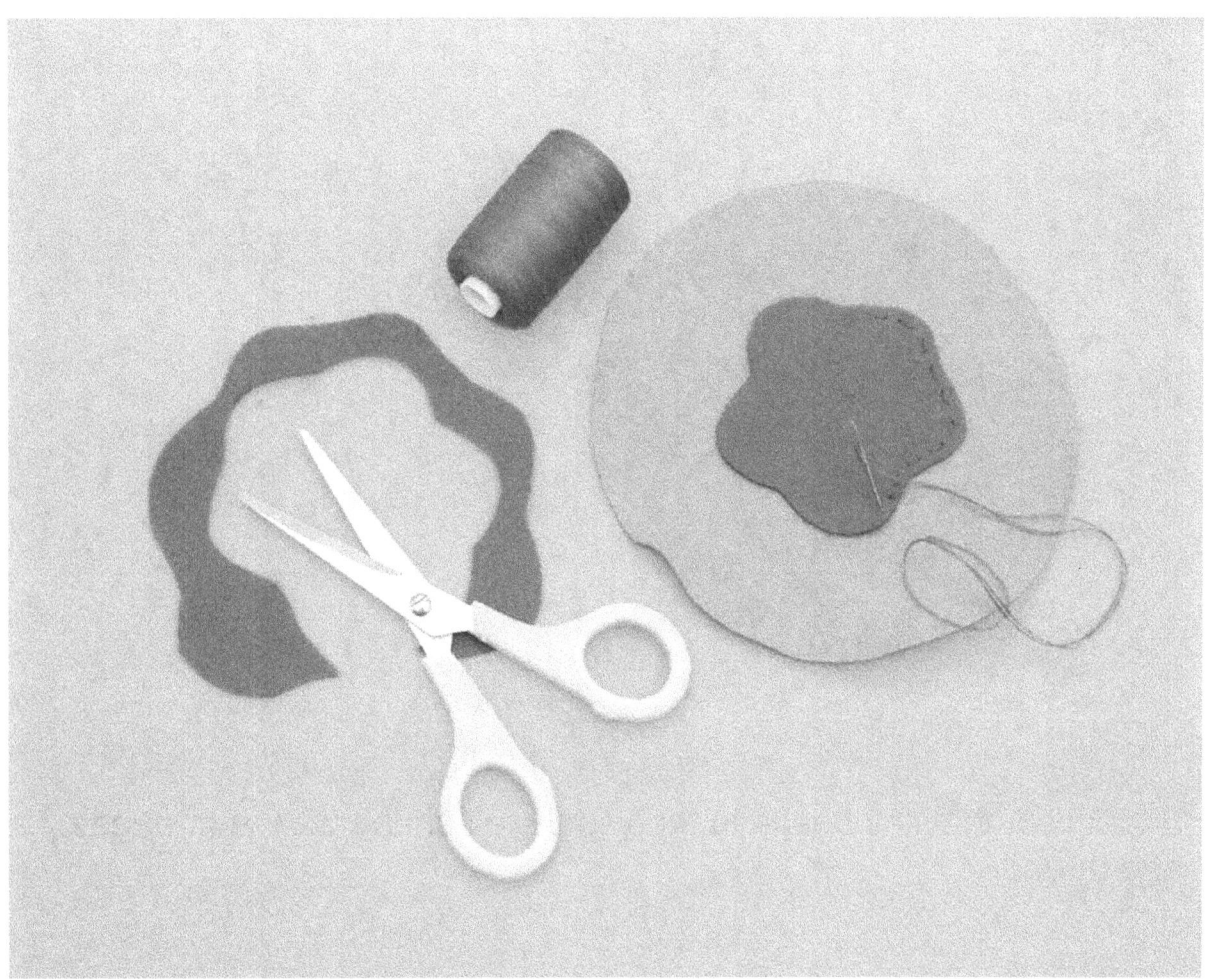

2. Cut out a 'splotch' shape with wiggly edges that is smaller than the circle. Stitch it on using a running stitch.

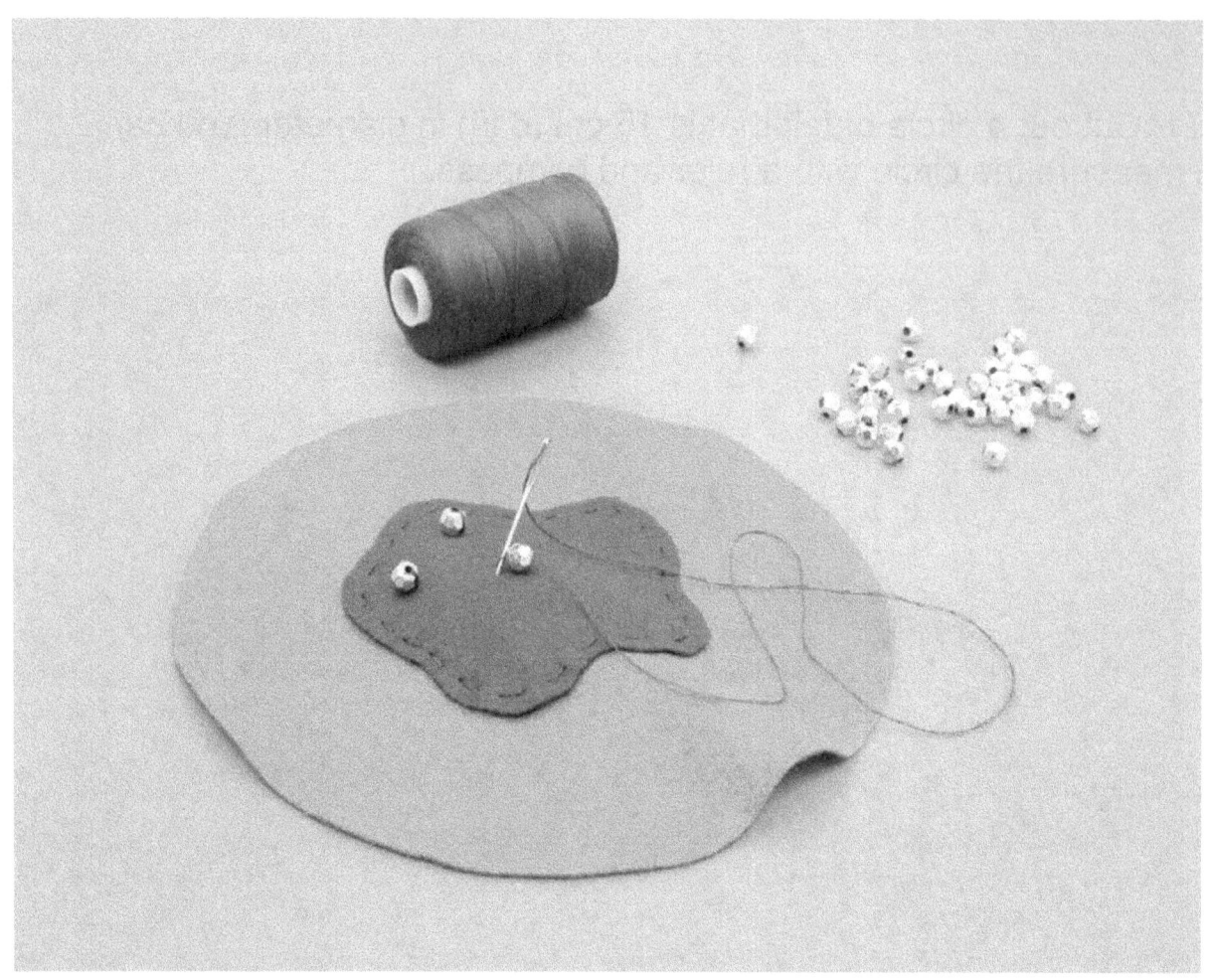

3. Sew some shiny beads to the wiggly felt shape with your needle and thread.

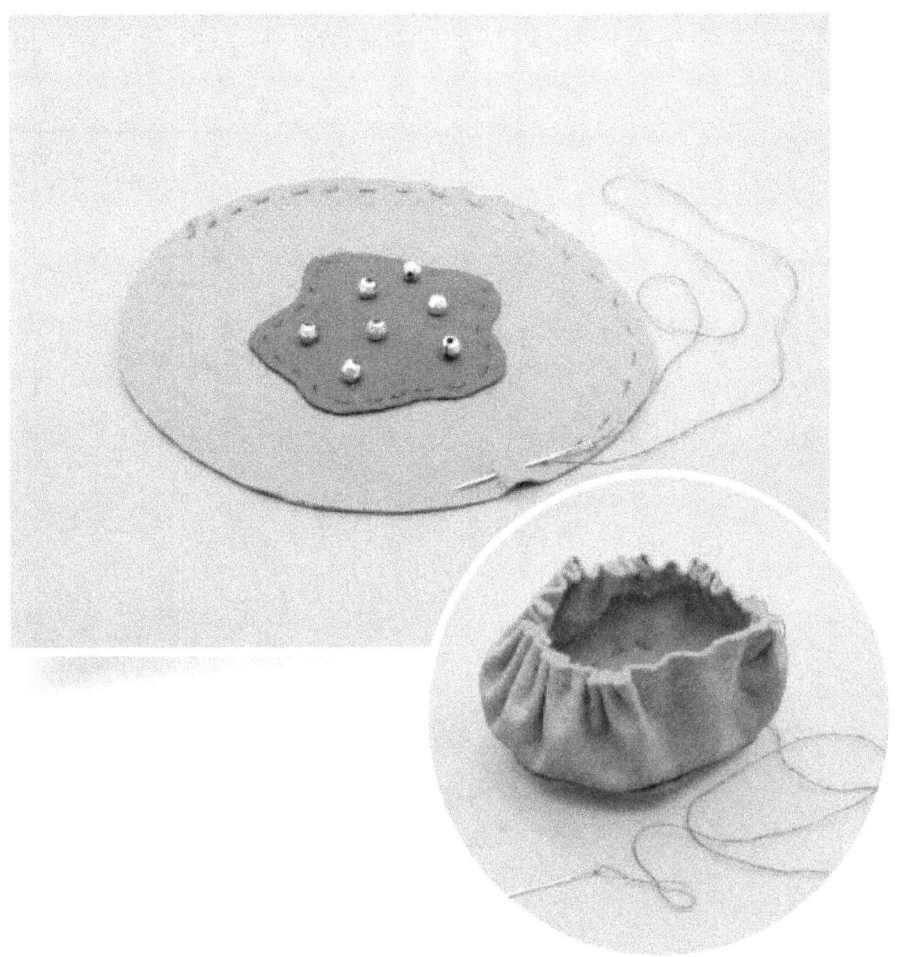

4. Sew a running stitch all around the edge of the felt circle. Leave the needle and thread still attached. Gather the running stitch slowly so that you start to make a pouch.

5. Roll some cushion filling in your hands so it makes a ball. Place it in the felt pouch, then pull the running stitch tightly together, and sew the fabric closed. Glue the felt ball into the silicone case and leave it to dry.

KNITTED PHONE CASE

Knitting is easy to learn. You will get faster with practice, and once you have got the hang of it you can knit all sorts of different things. Let's start by making a 'pooch pouch' for your phone!

You will need:

Wool

Knitting needles

Felt

Fabric glue

Darning needle

Scissors

Googly eyes

1. Tie your wool fairly loosely around a knitting needle in a double knot.

2. Pass a second needle through the wool loop from front to back. This will be the needle in your right hand.

3. Wind the wool under and over the tip of the right-hand needle and pull firmly. Slide the right-hand needle from behind the left, drawing the wool through the loop to form a new stitch.

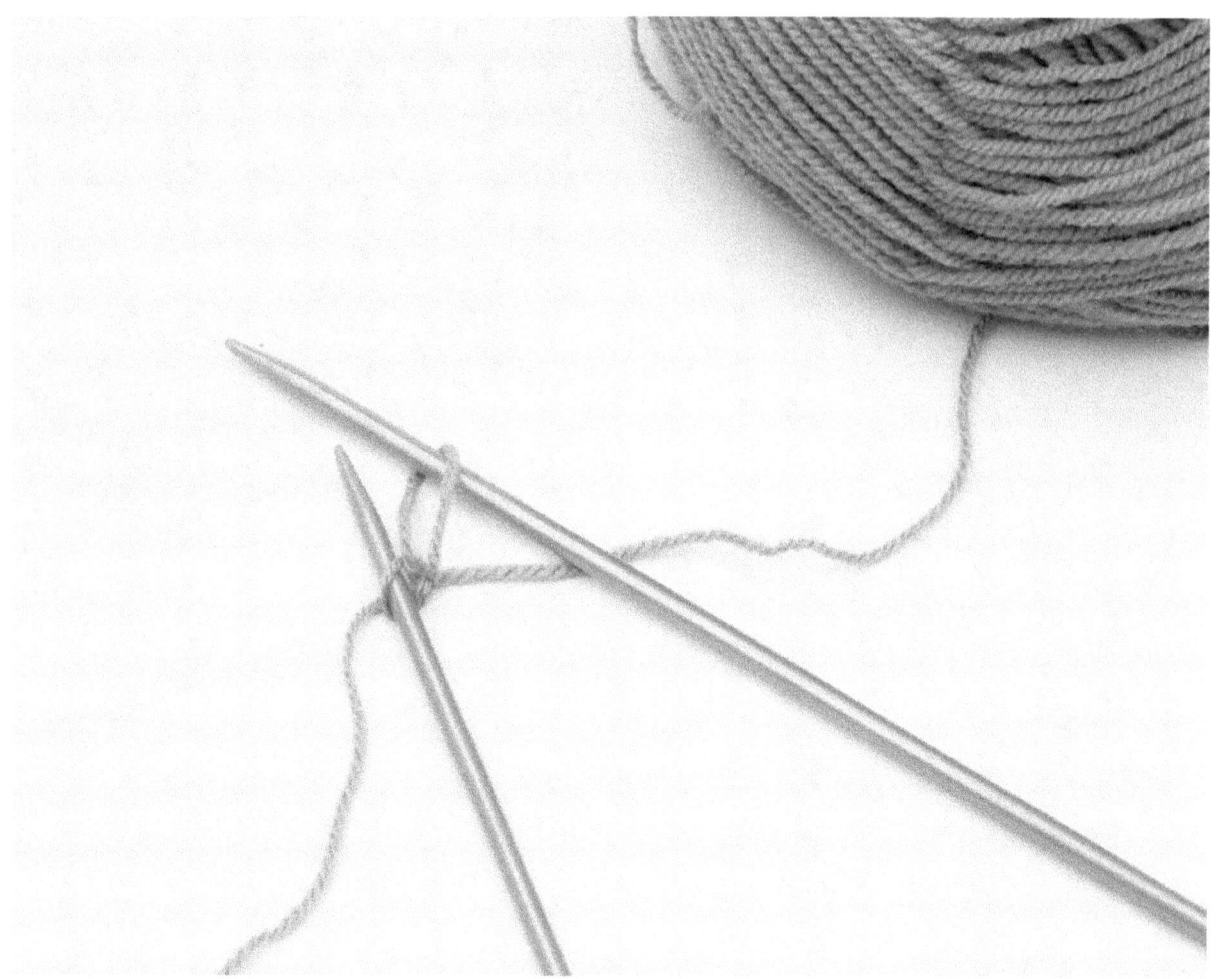

4. Put the new stitch onto the left-hand needle and withdraw the right-hand needle. Pull on the wool to tighten the stitch. Place the right-hand needle into the back of the stitch you have just made and then repeat steps 3–4 30 times.

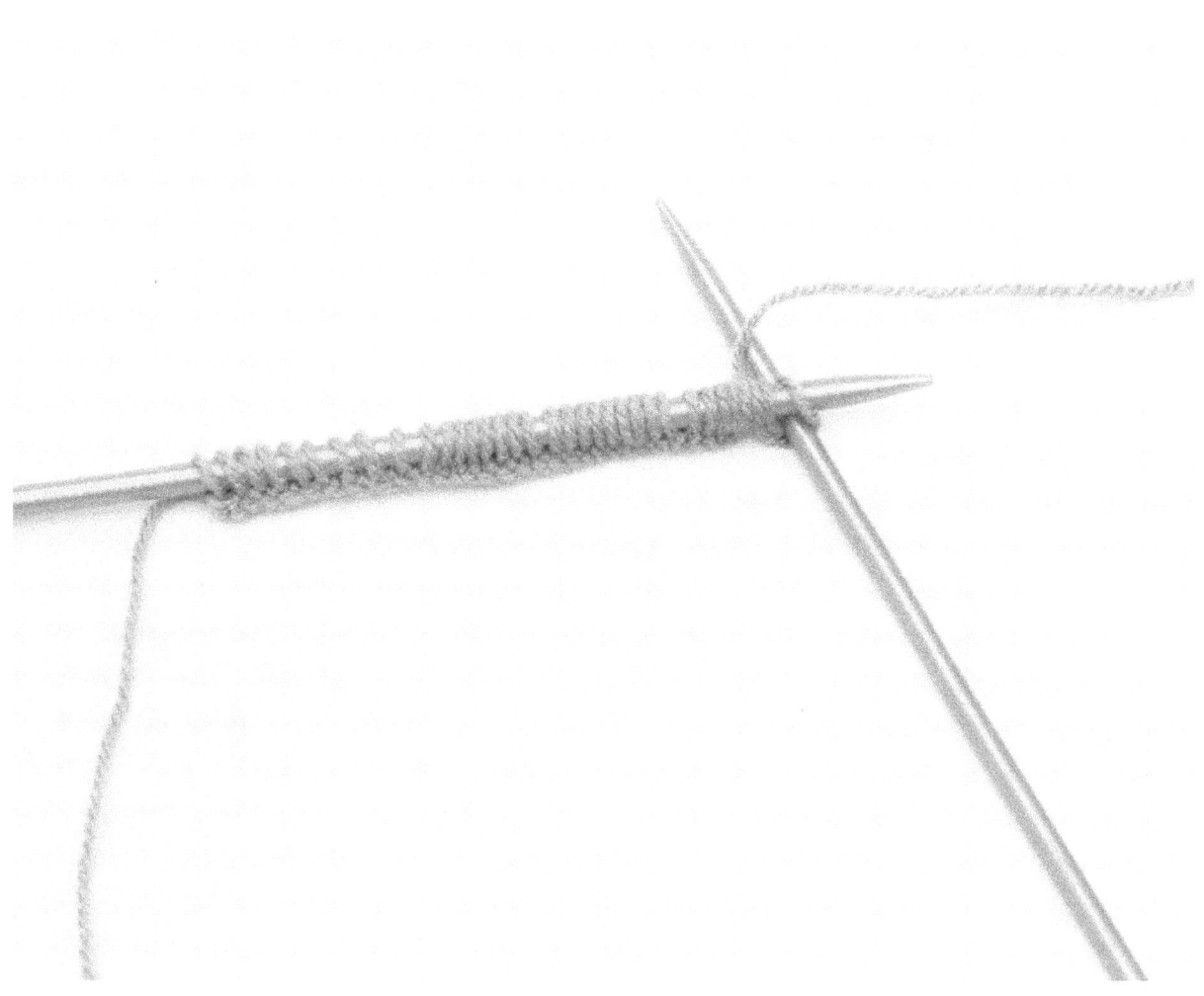

5. With the wool at the back, slide your right-hand needle into the stitch that is closest to the tip of your left-hand needle, from front to back. Loop the wool under and over the tip of the right-hand needle.

6. Make a new loop by sliding the tip of the right-hand needle up and over the left. Draw the wool completely through the stitch on the left-hand needle. Then slip one stitch off of the left-hand needle.

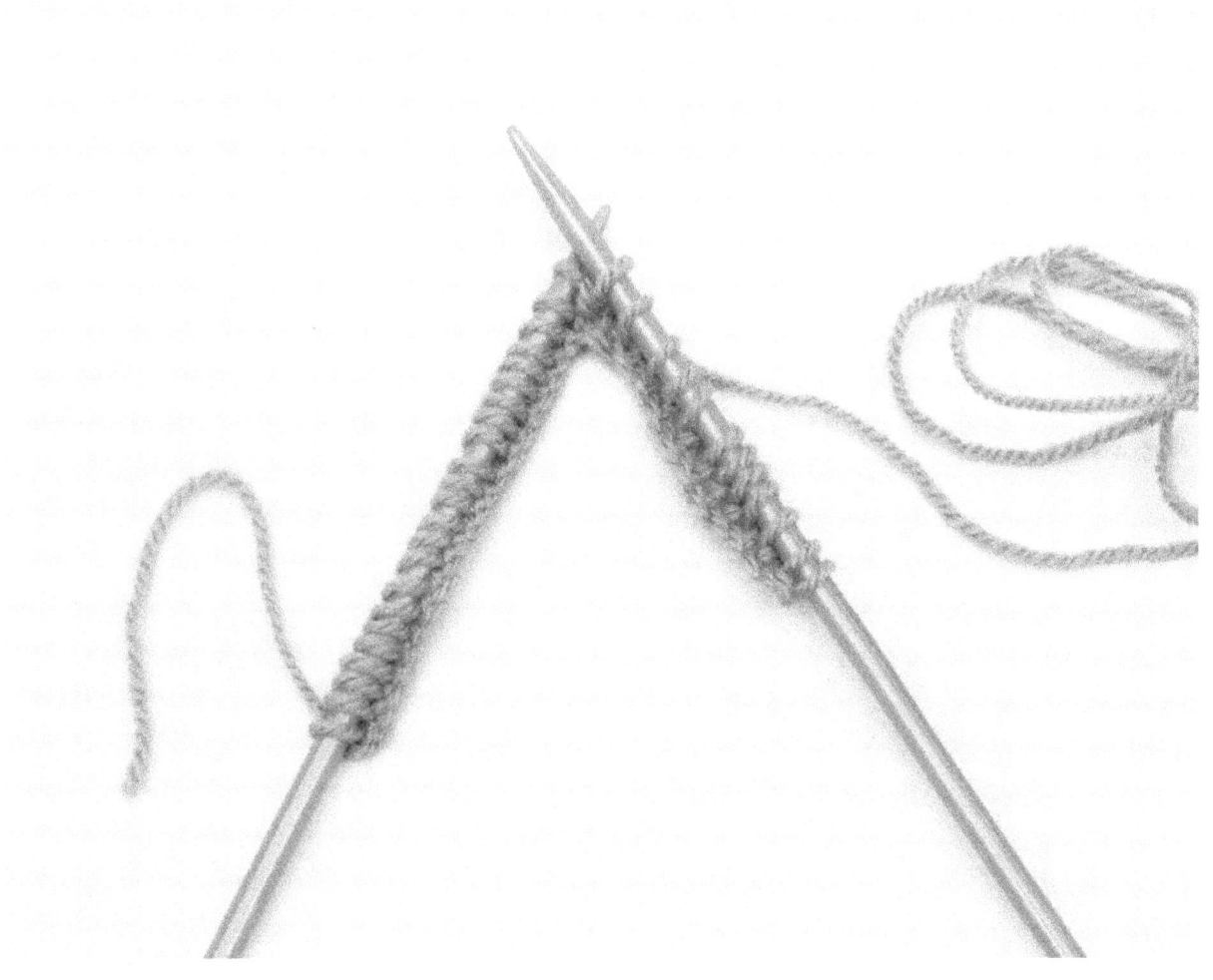

7. Repeat steps 5–6. Keep going until you have transferred all the stitches.

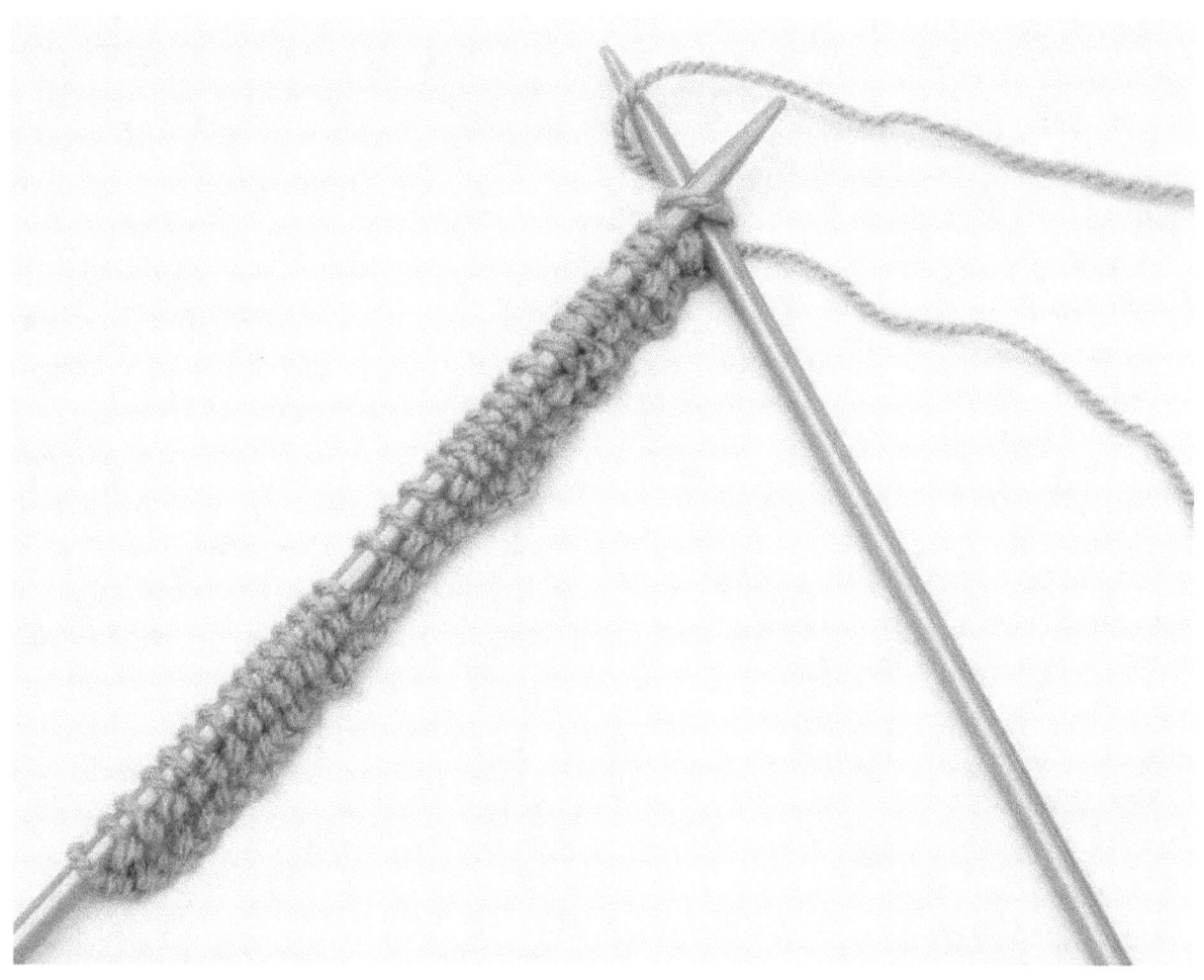

8. Swap your needles around and start again. Repeat 20 times until you have made 22 rows in total.

9. Knit two stitches onto the right-hand needle. Use the tip of the first needle to take the first stitch over the second and off the needle. This is called casting off.

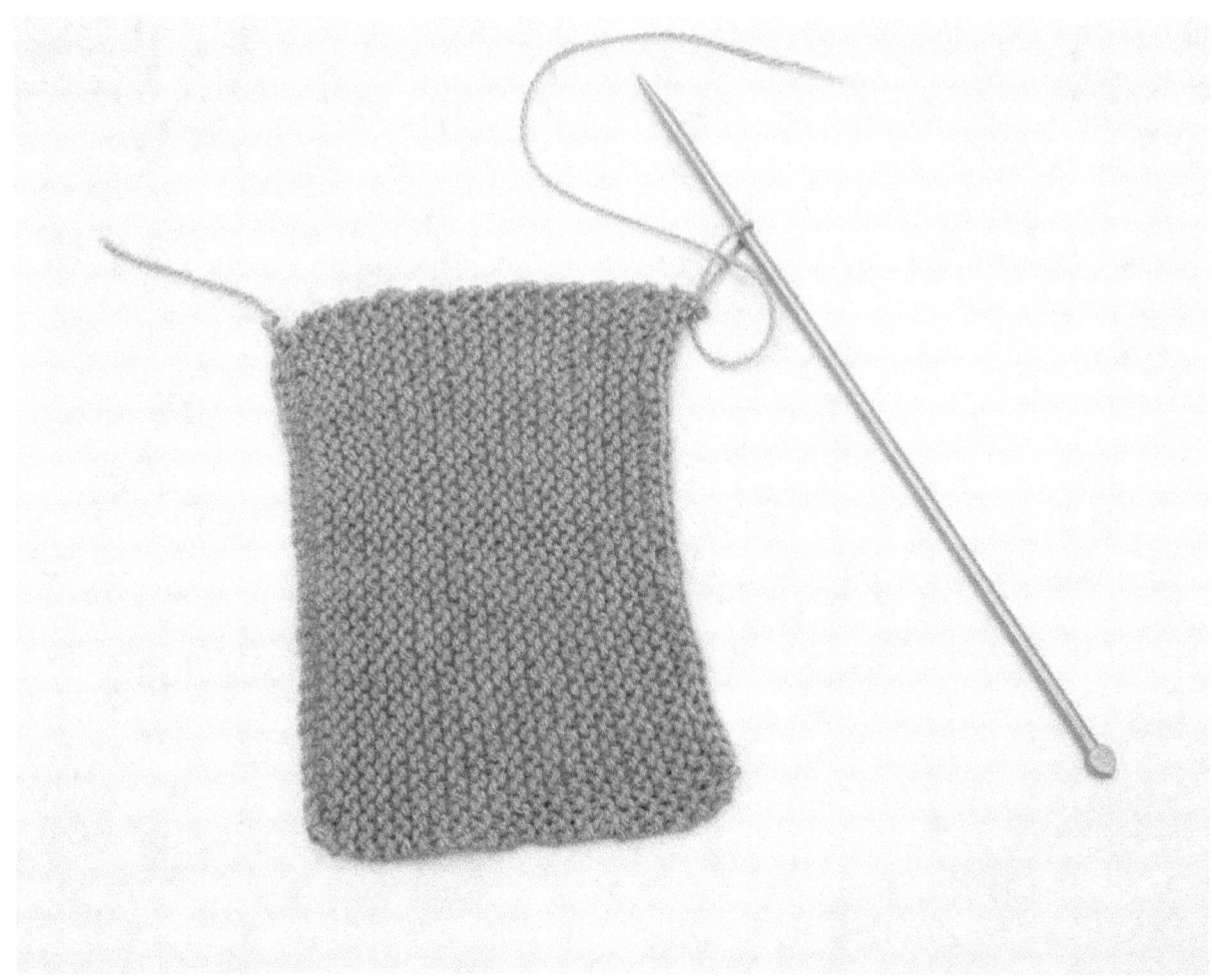

10. Make another stitch onto the second needle and repeat. Cast off until you have reached the end of the row and you have one stitch left. Take this off the needle and pull the wool through the last loop and knot in place.

11. Fold the rectangle in half and sew up one long and one short side using a darning needle and wool. Then turn it inside out, to hide your stitches.

12. Cut out felt shapes for your pooch's face, and glue them onto your pouch with fabric glue. Add some googly eyes.

GLOSSARY

acetate: A transparent sheet of plastic.

acrylic paint: A type of fast-drying paint, available in bright colours.

air-drying clay: A type of modelling clay used for making arts and crafts items.

bonsai: An ornamental, miniature tree, artificially prevented from growing to its full size.

compass: An instrument for drawing circles, consisting of two arms, one ending in a sharp point and one ending in a pen or pencil.

concertina fold: Continuous folding that results in a zigzag shape.

container: An object designed for storing or transporting one or more other objects.

corduroy: A thick cotton fabric with soft parallel raised lines on one side.

crescent: A shape that resembles a new moon.

découpage: A way of decorating by building up layers of paper cut-outs.

forage: To search over a large area.

freehand: Drawn by hand, without using guiding tools such as rulers.

customise: To make something in a special way to suit a particular person.

element: Part of an object.

ellipse: A shape like a squashed circle.

environment: The world of nature.

landfill: The disposal of waste by burying.

mosaic: A piece of art created by arranging small pieces of hard, coloured material (such as stones, tiles or glass) to make a picture.

papier mâché: A hard material made by layering paper and glue.

polystyrene: A type of plastic, which can be either stiff or a kind of foamy material.

quilling: A craft technique where paper or fabric is layered and folded to make patterns.

relief printing: A printing technique where raised shapes or letters are covered in ink, before being pressed onto a surface.

ruched: A gather created by passing a running stitch through a length of fabric and pulling the thread tight.

shredder: A machine for cutting paper into strips.

silicone: A heat resistant, synthetic material.

stencil printing: A printing technique where ink or paint is pushed through a pattern that has been cut into a sheet of plastic, card or metal.

stippling: A technique in drawing or painting where the artist makes a series of small dots or marks.

surgical spirit: A type of rubbing alcohol used as an antiseptic and cleanser.

template: An object that can be copied.

tote: A large bag.

turret: A small tower attached to a larger tower.

washer: A small metal ring used in plumbing.

Copyright 2023
Any person or persons who do any unauthorised act in relation to this publication may be liable to criminal prosecution and civil claims for damages.